PEOPLE AND ORGANISATIONS

Essentials of Employment Law

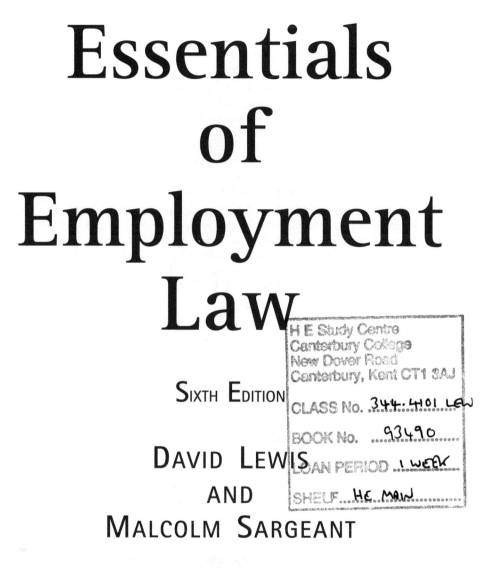

SIXTH EDITION

DAVID LEWIS
AND
MALCOLM SARGEANT

CHARTERED INSTITUTE OF PERSONNEL AND DEVELOPMENT

© David Lewis and Malcolm Sargeant 2000

First published in 2000
Reprinted 2000 (twice)

© David Lewis 1983, 1986, 1990, 1994, 1997

First published 1983
Second edition 1986
Reprinted 1987
Third edition 1990
Reprinted 1991, 1992
Fourth edition 1994
Reprinted 1995
Fifth edition 1997
Reprinted 1998 (twice)

Design by Curve

Typeset by Fakenham Photosetting Ltd, Fakenham, Norfolk

Printed in Great Britain by
the Short Run Press, Exeter

British Library Cataloguing in Publication Data
A catalogue record of this book is available from
the British Library

ISBN 0-85292-796-7

The views expressed in this book are the authors' own and
may not necessarily reflect those of the CIPD.

CIPD House, Camp Road, London SW19 4UX
Tel: 020-8971 9000 Fax: 020-8263 3333
E-mail: cipd@cipd.uk Website: www.cipd.co.uk
Incorporated by Royal Charter. Registered Charity No. 1079797.

Essentials of Employment Law

Sixth Edition

David Lewis is professor of employment law at Middlesex University and head of the Centre for Research in Industrial and Commercial Law. Apart from teaching on a wide range of degree courses and being a regular contributor to specialist commercial seminars, he has considerable experience as a consultant. He is a member of the editorial committee of the *Industrial Law Journal* and was appointed an ACAS arbitrator in 1999.

Dr Malcolm Sargeant is a senior lecturer in employment law at Middlesex University Business School. He has written widely on employment law subjects, especially on issues related to transfers of undertakings, discrimination in employment and parental rights. Prior to becoming an academic, he was personnel manager of a large financial services organisa... ...t and management consultancy.

Other titles in the series:

The Chartered Institute of Personnel and Development is the leading publisher of books and reports for personnel and training professionals, students, and all those concerned with the effective management and development of people at work. For details of all our titles, please contact the Publishing Department:

tel 020 8263 3387
fax 020 8263 3850
e-mail publish@cipd.co.uk

The catalogue of all CIPD titles can be viewed on the CIPD website:

www.cipd.co.uk/publications

Contents

Abbreviations

AC	Appeal Cases
ACAS	Advisory, Arbitration and Conciliation Service
ACOP	Approved Code of Practice
All ER	All England Law reports
AMRA	Access to Medical Reports Act 1988
CA	Court of Appeal
CAC	Central Arbitration Committee
Ch	Chancery Division
CMLR	Common Market Law Reports
CO	Certification Officer
CRE	Commission for Racial Equality
CRTUPEA	Collective Redundancies and Transfers of Undertakings (Protection of Employment) (Amendment) Regulations 1999
DDA	Disability Discrimination Act 1995
EAT	Employment Appeal Tribunal
EC	European Community
ECA	European Communities Act 1972
ECJ	European Court of Justice
ECR	European Court Reports
EOC	Equal Opportunities Commission
EPA	Equal Pay Act 1970
ERA	Employment Rights Act 1996
ERel	Employment Relations Act 1999
ETA	Employment Tribunals Act 1996
EU	European Union
HASAWA	Health and Safety at Work Act 1974
HMSO	Her Majesty's Stationery Office
HRA	Human Rights Act 1998
HSC	Health and Safety Commission
HSCE	Health and Safety (Consultation with Employees) Regulations 1996
HSE	Health and Safety Executive
ICR	Industrial Cases Reports
IRLB	Industrial Relations Law Bulletin

IRLR	Industrial Relations Law Reports
LWTL	Lawtel
MHSW	Management of Health and Safety at Work Regulations 1992
MLP	Maternity Leave Period
MPL	Maternity and Parental Leave Regulations 1999
MPP	Maternity Period Pay
NMW	National Minimum Wage
QB	Queen's Bench
RIDDOR	Reporting of Injuries, Diseases and Dangerous Occurrences Regulations 1995
RRA	Race Relations Act 1976
RTOST	Right to Time off for Study Regulations 1999
SDA	Sex Discrimination Act 1975
SI	Statutory Instrument
SMP	Statutory Maternity Pay
SRSC	Safety Representatives and Safety Committees Regulations 1977
SSCBA	Social Security and Benefits Act 1992
SSP	Statutory Sick Pay
Transfer Regulations	Transfer of Undertakings (Protection of Employment) Regulations 1981
TULRCA	Trade Union and Labour Relations (Consolidation) Act 1992
TURERA	Trade Union Reform and Employment Rights Act 1993
WLR	Weekly Law Reports
WT Regulations	Working Time Regulations 1998

List of cases cited

Preface

This is the sixth edition of *Essentials of Employment Law*, and it comes at a time of important changes in employment law as a result of the Government's programme of legislation and the continuing influence of European Union initiatives. It is also the first edition that has been jointly written.

The changes resulting from Employment Relations Act 1999 are included in this book, but it is important to note that, at the time of publication, a number of measures have not yet been the subject of commencement orders. This includes, for example, the legislation on the statutory recognition of trade unions. There are also a number of other measures that had not come into effect at the beginning of 2000. These include the Human Rights Act 1998, which comes into force on 1 October 2000 and the Data Protection Act 1998, which will be introduced over a period of time commencing 1 March 2000.

We would like to thank Professor Phil James of Middlesex University for his advice and Richard Goff of the CIPD for all the help and support that he has provided.

Finally, this edition is dedicated to the memory of Clarice Lewis, who gave pride of place on her bookshelf to the previous five editions.

David Lewis
Malcolm Sargeant

December 1999

1 The sources and institutions of employment law

This chapter will introduce you to both the way in which employment law is made and the institutions that develop, supervise and enforce it. We start with the distinction between civil and criminal law and a basic introduction to the legal system in this country. Employment law is created by primary and secondary legislation which is then interpreted by the courts, especially by employment tribunals and the Employment Appeal Tribunal. They are influenced by Codes of Practice and, importantly, by EU law and the decisions of the European Court of Justice. Finally we look at those organisations set up by Parliament to regulate industrial relations and dispute resolution.

CIVIL AND CRIMINAL LAW

Criminal law is concerned with offences against the state and, apart from private prosecutions, it is the state which enforces this branch of the law. The sanctions typically imposed on convicted persons are fines and/or imprisonment. Civil law deals with the situations where a private person who has suffered harm brings an action against (ie sues) the person who committed the wrongful act which caused the harm. Normally the purpose of suing is to recover damages or compensation. Criminal and civil matters are normally dealt with in separate courts which have their own distinct procedures.

In this book we shall be concentrating largely on civil law but we shall be describing the criminal law in so far as it imposes duties in relation to health and safety and restricts the activities of pickets. In employment law the two most important civil actions are those based on the law of contract and the law of tort. The essential feature of a contract is a binding agreement in which an offer by one person (for example, an employer) is accepted by someone else (for example, a person seeking work). This involves an exchange of promises. Thus, in a contract of employment there is a promise to pay wages in exchange for a promise to be available for work. As we shall see later, the parties to a contract are not entirely free to negotiate their own terms because Parliament imposes certain restrictions and minimum requirements. The law of tort places a duty on everyone not to behave in a way that is likely to cause harm to others, and in the employment field the tort of negligence has been applied so as to impose a duty on employers to take reasonable care of their employees during the course of their employment. Various torts have also been created by the judiciary in order to impose legal liability for industrial action, for example the tort of interfering with trade or business, but Parliament has intervened to provide immunities in certain circumstances (see Chapter 21).

LEGISLATION AND CODES OF PRACTICE

In this country the most important source of law governing industrial relations is legislation enacted by Parliament. Often the government will precede legislation by issuing Green Papers or White Papers. Traditionally the Green Paper is a consultative document and the White Paper is a statement of the government's policy and intentions, although this distinction does not always seem to be adhered to. The government will announce its legislative programme for the forthcoming session in the Queen's Speech. A Bill is then introduced into the House of Commons (sometimes this process can begin in the House of Lords) and is examined at a number of sessions (readings) in both the House of Commons and the House of Lords. The agreed Bill becomes an Act (or statute) when it receives the Royal Assent. It is then referred to (cited) by its name and year, which constitutes its 'short title' (eg Employment Rights Act 1996).

The provisions of an Act may not be brought into operation immediately, for the government may wish to implement it in stages. Nevertheless, once the procedure is completed, the legislation is valid. The main provisions of a statute are to be found in its numbered sections, whereas administrative details, repeals and amendments of previous legislation tend to be contained in the schedules at the back. Statutes sometimes give the relevant Secretary of State the power to make rules (regulations) to supplement those laid down in the Act itself. These regulations, which are normally subject to parliamentary approval, are referred to as statutory instruments (SI) and this process of making law is known as delegated or subordinate legislation. Statutory instruments are cited by their name, year and number (eg the Employment Tribunal (Constitution and Rules of Procedure) Regulations 1993, SI No 2678).

Codes of Practice

Legislation sometimes allows for an appropriate Minister or a statutory body to issue Codes of Practice. The primary function of these codes is to educate managers and workers by publicising the practices and procedures which the government believes are conducive to, say, good industrial relations. Under section 199 of the Trade Union and Labour Relations (Consolidation) Act 1992 (TULRCA 1992) the Advisory, Conciliation and Arbitration Service (ACAS) has a general power to issue codes 'containing such practical guidance as [ACAS] thinks fit for the purpose of promoting the improvement of industrial relations'. Following representations by interested parties ACAS submits a draft code to the Secretary of State for approval before it is laid before Parliament. At the time of writing, ACAS Codes of Practice exist on the following topics: *Disciplinary Practice and Procedures in Employment*; *Disclosure of Information to Trade Unions for Collective Bargaining Purposes*; and *Time Off for Trade Union Duties and Activities*. The Equal Opportunities Commission (EOC) and the Commission for Racial Equality (CRE) have also issued codes of the same standing as those of ACAS and, by virtue of section 16 of the Health and Safety at Work Act 1974 (HASAWA 1974), the Health and Safety Commission (HSC) has the power to approve Codes of Practice provided it obtains the consent of the Secretary of State on each occasion. Finally, sections 203–6 TULRCA 1992 entitle the Secretary of State to issue codes, but before publishing a draft he or she is obliged to consult ACAS. However, no such duty exists if a code is merely being revised to bring it into conformity with subsequent statutory provisions.[1] Although emerging by different means, all these codes have the same legal standing, ie nobody can be sued or prosecuted for breaching a code, but in any proceedings before a tribunal, court (if the code was issued under TULRCA 1992 or HASAWA 1974) or the Central Arbitration Committee (CAC) a failure to adhere to a recommendation 'shall be taken into account'.

COMMON LAW AND THE COURT HIERARCHY

The feature which distinguishes the English legal system from non-common-law systems is that in this country judicial decisions have been built up to form a series of binding precedents. This is known as the case-law approach. In practice this means that tribunals and judges are bound by the decisions of judges in higher courts. Thus employment tribunals, which are at the bottom of the English court hierarchy, are required to follow the decisions of the Employment Appeal Tribunal (EAT or Appeal Tribunal), the Court of Appeal and the Appeal Committee of the House of Lords, although they are not bound by other employment tribunal decisions. The Employment Appeal Tribunal is bound by the decisions of the Court of Appeal and the House of Lords and normally follows its own previous decisions. The Court of Appeal has a civil and criminal division and, while both are bound by the House of Lords' decisions, only the civil division is constrained by its own previous decisions. The House of Lords has stated that it will regard its own earlier decisions as binding unless in the circumstances of a particular case it is thought just to depart from them. In addition all English courts must follow the guidance given by the European Court of Justice (ECJ). Much of this guidance comes as a result of national courts' referring matters to the ECJ by a procedure under Article 234 of the EC Treaty (previously Article 177 EC). Thus when a court or tribunal decides that clarification of European law is required in order for it to make a decision, it will refer the matter to the ECJ for guidance.

What constitutes the binding element of a judicial decision is for a judge or tribunal in a subsequent case to determine. Theoretically what has to be followed is the legal principle or principles which are relied on in reaching the decision in the earlier case. In practice judges and tribunals have a certain amount of discretion, for they can take a broad or narrow view of the principles which are binding upon them. If they do not like the principles that have emerged, they can refuse to apply them so long as they are prepared to conclude that the facts of the case before them are sufficiently different from the facts in the previous decision. Not surprisingly, this technique is known as 'distinguishing'. Thus, while it is correct to argue that the doctrine of precedent imports an element of certainty, it is wrong to assume that there is no scope for innovation in the lower courts. In addition to interpreting the law, the judiciary can and does make law.

The court hierarchy
The court structure in England and Wales is shown in diagrammatic form in Figure 1 (page 6). Most proceedings involving individual employment rights are commenced at employment tribunals and appeals against an employment tribunal decision can normally be heard by the EAT only if there has been an error of law. This occurs when a tribunal has misdirected itself as to the applicable law, when there is no evidence to support a particular finding of fact, or when the tribunal has reached a perverse conclusion, ie one which cannot be justified on the evidence presented.[2] Further appeals can be made on a point of law to the Court of Appeal and the House of Lords, but only if permission is granted by either the body which made the decision or the court which would hear the appeal. Other civil actions can be started in the County Court or High Court. Appeals on a point of law against a decision made by either court can be lodged with the Court of Appeal and, if permission is granted, further appeal lies to the House of Lords. There is also a 'leapfrog procedure' which enables an appeal against

a decision of the High Court to go directly to the House of Lords so long as all the parties involved give their consent.

Criminal proceedings are normally commenced in magistrates' courts, for example if pickets are charged with obstructing police officers in the execution of their duty. The defence can launch an appeal on fact which goes to the Crown Court but it is also possible for either party to appeal on a point of law to the Divisional Court of the Queen's Bench and then on to the House of Lords. Prosecutions for serious offences, for example under section 33 of HASAWA 1974, are dealt with in the Crown Court and appeals on a point of law go to the Court of Appeal and the House of Lords in the usual way.

Figure 1 Court structure in England and Wales

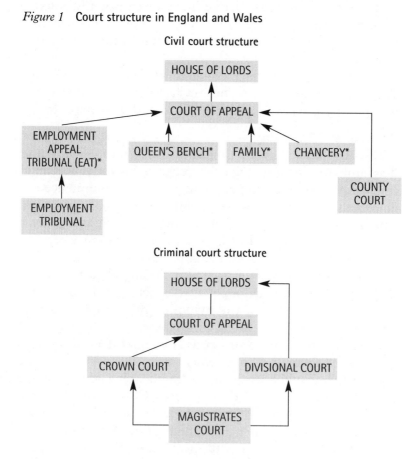

Civil court structure

Criminal court structure

*All divisions of the High Court

EUROPEAN LAW

The United Kingdom joined the European Economic Community in 1973. Since then there have been a number of Treaties by which the Member States have agreed to develop the scope of the law of the European Union (EU), the most recent being the Treaty of Amsterdam 1998. Article 249 of the EC Treaty (previously Article 189 EC) allows the EU to introduce different types of legislation, the most important ones being regulations and directives. Regulations tend to be of a broad nature and are directly applicable in all Member States. Most EU legislation that affects employment law is introduced, however, in the form of directives. Directives are legislative instruments that require a Member State to translate (transpose) the contents of the directive into national law. Member States are usually given a period of two to three years to carry this out.

If a Member State fails to do this, a citizen may, in certain circumstances, rely on the EU law rather than on existing national laws. The directive is then said to have direct effect. This can be the result of the Member State's either failing to transpose the directive or inadequately transposing it. Direct effect is, however, usually only vertically effective, ie it can only be relied upon against the state or 'emanations' of the state.[3] This concept of direct effect has proved an important tool in the enforcement of Community law, especially with respect to Article 141 EC (previously Article 119 EC) on equal pay.

Early cases in the European Court of Justice established the supremacy of Community law over national law.[4] National courts also have an obligation to interpret national law so that it gives effect to EU law.[5] This means that national legislation should be interpreted in a way that is consistent with the objects of the Treaty, the provisions of any relevant directives and the rulings of the European Court of Justice.[6] In relation to the interpretation of directives, this principle applies whether the national legislation came after or preceded the particular directive.[7]

It is the European Communities Act 1972 (ECA 1972)

which gives effect to the UK's membership of the EU. Firstly, section 2(1) enables directly effective EU obligations to be enforced as free-standing rights. Thus in *McCarthys Ltd v Smith*[8] Article 141 EC (previously Article 119 EC) on equal pay was applied following a reference to the European Court of Justice. Secondly, section 2(2) facilitates the introduction of subordinate legislation to achieve compliance with EU obligations, eg The Working Time Regulations 1998.[9] Articles 226 EC and 228 EC (previously 169 and 171 EC) enable the European Commission to take steps to ensure that the UK complies with its obligations to give effect to directives.[10] In addition, an individual may be able to obtain damages as a result of a Member State's failure to carry out its obligations under European law.[11]

THE KEY INSTITUTIONS

Employment tribunals

Industrial tribunals were first established under the Industrial Training Act 1964 but their jurisdiction has now been extended to cover applications relating to the matters listed in the Appendix. Their name was changed to 'employment tribunals' by section 1 of the Employment Rights (Dispute Resolution) Act 1998. In this book they will always be referred to by this new name, even though many of the cases cited will refer to them as industrial tribunals.

The Employment Tribunal Service was established in 1997 to provide administrative and organisational support for employment tribunals and the Employment Appeal Tribunal. It has 13 regional offices in England and Scotland, although the Secretary of the Employment Tribunals for England and Wales is based in London and the Scottish counterpart is based in Glasgow.

The President of these tribunals is a barrister or solicitor of seven years' standing who is appointed by the Lord Chancellor for a five-year term. Normally tribunal cases are heard by legally qualified chairpersons and two other people who are known as lay members.[12] Tribunal appointments are for five years initially and, whereas the chairpersons are appointed by the Lord Chancellor and are subject to the same qualification requirements as the President, the lay members are appointed by the Secretary of State. There are some 2,500 lay members in 24 centres around the country. They are drawn from two panels; one is formed as a result of nominations made by employer organisations, and the other consists of nominees from organisations of workers. Since 1999 the government has also advertised in the press so that individuals may nominate themselves for one of the panels. Two important points should be noted in relation to the composition of employment tribunals. Firstly, while lay members are expected to have an understanding of workplace practices and how people work together, they are not supposed to act as representatives of their nominating organisations. Secondly, women and racial minorities are significantly under-represented as both chairpersons and lay members, a fact which causes concern in the light of the tribunals' role in enforcing anti-discrimination legislation.

Hearings at employment tribunals are relatively informal.[13] The parties, known as applicants and respondents, may represent themselves or be represented by a legal practitioner, a trade union official, a representative from an employers' association or any other person. In practice, employers tend to be legally represented more often than employees, one reason being the unavailability of legal aid at present. (Applicants may be able to obtain advice and assistance in preparing their case under the legal aid scheme.) Human resource managers should give very serious thought to the question of representation, because the manager who understands how the shop floor operates and is familiar with the types of argument that may be raised during the disciplinary process may prove more effective than a lawyer from outside.

Apart from appeals against improvement or prohibition notices issued under HASAWA 1974, costs are not normally awarded unless either party is deemed to have acted frivolously, vexatiously, abusively, disruptively, or otherwise unreasonably in bringing or conducting the proceedings.[14]

Tribunal decisions can be challenged either by review or by

appeal. The power of review, which enables the whole or part of a case to be re-heard and set aside or the original decision varied, may be exercised only on one of the following grounds:

(a) the decision was wrongly made as a result of error on the part of tribunal staff

(b) a party did not receive notice of the proceedings

(c) the decision was made in the absence of a person entitled to be heard

(d) new evidence has become available since the making of the decision and its existence could not have been reasonably known of or foreseen

(e) the interests of justice require a review.[15]

Applications for review must be made within 14 days of the tribunal decision's being entered on the register which is kept by the Secretary of the tribunals. The review may be heard by the tribunal responsible for the original decision or by a differently constituted one. An appeal to the Employment Appeal Tribunal can normally be made only on a point of law and must be lodged within 42 days of the decision or order being sent to the appellant.[16]

The Employment Appeal Tribunal (EAT)

The EAT, which was established in 1976, is serviced by Employment Tribunal Service offices in London and Edinburgh. It can sit anywhere in England, Wales or Scotland and consists of High Court judges nominated by the Lord Chancellor (one of whom serves as President) and a panel of lay members who are appointed on the joint recommendation of the Lord Chancellor and the Secretary of State. This panel consists of nominees from employers' and workers' organisations. Appeals are heard by a judge and either two or four lay persons, all of whom have equal voting rights. However, a judge can sit alone where the appeal arises from proceedings before an employment tribunal consisting of the chair alone.

Parties can be represented by whomsoever they please, and costs will be awarded only where the proceedings are deemed to have been unnecessary, improper, or vexatious or where there has been unreasonable conduct in bringing or conducting the proceedings.[17] Apart from appeals on points of law, this body can hear appeals on fact from a decision of the Certification Officer under section 2 TULRCA 1992 (entry on the list of trade unions), and section 6 TULRCA 1992 (certificates of independence). The EAT has the same review powers as employment tribunals. Finally, the Appeal Tribunal may adjourn proceedings where there is a reasonable prospect of a conciliated settlement being reached.[18]

The Advisory, Conciliation and Arbitration Service (ACAS)

ACAS has been in existence since 1974. Its work is directed by a council consisting of a chairperson and nine members appointed by the Secretary of State. Three members are appointed after consultation with trade unions, three following consultation with employers' organisations and the remainder are independent. The Service is divided into eight regions which perform most of the day-to-day work, for example, handling direct enquiries from the public. Although ACAS is financed by the government, section 247(3) TULRCA 1992 states that it shall not be 'subject to directions of any kind from any Minister of the Crown as to the manner in which it is to exercise its functions'.

As a result of an amendment made by the E Rel Act 1999, ACAS is now charged with the general duty of promoting the improvement of industrial relations.[19] It also has specific functions which merit separate consideration:

(i)   *Advice*
      ACAS may, on request or on its own initiative, provide advice to employers, their associations, workers and trade unions on any matter concerned with or affecting industrial relations.[20] In practice the forms of advice range from telephone enquiries to in-depth projects,

diagnostic surveys and training exercises. In 1998, 2,039 advisory meetings were held and 530 advisory mediation projects were completed.

(ii) *Conciliation*

Where a trade dispute exists or is likely to arise, ACAS may, on request or of its own volition, offer assistance to the parties with a view to bringing about a settlement. This may be achieved by conciliation or other means, for example the appointment of an independent person to render assistance. Before attempting to conciliate in collective trade disputes, ACAS is required to 'have regard to the desirability of encouraging the parties to a dispute to use any appropriate agreed procedures'.[21] According to its Annual Report for 1998, in over 90 per cent of the cases completed, industrial action was avoided and mutually acceptable solutions found. Pay and other terms and conditions of employment were the most frequent issues in the disputes conciliated (48 per cent) and 41 per cent of requests for assistance came from both parties jointly.

In addition to collective matters, ACAS has the task of conciliating in employment tribunal cases. Particular officers have been designated and are known as 'Conciliation Officers (Tribunals)'. When a complaint is presented to an employment tribunal, a copy of it will be sent to one of these officers who has the duty to promote a settlement without the matter's having to go to a hearing. Conciliation officers can intervene if requested to do so by the parties or where they believe they could act with a reasonable prospect of success. At the instigation of either party the officer may act before a complaint has been presented in respect of a matter which could be the subject of tribunal proceedings (for the conciliation officer's particular duty in unfair dismissal cases, see Chapter 16). So as not to undermine the conciliation process it is stipulated that anything communicated to an officer in connection with the performance of her or his functions shall not be admissible in evidence in any proceedings before an employment tribunal without the consent of the person who communicated it.

The ACAS report for 1998 reveals that 27 per cent of tribunal applications reached a hearing although the rate of settlement, withdrawal and abandonment varied according to the particular jurisdiction. In 1998, of the 113,636 cases received for conciliation 40,153 were concerned with unfair dismissal, 16,260 were concerned with discrimination, 24,981 were concerned with the protection of wages, 23,578 were breach of contract cases, and 8,664 involved other employment protection provisions.

(iii) *Arbitration*

At the request of one party but with the consent of all the parties to a collective dispute (or potential dispute), ACAS may appoint an arbitrator or arbitration panel from outside the Service or refer the matter to be heard by the Central Arbitration Committee (CAC). In performing this function ACAS is obliged to consider whether the dispute could be resolved by conciliation, and arbitration is not to be offered unless agreed procedures for the negotiation and settlement of disputes have been exhausted (save where there is a special reason which justifies arbitration as an alternative to those procedures).[22] CAC awards can be published only with the consent of all parties involved. According to the ACAS report for 1998, 65 per cent of the 51 cases referred to arbitration and mediation involved disputes over pay and terms and conditions of employment, and 25 per cent were concerned with discipline and dismissal; 40 cases went to a single arbitrator, two to a board of arbitration and eight to a single mediator.

In addition, the Employment Rights (Dispute Resolution) Act 1998 allowed ACAS to set up an arbitration scheme to enable parties to unfair dismissal disputes to submit their dispute to arbitration. This can be done only with the agreement of all parties to the dispute, who must also agree to be bound by the arbitrator's decision. These decisions have the same status as those of employment tribunals.

(iv) *Inquiry*

ACAS may inquire into any question relating to industrial relations generally, in a particular industry or in a particular undertaking. Any advice or findings which emerge may be published so long as the views of all concerned parties have been taken into account.[23]

(v) *Other duties*

Apart from the general power to issue codes of practice, ACAS has an important conciliation role to play in statutory recognition claims and in those situations where a recognised union has lodged a complaint that an employer has failed to disclose information which it requires for collective bargaining purposes (see Chapter 19).

The Central Arbitration Committee (CAC)

The CAC consists of a chairperson, deputy chairpersons and other members all of whom are appointed by the Secretary of State after consultation with ACAS. The members must have experience as employer or worker representatives, while the deputy chairpersons tend to be lawyers or academic experts in industrial relations. Like ACAS, the CAC is not subject to directions from a Minister. Apart from receiving requests to arbitrate directly from parties to a dispute, the CAC receives arbitration requests from ACAS (see above). Additionally the CAC is required to make determinations under sections 183–5 TULRCA 1992 (dealing with complaints arising from a failure to disclose information). CAC awards are published and take effect as part of the contracts of employees covered by the award. Unless it can be shown that the CAC exceeded its jurisdiction,[24] breached the rules of natural justice or committed an error of law,[25] no court can overturn its decisions. According to the CAC Annual Report for 1997, 22 complaints about disclosure of information were received but only three cases went to a hearing.

The Employment Relations Act 1999 (ERel Act) added an important new role for the CAC in applications for statutory recognition and de-recognition of trade unions. The CAC receives the application for recognition and supervises the process, including the holding of a ballot amongst the affected employees, leading to a decision on whether recognition or de-recognition should be granted (see Chapter 19). It is required to establish a panel consisting of an independent chair and an experienced representative of employers and an experienced representative of workers to fulfil these functions. In dealing with these cases the Act requires the CAC to have regard to the object of encouraging and promoting fair and efficient practices in the workplace (so far as is consistent with its other obligations under the Act).

The Certification Officer

The Certification Officer is also appointed by the Secretary of State after consultation with ACAS and is required to produce an annual report for them. He or she is responsible for maintaining a list of trade unions and employers' associations and if an application is submitted has to determine whether or not a listed union qualifies for a certificate of independence. If the application is rejected, the union can appeal to the EAT on a point of law or fact. The Certification Officer also handles:

(a) disputes which arise from trade union amalgamations and mergers and the administration of political funds. However, under these jurisdictions an appeal is only possible if a point of law is involved.

(b) complaints that the provisions of Chapter IV TULRCA 1992, concerning trade union elections, have been infringed (see Chapter 20), and can determine the procedure to be followed on any application or complaint received.[26]

Under the Trade Union Reform and Employment Rights Act 1993 (TURERA 1993) the Certification Officer can direct a trade union to produce documents relating to its financial affairs. Where there appears to have been impropriety, the

Certification Officer can appoint inspectors to investigate (see Chapter 19).[27]

Finally, the ERel Act 1999 abolished the offices of the Commissioner for the Rights of Trade Union Members (CROTUM) and the Commissioner for Protection Against Unlawful Industrial Action. The Act gave the Certification Officer powers to hear complaints involving most aspects of the law in which CROTUM had previously been empowered to assist.

KEY POINTS 2
Sources and institutions of employment law

- The most important source of law governing industrial relations is legislation enacted by Parliament.

- Legislation sometimes allows for a Minister or a statutory body to issue Codes of Practice.

- The most relevant Codes of Practice for employment law are issued by ACAS, EOC, CRE and the Secretary of State.

- The case-law approach of the courts means that they are bound by the decisions of judges in higher courts.

- National courts must follow the decisions and guidance given by the European Court of Justice.

- European laws take precedence and are directly effective against the state or emanations of the state if not transposed correctly.

- Employment Tribunals are specialist bodies, whose decisions can be appealed against, on points of law, to the Employment Appeal Tribunal.

- ACAS has the general duty of improving industrial relations and provides advice, individual and collective conciliation and arbitration services.

- The Central Arbitration Committee deals with

complaints about failure to disclose information for the purposes of collective bargaining.

- The Central Arbitration Committee also has an important role to play in the procedure for the statutory recognition of trade unions.

- The Certification Officer maintains lists of employers' associations and trade unions and issues certificates of independence.

NOTES

1 See section 205 TULRCA 1992
2 *British Telecom v Sheridan* (1990) IRLR 27
3 See *Marshall v Southampton and South West Hampshire Area Health Authority* Case 152/85 (1986) IRLR 140
4 See *Amministrazione delle Finanze v Simmenthal* Case 106/77 (1978) ECR 629
5 See *Litster v Forth Dry Dock Engineering Co Ltd* (1989) IRLR 161
6 *Pickstone v Freemans* (1988) IRLR 357
7 See *Marleasing SA v Comercial Internacional de Alimentacion SA* Case 106/89 (1990) ECR 4135
8 (1980) IRLR 208
9 SI 1998/1833
10 See *Commission v UK* (1994) IRLR 292
11 See Cases 46/93 and 48/93 *Brasserie du Pêcheur SA v Federal Republic of Germany* and *R v Secretary of State for Transport ex parte Factortame* (1996) ECR 1029
12 Certain claims can be heard by a chair sitting alone. See Employment Tribunals Act 1996 and the Employment Rights (Dispute Resolution) Act 1998
13 On tribunal practice and procedures see specialist texts
14 Rule 12 Schedule 1 Employment Tribunal (Constitution and Rules of Procedure) Regulations 1993 SI 1993/2678
15 Rule 11 (see note 14)
16 Rule 3 (see note 14)
17 Section 28 Employment Tribunals Act 1996
18 Rule 36 (see note 14)
19 Section 209 TULRCA 1992
20 Section 213 TULRCA 1992
21 Section 210(3) TULRCA 1992
22 See section 212(3) TULRCA 1992
23 See section 214 TULRCA 1992
24 See *R v CAC ex parte Hy-Mac Ltd* (1979) IRLR 461
25 See *R v CAC ex parte BTP Tioxide* (1982) IRLR 61
26 See section 256 TULRCA 1992
27 See sections 37A-E TULRCA 1992

2 Formation of the contract of employment (1): The sources of contractual terms

This chapter and the next one are concerned with the contract of employment and how it comes into existence. We consider the influences that contribute to establishing the contents of the contract. Express terms agreed between the employer and the employee, or the employee's representatives, normally take precedence over all other terms. There is a statutory requirement for the employer to issue written particulars of employment to new employees within two months of their start date. These particulars are considered in detail here, as is the influence of collective agreements, workforce agreements, works rules, and custom and practice.

CONTRACTS OF EMPLOYMENT

Apart from those of apprentices and merchant seamen, who can only be employed under written deeds and articles respectively, contracts of employment may be oral or in writing.[1] A contract of employment is like any other contract in the sense that it is subject to the general principles of law. In theory this means that the parties are free to negotiate the terms and conditions that suit them so long as they remain within the constraints imposed by statute and the common law. In practice a significant proportion of the workforce do not negotiate on an individual basis. An important proportion are engaged on such terms and conditions as are laid down in currently operative collective agreements. However, these agreements are, in practice, confined to the minority of employers because almost two thirds of workplaces in the UK do not have any employees covered by collective agreements.

Illegal contracts
One aspect of the common law which has been relied on, particularly in unfair dismissal cases, is the principle that

courts will not enforce an illegal contract.[2] Thus, if employees receive additional payments which are not taxed, they may be debarred from exercising statutory rights on the ground that they were not employed under valid contracts of employment. However, an occasional payment by an employer to an employee without deduction of tax does not render the contract of employment unenforceable.[3]

Whether the employee is affected by the illegal performance of the contract by the employer depends on whether the employee was a party to or knew of the employer's illegality.[4] In *Coral Leisure Ltd v Barnet*[5] the EAT ruled that a distinction had to be drawn between cases in which there was a contractual obligation to perform an unlawful act, and cases where contractual obligations were capable of being performed lawfully and were initially intended to be so performed, but which had, in fact, been performed by unlawful means. The doing of an unlawful act by a party does not, of itself, preclude the further enforcement of that contract. Thus in *Hewcastle Catering v Ahmed*[6] the employee's involvement in a VAT fraud devised by the employer, and from which only the employer benefited, did not preclude a claim of unfair dismissal. According to the Court of Appeal, the general principle that a contract is unenforceable on grounds of illegality applies if in all the circumstances the court would appear to encourage illegal conduct. However, the defence of illegality will not succeed where the employer's conduct in participating in the illegal contract is so reprehensible in comparison with that of the employee that it would be wrong to allow the employer to rely on its being unenforceable.

Although a contract of employment can be entered into quite informally, because of the consequences of having an employee on the books (see Chapter 4) a considerable degree of formality is desirable. Indeed, if practical as well as legal difficulties are to be avoided, great care should be taken to ensure that all the relevant terms and conditions are understood at the time employment commences.

EXPRESS TERMS AND STATUTORY STATEMENTS

Express terms are those which are expressly stated to form part of the contract and they are binding irrespective of whether they differ from those contained in a job advertisement.[7] Apart from statutorily implied terms, which cannot be undermined, express terms normally take precedence over all other sources, ie common law implied terms and custom and practice. Not later than two months after the start of employment of a person whose employment continues for a month or more, the employer must supply written particulars of key terms of employment.[8] The reasoning behind this is clear: if employees receive written statements of the main terms of employment, disputes over the nature and scope of their contracts will be minimised.

STATEMENT OF PARTICULARS

The following information must be given to employees individually, although in relation to the matters mentioned in (vi), (vii), (ix) and (xv) below it is sufficient to make the information reasonably accessible to them by means of a document to which they are referred.[9]

(i) *The identity of the parties*
     Sometimes the identity of the employer can be in dispute, eg where people are 'hired out' to other organisations[10] or where the employer consists of a management committee running a charity.[11]

(ii) *The date on which the employee's period of continuous employment began* (taking into account any employment with a previous employer which counts towards that period)

     Section 211 ERA 1996 defines the meaning of 'continuous employment' (see Chapter 17). It begins with the day that a person starts work for an organisation, except that any period worked before the age of 18 years does not count towards the length of service needed to qualify for a redundancy payment. Also not counted in the length of service are periods spent taking part in a strike (sections 215 and 216 ERA 1996). The period of continuous employment is important because certain statutory rights are associated with length of service, eg the right not to be unfairly dismissed and the right to redundancy payments (see Chapter 17).

Section 218 ERA 1996 acts to preserve continuity of employment where there is a change of employer, as do the Transfer of Undertakings (Protection of Employment) Regulations 1981[12] (Transfer Regulations). If continuity is not preserved, for whatever reason, qualified employees are entitled to redundancy payments from their previous employer. According to Regulation 5(1) of the Transfer Regulations, where there is a transfer of an undertaking (or part of an undertaking), employees who are transferred are to be treated as if they had originally made contracts with the transferee employer. This provision excludes even a consensual variation in the terms of the contract of employment if the transfer is the reason for the variation.[13] It should also be noted that Regulation 5(1) is not limited to those obligations that arise out of the particular contract in existence at the date of the transfer. It also applies to anything done before the transfer in respect of 'a person employed in that undertaking or part'.[14] (On the scope of the Transfer Regulations see Chapter 15.)

(iii) *The scale or rate of remuneration, or the method of calculating remuneration, and the intervals at which remuneration is paid*
The word 'remuneration' is not defined in the statute and ought to be regarded as including all financial benefits (see Chapter 5 on the National Minimum Wage Act 1998).

(iv) *Any terms and conditions relating to hours of work and normal working hours*
The concept of normal working hours is crucial (see Chapter 17), so in order to avoid confusion, employers should specify whether or not overtime is

mandatory, ie forms part of the normal working hours. Care is especially needed when considering annualised hours contracts, where it may still be advisable to define the working week for the purpose of calculating holiday entitlement and any overtime payments due to people who leave during the working year. The courts or tribunals will not necessarily be prepared to fill gaps left by agreements that are not comprehensive. In *Ali v Christian Salvesen*[15] the Court of Appeal concluded that the parties to a collective agreement, which was expressly incorporated into a contract of employment, might deliberately have omitted provisions dealing with termination of employment during the calculation period on the grounds that it was too complicated or too controversial to include. Working hours are usually a matter for the parties to determine, but see Chapter 11 on the impact of the Working Time Regulations.[16]

(v) *Any terms and conditions relating to holidays and holiday pay*

Employees are entitled to be paid if holidays are taken in accordance with the terms of their employment during their period of notice.[17] According to the EAT, unless there is an express term to the contrary, the annual wage or salary should be divided by the calendar days in the year rather than the number of working days.[18] Those employees protected by the Working Time Regulations are entitled to four weeks paid holiday per leave year (Regulation 13). The leave year can be the subject of agreement or, if there is no such agreement, it will commence on the day employment began and each subsequent anniversary thereafter (see Chapter 11).

(vi) *Any terms and conditions relating to incapacity for work owing to sickness or injury*

This includes any provision for sick pay (see Chapter 6).

(vii) *Any terms and conditions relating to pensions and pension schemes*

(viii) *A note stating whether a contracting-out certificate is in force*
Although this book does not generally address the complex issues of pension entitlement, two matters will be mentioned here. First, where it is a contractual term that employees are entitled to benefits under a pension scheme, employers must discharge their functions under such a scheme in good faith and, so far as it is within their power, procure the benefits to which the employees are entitled.[19] Second, anything not relating to old age, invalidity or survivors' benefits that is included in a pension scheme will be protected where the Transfer Regulations apply (see Chapter 15).[20]

(ix) *The length of notice which the employee is entitled to receive and is obliged to give*
See Chapter 12.

(x)   *The title of the job or a brief description of the employee's work*
If, in the interests of flexibility, a job description is widely drawn, it should be pointed out to employees that the ambit of their contractual obligations may be wider than the particular duties upon which they are normally engaged.[21]

(xi) *Where the employment is temporary, the period for which it is expected to continue or, if it is for a fixed term, the date when it is to end*

(xii) *The place of work or, if the employee is required or permitted to work at various places, an indication of the employer's address*
If an employee works in a number of different countries, the place of work has been defined by the European Court of Justice as the place where the employee habitually carries out his work.[22]

(xiii) *Any collective agreements which directly affect the terms and conditions of employment, including, where the employer is not a party, the person by whom they were made*
Such agreements can be incorporated into a contract of

employment (see below) and may even be transferred to a new employer by the Transfer Regulations.[23]

(xiv) *Where the employee is required to work outside the UK for more than a month*
The period of work outside the UK, the currency in which payment will be made, any additional pay and benefits to be provided by reason of the work's being outside the UK, any terms and conditions relating to the employee's return to the UK.

The Posted Workers Directive[24] provides added protection for people working in a Member State other than that in which they normally work. Any rules in force concerning terms and conditions of employment, as a result of law, regulation, administrative provision or by collective agreements in the State to which the employee is posted are to be guaranteed. These rules can include maximum work periods; rest periods; paid holidays; minimum rates of pay (although not supplementary occupational pensions); conditions for hiring out temporary workers; health and safety; protective measures for pregnant women and those that have recently given birth; and equal treatment between men and women.

(xv) *Any disciplinary rules applicable to the employee*

(xvi) *The name or description of the person to whom employees can apply if they are dissatisfied with any disciplinary decision or seek to redress a grievance*
The statement must indicate the manner in which any such application should be made.

(xvii)*Any further steps consequent upon an applicant expressing dissatisfaction over a disciplinary decision or grievance*
Three points should be noted here. If the employer has fewer than 20 employees on the date the employment commences, the statement need not refer to disciplinary rules or procedures.[25] Secondly, although ERA 1996 does not state that employers must have disciplinary rules, the *Code of Practice on Disciplinary Practice and*

Procedures emphasises their desirability (see Chapter 14). Finally, rules, disciplinary decisions, grievances and procedures relating to health and safety at work are exempted because separate rules and procedures are thought to be appropriate in this area and should be referred to in the information provided by employers under section 2 HASAWA 1974 (see Chapter 10).

If there are no particulars to be entered under any of the above headings, that fact must be mentioned in the written statement. It should also be noted that information relating to items (viii), (xi), (xiii), (xiv) and (xvi) may be given in instalments within the two-month period. The other items must be dealt with in a single document called a 'principal statement'.

Changes cannot be made to a contract of employment without the consent of the employee but, where there is a change in any of the details required by section 1, written notification must be given to the employee within one month.[26] The nature of the changes must be set out in full, although the employer may refer to other documents for the same matters and in the same manner as for the original provision of particulars. There is no provision for the changes to be notified in instalments.

The status of the statement of particulars

It is important to understand that the statement issued does not constitute a contract or even conclusive evidence of its terms, but is merely the employer's version of what has been agreed.[27] Indeed, in *Robertson v British Gas*[28] the Court of Appeal decided that a statutory statement could not even be used as an aid to the interpretation of the contract. If agreement has not been reached in a key area, management may choose to include in that statement what it considers to be reasonable arrangements. Technically the statement will be inaccurate (because the terms were on offer rather than agreed at the time they were issued) but if the employee accepts the arrangements or acquiesces in them, ie by not challenging them, the employer's proposals may be deemed to have contractual effect. However, the EAT has suggested that a distinction might be drawn between a matter which has immediate practical application and one which does not. In *Jones v Associated Tunnelling Co.*[29] it was thought that it would be asking too much of ordinary employees to require them to object to erroneous statements of terms which had no immediate practical impact on them. The law does not oblige employees to sign the written particulars or even acknowledge their receipt, but if they confirm that what has been issued is an accurate summary of the main employment terms, the particulars may be treated by the courts as having contractual status.[30]

Where an employee is given a complete but incorrect statement, ie some of the particulars are wrong in that they do not reproduce what was agreed between the parties, the employee can complain to an employment tribunal which has the power to confirm, amend or replace the particulars. If there is no written statement or an incomplete one is issued, the tribunal must determine what the missing particulars are.[31] According to the Court of Appeal,[32] the particulars required under (i), (ii), (iii), (ix) and (x) above are 'mandatory' terms in that actual particulars must be given under those headings. On the other hand, the particulars required under (iv)–(vii) were viewed as 'non-mandatory' in the sense that no particulars need to be inserted if none has been agreed. As regards 'non-mandatory' terms, the Court of Appeal held that an employment tribunal could not invent a term if nothing had been agreed by the parties. However, where a 'mandatory' term was omitted from a statement a tribunal would probably have to imply one. When the tribunal has decided what particulars should have been included, the employer is deemed to have provided the employee with a statement containing those particulars.[33]

COLLECTIVE AGREEMENTS

Terms may be derived from collective agreements as well as being individually negotiated. Such agreements tend to be classed as being of either a procedural or a substantive nature. A procedural agreement aims to govern the relationship between the signatories (employers and trade unions) by establishing methods of handling disputes, whereas a substantive agreement is intended to regulate the terms and conditions of employment of those who are covered by it. Like any other agreement, collective agreements will be construed by giving meaning to the words used in the factual context known to the parties at the time.[34] It is possible to conclude a collective agreement which is legally enforceable (see Chapter 19), although this is not normally the wish of either party. By what mechanism then do individual employees derive the legal right to claim the terms and conditions which have been negotiated on their behalf? The answer lies in the process of incorporation, for by this device collectively agreed terms become legally binding as part of the individual contract of employment.[35] The simplest way of ensuring that substantive terms are incorporated into an employee's contract is by an express provision to this effect. Thus, workers may be employed on the basis of 'terms and conditions of employment which are covered by existing collective agreements negotiated and agreed with specific trade unions or unions recognised ... for collective bargaining purposes'.[36] Commonly, collective agreements will be expressly incorporated because they are referred to in a section 1 ERA 1996 statement of particulars.

In relation to the matters specified above, section 2 ERA 1996 permits employers to refer to 'some document which is reasonably accessible', and this document may be a copy of the currently operative collective agreement. Equally, it is possible for terms to be incorporated from a collective agreement by implication, although that is less desirable because of the uncertainties involved.[37] This can occur when employees have specific knowledge of the collective agreement and there is conduct which demonstrates that they accept the agreement and are willing to work under it. While this might be relatively straightforward in the case of union members, difficulties can arise in establishing the legal position of non-members. If such employees have habitually accepted and abided by the terms negotiated by the union, an implication arises that they will be bound by future agreements. However, if at any stage non-members declare that they are no longer willing to be bound by such agreements, that implication is no longer valid.[38]

It is normally quite easy to decide which terms of a collective agreement are appropriate for incorporation into an individual contract of employment: it is the substantive terms (eg on wages, hours, etc) rather than the procedural ones.[39] However, difficulties have been experienced in relation to no-strike clauses. An undertaking by the union not to call a strike before relevant procedures have been exhausted imposes an obligation on the union alone, but the following clause is clearly capable of being incorporated into individual contracts of employment: 'Employees will not engage in a strike or other industrial action until the grievance procedure has been exhausted.' The situation has been clarified by section 180 TULRCA 1992 which provides that no-strike clauses are binding only if the collective agreement:

(a) is in writing and contains a provision stating that the clause may be incorporated into a contract of employment

(b) is reasonably accessible to the employees concerned

(c) is concluded by an independent trade union and the individual contract of employment expressly or impliedly incorporates the no-strike clause.

Such clauses can be useful in drawing an employee's attention to the illegality of industrial action, but strictly speaking they are unnecessary because most forms of industrial action are likely to breach an obligation on all employees by the common law, ie the duty not to impede the employer's business (see Chapter 21).

WORKFORCE AGREEMENTS

The Working Time Regulations 1998 and the Maternity and Parental Leave Regulations 1999 are examples of where it is possible for 'relevant' agreements to be reached which enable employers to agree variations to the Regulations directly with their employees or with their representatives. These 'relevant' agreements can be reached via a process of bargaining. Where there are no collective agreements, employers can reach workforce agreements with their employees or their representatives. Regulation 23 of the Working Time Regulations allows a workforce agreement to modify or exclude Regulation 4(3) concerning the reference period for calculating the 48-hour average, Regulations 6(1) to (3) and (7) concerning night work, Regulation 10(1) concerning the entitlement to an 11-hour break in each 24 hours, Regulations 11(1) and (2) concerning a weekly or fortnightly break, and Regulation 12(1) concerning rest breaks, provided certain conditions are met. These conditions are in Schedule 1. An agreement is a workforce agreement where:

(a) it is in writing

(b) it has effect for a specified period not exceeding five years

(c) it applies to all the relevant members of a workforce or all the relevant members who belong to a particular group

(d) it is signed by the representatives of the group[40]

(e) copies of the agreement are readily available for reading prior to the signing.

WORKS RULES AND POLICY GUIDANCE

The essential difference between collective agreements and works rules lies not so much in their subject matter but in the fact that the contents of the latter are unilaterally determined by the employer. While both can be expressly or impliedly incorporated into individual contracts of employment (using the mechanisms described above), works rules offer one great advantage to the employer: whereas a collective agreement can be altered only with the consent of the parties to it, management can lawfully change the content of works rules at any time. A refusal to adhere to the revised rules would amount to a breach of contract (ie a failure to obey lawful and reasonable orders) even if there had been no advance warning or consultation with the employees affected. Thus a contractual term to the effect that employees must abide by 'the currently operative works rules' affords management the maximum degree of flexibility.[41]

There may be rules that constitute employer guidance or policy and are therefore not appropriate as contractual terms. Such a situation might arise when the employer is setting out practice and procedures rather than conferring rights on individuals. This occurred in *Wandsworth London Borough Council v D'Silva*[42] where changes to a code of practice on staff sickness were made by the employer without consultation with employees or their representatives. The EAT held that these changes amounted to alterations to a code of good practice, rather than an attempt to unilaterally alter the contract of employment.

The dismissal of an employee for failing to comply with revised works rules or policy guidance will not necessarily be fair because it will depend on what an employment tribunal regards as being 'reasonable in all the circumstances' (see Chapter 14).

CUSTOM AND PRACTICE

In the days when written contracts of employment were less common and written statements of particulars were not required by statute, custom and practice played an important part in helping to identify the contractual terms. Today custom and practice is not such an important source of law, although it may still be invoked occasionally to fill gaps in the employment relationship. To do so, a custom or practice must be definite, reasonable and generally applied in the area or trade in question. If these criteria are met, the fact that the particular employee against whom the custom is applied is ignorant of its existence appears to be of no consequence.[43] In determining whether a policy drawn up unilaterally by management has become a term of the employee's contract on the grounds that it is an established custom and practice, all the circumstances have to be taken into account. Among the most important circumstances are whether the policy has been drawn to the attention of employees by management or has been followed without exception for a substantial period.[44]

The major drawback of custom and practice is its uncertain legal effect and therefore its unreliability. After what period of time can it be said that a non-union member who has always worked in accordance with current collective agreements is bound to accept future agreements? If a custom and practice is useful to management, it is logical that efforts should be made to convert it into an express term of the contract. This may not always be possible, either because of the imprecise nature of the custom or because unions might oppose such a move as being contrary to the interests of their members. It almost goes without saying that a union will be in a better position to modify a custom or practice if it has not become embodied in a contract of employment. Finally, it should be noted that there may still be a place for custom and practice as an aid to interpreting a contractual term, eg the meaning of 'reasonable overtime' at a particular workplace.

TERMS IMPLIED BY STATUTE AND REGULATIONS

There are a number of examples of legislation implying terms into contracts of employment:

(i) *Terms and conditions awarded by the CAC*
Under section 185 TULRCA 1992 (on disclosure of information) these terms operate as part of the contract of employment of each worker affected. However, the terms and conditions imposed may be superseded or varied by a collective agreement between the employer and the union 'for the time being representing the employee' or an express or implied agreement between the employer and the employee so far as that agreement effects an improvement in the terms and conditions awarded by the CAC.

(ii) *The equality clause*
This is inserted by virtue of section 1 of the Equal Pay Act 1970 (EPA 1970), as amended (see Chapter 7).

(iii) *The National Minimum Wage Act 1998*
This, in Section 2, allows the Secretary of State to make provision for determining what is the hourly rate to be

paid. Section 2(3) allows provision to be made with respect to when a person is to be treated as working and when he or she is not.

(iv) *The Working Time Regulations*
These provide for maximum hours to be worked in various situations and occupations (see Chapter 11).

TERMS IMPLIED BY THE COMMON LAW

There are two distinct types of common law implied terms. First, where there is a gap in the contract of employment it is possible to imply a term if a court can be persuaded that it is necessary to do so in the circumstances of the particular case (implied terms of fact). Second, there are terms which are regarded by the courts as being inherent in all contracts of employment (implied terms of law). The next chapter will examine the major obligations which are automatically imposed on the parties to a contract of employment.

It is a basic principle that a contractual term can be implied only if it is consistent with the express terms of the contract. However, despite the increased use of written contracts and statements, it is not unusual for the parties to discover that they have failed to provide for a particular contingency. If there is a dispute over something which is not expressly dealt with in the contract of employment, a court or tribunal may be asked to insert a term to cover the point at issue. The party wishing to rely on an implied term must satisfy a court either that such a term was so obvious that the parties did not think it necessary to state it expressly (the 'officious bystander' test) or that such a term was necessary to give 'business efficacy' to the relationship.[45]

KEY POINTS 2
Formation of the contract of employment

- Express terms normally take precedence over all other terms apart from those implied by legislation.

- Not later than two months after the start of employment the employer must supply written particulars of employment, as provided in sections 1–3 ERA 1996.

- The statement does not constitute a contract of employment. It is merely the employer's version of what has been agreed.

- Terms of a contract may be derived from collective agreements as well as being individually negotiated.

- Substantive terms from a collective agreement may be expressly incorporated into an employee's contract of employment.

- Substantive terms from a collective agreement may also be impliedly incorporated into a contract of employment provided employees have knowledge of the agreement and their conduct demonstrates acceptance.

- Workforce agreements can provide for a variation in the Working Time Regulations and other statutory rights contained in the ERel Act 1999, where there is no collective agreement.

- Works rules are normally determined by the employer and can be expressly or impliedly incorporated into a contract of employment.

- Custom and practice, if it is definite, reasonable and generally applied, can be used to fill gaps in the employment relationship.

- Terms, such as the equality clause in section 1 EPA 1970, can be implied in the contract of employment by statute.

- Terms can also be implied by the common law if they are consistent with the express terms.

NOTES

1 On the distinction between a contract of apprenticeship and a contract of employment or training contract see *Wallace v C.A. Roofing Ltd* (1996) IRLR 435

2 Although tribunal jurisdiction in anti-discrimination cases may not depend on the existence of an enforceable contract of employment; see *Leighton v Michael* (1996) IRLR 67

3 See *Annandale Engineering v Samson* (1994) IRLR 59

4 See *Salvesson v Simons* (1994) IRLR 52

5 (1981) IRLR 204

6 (1991) IRLR 473

7 See *Deeley v British Rail Engineering Ltd* (1980) IRLR 147

8 Sections 1–2 ERA 1996

9 See sections 2(2) and (3) ERA 1996

10 For a discussion of this see *Secretary of State v Bearman* (1998) IRLR 431

11 See *Affleck v Newcastle Mind* (1999) IRLR 405

12 SI 1981/1794

13 See *British Fuels v Baxendale* and *Wilson v St Helens Borough Council* (1998) IRLR 706

14 See Regulation 5(2)(b) Transfer Regulations and *DJM International v Nicholas* (1996) IRLR 76

15 (1997) IRLR 17

16 SI 1998/1833

17 See section 88(1)(d) ERA 1996

18 See *Thames Water v Reynolds* (1996) IRLR 186 and *Morley v Heritage plc* (1993) IRLR 400

19 See *Mihlenstedt v Barclays Bank* (1989) IRLR 522

20 Regulation 7 Transfer Regulations and *Adams v Lancashire County Council* (1996) IRLR 154

21 See *Glitz v Watford Electrical* (1978) IRLR 89

22 See *Rutten v Cross Medical Ltd* (1997) IRLR 249

23 See *Whent v T. Cartledge* (1997) IRLR 153

24 Directive 96/71

25 See section 3(3) ERA 1996

26 See section 4 ERA 1996

27 See *Systems Floors (UK) Ltd v Daniel* (1981) IRLR 475

28 (1983) IRLR 302

29 (1981) IRLR 477; see also *Aparau v Iceland Foods* (1996) IRLR 119

30 See *Gascol Conversions v Mercer* (1974) IRLR 155

31 Section 11 ERA 1996

32 *Eagland v British Telecom plc* (1992) IRLR 323

33 Section 12(2) ERA 1996

34 See *Adams v British Airways* (1996) IRLR 574

35 See *Gibbons v Associated British Ports* (1985) IRLR 376

36 See *Airlie v City of Edinburgh District Council* (1996) IRLR 516

37 See *Hamilton v Futura Floors* (1990) IRLR 478

38 See *Singh v British Steel* (1974) IRLR 478

39 On the enforceability of redeployment and redundancy agreements see *Marley v Forward Trust Ltd* (1996) IRLR 369; on the enforceability of a recognition agreement see *NCB v NUM* (1986) IRLR 439

40 There are provisions which allow employers with less than 20 employees

to have the majority of those employees sign in order for a workforce agreement to come into being

41 See *Cadoux v Central Regional Council* (1986) IRLR 131
42 (1998) IRLR 193
43 See *Sagar v Ridehalgh* (1931) Ch 310
44 See *Quinn v Calder* (1996) IRLR 126
45 See *United Bank v Akhtar* (1989) IRLR 507

3 Formation of the contract of employment (2): Implied terms of law

In the previous chapter we looked at the different ways in which contractual terms may come into existence and observed that certain terms could be implied into all contracts of employment. We must now examine the major obligations imposed on both employers and employees by law. Some of these are based on long-established common law principles, while others (such as those to do with unfair dismissal) are of relatively recent origin having emerged as a result of legislative intervention.

DUTIES OF THE EMPLOYER

To pay wages

This is the most basic obligation of employers and is normally dealt with by an express term. In certain circumstances, however, the law does not leave the parties entirely free to determine the amount of remuneration payable, eg in the application of the national minimum wage or if an equality clause operates. Pay issues are considered in Chapters 5 and 6.

To provide work

Employers are generally not obliged to provide work and most employees who receive their full contractual remuneration cannot complain if they are left idle. Nevertheless, in certain circumstances the failure to provide work may amount to a breach of contract.

(i) *If a person's earnings depend upon work's being provided*
Employees who are paid by results or commission or who receive shift premiums must be given the opportunity to work because the payment of basic wages alone would deprive them of a substantial part of what they had bargained for – the opportunity to earn more.

(ii) *Where the lack of work could lead to a loss of publicity or affect the reputation of an employee*

Indeed, in one tribunal case it was held that the higher a person is in the management structure, the more important it is for work to be given when it is available.[1]

(iii) *Where an employee needs to practise in order to preserve his or her skills*

The Court of Appeal has suggested that such employees should be given the opportunity of performing work when it is available.[2] This is linked to the issue of 'garden leave' (see below), which is the practice of continuing to pay an employee for a period, but not allowing him or her to work during that time. It has sometimes been used to prevent a valuable employee from leaving and immediately taking up employment with a competitor. A problem arises when such a period without work can have a detrimental affect on an employee's skills. In *William Hill Organisation Ltd v Tucker*[3] the Court of Appeal held that the employer in this case did have an obligation to provide work when the work was available. This was partly because of the need to practise and partly because there was a contractual obligation on the employee to 'work those hours necessary to carry out his duties in a full and professional manner'.

To co-operate with the employee

Originally this duty amounted to little more than an obligation not to impede the employees in the performance of their contracts. However, one of the effects of the unfair dismissal provisions has been that the courts have displayed a greater willingness to accept that employers have a positive duty to ensure that the purposes of the contract are achieved. Thus it has frequently been stated that employers must not destroy the mutual trust and confidence upon which co-operation is built, although there are limits as to how positive this obligation should be. In *University of Nottingham v Eyett*,[4] for example, a failure by an employer to warn an employee who was proposing to exercise important rights in connection with pension benefits that the way that employee was proposing to exercise those rights was not the most financially advantageous was not seen as breaching a duty of mutual trust and confidence. Each case depends on its particular set of facts, but some examples of situations in which employers have been held to be in breach of this implied term are:

(a) the changing of the terms of a transferred employee's bridging loan to his or her detriment;[5]

(b) the operation by an employer of a business in a dishonest and corrupt manner which damaged an innocent employee's reputation,[6] although the employee may only be able to claim damages if he or she can show that the damage to their reputation has actually caused financial loss;[7]

(c) an employer's discretion under a mobility clause being exercised in a way that made it impossible for the employee to comply with a contractual obligation to move;[8]

(d) a failure to investigate a genuine safety grievance;[9]

(e) employees' not being afforded a reasonable opportunity to obtain redress of a grievance;[10]

(f) a false accusation of theft on the basis of flimsy evidence;[11]

(g) the persistent attempt by an employer to vary an employee's conditions of service.[12]

Similarly it has been suggested that this duty might require those who employ large numbers to permit reasonable time off in an emergency[13] and should also inhibit employers from issuing unjustified warnings which are not designed to improve performance but to dishearten employees and drive them out.[14]

The House of Lords has also accepted that in certain circumstances it will be necessary to imply an obligation on the employer to take reasonable steps to bring a contractual term to the employee's attention. Such a duty will arise when:

(a) the contractual terms have not been negotiated with individuals but result from collective bargaining or are otherwise incorporated by reference

(b) a particular term makes available to employees a valuable right contingent upon action being taken by them to avail themselves of its benefit

(c) employees cannot in all the circumstances reasonably be expected to be aware of the term unless it is drawn to their attention.[15]

To take reasonable care of the employee

In addition to this duty implied by law, there are a number of key statutes in the area of health and safety. We shall be looking at the legislation in Chapter 10, although it is important to note at this stage that a person who is injured in the course of employment in a factory may be able to bring an action for damages based either on the common-law duty or breach of statute or other regulations. 'In the course of employment' means the claimant was doing something that he or she was employed to do, or something reasonably incidental to those things. In *Chief Adjudication Officer v Rhodes*,[16] an employee of the Benefits Agency was assaulted at her home, when off sick from work, by a neighbour whom she had reported for suspected fraud. The Court of Appeal decided that although the incident arose out of her employment it did not take place in the course of that employment.

Recognising that employers cannot guarantee that no employees will be injured at work, the standard of care which the law demands is that which 'an ordinary prudent employer would take in all the circumstances'.[17] Generally speaking, if a job has risks to health and safety which are not common knowledge but about which an employer knows or ought to know, and against which she or he cannot guard by taking precautions, then the employer should tell anyone to whom employment is offered what those risks are if, on the information then available, knowledge of those risks would be likely to affect the decision of a sensible prospective employee about accepting the offer.[18] Thus the common law accepts that employers should be held liable only if they fail to safeguard against something which was reasonably foreseeable.[19] In *Pickford v Imperial Chemical Industries*[20] it was held that it was not reasonably foreseeable that a secretary spending 50 per cent of her time in typing would suffer, as a result, from repetitive strain injury. Indeed, it was assumed that a person of intelligence and experience would be able to intersperse the typing with other activities without being told to do so.

It should also be observed that the general duty of care does not extend to taking all reasonable steps to protect the economic welfare of employees, whether by insuring them against special risks known to the employer or by advising them of those risks so that they can obtain appropriate cover. Thus, in the absence of a contractual term to the contrary, the employer's duty is limited to the protection of the employee against physical harm or disease.[21]

Employers are entitled to follow recognised practices in their industry, unless the practices are obviously unsafe, but must make arrangements to ensure that they keep abreast of current developments, eg by joining an employers' association. Once an employer knows of a source of danger, or could have been expected to know of it, it is necessary to take all reasonable steps to protect employees from risks which have hitherto been unforeseeable.[22] The duty is to assess the likelihood of injury and to weigh the risk against the cost and inconvenience of taking effective precautions to eliminate it. Employers owe a single personal duty of care to each of their employees, having proper regard to the employee's skill and experience, etc. Thus even if the employer delegates this duty to another person who is reasonably believed to be competent to perform it, the employer will remain personally liable for injuries to an employee caused by that other person's negligence.[23] Similarly, where an employee's labour is subcontracted, the employer's duty of care is still owed.[24]

Having considered some general issues, it may be useful to subdivide this duty into the following headings:

(i) *Safe premises*

The case of *Latimer v AEC Ltd*[25] provides a suitable illustration of what is required of employers in this connection. Owing to exceptionally heavy rainfall, a factory was flooded. A layer of oil and grease was left on the floor which the employers attempted to cover with sawdust. However, this was not spread across all of the factory floor and an employee slipped in an area which was uncovered. It was held by the House of Lords that the employers had taken reasonable precautions and they could not be expected to close down their factory in order to avoid what was a fairly small risk of injury.[26] More recently it has been acknowledged that in certain circumstances UK-based employers may have to satisfy themselves as to the safety of overseas sites. According to the Court of Appeal, the employer's duty to take all reasonable steps to ensure the safety of employees applies whether the premises where the employee is required to work are occupied by the employer or by a third party.[27]

(ii) *Safe plant, equipment and tools*

If employers know that a tool or a piece of machinery could be a source of danger, it is incumbent upon them to take reasonable precautions to safeguard employees. Where tools or equipment are purchased from a reputable supplier and employers have no reason to suspect that they are defective, they cannot be held liable at common law. If in these circumstances an employee were to sustain an injury as a result of a defect, he or she would be obliged to sue the person responsible, such as the supplier or manufacturer, under the general law of negligence in order to recover damages.

(iii) *Safe system of work*

Under this heading are included all the matters which relate to the manner in which the work is performed: job design, working methods, the provision of protective clothing, training and supervision. Indeed, the High Court has accepted that employers have a duty not to cause their employees psychological damage by the volume or character of the work that they are required to perform.[28] In another case it was argued that following a wages snatch, the employer had been negligent in not hiring an outside firm of security specialists to collect wages. However, the Court of Appeal held that no more could be expected of an employer who had provided proper instruction in ways of reducing the risk of injury.[29] If safety rules and procedures exist, employees must be informed of their content, and if safety clothing or equipment is required, it must be readily available.[30] Clearly the more dangerous the task or workplace situation, the greater is the need for precautions to be taken – but how far must an employer go to ensure that safety devices are properly utilised?

In *Crouch v British Rail Engineering*[31] the Court of Appeal decided that where an employee is regularly performing tasks which involve a reasonably foreseeable risk to the eyes, the employer has the duty actually to put goggles into the employee's hands. Similarly, employees who are likely to do a great deal of typing should be told that they must take breaks and rest pauses.[32] In *Pape v Cumbria County Council*[33] the High Court ruled that an employer has a duty to warn cleaners of the dangers of handling chemical cleaning materials with unprotected hands and to instruct them on the need to wear gloves at all times. It would seem that the circumstances that have to be considered in ascertaining the extent of the duty of care include: the risk of injury; the gravity of any injury which might result; the difficulty of providing protective equipment or clothing; the availability of that equipment or clothing and the distance the worker might have to go to fetch it; the frequency of occasions on which the employee is likely to need the protective equipment or clothing; and the experience and degree of skill to be expected of the employee. Bearing in mind both this common-law duty and the obligations imposed by legislation (see

Chapter 10), managers would be advised to ensure that an unreasonable refusal to follow safety rules or procedures is classed as a breach of discipline which could ultimately lead to dismissal for misconduct.

(iv) *Competent and safe colleagues*

Employers are required to take reasonable steps to ensure that employees do not behave in such a fashion that they are a source of danger to others. This means that employers must engage competent staff, or train recruits to a safe worker level, must instruct their employees in safe working methods, and must then provide adequate supervision to check that these methods are being adhered to. Practical jokers cannot be tolerated, and if they do not respond to warnings their employment should be terminated in accordance with disciplinary procedures. Such people are a threat to everyone and are unlikely to attract the sympathy of their workmates.

This duty extends to a working environment in which an employee's colleagues smoke. In *Walton & Morse v Dorrington*[34] a secretary worked in the same office as a number of others, some of whom smoked. This was not a problem to her when working in a well ventilated room. When they were moved to an office where this was not the case, the smoke became a source of irritation and discomfort. Eventually she left when her employers would not make any changes. The EAT held that her employers were in breach of an implied term to provide their employees with, so far as was reasonably practicable, 'a working environment which is reasonably suitable for the performance by them of their contractual duties'.

To provide references

Strictly speaking, this concerns a duty of care owed to ex-employees, but it is an issue on which human resource professionals need to take care. In *Spring v Guardian Assurance plc*[35] the complainant argued that a reference provided by a former employer was a malicious falsehood and/or a negligent misstatement and/or a breach of an implied term in the contract of employment that any reference would be compiled with all reasonable care. The House of Lords concluded that an employer did normally have a duty both to supply a reference and to take reasonable care in compiling it by ensuring the accuracy of the information upon which it was based. This duty is to provide a reference which is in substance true, accurate and fair.[36] The provider of a reference must not give an impression that is unfair or misleading overall, even if the component parts of the reference are accurate. This can clearly mean the inclusion of matters not in the ex-employee's favour as well as those that are. Failure to provide a reference for an ex-employee might also be interpreted as coming within section 6(2) of the SDA 1975, which makes it unlawful to discriminate against employees by subjecting them to any detriment in relation to their employment (see Chapter 7).[37]

DUTIES OF THE EMPLOYEE

To co-operate with the employer

We are concerned here with the duty to obey lawful and reasonable orders and the duty not to impede the employer's business. In this context the obligation to carry out lawful orders has two distinct aspects. First, it means that employees are not required to comply with an order if to do so would break the law, for example by producing false accounts. Second, it also means that employees are not obliged to accept orders which fall outside the scope of the contract. This is consistent with the view that (at least in theory) the terms of a contract cannot be varied unilaterally. However, as we shall discover later (Chapter 14), this does not prevent employees from being fairly dismissed for refusing to follow instructions which may be outside their contractual obligations.[38]

As regards the duty not to impede the employer's business, it is clear that going on strike breaches a fundamental term of the contract: the essence of the employment relationship is that the employee is ready and willing to work in exchange for remuneration. However, is there a duty on employees not to engage in industrial action which falls short of a strike? In the leading case of the *Secretary of State v ASLEF*,[39] which involved a work to rule on the railways, the Court of Appeal gave different reasons in reaching the conclusion that such a duty exists. Lord Justice Roskill thought that there is an implied term that employees ought not to obey lawful instructions in such a way as to disrupt the employer's business. Lord Justice Buckley extended the notion of fidelity (see below) and proclaimed that 'the employee must serve the employer faithfully with a view to promoting those commercial interests for which he is employed'. Lord Denning chose to focus attention on motive, ie the wilfulness of the disruption caused, and his formulation leads to the conclusion that all forms of industrial action are likely to be unlawful. The High Court has also ruled that it is a professional obligation of teachers to co-operate in running schools and that the failure to cover for absent colleagues amounts to a breach of contract.[40] (On the options open to an employer where an employee only part-performs the contract see Chapter 12.)

Fidelity
Employees must avoid putting themselves in a position whereby their own interests conflict with the duty they owe their employer or an employer to whom they have been seconded.[41] Thus employees must not accept any reward for their work other than from their employer, eg a gift or secret commission. However, employees have no contractual duty to disclose their own misconduct, and whether there is a duty to report the misconduct of fellow employees depends on the individual contract of employment and the circumstances.[42] There are two particular aspects to this duty which we must now consider: the obligation not to compete with the employer, and the obligation not to disclose confidential information.

(i)   *The obligation not to compete with the employer*
      Generally the spare-time activities of employees are no business of the employer, although an injunction may be granted to prevent employees from working for competitors during their spare time if it can be shown

that the employer's business would be seriously damaged. However, in *Nova Plastics Ltd v Froggatt*[43] the EAT rejected the argument that there is a general implication that any work for a competitor should be regarded as being a breach of trust or a failure to give loyal service. It should be noted that the intention to set up in competition with the employer is not in itself a breach of the implied duty of loyalty, although there is a line over which the employee must not go. The renting and equipping of premises in an employee's spare time, and the arranging of financial backing to set up in competition may be construed as a breach of an implied duty of fidelity.[44] If the employer has reasonable grounds for believing that the employee has committed or is about to commit some wrongful act, dismissal may be justified (see Chapter 14).[45]

Normally ex-employees are entitled to make use of the skills and knowledge which they have acquired, and are allowed to compete with a former employer provided they do not rely on confidential information (see below). However, this is not the position if there is an express clause in the contract of employment which restrains competition by employees when they leave.[46] Such restraint clauses (restrictive covenants) will be enforced by the courts only if they provide protection against something more than competition alone, if they are shown to be reasonable in the circumstances, and if they are not contrary to the public interest.[47] A clause stopping an ex-employee ever dealing with any of the plaintiff's customers with whom he or she dealt might be unreasonable, but one restricting contact with customers dealt with during the last six months might be acceptable.[48] The reasonableness of the restraint is to be assessed as at the date the contract was made.[49] Non-competition clauses in a contract may be reasonable to protect the employer's proprietary interests in the customer connections that have been built up by the departing employees, although non-solicitation clauses should not be too broad. It would be an unreasonable restraint of trade to stop employees, or ex-employees, soliciting even the most junior of employees.[50]

What about the enforcement of 'garden leave' clauses, ie clauses which provide that during the period of notice an employee is not obliged to work but will receive full pay and meanwhile must not work for anyone else? Such clauses will not be enforced if it appears that the business for which the employee wishes to work before the notice expires has nothing to do with the employer's business. On the other hand, where the period during which the employee is not required to work is not excessive and there is a risk of damage to the employer's business, it may be appropriate to restrain the employee from taking other employment during the notice period, either under a specific clause or as a breach of duty of fidelity.[51] However, the wrongful or unfair dismissal of an employee will prevent the employer from relying on a restrictive covenant.[52]

Finally, one effect of Regulation 5 of the Transfer Regulations (see Chapter 15) is that the transferee may benefit from a restrictive covenant in contracts of employment made with the transferor. Thus an employee may be restrained from doing or seeking to do business with anyone who had dealt with the transferor during the period stipulated in the original contract.[53] Even if the employee has entered into an agreement, in return for payment, that he or she will not work for a competitor, the employer may find it difficult to enforce this agreement if it took place by a variation of contract as a result of a transfer of the undertaking.[54]

(ii) *The obligation not to disclose confidential information*
The following principles have been enunciated by the Court of Appeal.[55] First, an individual's obligations are to be determined by the contract of employment, and in the absence of any express term the employee's obligations in respect of the use and disclosure of information are the subject of implied terms. Second, while the individual remains in employment the obligations are included in the implied term which

imposes a duty of fidelity on the employee. The extent of this duty varies according to the nature of the contract and would be broken if an employee copied a list of the employer's customers for use after the employment ended, or deliberately memorised such a list.[56] Third, the implied term which imposes an obligation on the employee as to his or her conduct after the employment has terminated is more restricted than that imposed by the duty of fidelity. The obligation not to use or disclose information might cover secret processes of manufacture or designs, or any other information of a sufficiently high degree of confidentiality as to amount to a trade secret.[57] However, this obligation does not extend to information which is only 'confidential' in the sense that any unauthorised disclosure to a third party while the employment subsisted would be a breach of the duty of fidelity. Fourth, in order to determine whether any particular item of information falls within the implied term thus preventing its use or disclosure after the employment has ceased, it is necessary to consider all the circumstances of the case. Among the matters to which attention must be paid are:

- the nature of employment. A high obligation of confidentiality might be imposed if the employment was such that confidential material was habitually handled.

- the nature of the information. In deciding whether there is a legitimate trade secret to be protected, a distinction needs to be made between information which can be legitimately regarded as the property of the employer and the skill, know-how and general knowledge which can be regarded as the property of the employee. The information needs to be identifiable, rather than a general assertion of a mass of knowledge.[58]

- whether the employer impressed on the employee the confidentiality of the information. However, an employer cannot prevent the use or disclosure of information merely by telling the employee that it is confidential.

In practice it can be very difficult to differentiate between use and abuse of the knowledge which an ex-employee possesses, for example of the former employer's customers. Thus employers should be advised to draft express restraint clauses which set precise limits on the future employment of key workers. Such clauses must be carefully worded, for it is a court's duty to give effect to covenants as they are expressed rather than to correct errors or remedy omissions.[59] Because breaches are relatively easy to identify, enforcing such clauses should be a fairly simple process. Indeed, the mere presence of a restraint clause can be valuable as a reminder to the employee that disclosure of confidential information will not be condoned. The employer who relies solely on the implied term is at a serious disadvantage because an employee can be stopped from disclosing confidential information only when the plaintiff employer has proved that such information has already been divulged. Only then will an aggrieved employer have a remedy against a third party to whom the employee has passed trade secrets or confidential information.[60]

Two further points need to be considered. First, in an appropriate case a court has power to grant injunctions against ex-employees to restrain them from fulfilling contracts already concluded with third parties.[61] Second, although the Data Protection Act 1998 now imposes additional constraints on an employee's ability to disclose information (see Chapter 18), the Public Interest Disclosure Act 1998 protects workers who make certain disclosures in the public interest.

To take reasonable care

Employees must exercise reasonable skill and care in the performance of their contracts.[62] If they do not do so, apart from any disciplinary action that may be taken against them, there is an implied duty to indemnify the employer in respect of the consequences of their negligence.[63] In theory, therefore, if by virtue of the doctrine of vicarious liability (see Chapter 4) an employer is required to pay damages to an injured third party, the amount paid out could be recovered by suing the negligent employee. In practice, such embarrassing litigation is avoided because it is the employer's insurance company that actually pays the damages.

PUBLIC INTEREST DISCLOSURES

The purpose of the Public Interest Disclosure Act 1998, which primarily amended the ERA 1996, is to protect individuals who make certain disclosures of information in the public interest. Section 43A ERA 1996 defines a 'protected disclosure' as a qualifying disclosure which is made to the persons mentioned in Sections 43C–43H ERA 1996 (below). Section 43B(1) defines a 'qualifying disclosure' as one which a worker *reasonably believes* tends to show one or more of the following: (a) a criminal offence; (b) a failure to comply with any legal obligation; (c) a miscarriage of justice; (d) danger to the health and safety of any individual (ie not necessarily a worker); (e) damage to the environment; or (f) the deliberate concealment of information tending to expose any of the matters listed above. Three general points about these categories should be noted. Firstly, they are not restricted to confidential information. Secondly, there is no requirement for any link between the matter disclosed and the worker's employment. Thirdly, the matter disclosed may have occurred in the past, be currently occurring, or be likely to occur.

Section 43C(1) ERA 1996 protects workers who make qualifying disclosures *in good faith* to their employer or to another person who is responsible for the matter disclosed. According to Section 43C(2) ERA 1996, workers are to be treated as having made disclosures to their employer if they follow a procedure which the employer has authorised, even if the disclosure has been made to someone else such as an independent person or organisation. Thus there is a danger that workers may lose protection if they refuse to follow a procedure which they believe to be defective, for example, because of a lack of confidentiality. Section 43D ERA 1996 enables workers to seek legal advice about their concerns and to reveal to their adviser the issues about which a disclosure may be made. Under these circumstances, Section 43B(4) ERA 1996 provides that the legal adviser is bound by professional privilege and cannot make a protected disclosure.

Section 43E ERA 1996 protects workers in government-appointed organisations if they make a disclosure in good faith to a Minister of the Crown rather than to their legal employer. Section 43F(1) ERA 1996 protects workers who make disclosures in good faith to a person prescribed for the purpose by the Secretary of State.[64] However, the worker must reasonably believe that (a) the matter falls within the remit of the prescribed person, and (b) that the information and any allegation contained in it are substantially true.

Section 43G ERA 1996 enables workers to make a protected disclosure in other limited circumstances. In order to be protected workers must:

(a) act in good faith;

(b) reasonably believe that the information and any allegation contained in it are substantially true;

(c) not act for personal gain (according to Section 43L(2) ERA 1996, in determining whether a person has acted for personal gain, a reward payable under any enactment will be disregarded);

(d) have already disclosed substantially the same information to the employer or to a person prescribed under Section 43F ERA 1996, unless they reasonably believe that they would be subject to a detriment for doing so, or that the employer would conceal or destroy the evidence if alerted;

(e) act reasonably. For these purposes regard shall be had, in particular, to:

(i) the identity of the person to whom the disclosure

is made (for example, disclosure to an MP may be reasonable whereas disclosure to the media may not be)

(ii) the seriousness of the matter

(iii) whether there is a continuing failure or one likely to recur

(iv) whether the disclosure is made in breach of a duty of confidentiality owed by the employer to another person

(v) any action the employer (or prescribed person) has taken or might have been expected to take in relation to a previous disclosure

(vi) whether the worker has complied with any procedure authorised by the employer for making a disclosure.

Section 43H ERA 1996 deals with disclosures about exceptionally serious wrongdoing. Again, in order to be protected:

(a) workers must act in good faith;

(b) they must reasonably believe that the information and any allegation contained in it are substantially true;

(c) they must not act for personal gain;

(d) the relevant failure must be of an exceptionally serious nature; and

(e) in all the circumstances it must be reasonable to make the disclosure. In this respect particular regard will be had to the identity of the person to whom the disclosure is made.

Section 43J ERA 1996 prevents employers from generally contracting out of the provisions in Part IVA. In particular, it deals with 'gagging clauses' by invalidating a worker's agreement (whether contained in a contract or settlement of legal proceedings) not to make a protected disclosure.

Section 43K(1) ERA 1996 is designed to enable everyone who works to benefit from Part IVA, irrespective of whether they fall within the Section 230 ERA 1996 definition of 'employee' or 'worker'. Thus for these purposes the definition of 'worker' is extended to include certain agency workers; certain workers who would not otherwise be covered because they are not obliged to carry out all of their duties personally; NHS practitioners such as GPs, certain dentists, pharmacists and opticians; and certain trainees. Section 43K(2) ERA 1996 extends the definition of 'employer' accordingly.

Section 47B(1) ERA 1996 gives workers the right not to be subjected to any detriment for making a protected disclosure. For these purposes, the extended meaning of 'worker' in Section 43K applies, and it is made clear that 'detriment' covers both actions and a deliberate failure to act. Thus the following would be covered: discipline or dismissal, or being denied a pay rise or facilities that would otherwise be provided.

In addition, workers who have been dismissed for making a protected disclosure and are not qualified to claim unfair dismissal under Part X of the ERA 1996 (the general unfair dismissal provisions) can bring a claim under new Section 47B ERA 1996. The obvious example here is a worker who does not have a contract of employment. Section 48(1A) ERA 1996 enables a worker to complain to an employment tribunal that Section 47B has been infringed.

Section 103A ERA 1996 makes it automatically unfair to dismiss employees on the grounds that they have made a protected disclosure. No qualifying period of service is required and no age restriction operates in these circumstances. Similarly, Section 105(6A) ERA 1996 makes it unfair to select employees for redundancy if the reason for doing so is that they have made a protected disclosure. Finally, it should be noted that there is no limit on the compensation that can be awarded by an employment tribunal if Section 103A ERA 1996 applies.

THE LAW GOVERNING INVENTIONS AND COPYRIGHT

Since section 39(1) of the Patents Act 1977 came into force, an invention belongs to an employer if:

(a) it was made in the course of the employee's normal duties or those specifically assigned to him or her, and the circumstances in either case were such that an invention might reasonably be expected to result from the carrying out of those duties; or

(b) it was made in the course of the employee's duties and at the time of making the invention, because of the nature of the duties and the particular responsibilities arising from them, there was a special obligation to further the interests of the employer's undertaking.

In all other circumstances the invention belongs to the employee notwithstanding any contractual term to the contrary. This section was considered in *Reiss Engineering v Harris*[65] where the Patents Court held that for these purposes employees' normal duties are those which they are actually employed to do. Section 39(1)(a) was interpreted as referring to an invention which achieves or contributes to achieving whatever was the aim or object to which the employee's efforts in carrying out his or her duties were directed, ie an invention similar to that made but not necessarily the precise invention as that actually made. The extent and nature of the 'special obligation' in section 39(1)(b) will depend on the status of the employee and the attendant responsibilities and duties of that status.

Even if the invention belongs to the employer, an employee can apply to the Patents Court or Controller of Patents for an award of compensation. This may be granted if the patent is of outstanding benefit (in money or money's worth) to the employer and it is just to make an award. The burden of proof lies on the employee to show that the employer has derived benefit from the patented invention. Where inventions belong to employees and their interests have been assigned to the employer, they are still entitled to seek compensation if they can show that the financial benefit they have derived is inadequate in relation to the benefit derived by the employer from the patent and it is just that additional compensation should be paid. However, no compensation can be paid if, at the time the invention is made, there is in force a 'relevant collective agreement' (an agreement between a trade union to which the employee belongs and the employer or an association to which the employer belongs) which provides for the payment of compensation for inventions made by the employee. It is expected that collective agreements will improve upon the statutory rights, yet there appears to be nothing to prevent employers and unions from negotiating less favourable compensation schemes.

According to section 11 of the Copyright, Designs and Patents Act 1988, where a literary, dramatic, musical or artistic work is made by an employee in the course of employment, the employer is the first owner of any copyright subject to any agreement to the contrary.

KEY POINTS 3
Implied terms of law

The law regards employers and employees as having certain obligations to each other. These obligations arise out of long-established common-law principles and more recent statutory intervention in the employment relationship.

The duties of the employer include

- paying wages if an employee is available for work, and not making unlawful deductions

- providing work in circumstances where a lack of work will affect an employee's earnings or reputation or his or her skills

- co-operating with the employee and preserving the

mutual trust and confidence upon which this co-operation depends

- taking reasonable care of the employee by providing a safe working environment and safe working practices

- special care with regard to references for ex-employees.

The duties of the employee include

- co-operating with the employer and obeying lawful and reasonable instructions

- not damaging the employer's business by competing with the employer in breach of a duty of fidelity

- not disclosing certain confidential information to competitors

- taking reasonable care and exercising reasonable skills in the performance of his or her contract.

NOTES

1 *Bosworth v A Jowett* (1977) IRLR 341
2 *Longston v AUEW* (1974) ICR 180
3 (1998) IRLR 313
4 (1999) IRLR 87
5 *French v Barclays Bank* (1998) IRLR 647
6 *Malik v Bank of Credit and Commerce* (1997) IRLR 462; but there is no obligation on the employer to disclose that it has committed such breaches of contract prior to entering into an agreement to compromise any employee claims; see *Bank of Credit and Commerce v Ali* (1999) IRLR 226
7 See *Bank of Credit and Commerce International v Ali (No. 3)* (1999) IRLR 508
8 *United Bank v Akhtar* (1989) IRLR 507
9 *BAC v Austin* (1978) IRLR 332
10 *Goold Ltd v McConnell* (1995) IRLR 516
11 *Robinson v Crompton Parkinson* (1978) IRLR 61
12 *Woods v WM Car Services* (1982) IRLR 413
13 *Warner v Barber's Stores* (1978) IRLR 109; see also the provisions for time off for dependants in the Employment Relations Act 1999
14 *Walker v J Wedgewood Ltd* (1978) IRLR 105
15 See *Scally v Southern Health Board* (1991) IRLR 522
16 (1999) IRLR 103

17 *Paris v Stepney Borough Council* (1951) AC 376
18 See *White v Holbrook Ltd* (1985) IRLR 215
19 See *Hewett v Brown Ltd* (1992) ICR 530 on the duty owed to the employee's family
20 (1998) IRLR 436
21 See *Reid v Rush & Tompkins* (1989) IRLR 265
22 See *Baxter v Harland & Wolff* (1990) IRLR 516
23 See *McDermid v Nash Dredging* (1987) IRLR 334
24 See *Morris v Breaveglen Ltd* (1993) IRLR 350
25 (1953) AC 643
26 See also *Smith v Scot Bowyers Ltd* (1986) IRLR 315
27 See *Cook v Square D Ltd* (1992) IRLR 34
28 See *Walker v Northumberland County Council* (1995) IRLR 35
29 *Charlton v Forest Ink* (1980) IRLR 331
30 See *Pentney v Anglian Water Authority* (1983) ICR 463
31 (1988) IRLR 404
32 See *Pickford v Imperial Chemical Industries* (1996) IRLR 622
33 (1991) IRLR 404
34 (1997) IRLR 488
35 (1994) IRLR 460
36 See *Bartholomew v London Borough of Hackney* (1999) IRLR 246
37 See *Coote v Granada Hospitality Ltd* (1999) IRLR 452
38 See *Farrant v The Woodroffe School* (1998) IRLR 176
39 (1972) QB 443
40 See *Sim v Rotherham MBC* (1986) IRLR 391
41 *MacMillan Inc v Bishopsgate Investment* (1993) IRLR 393
42 See *Sybron Corporation v Rochem Ltd* (1983) IRLR 253
43 (1982) IRLR 146
44 See *Lancashire Fires Ltd v SA Lyons & Co Ltd* (1997) IRLR 113
45 See *Laughton v Bapp Industrial Ltd* (1986) IRLR 245 and *Adamson v B & L Cleaning Ltd* (1995) IRLR 193
46 On non-solicitation and non-poaching covenants see *Alliance Paper v Prestwich* (1996) IRLR 25
47 See *Office Angels Ltd v Rainer-Thomas* (1991) IRLR 214 and *Hanover Insurance Brokers Ltd v Schapiro* (1994) IRLR 82
48 See *Dentmaster (UK) Ltd v Kent* (1997) IRLR 636
49 See *D v M* (1996) IRLR 192
50 See *Dawnay, Day & Co v de Bracconier d'Alphen* (1997) IRLR 285
51 See *Eurobrokers Ltd v Rabey* (1995) IRLR 206 and *Credit Suisse Ltd v Armstrong* (1996) IRLR 450
52 See *Cantor Fitzgerald International v Callaghan* (1999) IRLR 234 and *Rock Refrigeration Ltd v Jones* (1996) IRLR 675
53 See *Morris Angel v Hollande* (1993) IRLR 169
54 See *Credit Suisse First Boston Ltd (Europe)v Padiachy* (1998) IRLR 504
55 See *Faccenda Chicken Ltd v Fowler* (1986) IRLR 69
56 See *Bullivant Ltd v Ellis* (1987) IRLR 491
57 See *Lancashire Fires Ltd v SA Lyons & Co* (note 44)
58 See *FSS Travel and Leisure Systems Ltd v Johnson* (1998) IRLR 382
59 See *WAC Ltd v Whillock* (1990) IRLR 23; on the possibility of severing unlawful clauses and enforcing the remainder see *Marshall v NM Financial Management* (1996) IRLR 20
60 See *Sun Printers Ltd v Westminster Press* Ltd (1982) IRLR 92

61 See *PSM International v McKechnie* (1992) IRLR 279
62 See also section 7 HASAWA 1974 (Chapter 10)
63 See *Janata Bank v Ahmed* (1981) IRLR 457
64 See The Public Interest Disclosure (Prescribed Persons) Order 1999 SI 1549
65 (1985) IRLR 232

4 Recruitment and selection

At the beginning of this chapter we raise some of the issues which will have to be considered by the human resources department. Firstly, is it preferable to hire employed or self-employed persons? Secondly, what are the possible implications of outsourcing the work to be done? Thirdly, if employees are engaged, should they have indefinite, fixed-term, or some other type of contract of employment? Fourthly, what are the issues concerned with employing workers on a temporary basis? Lastly, is it necessary to impose a probationary period on new recruits? The latter part of the chapter deals with some of the regulatory constraints which impinge upon the process of recruitment and selection. Rules concerning rehabilitated offenders and rules contained in the Asylum and Immigration Act 1996 are outlined here, as well as government initiatives for combating age discrimination in employment. The law relating to refusal of employment on union grounds, to the employment of disabled persons, and to sex and race discrimination are dealt with in Chapters 7 and 8.

EMPLOYEES OR INDEPENDENT CONTRACTORS?

Perhaps one of the most important decisions to be made is whether workers are to be hired under contracts of service (ie as employees) or contracts for services (ie as independent contractors). Although some statutes apply to all workers, for example the Sex Discrimination Act 1975 (SDA 1975),[1] there are still significant legal differences drawn between employed and self-employed persons.

Employees gain the benefit of a number of statutory employment rights and are subject to the unwritten general obligations implied in all contracts of employment (see Chapter 3). When employed, as opposed to self-employed, persons are engaged, employers are required by statute to deduct tax under Schedule E and social security contributions. In addition, employers are obliged to pay employers' National Insurance contributions and to insure against personal injury claims brought by employees. Perhaps the most significant difference at common law is that the doctrine of vicarious liability applies to employees but not to the self-employed, although in exceptional circumstances employers will be liable for the tortious acts of their independent contractors, eg if they authorise the commission of the wrongful act or have a responsibility which cannot, by law, be delegated to someone else.

The essence of the doctrine of vicarious liability is that employers are held liable to third parties for the civil wrongs committed by employees in the course of their employment. Determining what is 'in the course of employment' has caused immense difficulties over the years but the position today appears to be as follows. Clearly employees act 'in the course of employment' where they carry out acts which are authorised by the employer. Similarly, where their actions are so closely connected with the employment as to be incidental to it, although prohibited and unauthorised by the employer, employees act 'in the course of employment'. However, if an employee's action is so outside the scope of employment as to be not something the employee was employed to do, then the employer is not liable.[2] In *ST v North Yorkshire County Council*[3] a pupil was sexually assaulted by a deputy headmaster whilst away on a school trip. The Court of Appeal held that the employer could not be held vicariously liable. The deputy headmaster was employed to supervise the student's welfare while on the holiday, and sexual assault could not be described as carrying out that duty.

As regards travelling in the course of employment, the House of Lords has laid down the following six propositions:

(a) Employees travelling from their ordinary residence to their regular place of work, whatever the means of transport and even if provided by the employer, are not normally acting in the course of employment. However, if they are contractually obliged to use the employer's transport, they will normally, in the absence of an express condition to the contrary, be regarded as acting in the course of employment while doing so.

(b) Travelling in the employer's time between workplaces could be in the course of employment.

(c) Receipt of wages, although not the receipt of a travelling allowance, would indicate that the employee was travelling in the course of employment. The fact that an employee may have discretion as to the mode and time of travelling would not take the journey out of the course of employment.

(d) Employees travelling in their employer's time from their ordinary residence to a workplace other than their regular workplace or in the course of a peripatetic occupation or to the scene of an emergency would be acting in the course of employment.

(e) A deviation from or interruption to a journey undertaken in the course of employment, unless the deviation or interruption was merely incidental to the journey, would for the time being take the employee out of the course of employment.

(f) Return journeys are to be treated on the same footing as outward journeys.

These propositions are not intended to exhaustively define when travelling time is in the course of employment and are subject to any express arrangements between employer and employee.[4]

Before an employer can be held vicariously liable, some nexus has to be established between the employee's wrongful act and the circumstances of employment. Thus a contractor engaged to clean offices (including telephones) was not vicariously liable when one of the contractor's employees dishonestly used the phones for his own purposes.[5] Employees remain personally liable for their own acts and theoretically may be required to reimburse the employer for any damages paid out as a result of their failure to take care (see Chapter 3). It should also be noted that in some cases the criminal law regards an employee's act as being that of the employer, in which case the latter will be responsible for the wrongs committed by the former.

Additionally, a company might be liable as a substitute employer for the negligence of employees not directly employed by them if it can be shown that the substitute employer had sufficient power of control and supervision properly to be regarded as the effective employer at the critical time.[6]

Distinguishing employees from other types of worker

Given all the consequences of having an employee on the books, is it always possible to discern whether a contract is a contract of service or a contract for services? Unfortunately, the answer must be in the negative, for the courts have ruled that the intention of the parties cannot be the sole determinant of contractual status; otherwise it would be too easy to contract out of employment protection legislation. It is the operation of the contract in practice that is crucial rather than its appearance. According to the Court of Appeal[7] tribunals have to consider: 'all aspects of the relationship, no single feature being in itself decisive and each of which may vary in weight and direction, and having given such balance to the factors as seems appropriate to determine whether the person was carrying on business on his own account'. Thus in *Hall v Lorimer*[8] the Court of Appeal considered the position of a person who gave up their employment to pursue the same occupation on a freelance basis. The person concerned carried out all their tasks at employers' premises using equipment provided by the employers. The Court held that there was no single path to deciding whether the contracts under which a person worked were contracts of service or contracts for services. One had to stand back from the detail and take an informed and considered view of the whole picture. In this case the crucial factor was that the employee worked for a number of different companies.

Although the element of control is important, it may not be

decisive in the case of skilled workers who decide for themselves how their work should be done. In such cases the question is broadened to 'Whose business is it?'[9] The fact that workers pay their own tax and National Insurance cannot be conclusive in determining employment status,[10] and the cases show that people who perform work at home may be classed as employees so long as there is an element of continuing mutual contractual obligation.[11] Of crucial importance is whether one person working for another is required to perform his or her service in person or not. In *Express and Echo Publications v Tanton*[12] a contract allowed a worker to provide a substitute if he was not available. This prevented the worker from being defined as an employee because the obligation to do the work in person was, according to the Court of Appeal, an 'irreducible minimum'.

Unless the relationship is dependent solely upon the true construction of a written contract, whether a person is engaged under a contract of employment is a question of fact for a court or tribunal to determine.[13]

OUTSOURCING

Increasingly employers are choosing to outsource parts of their non-core activities. Outsourcing can mean an arrangement whereby a contractor supplies staff who will be under the supervision of the hirer, or it can mean the outsourcing of the complete activity so that the hirer is concerned only with the outcomes rather than with the means of achieving them. Activities that are commonly outsourced include in-house catering and the cleaning of premises.

When an organisation decides on outsourcing an activity it must also decide what is to happen to its current employees who work in the part to be contracted out. It also has an obligation to inform and consult those employees at the earliest opportunity. There may be no need for redundancies because the employees currently working in the part to be transferred may be protected by the Transfer of Undertakings (Protection of Employment) Regulations 1981[14] (these

Regulations will be further considered in Chapter 15). Their contracts of employment and their employment relationship are likely to transfer with the outsourcing contract. The contractor will become their employer and be liable for all and any debts arising out of the employment relationship. It will be as if they signed their original contract of employment with the new contractor. Any outstanding claims from employees, whether they concern contractual or other obligations, will transfer. In a case, for example, where two employees had an outstanding claim for sex discrimination at the time of the transfer, the claim was transferred to the contractor who was faced with the need to settle a dispute in which it had not taken part.[15]

Examples of outsourcing situations where the Transfer Regulations have been held to apply include the contracting out of a local authority refuse collection and cleansing work,[16] a contract to deliver Audi and Volkswagen cars around the country,[17] and the transfer of a security guarding contract.[18]

It is not always clear whether the Transfer Regulations apply (see Chapter 15) and there has been much litigation on the meaning of a transfer of an undertaking or business. If outsourcing does take place and there is no application of the Transfer Regulations, then the outsourcing employer may be faced with significant redundancy payments and the contractor may be faced with possible litigation. It might be considered good practice for the outsourcing employer to decide that the Regulations apply and make them a condition of the tendering and contracting process.

FIXED-TERM OR INDEFINITE CONTRACT?

Assuming that a decision has been taken that the organisation will engage employees itself, another matter for consideration is whether to hire for a fixed term or for an indefinite period.[18a] From the employer's point of view one of the advantages of the fixed-term contract had been that if it was for two years or more it was possible to remove an employee's right to claim unfair dismissal and/or redundancy while retaining the right to give notice.[19] The Employment Relations Act 1999 removed the ability of employers to have clauses in the contract excluding unfair dismissal claims. The possibility remains for such clauses to exclude redundancy claims. However, if there is no written clause, the expiry of a fixed-term contract without its renewal on the same terms amounts to a dismissal in law (see Chapter 13).

SHOULD TEMPORARY EMPLOYEES OR AGENCY STAFF BE HIRED?

In deciding whether to employ on a temporary or 'permanent' basis (see Chapter 12 on notice provisions), it should be noted that temporary staff have exactly the same statutory rights as other employees so long as they possess any necessary qualifying period of service. The only two exceptions to this proposition arise where an individual is employed on a temporary basis as a replacement for a woman on maternity leave or to replace someone absent from work under the statutory provisions relating to medical suspension (see Chapters 9 and 6 respectively).

Occasionally an organisation may ask an agency to provide staff, and if the worker engaged by the client organisation is under a personal obligation to perform the work, a contract of employment may exist. However, if the agency does not undertake to send a specific person, then the person supplied is unlikely to be an employee. If the client organisation pays the agency for the labour provided and the latter pays the worker, then a contract of employment could only exist between the agency and the worker concerned. In these circumstances, whether a written contract is one of employment is a question of law to be determined upon the true construction of the document, but it is possible for a short-term contract between the agency and the worker to be a contract of employment.[20]

SHOULD A PROBATIONARY PERIOD BE IMPOSED?

We shall see in Chapter 17 that (save in exceptional

circumstances) only those who have been continuously employed for one year can claim that they have been unfairly dismissed. In a sense this requirement serves to impose a probationary period but some employers may regard one year as excessive for the purpose of establishing whether a person's appointment should be confirmed. Often a shorter period will be deemed appropriate. Some employers prefer to make an assessment within four weeks in order to avoid having to give statutory notice to terminate the contract (see Chapter 12). The great advantage of operating a probationary period is that new recruits are made aware that they are on trial and must therefore establish their suitability.

REGULATORY CONSTRAINTS

At common law, employers have the right to decide what policies to adopt in relation to recruitment, but this position has now been altered by a series of statutory and non-statutory interventions designed to protect certain categories of job applicant. Such interventions mostly concern provisions designed to prevent discrimination in recruitment and employment on the grounds of gender, race, disability and membership or non-membership of a trade union. These issues will be considered in Chapters 7 and 8. Other matters will be considered here, including the selection and recruitment aspects of age discrimination in employment.

Rehabilitation of Offenders Act 1974
The law does not require applicants to disclose facts about themselves which could hinder them in getting jobs (unless their silence amounts to fraud). Thus if employers believe that certain information is important, they should seek it specifically before the job is offered.

Section 4 of this Act relieves certain rehabilitated persons from the obligation to disclose 'spent' convictions to a prospective employer and makes it unlawful for an employer to deny employment on the grounds that the applicant had a conviction which was 'spent'. It is the policy of the Act that applicants should not be questioned about spent convictions, although if this situation does arise applicants are entitled to deny that they have ever been convicted. However, under an exemption order, protection is not afforded to those applying for a whole range of jobs, eg as a doctor, nurse, teacher, social worker or probation officer.[21]

Sentences of over two-and-a-half years' imprisonment never become 'spent'; otherwise, convictions become 'spent' after periods which are related to the gravity of the sentence imposed. Thus for a sentence of imprisonment of between six months and two-and-a-half years the rehabilitation period is 10 years. Imprisonment for less than six months requires a seven-year rehabilitation period, and fines or community service orders take five years to become 'spent'. A probation order, conditional discharge or binding over need not be disclosed after a year or until the order expires (whichever is the longer), and absolute discharges can be concealed if six months have elapsed since sentence. Despite the existence of the Act, the courts cannot compel an employer to engage a rehabilitated offender: they can only declare the exclusion of the applicant to be unlawful.

Asylum and Immigration Act 1996

Section 8 of this Act is concerned with restrictions on employment of persons subject to immigration control. Employers commit an offence if they employ a person of 16 years or over if either the employee has not been granted leave to enter or remain in the United Kingdom, or if his or her stay in the United Kingdom is subject to a condition that precludes them from taking up employment.[22] However, if before the employment began the potential employee produced suitable documentation and the employer retained it or kept a photocopy, then this may be a defence. Suitable documentation includes[23]

(a) a document issued by a previous employer or a government department, such as the Inland Revenue or the Benefits Agency, which contains the person's National Insurance number;

(b) a passport which gives the person the right of abode or of readmission to the United Kingdom, or which contains a Certificate of Entitlement issued by the government;

(c) a birth certificate issued in the United Kingdom, the Republic of Ireland, the Channel Islands or the Isle of Man;

(d) a passport or identity card issued by a Member State of the European Economic Area.

It is not a defence if the employer knew that the applicant was not entitled to work in the United Kingdom.[24] If this offence is committed by a corporate body, then that body will be liable to a fine, as will those senior individuals in the corporate body who connived in the offence.

AGE DISCRIMINATION IN RECRUITMENT AND SELECTION

In 1999 the government issued a Code of Practice on Age Diversity in Employment. One of the purposes of the Code is to show how businesses and employers can take steps to ensure that they select, retain and develop the best person for the job by eliminating age as an employment criterion. The Code of Practice is a voluntary one, but the government clearly hopes that employment tribunals will take it into account in their deliberations. Other countries such as Ireland, Australia and the United States of America have adopted legislation to make discrimination on the basis of age unlawful. The UK government prefers a voluntary route aimed at persuading employers that it is in their best interests to adopt the policies in the Code.

It should be noted that discrimination on the basis of age is not unlawful in the United Kingdom, unless it amounts to indirect sex discrimination. It is not unlawful to place recruitment advertisements in the press which stipulate a required or preferred age range for applicants. The government is hoping that it will become good practice not to do so. The Institute of Personnel and Development adopted this approach as long ago as 1993 by not allowing recruitment advertisements which contain age references in its journals.

The Code of Practice considers the employment cycle and makes recommendations for good practice in each. The stages of the cycle are recruitment, selection, promotion, training and development, redundancy, and finally, retirement.

Recruitment

The recommendations under the heading of recruitment concern how to ensure that the best person applies for the job. The Code suggests this is to be done, firstly, by not using age limits or age ranges in job adverts; secondly, by placing job advertisements specifying the skills and abilities required for the post; thirdly, by avoiding phrases which imply an age restriction; and lastly, by thinking about where to advertise. Different journals are aimed at different markets, including age markets. The Code says that the selection process requires employers to

(a) focus on skills, abilities and potential when sifting applications;

(b) ensure that interviewers are aware of the need to ask job-related questions;

(c) use a mixed-age interviewing panel;

(d) ensure that all interviewers are trained to avoid basing decisions on prejudice and stereotypes;

(e) avoid making age an integral part of the application form or process;

(f) select on merit, based on information provided in the application form and interview.

Selection

This is about selecting the best candidate on the basis of merit: partly about focusing on the skills, abilities and potential of the candidates when deciding on whom to interview, and partly about the need to ensure that the interviewers

(a) are aware of the need to ask job-related questions;

(b) are trained to avoid basing decisions on prejudices and stereotypes; and

(c) constitute, where possible, a mixed-age interviewing panel.

These are, of course, important objectives, and are so not just in the context of age discrimination. Such training ought to be essential in relation to all forms of discrimination, perhaps especially that related to sex, race and disability.

KEY POINTS 4
Recruitment and selection

- Organisations have to decide whether to use employees or independent contractors; there are differences in taxation and employment costs as well as vicarious liability.

- It is not always clear whether a worker is employed under a contract of service or is working under a contract for services; the intention of the parties is important, but may not be the deciding factor.

- The current test for distinguishing between an employee or a self-employed contractor is whether the person concerned was carrying on business on his or her own account.

- Outsourcing is an option for many employers, but it is important to be aware of the effect of the Transfer of Undertakings (Protection of Employment) Regulations 1981.

- Should employment be on fixed-term or an indefinite contract of employment? Those on a fixed-term contract can be asked to give up any potential claims towards redundancy payments.

- Is it better to hire temporary employees rather than permanent ones? Temporary staff, if obtained through an employment agency, are unlikely to be seen as employees of the host organisation.

- Probationary periods may be useful in deciding whether to confirm an appointment; the law normally places a requirement for one year's continuous employment before there is a right to claim unfair dismissal.

- Discrimination on the grounds of age is not unlawful, but discouraged by a government Code of Practice.

- Rehabilitated offenders have the right, in certain circumstances, not to reveal information about spent convictions.

- There may be a need to obtain documentation to prove that a person has the right to work in the United Kingdom, in order for his or her employer to avoid committing an offence.

NOTES

1 See *Mirror Group Ltd v Gunning* (1986) IRLR 27
2 See *Chief Adjudication Officer v Rhodes* (1999) IRLR 103
3 (1999) IRLR 98
4 See *Smith v Stages* (1989) IRLR 177
5 See *Heasmans v Clarity Cleaning* (1987) IRLR 286
6 See *Sime v Sutcliffe Catering* (1990) IRLR 228
7 *O'Kelly v Trust House Forte* (1983) IRLR 286
8 *Hall v Lorimer* (1994) IRLR 171
9 See *Lane v Shire Roofing* (1995) IRLR 493
10 See *Young & Woods v West* (1980) IRLR 201
11 See *McCleod v Hellyer Bros* (1987) IRLR 232
12 (1999) IRLR 367
13 See *Clark v Oxfordshire Health Authority* (1998) IRLR 125
14 SI 1981/1794
15 See *DJM International Ltd v Nicholas* (1996) IRLR 76
16 *Wren v Eastbourne Borough Council* (1993) IRLR 425
17 *ECM (Vehicle Delivery Services) Ltd v Cox* (1998) IRLR 416

18 *Securicor Guarding Ltd v Fraser Security Services* (1996) IRLR 552

18a An EU Directive on Fixed-Term Work must be implemented by 28 June 2001.

19 See section 197 ERA 1996 and *BBC v Kelly-Phillips* (1998) IRLR 294

20 See *McMeechan v Secretary of State for Employment* (1997) IRLR 353

21 Rehabilitation of Offenders Act 1974 (Exemption) Order 1975; see *Wood v Coverage Care Ltd* (1996) IRLR 264

22 Section 8(1) Asylum and Immigration Act 1996

23 See The Immigration (Restrictions on Employment) Order 1996 SI 1996/3225 for a complete list of documentation

24 Sections 8(2) and 8(3) Asylum and Immigration Act 199

5 Pay issues (1)

This chapter is concerned with a number of issues related to pay, beginning with the duty to pay wages or salaries. There is then some detailed consideration of the National Minimum Wage Act 1998 and the complexities associated with trying to establish the actual rates paid in a variety of work circumstances. We then discuss the employer's duty to provide pay statements and what employee rights are in connection with guaranteed payments when not provided with work.

THE DUTY TO PAY WAGES

This is a basic obligation of employers and is normally dealt with by an express term. There are a number of issues to be considered.

(i) *An employer may be required to pay wages even if there is no work for the employee to do*

The general rule is that wages must be paid if an employee is available for work,[1] but everything will depend on whether there is an express or implied term of fact in the contract which deals with the matter. Thus an express term to the effect that 'no payment shall be made during a period of lay-off' will eliminate the possibility of a contractual claim being brought in such a situation.

(ii) *Deductions from wages or payment by the employer are unlawful unless required or authorised by statute, for example PAYE or social security contributions, or the worker has agreed to it*[2]

Section 27(1) ERA 1996 defines 'wages' as 'any sum payable to the worker in connection with his employment'. This includes commission earnings which are payable after an employee has left. Before payment of such 'wages' the employer would be entitled to deduct an amount to repay any advances that had been given to the employee.[3]

The worker must give oral or written consent to the deduction before it is made,[4] and where the agreement constitutes a term of the contract of employment it must be in writing and drawn to the employee's attention (or its effect must have been notified to the worker in writing).[5] To satisfy the requirements of the Act there must be a document which clearly states that a deduction is to be made from the employee's wages and that the employee agrees to it.[6] Even if an employee has entered into a compromise agreement to settle an unfair dismissal dispute over non-payment of wages, he or she may still be able to make a claim for that underpayment.[7] If a tribunal is not persuaded on the evidence that a deduction was authorised by a provision of the employee's contract, the individual is entitled to be paid the money deducted.[8] If, however, the contract of employment allowed the employer to change the hours or shift-patterns of an employee, then the employer would be entitled to adjust the pay levels to reflect those changes.[9]

For these purposes there is no valid distinction between a deduction and a reduction of wages. The issue is whether, for whatever reason, apart from an error of computation, the worker is paid less than the amount of wages properly payable.[10] However, employers who take a conscious decision not to make a payment because they believe that they are contractually entitled to take that course are not making an error of computation.[11] Although section 13(4) refers to an 'error of any description' it does not include an error of law.[12] Where there is a dispute over the justification for a deduction, it is the employment tribunal's task to resolve it.[13] However, tribunals do not have jurisdiction to determine whether a deduction by reason of industrial action was contractually authorised.[14]

Written agreements under which employers pay a proportion of wages to third parties are not affected by this Act, and in retail employment deductions or payments made to an employer in relation to stock or cash shortages are subject to a limit of one-tenth of gross pay, except for the final payment of wages.[15]

(iii) *Payments in lieu are not wages within the meaning of ERA 1996 if they relate to a period after the termination of employment*

According to the House of Lords, in *Delaney v Staples*,[16] the Act requires wages to be construed as payments in respect of the rendering of services during employment. Thus the only payments in lieu covered by the legislation are those in respect of 'garden leave', since these can be viewed as wages owed under a subsisting contract of employment. In the same case the Court of Appeal accepted that non-payment of wages constitutes a deduction for these purposes, as does the withholding of commission and holiday pay.[17] Indeed, the withholding of commission may amount to an unlawful deduction even where it is discretionary so long as commission was normally expected by the employee.[18]

(iv) *A complaint that there has been an unauthorised deduction must normally be lodged with an employment tribunal within three months of the deduction's being made*[19]

If the complaint is well-founded, the tribunal must make a declaration to that effect and must order the reimbursement of the amount of the deduction or payment to the extent that it exceeded what should lawfully have been deducted or received by the employee. This does not affect the ability of the tribunal to consider references about itemised pay statements under section 11 ERA 1996. The total awarded, however, must not exceed the total amount of the deductions.[20] The only method of contracting out of the requirements of this Act is if an agreement is reached following action taken by ACAS or there is a valid compromise agreement (see Chapter 16).

(v)   *Overpayments*

Employers may be entitled to restitution of over-payments made to an employee owing to a mistake of fact but *not* a mistake of law, eg an overpayment which arose as the result of a misunderstanding of the National Minimum Wage Act would be irrecoverable.[21] Indeed, employees may commit theft if they fail to notify the employer of an accidental overpayment.[22] Section 16(1) ERA 1996 makes specific provision for the recovery of overpayments, and tribunals cannot inquire into the lawfulness of a deduction for this purpose.[23]

THE NATIONAL MINIMUM WAGE

The National Minimum Wage Act 1998 (NMWA 1998) established a minimum hourly wage for workers from 1 April 1999. 'Worker' is defined, in Section 54(3), as someone working under a contract of employment or any other contract under which an individual undertakes to do or perform in person any work or service for another. The standard rate was established by the National Minimum Wage Regulations 1999 (NMW Regulations 1999)[24] as £3.60 per hour. Regulation 13 set a lower rate of £3.00 per hour for workers who were aged between 18 years and 22 years. It also set a rate of £3.20 per hour for those aged over 22 years who were in their first six months with an employer and who were receiving at least 26 days of approved training during those six months. Regulation 12 describes those who do not qualify for the national minimum wage at all. These include

(a)   those under 18 years of age;

(b)   a worker under the age of 26 years who is employed under a contract of apprenticeship and is in the first 12 months of that contract, or who has not reached the age of 19 years;

(c)   a worker who is participating in a scheme designed to provide him or her with training, work, or temporary work, or which is designed to assist him or her to obtain work;

(d) a worker who is attending higher education up to first degree level or a teacher-training course;

(e) a homeless person who is provided with shelter and other benefits in return for performing work.

Workers who work and live in the employer's household and who are treated as members of the family are also excluded.[25]

The hourly rate is calculated by adding up the total remuneration, less reductions, and dividing by the total number of hours worked[26] during a pay reference period.[27] Total remuneration[28] in a pay reference period is calculated by adding together

(a) all money paid by the employer to the worker during the reference period

(b) any money paid by the employer to the worker in the following reference period which is in respect of work done in the current reference period

(c) any money paid by the employer to the worker later than the end of the following pay reference period in respect of work done in the current reference period and for which the worker is under an obligation to complete a record and has not done so

(d) the cost of accommodation, calculated by an approved formula.[29]

Deductions that can be made from this total remuneration figure are set out in Regulation 31 and include:

(a) any payments made by the employer to the worker in respect of a previous pay reference period

(b) in the case of non-salaried work, any money paid to the worker in respect of periods when the worker was absent from work or engaged in taking industrial action

(c) in the case of time-work, the difference between the lowest rate of pay and any higher rates of pay paid during the reference period

(d) any amounts paid by the employer to the worker that represent amounts paid by customers in the form of service charge, tips, gratuities or cover charge – that is, not paid through the payroll

(e) the payment of expenses.

The calculation of the hours worked can be complex. There are four different types of hours of work. These are:

(i) *salaried hours work*[30]
This is where the worker is paid for a number of ascertainable hours in a year (the basic hours) and where the payment, which normally consists of an annual salary and perhaps an annual bonus, is paid in equal instalments, weekly or monthly.

(ii) *time-work*[31]
This is work that is paid for under a worker's contract by reference to the time worked, and is not salaried hours work.

(iii) *output work*[32]
This is work that is paid for by reference to the number of pieces made or processed, or by some other measure of output such as the value of sales made or transactions completed. The output hours, in a reference period, will be the total number of hours spent by the worker in doing output work.[33] It is possible, according to regulation 25, for the employer and worker to reach a 'fair estimate' agreement on what number of hours to use.

(iv) *unmeasured work*[34]
This is any work that is not salaried hours work, time-work or output work, especially work where there are no specified hours and the worker is required to work when needed or whenever work is available. The unmeasured output hours will be the total hours, in a pay reference period, spent by the worker in carrying out his or her contractual duties.[35] Regulation 28 allows for a 'daily average' agreement to be reached between the employer and the worker.

Section 9 of the Act[36] allows the Secretary of State to require employers to keep and preserve records for at least three years. Workers have the right to inspect these records if they believe, on reasonable grounds, that they are being paid at a rate less than the national minimum wage.[37] When inspecting these records a worker may be accompanied by another person of his or her choice.[38] This must be stated in the 'production notice' that the worker gives to the employer requesting the production of the records.[39] The employer must then produce these records within 14 days following receipt of the notice and must make them available at the worker's place of work or some other reasonable place.[40] Failure to produce the records or to allow the workers to exercise their rights can lead to a complaint at an employment tribunal.[41] In these circumstances the tribunal can make an award of up to 80 times the national minimum wage. If a worker has been remunerated, during the reference period, at a rate less than the national minimum wage, then there is a contractual entitlement to be paid the amount underpaid.[42] There is a reversal of the normal burden of proof in that the presumption is that the worker qualifies for the national minimum wage and that he or she is underpaid.[43]

Sections 5–8 of the NMW Act 1998 established the Low Pay Commission and gave the Secretary of State discretion to refer matters to it. Additionally, the Secretary of State may appoint officers to inspect records and enforce the Act's requirements.[44] If the officers discover workers not being paid the national minimum wage, they may, according to Section 19, issue enforcement notices requiring payment of the national minimum wage and the payment of arrears. Section 20 allows an enforcement officer to complain, on behalf of a worker, to an employment tribunal if the enforcement order is not complied with. The tribunal may impose a penalty of twice the hourly rate recommended for as long as the lack of compliance takes place.

Workers have a right not to suffer detriment[45] if they assert, in good faith, their right to the national minimum wage or their right to inspect records or their right to recover underpayment.

PAY STATEMENTS

Under section 8 ERA 1996 employers must give their employees an itemised pay statement. The statement must contain the following particulars:

(a) the gross amount of wages or salary

(b) the amount of any variable or fixed deductions and the purposes for which they are made (on the legality of such deductions, see above)

(c) the net wages or salary payable and, where the net amount is paid in different ways, the amount and method of payment of each part payment.

Such a statement need not contain separate particulars of a fixed deduction, eg of union dues, if it specifies the total amount of fixed deductions and each year the employer provides a standing statement of fixed deductions which describes the amount of each deduction, its purpose and the intervals at which it is made. If no pay statement is issued, an employee may refer the matter to an employment tribunal to determine what particulars ought to have been included. Where a tribunal finds that an employer failed to provide such a statement or the statement does not contain the required particulars, the tribunal must make a declaration to that effect. Additionally, where it finds that any unnotified deductions have been made during the 13 weeks preceding the application, it may order the employer to pay compensation to the employee. This refund cannot exceed the total amount of unnotified deductions.[46] Thus unlike the provisions relating to the enforcement of section 1 ERA 1996 statements, there is here a penal aspect to the discretion which tribunals have to exercise.

GUARANTEE PAYMENTS

Employees with one month's continuous service qualify for a guarantee payment if they are not provided with work throughout a day in which they would normally be required to work in accordance with their contract of employment because of:

(a) a diminution in the requirements of the employer's business for work of the kind which the employee is employed to do; or

b) any other occurrence that affects the normal working of the employer's business in relation to work of that kind.[47]

However, if a contract of employment is not expected to last more than three months, there is no right to a guarantee payment unless the person is in fact employed for more than three months.[48] The words 'normally required to work' are significant for two reasons. First, an employee who is not obliged to work when requested may be regarded as not being subject to a contract of employment.[49] Second, if contracts of employment are varied to provide for a reduced number of working days, for example four instead of five, employees will be unable to claim a payment for the fifth day because they are no longer 'required to work' on that day. 'Any other occurrence . . .' would seem to contemplate something like a power failure or natural disaster rather than works holidays.

No guarantee payment is available if the workless day is a consequence of a strike, lock-out or other industrial action involving any employee of the employer or any associated employer.[50] The entitlement to a guarantee payment may be lost in two other circumstances:

(a) where the employer has offered to provide alternative work which is suitable in the circumstances (irrespective of whether it falls inside or outside the scope of the employee's contract) but this has been unreasonably refused;[51] and

(b) where the employee does not comply with reasonable requirements imposed by the employer with a view to ensuring that his or her services are available.[52] This is to enable the employer to keep the workforce together, perhaps in the hope that the supplies which have been lacking will be delivered.

A guarantee payment is calculated by multiplying the number

of normal working hours on the day of lay-off by the guaranteed hourly rate. Accordingly, where there are no normal working hours on the day in question, no guarantee payment can be claimed.[53] The guaranteed hourly rate is one week's pay divided by the number of normal hours in a week, and where the number of normal hours varies, the average number of such hours over a 12-week period will be used.[54] Payment cannot be claimed for more than five days in any period of three months,[55] although the Secretary of State may vary, by order, both the length of the period and the amount paid.[56] It should be noted that contractual payments in respect of workless days not only discharge an employer's liability to make guarantee payments for those days[57] but are also to be taken into account when calculating the maximum number of days for which employees are entitled to statutory payments.[58] Where guaranteed weekly remuneration has been agreed, this sum is to be 'apportioned rateably between the workless days'.[59] If an employer fails to pay the whole or part of a guarantee payment, an employee can complain to an employment tribunal within three months of the last workless day. Where a tribunal finds a complaint to be well-founded, it must order the employer to pay the amount which it finds owing to the employee.[60]

If guaranteed remuneration is the subject of a collective agreement currently in force, all the parties may choose to apply for an exemption order. So long as the Secretary of State is satisfied that the statutory provisions should not apply, the relevant employees will be excluded from the operation of section 28 ERA 1996. However, the Secretary of State cannot make an order unless a collective agreement permits employees to take a dispute about guaranteed remuneration to arbitration, an independent adjudicating body or an employment tribunal.[61]

KEY POINTS 5
Pay issues

- Normally one would expect pay matters to be settled by express terms, but sometimes statute implies terms affecting pay such as the equality clause implied by the EPA 1970 and the minimum wage by the NMWA 1998.

- Subject to express or implied contractual terms, an employer is normally obliged to pay wages if there is no work.

- Deductions from wages are unlawful unless approved by statute or by agreement with the employee.

- The national minimum wage was set at £3.60 per hour in 1999, with a lower rate for those under 19 years and an intermediate rate for those between 22 and 26 years who are within the first 6 months of their employment and receiving a certain amount of training.

- The types of hours worked, for the purposes of the NMWA 1998, are salaried hours work, time-work, output work and unmeasured work.

- Employers must give their employees itemised pay statements.

- Employees with one month's continuous service may be eligible for a guarantee payment if they are not provided with work.

NOTES

1 See *R v Liverpool City Corporation* (1985) IRLR 501
2 See sections 13(1) and 15(1) ERA 1996; a worker is defined in section 230(3) ERA 1996
3 See *Robertson v Blackstone Franks Investment Management Ltd* (1998) IRLR 376
4 See *Discount Tobacco v Williams* (1993) IRLR 327
5 Section 13(2) ERA 1996; see *Kerr v The Sweater Shop* (1996) IRLR 424
6 See *Potter v Hunt Contracts Ltd* (1992) IRLR 108

7   See *Dattani v Trio Supermarkets Ltd* (1998) IRLR 240
8   See *Davies v Hotpoint Ltd* (1994) IRLR 538 on the impact of collective agreements
9   *Hussman Manufacturing Ltd v Weir* (1998) IRLR 288
10 See sections 13(3) and (4) ERA 1996 and *Bruce v Wiggins Teape* (1994) IRLR 536. On the distinction between a deduction in respect of wages and a deduction in respect of expenses see *London Borough of Southwark v O'Brien* (1996) IRLR 240
11 See *Yemm v British Steel* (1994) IRLR 117
12 See *Morgan v West Glamorgan County Council* (1995) IRLR 68
13 See *Fairfield Ltd v Skinner* (1993) IRLR 3
14 See section 14(5) ERA 1996 and *Sunderland Polytechnic v Evans* (1993) ICR 196
15 See section 13 ERA 1996
16 (1992) IRLR 191
17 *Delaney v Staples t/a De Montfort Recruitment* (1991) IRLR 112
18 See *Kent Management Services v Butterfield* (1992) IRLR 394
19 'Or, within such further period as the tribunal considers reasonable in a case where it is satisfied that it was not reasonably practicable for the complainant to be presented within three months': sections 23(2)–(4) ERA 1996. This 'escape clause' applies to other statutory provisions and throughout the rest of the book will be referred to as the 'time-limit escape clause'; see *Taylorplan v Jackson* (1996) IRLR 184
20 See section 26 ERA 1996
21 See *Avon County Council v Howlett* (1993) 1 All ER 1073
22 See *Attorney General's reference* (No 1 of 1983) 1 All ER 369
23 See *SIP Ltd v Swinn* (1994) IRLR 323
24 SI 1999/584
25 Regulation 2 NMW Regulations 1999
26 Regulation 14 NMW Regulations 1999
27 Regulation 10 NMW Regulations 1999; a pay reference period is one month or a shorter period if a worker is usually paid at more frequent intervals
28 Regulation 30 NMW Regulations 1999
29 Regulation 36 NMW Regulations 1999
30 Regulation 16 NMW Regulations 1999
31 Regulation 15 NMW Regulations 1999
32 Regulation 17 NMW Regulations 1999
33 Regulation 24 NMW Regulations 1999
34 Regulation 18 NMW Regulations 1999
35 Regulation 27 NMW Regulations 1999
36 See also regulation 38 NMW Regulations 1999
37 Sections 10(1) and 10(2) NMW Regulations 1999
38 Section 10(4)(b) NMW Regulations 1999
39 Sections 10(5) and 10(6) NMW Regulations 1999
40 Sections 10(8) and 10(9) NMW Regulations 1999
41 Section 11 NMWA 1998; section 11(3) requires that the complaint should normally be made within three months of the end of the 14-day notice period
42 Section 17 NMWA 1999
43 Section 28 NMWA 1998
44 Sections 13–17 NMWA 1998

45 Section 23 NMWA 1998
46 Section 12(4) ERA 1996
47 Section 28(1) ERA 1996
48 Section 29(2) ERA 1996
49 See *Mailway (Southern) Ltd v Willsher* (1978) IRLR 322
50 Section 29(3) ERA 1996; 'associated employer' is defined by section 231 ERA 1996
51 Section 29(4) ERA 1996
52 Section 29(5) ERA 1996
53 Section 30(1) ERA 1996
54 Section 30(2)–(4) ERA 1996
55 Section 31(1)–(3) ERA 1996
56 Section 31(7) ERA 1996
57 Section 32(2) ERA 1996
58 See *Cartwright v Clancey Ltd* (1983) IRLR 355
59 Section 32(3) ERA 1996
60 Section 34(3) ERA 1996
61 Section 35 ERA 199

6 Pay issues (2)

This chapter is concerned with those pay issues that are related to sickness. We consider the common-law right to sick pay and whether a duty to make such a payment can be implied in a contract of employment. We then look at statutory rights to payments and we examine the complex rules regarding statutory sick pay by looking at the qualifying conditions, the rules governing notification of sickness, the amounts payable, together with ways of enforcing the right, and the duty of employers to keep records. Also considered is the right of employers to suspend employees on medical grounds.

THE RIGHT TO SICK PAY AT COMMON LAW

In the absence of an express term in the contract of employment, the correct approach to finding out if there is an obligation upon the employer to pay wages to an employee absent through sickness is to look at all the facts and circumstances to see whether such a term is implied. Such a term may be implied from the custom or practice in the industry or from the knowledge of the parties at the time the contract was made. The nature of the contract will have to be taken into account and, on occasions, it will be permissible to look at what the parties did during the period of the contract. Only if all the factors and circumstances do not indicate what the contractual term is will it be assumed that wages should be paid during sickness. If such a term is implied, it is likely to provide for the deduction of sums received under social security legislation.[1] In *Howman & Sons v Blyth*[2] it was held that the reasonable term to be implied in respect of duration in an industry where the normal practice is to give sick pay for a limited period only is the term normally applicable in the industry. The EAT did not accept that where there is an obligation to make payments during sickness, in the absence of an express term to the contrary, sick pay is owed so long as the employment continues.

The courts have intervened to ensure that employees' entitlements to disability benefits under health insurance schemes have not been frustrated by a strict interpretation of the contract of employment. In *Adin v Sedco Forex International*[3] an employee's contract of employment included provisions for short-term and long-term disability benefits. It also contained a clause which allowed the employer, at their sole discretion, to terminate the contract for any reason whatsoever. The Court of Session concluded that because the right to these benefits was established in the contract of employment, the employer could not take them away by dismissing the employee. The courts are also willing to infer terms in contracts which will give effect to agreed health insurance schemes. In *Aspden v Webbs Poultry Group*[4] a management employee had a contract of employment which did not mention the generous health insurance scheme which, the High Court held, had been mutually agreed by the employers and the senior management staff. The employee was dismissed while on sick leave as a result of angina. It was claimed that there was an implied term that the employee would not be dismissed while incapacitated because this would frustrate the permanent health insurance scheme. The court accepted this argument, even though there was an express term in the contract that allowed the employer to dismiss employees for reasons of prolonged incapacity.

An employee can rely on contractual terms to pay long-term benefits, even if the employer has stopped paying the premiums on their health insurance policy.[5] In *Hill v General Accident*[6] an employee was dismissed for reasons of redundancy whilst in receipt of sick pay. The employee was only four months short of qualifying for an ill-health retirement pension. The contract of employment contained an express provision for the retention of sick employees for a period of two years' absence before they were able to qualify for the ill-health retirement scheme. It was held that this express provision did not exclude the possibility of the employee's being dismissed through redundancy, despite the unfortunate consequences. To allow this exclusion would put sick employees at an advantage as compared to those who were well and at work when it came to selecting those who would be dismissed.

STATUTORY SICK PAY

The Social Security Contributions and Benefits Act 1992 (SSCBA 1992) and the Statutory Sick Pay Act 1994 make employers responsible for paying statutory sick pay (SSP) to such of their employees as work within the EU.[6a] SSP will be paid for up to 28 weeks of absence due to sickness or injury in any single 'period of entitlement' (see below).[7] As well as those who pay full Class 1 National Insurance contributions, married women and widows paying reduced contributions are eligible for SSP. Part-timers who earn more than the current earnings limit (£66 per week) are to be treated in the same way as full-time employees, and there is no minimum service qualification. Indeed, an employee may be entitled to SSP under more than one contract or with more than one employer if the relevant conditions are satisfied.

The qualifying conditions and limitations on entitlement

SSP is available for a 'day of incapacity for work' (not part of a day) which falls within 'a period of entitlement'.[8] In addition, a payment will be made only for the fourth and subsequent 'qualifying days' within that period of entitlement, and employees must comply with provisions requiring them to notify the employer of incapacity to work.[9] According to section 151(4) SSCBA 1992 a day of incapacity for work is a day on which the employee is (or is deemed to be) 'incapable by reason of some specific disease or bodily or mental disablement of doing work of a kind which he might reasonably be expected to do' under his or her contract of employment.[10] When an employee has four or more consecutive 'days of incapacity for work' a 'period of incapacity for work' is formed. These successive days include non-working days, eg Sundays or bank holidays. 'Periods of incapacity for work' which are separated by eight weeks or less are treated as one for these purposes (the 'linking mechanism') so employees are not obliged to wait another three days to qualify for SSP.[11] However, a single period of incapacity cannot extend beyond three years.[12]

A 'period of entitlement' commences with the first 'day of incapacity for work' and ends when whichever of the following first occurs:[13]

(a) the period of incapacity for work ends

(b) SSP entitlement is exhausted

(c) a pregnant employee reaches the 'disqualifying period', ie the period of 18 weeks that begins the eleventh week before the expected week of confinement

(d) the employee is detained in legal custody or sentenced to a term of imprisonment[14]

(e) the employee's contract of service terminates.[15] Regulation 4 of the SSP Regulations 1982 deals with the situation where an employee is dismissed solely or mainly for the purpose of avoiding SSP liability. If on the day the contract is brought to an end the employee has a period of entitlement, the employer must pay SSP until the period of entitlement would have ended under (a–d) above or, if earlier, the date on which the contract would have expired

(f) a period of three years has elapsed since entitlement commenced. At this point the employee will be transferred to state incapacity benefit.

However, a 'period of entitlement' will not arise[16]

(a) if at the 'relevant date' the employee is over state pension age

(b) if the employee was engaged for a specified period of three months or less and that period is not exceeded. Where an individual has been employed by the same employer within the previous eight weeks, regard is to be had to the aggregate period of employment

(c) if at the 'relevant date' the employee's normal gross weekly earnings (ie average earnings including overtime and bonuses) are less than the current earnings limit for social security purposes[17]

(d) if the employee's first 'day of incapacity for work' is within 57 days of entitlement to an invalidity pension, a severe disablement allowance or incapacity benefit

(e) if the employee has done no work for the employer under the contract of service. Where the employee has been employed by the same employer within the previous eight weeks, the two contracts are to be treated as one[18]

(f) if on the 'relevant date' there is a stoppage of work due to a trade dispute at the employee's place of employment, unless the employee can prove that he or she did not have a direct interest in the dispute[19]

(g) if before the 'relevant date' the employee has exhausted his or her SSP entitlement from the employer

(h) if the employee is pregnant and the 'relevant date' falls within the 'disqualifying period' (see above)

(i) if on the first day of the period of incapacity for work the employee is in legal custody or serving a prison sentence.[20]

In this context the 'relevant date' is the date on which a period of entitlement would have begun if schedule 11 did not prevent its arising.[21]

If a period of incapacity for work has been formed but the employee is excluded from SSP, the employer must complete an 'exclusion form' and give or send it to the employee within seven days.[22] Similarly, employers must issue a transfer form to employees off sick at the start of the twenty-third week of SSP entitlement.[23] When completed, these forms will reveal why the employer is not paying SSP and will enable the employee to claim state sickness or incapacity benefits. When requested, employers must also provide 'leaver's statements' to those who are leaving employment and who have had a period of incapacity for work not more than eight weeks before the contract ends.[24] Employers will generally be required not later than the seventh day[25] after the date the contract terminates to issue a statement to the employee which contains the following information:

(a) the first day of sickness in the period of incapacity for work (including linked periods)

(b) the number of weeks of SSP paid or due to be paid (to the nearest whole week)

(c) the last day for which SSP was paid.

If the employee falls ill within eight weeks of the last date on which SSP was paid, a new employer who has received a statement must take the weeks of SSP shown on it into account in calculating his or her own 28 weeks' liability. However, the new employer need only consider a leaver's statement if it is received or posted on or before the seventh calendar day after the first qualifying day in a period of incapacity or such later date as the employer may require. Employers can accept the late receipt of a leaver's statement if they are satisfied that there was good cause for delay, but there is an absolute limit of 91 days after which the statement must be ignored. Employers should retain copies of any leaver's statements they issue and have received for a period of three years after the tax year to which the statement relates. Although employees are not obliged to give leaver's statements to their new employer, it is clearly in the employer's interest to ask recruits whether they have been given such a form.

There must be at least one 'qualifying day' in each week.[26] Although such days may be agreed between the employer and the employee, they are prevented from arranging that the qualifying days are those on which the employee was incapable for work. According to Regulation 5(2) of the SSP Regulations 1982, where the employer and employee have not reached agreement the qualifying day or days will be:

(a) the day or days on which the parties agreed that the employee was required to work; or

(b) on Wednesday, if it is agreed that there is no day on which work would be done.

Notification of sickness absence and proof of incapacity

Notification of absence is distinct from evidence of sickness. Notice of any day of incapacity for work must be given to the employer by (or on behalf of) an employee:[27]

(a) where the employer has a fixed time-limit and has taken reasonable steps to make it known to the employee, within that time-limit. However, an employee cannot be required to notify 'earlier than the first qualifying day ... or by a specified time during that qualifying day'

(b) in any other case before the end of the seventh day after that day of incapacity.

Notice of a day of incapacity can be given one month later than as mentioned in (a) or (b) if there is a 'good cause' for doing so, or it was not practicable in the particular circumstances, but in any event it must be submitted before the end of the ninety-first day after the day of incapacity. Where the employer has taken reasonable steps to make the desired manner of notification known to the employee, that manner must be followed. However, the employer cannot insist on notice being given:

(a) in person, or

(b) in the form of medical evidence, or

(c) more than once in every seven days during a period of entitlement, or

(d) on a document supplied by him or her, or

(e) on a printed form.

Employees can notify in any way they wish provided they do so in writing (unless otherwise agreed). Where the employee fails to comply with the notification procedure, the employer may withhold SSP for the unnotified days, although the employee's maximum entitlement will be unaffected.[28]

Section 14(1) of the Social Security Administration Act 1992 stipulates that an employee must provide such information as may reasonably be required to enable the employer to determine whether there is a period of entitlement, and if so, its duration. Evidence of sickness must be supplied by means of a doctor's statement in a prescribed form.[29] On it the medical practitioner must specify that the employee has been advised that he or she should refrain from work for a period (usually up to six months) specified in the statement. It should be noted that medical information cannot be required in respect of the first seven days of absence in any period of incapacity for work.

The amounts payable and recoverable by employers

The current rate of SSP is £59.55 per week, and the daily rate will be the appropriate weekly rate divided by the number of 'qualifying days' in the week (starting with Sunday).[30] Employers must pay the stipulated amount of SSP for each day that an employee is eligible, but any other sums paid in respect of the same day can count towards the SSP entitlement, eg normal wages.[31] Any agreement which purports to exclude, limit or modify an employee's right to SSP or which requires an employee to contribute (directly or indirectly) towards any cost incurred by the employer will be void.[32] For many employees SSP will be worth less than state sickness benefit because the former is subject to tax and National Insurance contributions and will be paid at a flat rate without additions for dependants. It is therefore hardly surprising that trade unions endeavour to negotiate sick pay schemes which ensure that their members do not suffer any detriment as a result of this legislation.

Normally employers cannot recover the sums they pay out by way of SSP. However, if in any tax month the amount of SSP exceeds 13 per cent of National Insurance contributions' liability for that month, the employer can recoup the excess from the contributions due.[33]

Enforcing the right to SSP

Section 14(3) of the Social Security Administration Act 1992 gives employees the right to ask their employer for a written statement, in relation to a period before the request is made, of one or more of the following matters:

(a) the days for which the employer regards himself or herself as liable to pay SSP

(b) the reasons the employer does not consider himself or herself liable to pay for other days

(c) the amount of SSP to which the employer believes the employee is entitled

and, to the extent to which the request is reasonable, the employer must comply with it within a reasonable time.

Unless it is reserved for the determination of the Secretary of State, any question over entitlement to statutory sick pay can be referred to an adjudication officer who, so far as it is practicable, must dispose of it within 14 days or refer it to a Social Security Appeal Tribunal. Appeals against an adjudication officer's decision go to the Social Security Appeal Tribunal and must normally be lodged within 28 days.[34] Further appeals (with leave) go to the Social Security Commissioners and then the Court of Appeal. Any party to proceedings who is notified by the Secretary of State that information is required from him or her for the determination of any question arising in connection with those proceedings must provide the information sought within ten days of receiving the notification.[35]

According to Regulation 9 of the SSP Regulations 1982, SSP must be paid not later than the first pay day after:

(a) where an appeal has been brought, the day on which the employer receives notification that it has been finally disposed of

(b) where leave to appeal has been refused and there is no further opportunity to apply for leave, the day on which the employer receives notification of the refusal

(c) in any other case, the day on which the time for lodging an appeal expires.

Where as a result of the employer's methods of accounting for and paying remuneration it is impracticable to comply with the above requirement, it must be met not later than the next following pay day. Once entitlement to SSP is established, any outstanding sums can be recovered through the county courts if necessary, although to the extent that SSP has not been paid by the employer, liability passes to the Secretary of State.[36]

The duty to keep records

Employers are obliged to keep records showing:

(a) the amount of SSP paid to each employee on each pay day

(b) the amount of SSP paid to each employee during each tax year

(c) the total amount of SSP paid to all employees during the tax year.

Additionally, Regulation 13 of the SSP Regulations 1982 (as amended) stipulates that for three years after the end of each tax year employers must in relation to each employee keep a record of the following matters:

(a) any day in that tax year which was one of four or more consecutive days of incapacity for work, whether or not the employee would normally have been expected to work on that day

(b) any day recorded under (a) for which the employer paid SSP.

Penalties

An employer who knowingly produces false information in order to recover a sum allegedly paid out as SSP commits an offence. The maximum penalty for knowingly making a false claim is a fine not exceeding level 5 on the standard scale or three months' imprisonment, or both. A reckless claim may lead to a fine not exceeding level 4 on the standard scale. Any person who without reasonable excuse fails to:

(a) comply with the time-limit for paying SSP, or

(b) maintain the records required, or

(c) provide the information sought by the Secretary of State in connection with proceedings, or

(d) provide information to employees in accordance with Regulation 15 of the SSP Regulations 1982

may receive a fine not exceeding level 3 on the standard scale. If the contravention continues after conviction, a daily fine may be imposed.[37] Where an offence is proved to have been committed with the consent or connivance of, or to have been attributable to neglect on the part of, any director, manager, secretary or other similar officer, that person as well as the company may be found guilty of an offence.

SUSPENSION ON MEDICAL GROUNDS

Employees with at least one month's continuous service who are suspended from work in consequence of a requirement imposed by specified health and safety provisions or a recommendation contained in a code of practice issued or approved under section 16 HASAWA 1974 are entitled to a week's pay (see Chapter 10) for each week of suspension up to a maximum of 26 weeks.[38] The relevant health and safety provisions are listed in section 64(3) ERA 1996 and cover hazardous substances and processes, eg lead and ionizing radiation. It should be observed that this statutory right can be invoked only where the specified safety legislation has affected the employer's undertaking and not the employee's health. Employees are therefore not entitled to remuneration under this provision for any period during which they are incapable of work by reason of illness or injury. Additionally, if employees unreasonably refuse to perform suitable alternative work (whether or not it is within the scope of their contract), or they do not comply with reasonable requirements imposed by their employer with a view to ensuring that their services are available, no payment is owed.[39]

It is important to note that these sections do not grant employers the right to suspend: they merely give rights to employees who are lawfully suspended. If there is no contractual right to suspend, employees will be entitled to sue for their full wages anyway, although any amounts already paid in respect of this period can be set off against these wages.[40] Where the employer fails to pay remuneration which is owed to the employee by virtue of the statute, the employee can apply to an employment tribunal normally within three months. Section 70(3) ERA 1996 provides that if the tribunal finds a complaint to be well-founded, the employer must be ordered to pay the amount due to the employee. As long as any replacement for a suspended employee is informed in writing by the employer that the employment will be terminated at the end of the suspension, dismissal of the replacement in order to allow the original employee to resume work will be deemed to have been for a 'substantial reason of a kind such as to justify the dismissal of an employee holding the position which that employee held'.[41] However, an employment tribunal must be still satisfied that it was reasonable in all the circumstances to dismiss (see Chapter 14).

KEY POINTS 6
Pay issues and sickness

- A right to sick pay may be inferred in the contract of employment as a result of custom and practice or the knowledge of the parties at the time the contract was entered into.

- Employers are responsible for paying statutory sick pay for up to 28 weeks of absence in a single period of entitlement.

- A period of entitlement commences with the first day of incapacity for work.

- Notification of absence is different from evidence of sickness.

- Notification of absence must be given to the employer in accordance with rules made known to employees; this notification can be given up to one month later if there is 'good cause' for doing so.

- Employers are obliged to keep records showing the amount paid to each employee.

- Employers who knowingly produce false information on payments can be fined and/or imprisoned; those who fail to pay statutory sick pay or provide information may be liable to fines.

- Employees who are suspended from work as a result of a requirement imposed by any provisions or code of practice under the HASAWA 1974 are entitled to a week's pay for each week of suspension up to a maximum of 26 weeks.

NOTES

1 See *Mears v Safecar Security* (1982) IRLR 501
2 (1983) IRLR 139
3 (1997) IRLR 280
4 (1996) IRLR 521
5 See *Bainbridge v Circuit Foil UK Ltd* (1997) IRLR 305
6 (1998) IRLR 641
6a The SSP (General) Amendment Regulations 1996 S.T. 3042 allow employers to opt out of this scheme if they make contractual payments that equal or exceed the SSP level
7 Section 155 SSCBA 1992 sets the entitlement limit at '28 times the appropriate weekly rate'
8 Sections 152–3 SSCBA 1992
9 Sections 154 and 156 SSCBA 1992
10 Regulation 2 of SSP (General) Regulations 1982 describes the circumstances in which a person may be deemed incapable of work
11 Section 152 SSCBA 1992
12 See Regulation 3 SSP (General) Amendment Regulations 1986
13 Section 153(2) SSCBA 1992
14 Regulation 3(1) of SSP (General) Regulations 1982
15 See *Brown v Chief Adjudication Officer* (1997) IRLR 110
16 See Schedule 11 paragraph 2 SSCBA 1992
17 The meaning of 'earnings' and 'normal weekly earnings' is dealt with in Regulations 17 and 19 of SSP (General) Regulations 1982 (as amended)
18 See Regulation 20 SSP (General) Regulations 1982

19 See also Schedule 11 paragraph 7 SSCBA 1992
20 Regulation 3(2) of SSP (General) Regulations 1982
21 See Schedule 11 paragraph 3 SSCBA 1992
22 Where in the particular circumstances it is not practicable for the employer to furnish the information in time, it must be provided to the employee not later than the immediately following pay day
23 See Regulation 15 of SSP (General) Regulations 1982 (as amended)
24 See Regulation 15A of SSP (General) Regulations 1982 (as amended)
25 See note 21 above
26 Section 154 SSCBA 1992
27 See Regulation 7 of SSP (General) Regulations 1982 (as amended)
28 See section 156(2)(3) SSCBA 1992
29 See SSP (Medical Evidence) Regulations 1985 (as amended)
30 See section 157 SSCBA 1992
31 See Schedule 12 paragraph 2 SSCBA 1992
32 Section 151(2) SSCBA 1992
33 SSP Percentage Threshold Order 1995 SI 1995/512
34 See Social Security (Adjudication) Regulations 1986 SI 1986/2218
35 See Regulation 14 SSP (General) Regulations 1982
36 See Regulation 9A SSP (General) Regulations 1982 (as amended)
37 See Regulation 22 SSP (General) Regulations 1982 (as amended
38 Section 64(1) ERA 1996
39 Section 65 ERA 1996
40 See section 69(3) ERA 1996
41 See section 106(3) ERA 1996

7

Discrimination against employees on the grounds of sex or race

Here we consider three important pieces of anti-discrimination legislation: the Equal Pay Act 1970, the Sex Discrimination Act 1975 and the Race Relations Act 1976. Included in this is the important role played by the EU and decisions of the European Court of Justice. We begin with an explanation of the differences between direct and indirect discrimination and then look at those occasions when discrimination is lawful, eg when there is a genuine occupational qualification. There is an examination of issues raised by the Equal Pay Act and we look at the meaning of such terms as 'like work' and 'work rated as equivalent'.

THE SEX DISCRIMINATION ACT 1975 AND THE RACE RELATIONS ACT 1976

It is important to note that the titles of these statutes do not fully reflect the matters that are covered. The Sex Discrimination Act 1975 (SDA 1975) outlaws, for example, discrimination against married (but not single) persons on the grounds of marital status. The Race Relations Act 1976 (RRA 1976) defines 'racial grounds' as meaning colour, race, nationality, national or ethnic origins.[1] A racial group that is defined by colour may include people of more than one ethnic origin.[2] In *Mandla v Lee*[3] the House of Lords held that 'ethnic origins' meant a group which was a segment of the population distinguished from others by a sufficient combination of shared customs, beliefs, traditions and characteristics derived from a common or presumed common past. This was so even if not drawn from what in biological terms was a common racial stock, in that it was that combination which gave them a historically determined social identity in their own eyes and in the eyes of those outside the group.[4] Although a racial group cannot be defined by language or religion alone,[5] it has been accepted that Sikhs,

Jews and gypsies all fall within the scope of the Race
Relations Act 1976. In contrast, in *Dawkins v Department of
the Environment*[6] it was accepted that Rastafarians are a
separate group with identifiable characteristics, but the Court
of Appeal concluded that they have not established a separate
identity by reference to their ethnic origins and are therefore
not protected by the 1976 Act.

Both the Equal Opportunities Commission (EOC) and the
Commission for Racial Equality (CRE) have issued Codes
of Practice for the purpose of eliminating discrimination in
employment.[7] A failure to observe any of the provisions of
these codes does not render a person liable to legal
proceedings but the Commissions' recommendations are
admissible in evidence before employment tribunals.[8]

Both statutes recognise that discrimination can be either
direct or indirect.

Direct discrimination

Direct discrimination occurs where on the grounds of sex,
marital status or race a person is treated less favourably than
a person of the opposite sex, a single person or a person not
of the same racial group would be treated.

Section 1(1)(a) RRA 1976 covers all cases of discrimination
on racial grounds whether the racial characteristics in
question are those of the person treated less favourably or
some other person. Thus in *Weathersfield Ltd v Sargent*[9] it was
held that a white European woman was unlawfully
discriminated against on grounds of race when she resigned
as a result of being given an unlawful instruction to
discriminate on racial grounds against black and Asian
people.

Section 1(2) RRA 1976 states that segregation on racial
grounds amounts to less favourable treatment, although it
has been decided that allowing members of a racial group to
congregate voluntarily, eg in a particular department, will not
render an employer liable.[10] It cannot be inferred that
because a person received treatment falling below what was
expected from a reasonable employer, he or she had been

treated less favourably than others. It might need to be shown that the employer does not treat everyone in this same manner.[11]

It appears that the phrase 'on the grounds of sex' does not refer to the alleged discriminator's reason or motive but to the intention to provide less favourable treatment. According to the House of Lords, the relevant question is: 'Would the complainant have received the same treatment but for his or her sex?'[12] Words or acts of discouragement can amount to less favourable treatment.[13] The dismissal of a transsexual for a reason related to a gender reassignment would be contrary to Article 5(1) of the Equal Treatment Directive and the Sex Discrimination (Gender Reassignment) Regulations 1999.[14]

Sexual and racial harassment

The phrase 'on the grounds of' covers cases of harassment and where the reason for the discrimination is a generalised assumption that people of a particular sex, marital status or race possess or lack certain characteristics.[15] Sexual harassment has been defined as 'unwanted conduct of a sexual nature, or other conduct based on sex affecting the dignity of women and men at work'.[16] In *Reed and Bull Information Systems v Stedman*[17] the EAT said that the essential characteristic of sexual harassment is that it is words or conduct which is unwelcome to the recipient. It is for the recipient themselves to decide what is acceptable and what is unwelcome or offensive. Provided that any reasonable person would understand her/him to be rejecting the conduct of which she/he is complaining, then a continuation of that conduct would generally be regarded as harassment.

It is worth noting that both employment tribunals and the EAT are allowed to make a 'restricted reporting order' in cases where allegations of sexual misconduct are made. Whether such an order is made is up to the discretion of the tribunal, and its effect will be to prohibit the publication or broadcasting of anything likely to lead the public to identify either the person making the allegation or any person affected by it. This only relates to individuals, so tribunals do not have the ability to make a restricted reporting order protecting a corporate body.[18] Unless revoked earlier, an order will lapse when the tribunal makes its decision.[19]

In *Jones v Tower Boot Co Ltd*[20] an employee whose mother was white and father black was held to have been racially harassed as a result of a number of incidents at work which included being called offensive names and having an arm burned with a hot screwdriver. The employer was held to be vicariously liable for the harassment because the acts were carried out 'during the course of employment'.[21] This phrase has been given a broad interpretation. It includes, for example, actions that take place during a social event held immediately after work and during a leaving party for a colleague.[22]

Section 1(1) of the Protection from Harassment Act 1997 declares that a person must not pursue a course of conduct which amounts to the harassment of another or which she or he knows, or ought to know, amounts to harassment of another. Section 2 makes such action a criminal offence, and section 3 provides for a civil remedy against the offender. The Act may be of limited use in the workplace because employees who suffer from harassment may see the solution to their problem as resting with the employer rather than with those individuals who are carrying out the harassment.

The CRE booklet on racial harassment explains the policies and procedures employers need to adopt.[23] It defines such harassment as 'unwanted conduct of a racial nature, or other conduct based on race affecting the dignity of women and men at work'. It is additionally worth noting that it is also a criminal offence intentionally to cause another person harassment, alarm or distress. This applies not only to sexual and racial harassment but also to other grounds, for example sexual orientation or disability.[24]

Indirect discrimination
A person can complain of indirect discrimination where an employer applies a requirement or condition which would apply equally to a person of the opposite sex (single people or persons not of the same racial group) but which is such

that the proportion of the applicant's sex (marital status or racial group) who can comply with it is considerably smaller than the proportion of persons of the opposite sex (single people or persons not of the same racial group). The applicant must also show that he or she suffered a detriment as a result of being unable to comply with the requirement or condition. Employers can avoid liability by demonstrating that the requirement or condition is 'justifiable' irrespective of the sex, marital status or race of the person to whom it is applied.[25] Both statutes stipulate that when drawing comparisons the relevant circumstances must be the same or not materially different.[26]

(i) *Requirement or condition*

The words 'requirement or condition' are of wide import and are capable of including any obligation of service, for example an obligation to work full-time or be mobile.[27] Indeed, the mere fact that the employer requires workers to perform the jobs they were employed to do may be regarded as 'applying a requirement'.[28] Similarly, the inclusion of a contractual term can amount to an application of a requirement or condition even though that term has not been invoked.[29] However, in *Brook v London Borough of Haringey*[30] the EAT upheld the employment tribunal's decision that a requirement to obtain a prescribed number of points by reference to multiple factors in order to avoid redundancy did not amount to a 'condition'. A requirement or condition can be discriminatory even if it is only expressed as being desirable, rather than essential. In *Falkirk Council v Whyte*[31] some prison officers failed to gain promotion because management training and supervisory experience was desirable before a promotion could be agreed. In practice this requirement turned out to be essential, and because most of the people in the basic grade posts were women, it was held to be discriminatory.

(ii) *Can comply*

The courts have interpreted the words 'can comply' to mean 'can in practice comply' rather than physically or theoretically comply. Thus it has been held that an age-limit of 28 for recruitment could amount to indirect discrimination against women since they are less likely than men to be available for work below that age owing to child-bearing and rearing.[32] However, the expression 'can comply' cannot be equated with 'may wish to comply'; ultimately it is a question of reasonableness, taking into account all the surrounding circumstances. In *Clarke and Powell v Eley (IMI) Kynoch Ltd*[33] the issue arose whether the words 'can comply' and 'cannot comply' include past opportunities to comply. The EAT decided that the date on which the detriment must be demonstrated was the date the discriminatory conduct operated so as to create the alleged detriment.

(iii) *Proportion*

As regards the relative proportion of persons who can comply, much will depend on the tribunal's own knowledge and experience and its selection of the appropriate section of the population for comparison. In *Jones v University of Manchester*,[34] for example, the Court of Appeal ruled that in finding that the requirement for a career adviser to be a graduate aged between 27 and 35 years had a disproportionate impact on women, the employment tribunal had erred in restricting the pool for comparison to mature students. According to the Court of Appeal, the appropriate pool was all men and women with the required qualifications not including the requirement complained of, in this case graduates with the necessary experience. In *Greater Manchester Police v Lea*[35] the EAT was keen to avoid a discussion about statistical bases and upheld the employment tribunal's decision that the proportion of men in the pool who could comply with the condition of not being in receipt of an occupational pension (95.3 per cent) was considerably smaller than the proportion of women (99.4 per cent). The decision on what is a considerably smaller proportion is a question of fact for the employment tribunal.[36]

Where a prima facie case of indirect discrimination has been established, the employer will have to satisfy the tribunal that the discriminatory requirement or condition was justifiable. In race discrimination cases this means that an objective balance has to be struck between the discriminatory effect of the requirement or condition and the reasonable needs of the party applying it.[37] Clearly, a nexus must be established between the function of the employer and the imposition of the requirement or condition. In addition, a tribunal must assess both the quantitative and the qualitative effects of the requirement or condition on those affected by it.[38]

The European Court of Justice has indicated that Article 141 EC (previously Article 119 EC) precludes national legislation which has a disproportionate effect on women unless the Member State concerned can show that the legislation is justified by objective factors unrelated to any discrimination on the ground of sex.[39] On this basis both the qualifying periods of service and the exclusion of part-timers from statutory rights have been successfully challenged in the UK courts.[40] The Court of Justice has also held that compensation for unfair dismissal can be treated as pay, meaning that it is possible to regard the two-year period (now one-year) of continuous service required to qualify for unfair dismissal as potentially discriminatory.[41] In order to justify a requirement or condition which has a disproportionate impact on one sex the employer must demonstrate that the requirement or condition is designed to meet a legitimate objective and that the means chosen are appropriate and necessary to achieving that objective.[42] Finally, it should be noted that neither sex nor race discrimination can be justified on the basis of customer or union preferences.[43]

RECRUITMENT AND SELECTION

It is unlawful to discriminate on the prohibited grounds in the arrangements made for the purpose of determining who should be offered employment, in the terms on which employment is offered, or by 'refusing or deliberately omitting' to offer employment.[44] These arrangements can include the interviewing and assessing of candidates for a post. If racial grounds, for example, are the reason for the less favourable treatment resulting from the arrangements made, then direct discrimination is established. The reason for the discrimination is not relevant.[45]

'Employment' covers engagement under a contract of service or a contract personally to execute any work or labour.[46] According to the Court of Appeal, the legislation contemplates a contract of which the dominant purpose is that the party contracting to provide services under it personally performs the work or labour which constitutes the subject matter of the contract.[47] Both statutes aim to prevent the emergence or continuation of discriminatory practices, ie conduct which does not, in itself, amount to unlawful discrimination but which in fact results in discriminatory treatment.[48] Thus if it becomes common knowledge that Asians are unlikely to get jobs with a particular organisation because of the stringent English language tests it imposes, it may be possible to establish the existence of a discriminatory practice even though there is no applicant for a post.[49]

Advertisements must not indicate, or reasonably be understood as indicating, an intention to discriminate unlawfully nor should they adopt a job title with a sexual connotation, eg waiter or stewardess, because this will be taken to indicate a discriminatory intent unless there is an indication to the contrary.[50] The word 'advertisement' is defined to include 'every form of advertisement, whether to the public or not'.[51]

It would seem to follow that human resource managers should ensure that application forms and interviewers ask only questions and insist on minimum qualifications that are relevant to the requirements of the job.[52] Thus a height requirement and certain conditions relating to past experience, eg having served an apprenticeship, might be difficult to justify under either Act. Clearly, word of mouth recruitment is suspect and refusing to employ those who live in a particular geographical area could amount to indirect discrimination if there was a racial imbalance in the population residing there.[53] Employers also need to be aware that failure to provide a reference for an ex-employee might be construed as victimisation.[54] In *Coote v Granada Hospitality Ltd*[55] an ex-employee who had settled a complaint of sex discrimination was able to rely upon Article 6 of the Equal Treatment Directive[56] to show that the failure to provide the reference was victimisation.

LAWFUL DISCRIMINATION

Despite what has been stated above, discrimination may be lawful in certain circumstances:

(i) *Genuine occupational qualifications*

The major exception, which is common to both statutes, is where sex or race is a genuine occupational qualification (GOQ). In the case of sex, this occurs where:[57]

(a) the essential nature of the job demands a particular physiology (excluding physical strength) or authenticity in entertainment

(b) the job needs to be held by a particular sex to preserve decency or privacy either because it is likely to involve physical contact in circumstances where members of the opposite sex might reasonably object to its being carried out (eg searching, for security purposes) or because people are in a state of undress or are using sanitary facilities. In *Sisley v Britannia Security*[58] it was held that this exclusion covered all matters reasonably incidental to an employee's work and is not confined to cases where the job itself requires the holder to be in a state of undress

(c) the nature or location of the employer's establishment makes it impracticable for the job-holder to live anywhere other than on the employer's premises and the premises are not equipped with separate sleeping accommodation and sanitary facilities for more than one sex and it is unreasonable to expect the employer to equip those premises with separate facilities or to provide separate premises (eg where the employment is on a remote site). The words 'to live in' involve the concept of residence (either permanent or temporary) and do not cover the situation where the employee is obliged to remain on the premises for a limited period eating or resting[59]

(d) the nature of the establishment demands a person of a particular sex because it is an establishment for persons requiring special care or attention and those persons are all of a particular sex and it is reasonable, 'having regard to the essential character of the establishment', that the job should not be held by a person of the opposite sex[60]

(e) the job-holder provides personal services which can most effectively be provided by a person of a particular sex (eg in a team of social workers)

(f) the job is one of two to be held by a married couple

(g) the job is likely to involve the holder's working or living in a private home and the job needs to be done by a member of one sex because objection might reasonably be taken to allowing someone of the other sex the degree of physical or social contact with a person living in the home or the knowledge of such a person's private affairs, which the job is likely to entail

(h) the job is likely to involve the performance of duties outside the UK in a country of which the laws or customs are such that the duties could not effectively be performed by a woman.

The only GOQs allowed for under the 1976 Act depend on authenticity in the provision of food and drink, in entertainment and modelling, and where the job-holder provides personal welfare services which can most effectively be provided by a person of a particular racial group. In relation to personal welfare services, the Court of Appeal has ruled that the word 'personal' indicates that the identity of the giver and the recipient of the services is important and appears to contemplate direct contact between the giver and the recipient.[61] Under both Acts, GOQs apply even though they relate to only some of the job duties, and unless a duty is so trivial that it ought to be disregarded altogether, it is not for tribunals to assess its importance.[62] However, a GOQ will not provide a defence if the employer already has sufficient employees capable of carrying out those duties and whom it would be reasonable to employ in that way.[63]

The GOQ defence is also unavailable if there is a discriminatory dismissal. In *Timex Corporation v Hodgson*[64] the EAT had to consider whether a GOQ could be used as a defence where a male supervisor had been selected for redundancy on sexual grounds. Rather surprisingly, it was held that the employers had discriminated by *selecting* a woman to do the revised job, and not in *dismissing* the man. Because the discrimination lay in 'deliberately omitting to offer' or failing to transfer to the revised job the GOQ defence could apply.

(ii) *It is lawful to discriminate if it is necessary to do so to comply with a requirement of an existing statutory provision whose purpose is to protect women as regards pregnancy or maternity or other circumstances giving rise to risks specifically affecting women*[65]

It is also lawful to discriminate if it is necessary to do so to comply with a requirement of Part 1 HASAWA 1974 (see Chapter 10), or certain other health and safety legislation. For this exception to apply, the employer must demonstrate not only that the discriminatory act was necessary to comply with the statutory duty but also that it was done for the purpose of protecting the woman in relation to pregnancy, maternity or other circumstances giving rise to risks specifically affecting women. It should be noted that section 2(2) of SDA 1975 prevents men from complaining that special treatment has been afforded to women in connection with pregnancy or childbirth.

UNEQUAL TREATMENT IN EMPLOYMENT AND DISMISSALS

Turning our attention to unequal treatment in the course of employment and to discriminatory dismissals, it is unlawful for employers to discriminate:[66]

(a) (under the RRA 1976) in the terms of employment afforded[67]

(b) in the way they afford access to opportunities for promotion, transfer or training, or to any other benefits, facilities or services, or by refusing or deliberately omitting to afford access to them

(c) by dismissing or subjecting the employee to any other detriment.

The following should be noted:

(a) Positive discrimination may be permissible in certain circumstances. The European Court of Justice has held that rules which allow women to be preferred for promotion over male colleagues are acceptable provided that the male and female candidates in question are equally qualified and that the sector in question is one in which women are under-represented.[68] Special arrangements can be made to train persons of a particular sex or racial group if it can be shown that within the previous 12 months only a small minority of that sex or racial group was performing a particular type of work.[69] A refusal to investigate complaints of unfair treatment may amount to a refusal of access to 'any other benefits, facilities or services'.[70]

(b) Occupational pensions schemes must contain an equal treatment rule which ensures that men and women are offered the same rights to join a scheme as well as being entitled to the same benefits.[71] However, equal treatment is enforceable only in relation to pensionable service after 17 May 1990. Enforcement is via the Equal Pay Act 1970 (see below) and actions can be brought against scheme trustees or managers.[72]

(c) Good motive cannot excuse discriminatory behaviour. Thus, despite the Court of Appeal's decision in *Peake's* case,[73] it is submitted that allowing one sex or racial group to arrive late or leave work early constitutes unlawful discrimination because those not specially favoured have been either denied access to a benefit or have suffered a detriment. The Court of Appeal has subsequently recognised that such arrangements cannot be condoned on the grounds of chivalry or administrative convenience and it is no trifling matter that an employer has introduced a sex-based scheme when the same objective could be achieved in a non-discriminatory fashion. The words 'subjecting ... to any other detriment' are to be given their broad ordinary meaning, so it is clear that almost any discriminatory conduct by an employer is potentially unlawful.[74] However, rules concerning appearance will not be discriminatory because their content is different for men and women so long as they enforce a common principle of smartness or conventionality and, taken as a whole, neither sex is treated less favourably in enforcing that principle.[75]

(d) When considering termination, it is automatically unfair to dismiss a woman, irrespective of her hours of work or length of service, if the reason for dismissal is that she is pregnant or if the reason is in any way connected with her pregnancy (see Chapter 9). The critical question is whether, on an objective consideration of all the surrounding circumstances, the treatment complained of is on the ground of pregnancy or some other ground. This must be determined by an objective test of causal connection. The event or factor alleged to be causative of the matter complained of need not be the only or even the main cause of the result complained of. It is enough if it is an effective cause.[76] Thus in *Caruana v Manchester Airport plc*[77] it was held that there had been unlawful sex discrimination when the employee's fixed-term contract was not renewed because she would be unavailable for work at its commencement owing to pregnancy.

(e)   The dismissal of a woman on the ground of age when a man of that age in comparable circumstances would not have been dismissed, or vice versa, will be unlawful. However, there is nothing in the SDA 1975 which prevents an employer from having a variety of retiring ages for different jobs, provided there is no direct or indirect discrimination based on gender.[78] In *Marshall v Southampton and South West Hampshire AHA*[79] the European Court of Justice held that a policy of dismissing a woman solely because she had attained, or passed, the qualifying age for a state pension constituted discrimination on the ground of sex, contrary to the Equal Treatment Directive.[80] Article 5(1) of this Directive prohibits any discrimination on the grounds of sex with regard to working conditions, including conditions governing dismissal, and can now be relied on as against the state or an emanation of the state acting in its capacity as an employer.

(f)   Selection for redundancy on the grounds of sex will also be unlawful. However, suppose a woman was selected for redundancy on the grounds that, although she had a longer period of *cumulative* service, she had less *continuous* service than a man. It could be argued that because women are likely to have shorter periods of continuous service than men as a consequence of child-bearing and rearing, such a basis for selection constitutes indirect discrimination and would therefore need to be justified.[81] In *Clarke's* case[82] the EAT decided that redundancy selection criteria which resulted in the selection of part-timers first was unlawful because they had a disproportionate impact on women and could not be justified on the particular facts of the case. Dismissal on the grounds of sex or race cannot be excused simply because there was pressure from other employees.

(g)   A term in a contract or collective agreement is void[83] where its inclusion renders the making of the contract unlawful by virtue of the SDA 1975 or it provides for the doing of an act which would be unlawful under this legislation. This section also applies to the rules of employers, employers' associations, professional or qualifying bodies and trade unions. Employees (or job-seekers) can complain to an employment tribunal that a term of a collective agreement or a works rule is void. However, to do so they must believe that the term or rule may have some effect on them in the future, or that the term provides for the doing of an unlawful discriminatory act which might be done to them, and the collective agreement was made by or on behalf of the employer or an employers' organisation to which the employer belongs. It is interesting to note that tribunals have no power to amend the term so as to make it non-discriminatory. Where the victim of the discrimination is a party to the contract, the term is unenforceable against that person.[84]

In *Kowalska v Freie und Hansestadt Hamburg*[85] the ECJ declared that Article 119 EC (now Article 141 EC) precludes the application of a provision of a collective agreement under which part-timers are excluded from the benefit of severance pay when it is clear that a considerably smaller proportion of men than women work part-time, unless the employer shows that the provision is justified by objective factors unrelated to sex discrimination. Where there is indirect discrimination in a collective agreement, members of the group that is disadvantaged must be treated in the same way as other workers in proportion to the hours they work. Similarly, it would be unlawful for a collective agreement to provide for the service of full-timers to be fully taken into account for regrading purposes when only half of such service is taken into account in the case of part-timers, and the latter group comprise a considerably smaller percentage of men than women, unless the employer can prove that such a provision is objectively justified.[86]

LIABILITY

If the provisions of the SDA 1975 or RRA 1976 are not

complied with, both the employing body and named individuals may be sued. Individuals may be liable for instructing or putting pressure on someone to perform an unlawful act and for knowingly aiding another person to do an unlawful act.[87] Employers are liable for the acts of employees in the course of employment, whether or not they were done with the employer's knowledge or approval, unless it can be proved that the employer 'took such steps as were reasonably practicable to prevent the employee from doing that act'.[88] Hence it is not sufficient to adopt an equal opportunities policy: it is also necessary to check that such a policy has been communicated to all staff, and has been understood and implemented. Additionally, employers should ensure that informal practices do not develop which could lead to an act of unlawful discrimination.[89]

Both statutes permit individuals to bring complaints before an employment tribunal within three months of an 'act complained of' occurring. For these purposes an act which extends over a period is to be treated as done at the end of that period. In *Owusu v London Fire Authority*[90] the EAT ruled that an act extends over a period if it takes the form of some policy, rule or practice in accordance with which decisions are taken from time to time. Over the years the courts have struggled to distinguish a continuing act from a one-off act with a continuing consequence. The following have been held to constitute continuing acts: the refusal of a mortgage subsidy;[91] the failure to re-grade and give an employee the opportunity to act up when opportunities arose;[92] an employer's failure to implement promised remedial measures,[93] and a requirement to work on less favourable pension terms.[94] Although in *Sougrin v Haringey Health Authority*[95] the Court of Appeal thought that the placing of a black nurse at a lower grade than a white colleague and the rejection of her appeal was not a continuing act, it is difficult to see why the appeal itself could not constitute a separate 'act complained of'. According to the EAT, in determining when the 'act complained of was done' the question is whether the cause of action had crystallised on the relevant date, not whether the complainant felt that he or she had suffered discrimination on that date.[96] Out-of-time claims can be heard if it is just and equitable to do so,[97] and in this respect the strength of the employee's complaint may be a factor.[98]

Only the Equal Opportunities Commission or the Commission for Racial Equality can commence proceedings where there has been discriminatory advertising, a discriminatory practice, or where there have been instructions or pressure to discriminate.[99] However, there is nothing to prevent an individual from complaining that an advertisement led to discrimination in the arrangements made for determining who should be offered employment.[100]

It is recognised that obtaining information can be particularly difficult where discrimination is alleged, and so Questions and Replies Orders were passed in 1975 (sex) and 1977 (race) to assist applicants in this respect. Although special forms are not necessary, an aggrieved person's questions and any reply by the employer are admissible in evidence. If there is a failure to reply within a reasonable period, or an 'evasive or equivocal' response is received, the inference may be drawn that an unlawful act has been committed.[101] Thus where an employer failed to answer all but one of nine questions asked by an unsuccessful job applicant, the reply was regarded as evasive and the inference drawn that the applicant had suffered unlawful discrimination in the selection arrangements.[102] Additionally, the House of Lords has ruled that the contents of documents must be disclosed if such 'discovery' (a technical legal term) is necessary to dispose fairly of the proceedings.[103] In this context 'fair disposal' means a disposal of the proceedings which is fair to the applicant.[104] However, a tribunal is not empowered to order an employer to disclose information which is not available at the time.[105]

Both Acts allow the Commissions to devote resources to assisting actual or prospective complainants,[106] and if they think it desirable they can instigate formal investigations of anyone believed to be discriminating unlawfully.[107] However, the Commissions cannot embark on a 'named person' investigation in the absence of any belief that the person named might have committed an unlawful act.[108] The Commissions also have the power to require the production of documents, to make recommendations, and, if necessary, to issue non-discrimination notices.[109] As a last resort, either body may seek a county court injunction to prohibit discriminatory acts.

In relation to the burden of proof, it is worth referring to the principles and guidelines set out by the Court of Appeal in *King v GB-China Centre*:[110]

(a) It is unusual to find direct evidence of discrimination.

(b) The outcome of a case will therefore usually depend on what inferences it is proper to draw from the facts found by the tribunal.

(c) A finding of discrimination and of a difference in race (or sex) will often point to the possibility of discrimination. In such circumstances it will be for the employer to explain. If no explanation is offered or the tribunal considers the explanation to be unsatisfactory, it will be legitimate to infer that the discrimination was on racial (or sexual) grounds.

(d) It is unnecessary and unhelpful to introduce the concept of a shifting evidential burden of proof. Tribunals should reach a conclusion on the balance of probabilities, bearing in mind the difficulties which face a person who complains of unlawful discrimination and the fact that it is for the complainant to prove his or her case.

Evidence of events subsequent to the alleged act of discrimination can be taken into account if it provides proof of a relevant fact.[111]

A European Council Directive on the burden of proof in sex discrimination cases[112] will place a much greater burden of proof on employers. Article 4 of the Directive states that once a complainant has established a set of facts from which there may be a presumption of direct or indirect discrimination, the burden is on the respondent to show that there has been *no breach* of the principle of equal treatment. This Directive is due to be implemented, in most countries, by January 2001.

If no settlement is reached,[113] and the complaint is held to be well-founded, three possible remedies are available:[114]

(a) The tribunal can make a declaration of the complainant's rights.

(b) It can require the respondent to pay unlimited compensation.[115] In principle, successful complainants should be restored to the position they would have been in but for the unlawful conduct.[116] However, the RRA 1976 provides that in cases of indirect discrimination no compensation can be awarded if the employer shows that there was no intention to discriminate.[117] For these purposes the requisite intention is established if, at the time the relevant act is done, the employer (i) wants to bring about the state of affairs which constitutes the unfavourable treatment; and (ii) knows that this prohibited result will follow from the act. It is clear that a claim for hurt feelings is almost inevitable in discrimination cases[118] and that exemplary damages are unavailable.[119]

(c) There may be a recommendation that the employer takes action within a specified period to reduce the effect of the discrimination which has taken place, such as by removing an age barrier to recruitment.[120]

Finally, both the SDA 1975 and RRA 1976 outlaw the victimisation of people simply because they have given evidence in connection with proceedings, have brought proceedings or intend to do so against someone (eg some other employer) under the Equal Pay Act 1970, the SDA 1975, or the RRA 1976.[121]

THE EQUAL PAY ACT 1970

According to the Equal Pay Act 1970, an equality clause operates when a person is employed on 'like work', work rated as equivalent or work of equal value to that of a person of the opposite sex in the same employment.[122] For these purposes men and women are to be treated as in the same employment if they are employed at the same establishment or at establishments in Great Britain which observe common terms and conditions of employment.[123] For these purposes 'common terms and conditions' means terms and conditions which are substantially comparable on a broad basis rather than the same terms and conditions.[124]

It should be noted that the class of comparators defined in Section 1(6) EPA 1970 is more restricted than applies under Article 141 EC (formerly Article 119 EC). Because Article 141 EC takes precedence, the crucial question is whether the applicant and the comparators are employed 'in the same establishment or service'. This same establishment, however, does not include employees who work for a section of the business that has been contracted out. Claimants are unable to use employees in the contracted-out business as comparators.[125]

The effect of the equality clause is that any term in a person's contract (whether concerned with pay or not) which is less favourable than in the contract of a person of the opposite sex is modified so as to be not less favourable. In *Evesham v North Hertfordshire Health Authority*[126] the EAT held that this meant being placed at the same point on an incremental scale as the comparator, not being placed on that scale at a level that was commensurate with her experience. It should also be noted that paragraph 2 of Article 141 EC states that 'pay' means 'the ordinary basic minimum wage or salary and any other consideration, whether in cash or in kind, which the worker receives, directly or indirectly, in respect of his employment from his employer'. According to the Court of Justice, a benefit is pay if the worker is entitled to receive it from his or her employer by reason of the existence of the employment relationship. Thus Article 141 EC covers not only occupational retirement and survivors' pensions,[127] travel concessions on retirement, and statutory and contractual severance payments, but also paid leave or overtime for participation in training courses given by an employer under a statutory scheme.[128] Section 6 of the EPA 1970 provides that an equality clause does not operate where there are terms affording special treatment to women in connection with pregnancy or childbirth.

The concept 'like work' focuses on the job rather than the person performing it. Once a person has shown that her or his work is of the same or broadly similar nature as that of a person of the opposite sex, unless the employer can prove that any differences are of practical importance in relation to terms and conditions of employment, that person is to be regarded as employed on 'like work'.[129] In comparing work, a broad approach should be taken and attention must be paid to the frequency with which any differences occur in practice as well as their nature and extent. Trivial differences or 'differences not likely in the real world to be reflected in terms and conditions of employment' are not to be taken into account.[130] Similarly, tribunals are required to investigate the actual work done rather than rely on theoretical contractual obligations. The performance of supervisory duties may constitute 'things done' of practical importance[131] but the time at which the work is done would seem to be irrelevant. In *Dugdale v Kraft Foods*[132] the men and women were employed on broadly similar work but only men worked the night shift. It was held that the hours at which the work was performed did not prevent equal basic rates being afforded because the men could be compensated for the night shift by an additional payment. Thus an equality clause will not result in equal pay if persons of one sex are remunerated for something which persons of the other sex do not do.[133] It is not permissible, however, to ignore part of the work which a person actually performs on the ground that his or her pay includes an additional element in respect of that work,[134] although there might be an exception where part of the work is, in effect, a separate and distinct job. Finally, in determining whether differences are of practical importance a useful guide is whether the differences are such as to put the two employments in different categories or grades in an evaluation study.[135]

According to section 1(5) EPA 1970, a person's work will only be regarded as rated as equivalent to that of a person of the opposite sex if it has been given equal value under a properly conducted job evaluation scheme, including the allocation to grade or scale at the end of the evaluation process. Thus in *Springboard Trust v Robson*[136] it was accepted that the applicant was employed on work rated as equivalent, notwithstanding that the comparator's job scored different points, where the result of converting the points to grades provided for under the evaluation scheme was that the jobs were to be treated as in the same grade.

A valid job evaluation exercise will evaluate the job and not the person performing it, and if evaluation studies are to be relied on they must be analytical in the sense of dividing a physical or abstract whole into its constituent parts. It is clearly insufficient if bench-mark jobs have been evaluated using a system of job evaluation whereas the jobs of the applicant and comparators have not.[137] Employers are not prevented from using physical effort as a criterion if the tasks involved objectively require a certain level of physical strength, so long as the evaluation system as a whole precludes all sex discrimination by taking into account other criteria.[138] If the work has been rated as equivalent, a complainant does not have to show that the employees concerned have actually been paid in accordance with the evaluation scheme.[139]

The House of Lords has ruled that an equal value claim can be pursued so long as the applicant's comparator is not engaged on like work or work rated as equivalent.[140] Where work has been given different ratings under a job evaluation study, however, an equal value claim cannot proceed unless a tribunal is satisfied that there are reasonable grounds for determining that the study was made 'on a system which discriminates on the grounds of sex.'[141] Section 2A(3) states that there is discrimination on the grounds of sex for these purposes where a 'difference, or coincidence, between values set by that system on different grounds under the same or different headings is not justifiable irrespective of the sex of the person on whom those demands are made'.

This would appear to cover both direct and indirect discrimination.

Where a woman, for example, can show that she is employed on like work, or work rated as equivalent, an employer can still defeat a claim for equal pay by proving on the balance of probabilities that the variation is 'genuinely due to a material difference (other than the difference of sex) between her case and his'.[142] If there is an equal value claim, the employer need only show that a variation between a woman's and a man's contract is genuinely due to a factor which is (a) material and (b) not the difference of sex. In this context 'material' means significant and relevant. The requirement for 'genuineness' is satisfied if the tribunal concludes that the reasons put forward were not a sham or pretence. For the material factors relied upon, it is sufficient to show that they were in fact a cause of the difference in pay and that this difference is not 'tainted by sex'.[143] According to the ECJ, the employer cannot rely on the fact that rates of pay have been set by collective bargaining even if the bargaining process is untainted by sex discrimination. In the same case the ECJ acknowledged that market forces cannot constitute a complete defence where they account only for part of the difference in pay.[144]

The objectively justified grounds need not be solely economic and could include administrative efficiency in appropriate cases.[145] It is worth noting that the following have been regarded as genuine material differences: the method of entering employment;[146] working in a different part of the country;[147] responsibility allowances;[148] financial constraints;[149] longer service; better academic qualifications; and higher productivity.

In *Jenkins v Kingsgate Clothing Ltd (No 2)*[150] the question of whether a female 'part-timer' was entitled to the same hourly rate as a 'full-time' man was referred to the ECJ. This court decided that a difference in pay between full- and part-time workers does not amount to discrimination prohibited by Article 141 EC (formerly Article 119 EC) unless it is in reality merely an indirect way of reducing the level of pay of part-timers on the ground that that group of workers is composed exclusively or predominantly of one sex. Having received no clear guidance from the European Court of Justice, the EAT chose to construe the EPA 1970 as requiring any difference in pay to be objectively justified.[151] However, it is not unlawful to provide overtime payments only for hours worked in excess of the normal working hours for full-timers. Thus part-timers who work in excess of their contractual hours can be excluded from overtime payments if their total hours do not exceed the normal hours of full-timers.[152] According to the ECJ, a system for classifying part-time workers converting from job-sharing to full-time work comes within the concept of pay, and any rules which put part-timers at a disadvantage when changing by applying criteria based on length of service in the post is contrary to Article 141 EC because the great majority of job-sharers are women.[153]

In the *Danfoss* case[154] the Equal Pay Directive 75/117 was interpreted as meaning that where employees do not understand how the criteria for pay increments are applied, if a woman establishes that the average pay of females is lower than that of men, the burden of proof is on the employer to show that the pay system is not discriminatory. Thus where vocational training or flexibility operate to the disadvantage of women, the employer will have to justify their application. According to the European Court of Justice, vocational training can be justified as a criterion if the employer shows that such training is important for the performance of specific work tasks. Similarly, in so far as flexibility refers to adaptability to variable work schedules rather than to the quality of the work, it can be justified by demonstrating that such adaptability is of importance for the performance of specific job duties.

In relation to piecework, the ECJ has ruled that where individual pay includes a variable element depending on each worker's output and it is impossible to identify the factors which determined how the variable element in pay was calculated, the burden of proving that the differences found are not the result of sex discrimination may shift to the employer. For these purposes any comparisons must cover a relatively large number of employees in order to ensure that the differences found are not purely fortuitous or differences in individual output.[155] As regards seniority, the ECJ has acknowledged that its objectivity depends on all the circumstances, notably on the relationship between the nature of the duties performed and the experience afforded by their performance after a certain number of working hours.[156]

The practice of drawing a circle around the names of those within a protected group – eg employees demoted through no fault of their own as the result of a reorganisation – is one device that needs to be scrutinised as a result of the EPA 1970. Such action may be perfectly lawful, eg where employees accept lower-paid work in a redundancy situation, but if the underlying reason for different treatment is sex-based it cannot be accepted as a defence.[157] Employers have to justify the inclusion of every employee in a red-circled group and must prove that at the time of admission to the circle the more favourable terms were related to a consideration other than sex.[158] Again, if a person's wages are protected on a transfer, perhaps because of age or illness, tribunals must be satisfied that this was not merely because of sex or that the new job was not one which was open only to one sex. The prolonged maintenance of a red circle may not only be contrary to good industrial relations practice but may in all the circumstances give rise to a doubt as to whether the employers have discharged the statutory burden of proof imposed on them by section 1(3) EPA 1970. In their Code of Practice on Equal Pay, the EOC recommends an internal pay review as the most appropriate method of ensuring that a pay system delivers equal pay free from sex bias.[159]

Where there is a dispute as to the effect of an equality clause, both the employee and the employer can apply to an employment tribunal. Complaints must be lodged within six months of the termination of employment, whether they are brought under the EPA 1970 or European law.[160] The employee can claim arrears of pay and damages and, following a judgment by the European Court of Justice,[161] the EAT has held that the two-year limitation on arrears of remuneration in section 2(5) of the EPA 1970 breaches European Community law. The EAT concluded that the six-year limit in the Limitations Act, from the date of commencement of proceedings, now applies to the EPA.[161a] Complainants must identify a comparable person of the opposite sex and cannot launch an application without some sort of prima-facie case.[162] Although a comparison cannot be made with a hypothetical person, the ECJ has decided that Article 141 EC allows a complainant to compare herself or himself with a previous job incumbent.[163]

Where an equal value claim is lodged, the employment tribunals must allow the parties to apply for an adjournment in order to reach a settlement.[164] A tribunal can reach a decision only if it is satisfied that there are reasonable grounds for determining that the work is of equal value, and it may ask for a report to be made by a member of the panel of independent experts.[165] An employment tribunal is not entitled to require an expert's report before deciding whether there are reasonable grounds.[166] However, it is entitled to hear evidence of a job evaluation scheme undertaken by the employer after the commencement of proceedings, provided it relates to facts and circumstances existing at the time the proceedings were initiated. Indeed, it is open to an employer to utilise such a scheme as evidence at any stage up to the final hearing.[167] The employer can ask the tribunal to hear the material factor defence before the matter is referred to an expert, but only in exceptional circumstances can this issue be raised again after the report has been submitted.[168] A minimum period of six weeks is allowed for the preparation of the report, and the parties have an opportunity to make representations before it is drawn up.[169] No method for comparing jobs is stipulated, although it is envisaged that this will involve evaluating factors such as effort, skill and decision. While there is a presumption in favour of admitting the report, it can be challenged on the following grounds:[170]

(a)   the expert failed to follow the designated procedure

(b)   the expert's conclusion was not reasonably reached

(c)   for 'some other material reasons' (excluding simple disagreement with the expert's conclusion or reasoning) the report is unsatisfactory.

The expert may be obliged to attend the tribunal hearing as a witness and may be required to explain any matter contained in the report. Indeed, the tribunal is entitled to take into account the expert's oral evidence in deciding whether to admit the report.[171] Each party is entitled to call one witness to give evidence on the equal value question, but a tribunal has no power to require a complainant to be interviewed by an expert appointed by the employer.[172] The tribunal can only hear factual evidence relating to a conclusion in the report if it relates to the genuine material factor defence, or a party has failed to provide information or produce documents for the expert. Finally, it should be remembered that the decision on whether an equal value claim succeeds is that of the tribunal and not the expert. The current attitude of the EAT is that an independent expert appointed by a tribunal has no greater standing than an expert called by either side.[173]

KEY POINTS 7
Sex and race discrimination

- The Sex and Race Discrimination Acts cover more than their names suggest; the SDA 1975, for example, covers discrimination against married persons, while the RRA 1976 defines racial grounds as meaning colour, race, nationality, and national or ethnic origins.

- Direct discrimination occurs when on the grounds of sex, marital status or race a person is treated less favourably than a person of the opposite sex, a single person or a person not of the same racial group.

- Indirect discrimination occurs where an employer applies a requirement or condition which would apply equally to a person of the opposite sex, or persons of a different racial group, but which is such that the proportion of the applicant's sex or racial group who can comply with it is considerably smaller than the proportion of persons of the opposite sex or not of the same racial group.

- There are occasions when it is lawful to discriminate; these include when there is a statutory requirement whose purpose is to protect women in relation to pregnancy or maternity provisions and when there is a genuine occupational qualification.

- The EPA 1970 inserts an equality clause into all contracts of employment when a person is employed on like work or work rated as equivalent or work of equal value to that of a person of the opposite sex in the same employment.

- An employer will need to show that any differences in pay are the result of a genuine material difference not related to the sex of either employee.

NOTES

1 Section 3(1) RRA 1976
2 See section 2(2) RRA 1976 and *London Borough of Lambeth v CRE* (1990) IRLR 231
3 (1983) IRLR 209
4 See *Northern Joint Police Board v Power* (1997) IRLR 610 for issues relating to English and Scottish racial groups
5 See *Gwynedd CC v Jones* (1986) ICR 833; *Nyazi v Rymans Ltd* (1988) IRLIB 367
6 (1993) IRLR 284
7 EOC Code of Practice for the elimination of discrimination on the grounds of sex and marriage and the promotion of equality of opportunity in employment 1985; CRE Code of Practice for the elimination of racial discrimination and the promotion of equality of opportunity in employment 1983; see also CIPD Equal Opportunities Code
8 Section 56A(10) SDA 1975 and section 47(10) RRA 1976
9 (1999) IRLR 94
10 See *FTAT v Modgill* (1980) IRLR 142
11 *Zafar v Glasgow City Council* (1998) IRLR 36
12 See *James v Eastleigh BC* (1990) IRLR 288
13 See *Tower Hamlets v Rabin* (1989) ICR 693
14 SI 1999/1102; see *P v S and Cornwall County Council* (1996) IRLR 347
15 See *Coleman v Skyrail Oceanic* (1981) IRLR 398; *Hurley v Mustoe* (1981) IRLR 208 and EOC Code para 13(a)
16 See European Commission Recommendation 91/131 on the protection of the dignity of women and men at work; see also CIPD statement on harassment at work and *Chief Constable of Lincolnshire Police v Stubbs* (1999) IRLR 81
17 (1999) IRLR 299
18 See *Leicester University v A* (1999) IRLR 352
19 Sections 11 and 13 ETA 1996; see also *Chessington World of Adventures v Reed* (1998) IRLR 56
20 (1997) IRLR 168
21 Section 32 RRA 1976 and section 41 SDA 1975
22 *CC of Lincolnshire Police v Stubbs* (note 16)
23 'Racial Harassment at work: what employers can do about it.' May 1995
24 Section 4A Public Order Act 1986
25 Section 1(1) of both Acts
26 Section 5(3) SDA 1975, section 3(4) RRA 1976; see *Wakeman v Quick Corporation* (1998) IRLR 424
27 See *Holmes v Home Office* (1984) IRLR 299 and *Meade-Hill v British Council* (1995) IRLR 478 respectively
28 See *Briggs v North Eastern Education and Library Board* (1990) IRLR 181
29 See *Meade-Hill v British Council* (note 27)
30 (1992) IRLR 478
31 (1997) IRLR 560
32 *Price v Civil Service Commission* (1978) IRLR 3
33 (1982) IRLR 482

34 (1993) IRLR 218

35 (1990) IRLR 372; see also *London Underground v Edwards* (1998) IRLR 364

36 *London Underground v Edwards* (note 35)

37 See *Hampson v DES* (1989) IRLR 69

38 See *Jones v University of Manchester* (note 34)

39 See Case 171/88 *Rinner-Kuhn v FWW Spezial Gebäudereinigung* (1989) IRLR 494

40 See *R v Secretary of State ex parte EOC* (1993) IRLR 10

41 Case 167/97 *R v Secretary of State for Employment ex parte Seymour-Smith and Perez* (1999) IRLR 253

42 See Case 170/84 *Bilka-Kaufhaus v Weber von Harz* (1986) IRLR 317

43 Section 40 SDA 1975 and section 31 RRA 1976 deal with inducement or attempted inducement to perform an unlawful act

44 Section 6(1) SDA 1975 and section 4(1) RRA 1976; *Brennan v Dewhurst Ltd* (1983) IRLR 357

45 See *Nagarajan v London Regional Transport* (1999) IRLR 572

46 See section 82(1) SDA 1975 and section 78(1) RRA 1976; on employment outside Great Britain see section 10 SDA 1975 and section 8 RRA 1976; *Haughton v Olau Line* (1985) ICR 711

47 See *Mirror Group Ltd v Gunning* (1986) IRLR 27; section 9 SDA 1975 and section 7 RRA 1976 outlaw discrimination against contract workers: see *Harrods Ltd v Remick* (1996) ICR 846

48 Section 37 SDA 1975 and section 28 RRA 1976

49 On language qualifications see *Raval v DHSS* (1985) IRLR 370; on language training see CRE Code 1.26–27

50 Section 38 SDA 1975 and section 29 RRA 1976

51 Section 82(1) SDA 1975 and section 78(1) RRA 1976

52 See EOC Code para 23; CRE Code 1.13–14 and CIPD Recruitment Code; see also *Martins v Marks and Spencer* (1998) IRLR 326

53 See EOC Code para 19; CRE Code 1.13–14 and CIPD Recruitment Code

54 Section 4 SDA 1975

55 (1999) IRLR 452

56 Directive 76/207

57 Section 7 SDA 1975

58 (1983) IRLR 404

59 *Sisley v Britannia Security* (note 58)

60 See *Lasertop Ltd v Webster* (1997) IRLR 498

61 See *London Borough of Lambeth v CRE* (note 2)

62 See *Tottenham Green Under-Fives v Marshall (No 2)* (1991) IRLR 161

63 See *Etam plc v Rowan* (1989) IRLR 150

64 (1981) IRLR 530

65 Section 51(1)(2) SDA 1975; compare section 41 RRA 1976 and *Hampson v DES* (1990) 3 WLR 42

66 Section 6(2) SDA 1975; section 4(2) RRA 1976; EOC Code paras 25, 28, 32 and CRE Code paras 1.1–17, 1.2–1

67 Section 4(2)a RRA 1976; in relation to sex, the EPA 1970 deals with discrimination in contractual matters

68 See *Marshcall v Land Nordrhein-Westfalen* (1998) IRLR 39

69 Section 47 SDA 1975 and section 37 RRA 1976

70 See *Eke v Commissioners of Customs and Excise* (1981) IRLR 384; EOC Code para 31 and CRE Code para 1.22

71 See sections 62–66 Pensions Act 1995. Section 64 deals with exclusions, for example, in relation to bridging pensions and actuarial factors

72 See Occupational Pension Schemes (Equal Treatment) Regulations 1995 SI 1995/3183

73 *Peake v Automotive Products* (1977) IRLR 365

74 See *Barclays Bank v Kapur* (1991) IRLR 136

75 See *Smith v Safeway plc* (1996) IRLR 456 and CRE Code para 1.24

76 See *O'Neill v Governors of St Thomas More School* (1996) IRLR 372

77 (1996) IRLR 378

78 See *Bullock v Alice Ottley School* (1992) IRLR 564

79 (1986) IRLR 140

80 Directive 76/207

81 See *Brook v London Borough of Haringey* (1992) IRLR 478

82 See note 33

83 Section 77 SDA 1975

84 See *Meade-Hill v British Council* (note 27)

85 Case 33/89 (1990) IRLR 447

86 Case 184/89 *Nimz v Freie und Hansestadt Hamburg* (1991) IRLR 222

87 Sections 30–40, 42 SDA 1975 and sections 30–1, 33 RRA 1976; see *AM v WC and SPV* (1999) IRLR 410

88 Section 41 SDA 1975 and section 32 RRA 1976; *Towerboot Co. v Jones* (note 21)

89 See EOC Code paras 33–40; CRE Code paras 1.33–43

90 (1995) IRLR 574

91 *Calder v Finlay* (1989) IRLR 55

92 *Owusu v London Fire Authority* (note 90)

93 *Littlewoods v Traynor* (1993) IRLR 54

94 *Barclays Bank v Kapur* (1991) IRLR 136

95 (1992) IRLR 416

96 See *Clarke v Hampshire Electro-Plating* (1991) IRLR 491

97 Section 76 SDA 1975 and section 68 RRA 1976; see *Hawkins v Barclays Bank* (1996) IRLR 258

98 See *Foster v South Glamorgan HA* (1988) IRLR 277

99 Section 72(4) SDA 1975 and section 63(4) RRA 1976; see *Cardiff Womens' Aid v Hartup* (1994) IRLR 390

100 See *Brindley v Tayside Health Board* (1976) IRLR 364

101 Section 74 SDA 1975 and section 65 RRA 1976

102 See *Virdee v ECC Quarries* (1978) IRLR 295

103 See *Nasse v Science Research Council* (1979) IRLR 465

104 See *British Library v Palyza* (1984) IRLR 307

105 See *Carrington v Helix Ltd* (1990) IRLR 6

106 Section 75 SDA 1975 and section 66 RRA 1976

107 Sections 57–8 SDA 1975 and sections 48–9 RRA 1976

108 See *Re Prestige plc* (1984) IRLR 166

109 Sections 59–60, 67 SDA 1975 and sections 50–51, 58 RRA 1976; see *R v CRE ex parte Westminster CC* (1985) IRLR 426

110 (1991) IRLR 513

111 See *Eke's* case (note 70) and *Chattopadhyay v Headmaster of Holloway School* (1981) IRLR 487

112 Directive 97/80

113 On conciliation see *Livingstone v Hepworth Refractories* (1992) IRLR 63

114 Section 65 SDA 1975 and section 56 RRA 1976

115 See Sex Discrimination and Equal Pay (Remedies) Regulations 1993 SI 1993/2798 and Race Relations (Remedies) Act 1994 which gave tribunals discretion to include interest on sums awarded
116 See *MOD v Cannock* (1994) IRLR 509
117 Section 57(3) RRA 1976
118 See *Orlando v Didcot Social Club* (1996) IRLR 262
119 *MOD v Meredith* (1995) IRLR 539
120 See *Noone v North West Thames RHA* (1988) IRLR 530
121 Section 4 SDA 1975 and section 2 RRA 1976
122 Section 1(2) EPA 1970; on work of greater value see *Murphy v Bord Telecom Eirann* (1988) IRLR 267
123 See section 1(6) EPA 1970
124 *British Coal v Smith* (1996) IRLR 404
125 See *Lawrence v Regent Office Care Ltd* (1999) IRLR 148
126 (1999) IRLR 155
127 See *Ten Oevers* case (1993) IRLR 601
128 See *Botel's* case (1992) IRLR 423
129 Section 1(4) EPA 1970
130 See *Capper Pass Ltd v Lowton* (1976) IRLR 366
131 See *Eaton v Nuttall* (1977) IRLR 71
132 (1976) IRLR 368
133 See *Thomas v NCB* (1987) IRLR 451 and *Calder v Rowntree Mackintosh* (1993) IRLR 212
134 See *Maidment v Cooper & Co* (1978) IRLR 462
135 See *British Leyland v Powell* (1978) IRLR 57
136 (1992) IRLR 261
137 See *Bromley v Quick Ltd* (1988) IRLR 249
138 See *Rummler v Dato-Druck GmbH* (1987) IRLR 32; on job evaluation generally see ACAS advisory booklet entitled *Job Evaluation: An Introduction*
139 See *O'Brien v Sim-Chem Ltd* (1980) IRLR 373
140 See *Pickstone v Freemans PLC* (1988) IRLR 357
141 Section 2A (1–2) EPA 1970
142 See *Financial Times v Byrne (No 2)* (1992) IRLR 163
143 See *Strathclyde Council v Wallace* (1998) IRLR 146
144 *Enderby v Frenchay Health Authority* (1993) IRLR 591
145 See *Rainey v Greater Glasgow HB* (1987) IRLR 26
146 *Rainey v Greater Glasgow HB* (note 145)
147 *NAAFI v Varley* (1976) IRLR 408
148 *Avon and Somerset Police Authority v Emery* (1981) ICR 229
149 *Beneviste v University of Southampton* (1989) IRLR 122
150 (1981) IRLR 388
151 See, for example, *Montgomery v Lowfield Distribution* (1996) IDS Brief 576 where part-timers worked fixed hours but full-timers had flexible shifts
152 See *Stadt Lengerich v Angelica Helmig* (1996) IRLR 35
153 See *Hill and Stapleton v Revenue Commissioners* (1998) IRLR 466
154 (1989) IRLR 532
155 See the *Dansk Industrie* case (1995) IRLR 648
156 See *Nimz v Freie und Hansestadt Hamburg* (1991) IRLR 222
157 See *Snoxell v Vauxhall Motors* (1997) IRLR 123
158 See *Methuen v Cow Industrial Polymers* (1980) IRLR 289

159 EOC 1996
160 See *Preston v Wolverhampton NHS Trust* (1998) IRLR 197, in which the House of Lords has referred to the ECJ the question whether the two-year limitation on retrospective recovery of compensation, in section 2(5) EPA 1970, contravenes Community law
161 Section 2(5) EPA 1970; Case 326/96 *Levez v TH Jennings* (1999) IRLR 36
161a *Levez v TH Jennings* (No 2) (1999) IRLR 764
162 See *Clwydd CC v Leverton* (1985) IRLR 197
163 See *McCarthys Ltd v Smith* (1980) IRLR 210
164 Rule 13 Schedule 2 Employment Tribunal (Constitution and Rules of Procedure) Regulations 1993 SI 1993/2687
165 Section 2A(1)(4) EPA 1970; see Sex Discrimination and Equal Pay (Miscellaneous Amendments) Regulations 1996 SI 1996/438
166 See *Wood v Ball Ltd* (1999) IRLR 773
167 *Dibro Ltd v Hore* (1990) IRLR 129
168 See Rule 9 Schedule 2 Employment Tribunal (Constitution and Rules of Procedure) Regulations 1993 SI 1993/2687
169 Rule 8A Schedule 2 Employment Tribunal Regulations 1993 (note 166)
170 See *Tennant's Textiles v Todd* (1989) IRLR 3
171 See *Aldridge v British Telecom* (1990) IRLR 10
172 See *Lloyds Bank v Fox* (1989) IRLR 103
173 See *Dibro Ltd v Hore* (note 167)

8 Discrimination on the grounds of disability, trade union membership and age

This chapter deals with discrimination by employers on the grounds of disability, trade union membership and age. The Disability Discrimination Act 1995 makes it unlawful for all but the smallest employers to discriminate against current or prospective employees for a reason relating to their disability. We examine how the Act defines disability and the duties of the employer to take such steps as are reasonable in the circumstances to stop any physical or other arrangements placing a disabled person at a disadvantage. We look at discrimination against employees or prospective employees on the grounds of trade union membership or non-membership and consider the issues of unlawful refusal of employment, the right not to suffer detriment and dismissals. Finally we examine the Code of Practice on Age Diversity in Employment, which is a voluntary code aimed at removing discrimination on the grounds of age from the workplace.

DISABILITY

The Disability Discrimination Act 1995 (DDA 1995) makes it unlawful for employers with fifteen[1] or more employees to discriminate against existing or prospective staff for a reason relating to their disability. People are also protected if they have recovered from a disability that is covered by this Act.[2] The DDA 1995 covers employees and contract workers, apprentices and those working under a contract to do any work (see page 138). It excludes police and prison officers, fire-fighters, the armed services and people working on board a ship, aircraft or hovercraft.[3]

According to section 1(1) DDA 1995, a person has a disability 'if he has a physical or mental impairment which has a substantial and long-term adverse effect on his ability to carry out normal day-to-day activities'. The definition covers impairments affecting the senses such as hearing and sight, together with learning difficulties or a mental illness that is clinically well-recognised. However, addictions, tattoos and body-piercing are all excluded from the protection of the Act.[4] For these purposes an impairment has a long-term effect only if it has lasted for at least 12 months, is likely to do so, or is likely to last for the rest of the life of the person affected. Long-term effects include those that are likely to recur.[5]

Day-to-day activities are normal activities carried out on a regular basis and must involve one of the following:

(a) mobility

(b) manual dexterity (this covers the ability to use hands and fingers with precision)

(c) physical co-ordination

(d) continence

(e) the ability to lift, carry or move everyday objects

(f) speech, hearing or eyesight

(g) memory or ability to concentrate, learn or understand

(h) perception of the risk of physical danger.

However, severe disfigurements are treated as disabilities although they have no effect on a person's ability to carry out normal day-to-day activities.[6]

Medication or equipment is not taken into account when assessing whether an impairment has a substantial effect. One exception to this is when people wear glasses or contact lenses.[7] Where a progressive condition has resulted in an impairment that has affected a person's day-to-day activities but the effect is not yet substantial, it is to be treated as having a substantial effect if that is the likely prognosis. The examples given of progressive conditions are: cancer, multiple sclerosis, muscular dystrophy and HIV infection.[8] It should be noted that the DDA 1995 does not cover those with a latent genetic predisposition to disability, for example Huntington's chorea, unless the disability develops.

The proper approach to the question of whether a person has a disability, within the meaning of the Act, was considered in *Goodwin v The Patent Office*.[9] The EAT concluded that a tribunal should look at the evidence by reference to four different conditions:

(i) *the impairment condition*
Does the applicant have an impairment which is either physical or mental? If there is any doubt whether the impairment condition is fulfilled in a mental illness case, reference should be made to the World Health Organisation International Classification of Diseases.

(ii) *the adverse effect condition*
Does the impairment affect the applicant's ability to carry out normal day-to-day activities as set out in paragraph 4(1) of Schedule 1 to the Act (see below)? This condition is concerned with the *ability* to carry out normal day-to-day activities whether at work or at home; eg a person may be able to cook, but only to do so with the greatest difficulty.

(iii) *the substantial condition*
Is the adverse condition substantial? The tribunal will need to look at how the person's abilities were affected at the material time while on medication, and then try to deduce what he or she would have been like without medication. The question is then whether the actual or deduced effects on the applicant's ability to carry out normal day-to-day activities is clearly more than trivial.

(iv) *the long-term condition*
Is the adverse condition long-term?

Section 5 declares that an employer discriminates against a disabled person if, for a reason relating to that person's disability,

(a) the employer treats him or her less favourably than the employer treats or would treat others to whom that reason does not or would not apply; and

(b) the employer cannot show that the treatment is justified.

Less favourable treatment can be justified only if such treatment is material to the circumstances of the individual case. Even so, employers must consider whether the reason could be overcome or made less substantial by making a reasonable adjustment.[10] The rights of an employee to have these reasonable adjustments made are additional rights and do not depend upon the employee's showing that discrimination has taken place under section 5(1) DDA 1995.[11] In *Clark v TGA Ltd t/a Novacold*[12] the Court of Appeal concluded that the test of less favourable treatment is based on the reason for the treatment of the disabled person and not on the fact of the disability. It did not, unlike the SDA 1975 and the RRA 1976, need a comparator to show that discrimination had taken place.

According to Section 6, where any of the employer's arrangements or any physical feature of the premises place a disabled person at substantial disadvantage, the employer must take such steps as are reasonable in all the circumstances to prevent the arrangements or feature having that effect. The following are examples of steps that an employer may have to take in order to comply with this obligation:

(a) making adjustments to premises

(b) allocating some of the disabled person's duties to another

(c) transferring the disabled person to fill an existing vacancy

(d) altering the disabled person's working hours

(e) assigning him or her to a different place of work

(f) allowing him or her to be absent during working hours for rehabilitation, assessment or treatment

(g) training or arranging for training to be given to him or her

(h) acquiring or modifying equipment

(i) modifying instructions or reference manuals

(j) modifying procedures for testing or assessment

(k) providing a reader or interpreter

(1) providing supervision.[13]

In deciding whether it is reasonable for an employer to take a particular step, regard will be had, in particular, to

(a) the extent to which taking the step would prevent the particular effect in question

(b) the extent to which it is practicable for the employer to take the step

(c) the financial and other costs which would be incurred and the extent to which taking it would disrupt the employer's activities

(d) the extent of the employer's financial and other resources

(e) the availability to the employer of financial and other assistance in making the adjustment.

There is a limit to the adjustments that an employer is required to make. They do not include the provision of personal carer services for a person that might need such help. They might, however, include the accommodation of such a carer if provided by others.[14]

The duty to make adjustments does not arise until a disabled person is employed or such a person applies or considers applying for a job. The applicant needs to make the employer aware of his or her disability and whether special interview arrangements are necessary. In *Rideout v T C Group*[15] a candidate suffering from a rare form of epilepsy was interviewed in surroundings which, it was suggested, were unsuitable for someone with her disability. Although the Code of Practice for the elimination of disability discrimination in employment[16] suggests that employers should think ahead in making arrangements for interviews, the EAT concluded that no reasonable employer could be expected to know, without being told by the applicant, that the arrangements for an interview might disadvantage such an applicant. It will be difficult to show that an employer is guilty of disability discrimination if they have not been told of the employee's condition. In *O'Neill v Symm & Co.*[17] an employee was dismissed after 15 months' employment which included a number of absences for a viral illness. The employee was diagnosed as suffering from ME/chronic fatigue syndrome and claimed discrimination on the grounds of her disability. The employer, however, did not know of this diagnosis, which meant that the reason for the dismissal was not the disability.

It is unlawful for employers to discriminate against disabled people

(a) in the arrangements made for determining who should be offered employment;[18]

(b) in the terms on which employment is offered; or

(c) by refusing or deliberately not offering employment.

It is also unlawful to discriminate against disabled employees

(a) in the terms of employment;

(b) in the opportunities afforded for promotion, training, transfer or receiving any other benefit;

(c) by refusing to afford or deliberately not affording any such opportunity; or

(d) by dismissing or subjecting the disabled person to any other detriment.[19]

Section 68(1) DDA 1995 defines the term 'employment' as employment under either a contract of service or a contract to personally do any work. The EAT has interpreted this to mean that the dominant purpose of the contract was the execution of personal work or labour. Thus, for example, a subpostmaster who, though answerable to the Post Office, was not obliged to carry out the work in person, was unable to claim discrimination on the grounds of a disability.[20]

Claims that the DDA 1995 has been infringed must normally be lodged with an employment tribunal within three months of the act complained of. As with other tribunal proceedings, ACAS conciliation officers will make their services available in order to assist the parties to reach a settlement. There is an obligation upon the tribunal to enquire about what steps the employer has taken and whether they were reasonable.[21] If, however, a tribunal finds that a complaint is well-founded, it may provide for any of the following remedies it considers just and equitable:

(a)   a declaration as to the rights of the parties

(b)   an order for compensation to be paid to the complainant

(c)   a recommendation that the employer takes action within a specified period for the purpose of obviating or reducing the adverse effect on the complainant of any matter to which the complaint relates.[22]

It is made clear that compensation is available for injury to feelings, and there is no limit on the amount of money that can be awarded.[23]

Where an advertisement might reasonably be understood to have indicated that a person might not get the job because of a disability or that an employer is unwilling to make adjustments for disabled people, and a disabled person who was not offered the post complains, the employment tribunal must take the advertisement into account. Unless it can be proved otherwise, the tribunal will assume that the reason the complainant did not get the job related to his or her disability.[24] It should be noted that, apart from Section 6, employers are not obliged to treat disabled persons more favourably than others, although such discrimination in itself will not necessarily be unlawful.[25] Thus, there is nothing in this statute which prevents positive discrimination.

Section 55 makes it unlawful for a person to victimise another for

(a)   bringing proceedings under the DDA 1995;

(b)   giving evidence or information in connection with such proceedings;

(c) doing anything under the DDA 1995; or

(d) alleging that another person contravened the DDA 1995 (unless the allegation was false and not made in good faith).

As with sex and race discrimination, anything done by a person in the course of employment is treated as also done by the employer, whether or not it was done with the employer's approval. However, employers will not be liable if they can show that they took such steps as were reasonably practicable to prevent the employee's action.[26] Similarly, section 57 provides that anyone who knowingly aids another to perform an unlawful act is to be treated as having committed the same unlawful act.

The Disability Rights Commission[27] will advise the government on ways to eliminate and reduce discrimination and on the operation of the Act generally. This Commission will be able to produce Codes of Practice and carry out formal investigations in particular sectors or where it is concerned that the law is not being followed. The Secretary of State can also produce Codes of Practice and has the power to appoint people to advise him or her on matters relating to the employment of disabled persons.[28]

TRADE UNION MEMBERSHIP OR NON-MEMBERSHIP

Unlawful refusal of employment

Section 137(1) of TULRCA 1992 makes it unlawful to refuse employment to people because

(a) they are or are not members of a trade union; or

(b) they refuse to accept a requirement that they become a member or cease to be a member, or a requirement that they suffer deductions if they fail to join.[29]

People are deemed to have been refused employment with an employer if that employer:

(a) refuses or deliberately omits to entertain the application or enquiry; or

(b) causes the applicant to withdraw or cease to pursue the application or enquiry; or

(c) refuses or deliberately omits to offer employment; or

(d) makes an offer of employment the terms of which are such as no reasonable employer who wished to fill the post would offer, and which is not accepted; or

(e) makes an offer of employment but withdraws it or causes the applicant not to accept it; or

(f) offers employment on terms which include a requirement within section 137(1), and the applicant declines the offer because of this requirement.

As regards job advertisements,[30] if an advertisement indicates, or might reasonably be understood as indicating, that employment is open only to people who are or are not union members, or that there is a requirement applying to the post of the sort mentioned in section 137(1)(b), then if people who do not meet the relevant condition are refused employment, it will be conclusively presumed that this was because they failed to satisfy the condition. Where it is the practice for trade unions to supply job applicants, non-members who are refused employment are deemed to have been so refused on account of their non-membership.

Section 138 makes it unlawful for an agency which finds employment for workers, or supplies employers with workers, to refuse its services to people because they are or are not union members or are unwilling to accept a condition or requirement of the type mentioned in section 137(1)(b). The provisions relating to advertisements also apply to such agencies.

Section 3 of the ERel Act 1999 gives the Secretary of State the power to make regulations with the purpose of prohibiting the compilation and use of lists which contain information about an individual's trade union membership or activities with a view to their being used by employers or employment agencies for the purposes of recruitment (see page 149).

A complaint about the infringement of sections 137–8 must

normally be presented to an employment tribunal within three months of the date of the conduct complained about. Under section 139 TULRCA 1992, the date of the conduct complained of will be:

(a) in the case of an actual refusal, the date of the refusal

(b) where there was a deliberate omission to offer employment or deal with an application or enquiry, the end of the period within which it was reasonable to expect the employer to act

(c) in the case of conduct that causes the applicant to withdraw or cease to pursue an application, the date of that conduct

(d) in a case where an offer was made but withdrawn, the date when it was withdrawn

(e) in a case where an offer was made but not accepted, the date the offer was made.

Provision is made for conciliation, but if a complaint is upheld, the tribunal must make a declaration to that effect and may make such of the following remedies as it considers just and equitable:[31]

(a) an order obliging the respondent to pay compensation, which is to be assessed on the same basis as damages for breach of statutory duty and may include damages for injury to feelings

(b) a recommendation that the respondent takes such action as the tribunal thinks practicable to obviate or reduce the effect on the complainant of the conduct to which the claim relates. If such a recommendation is not complied with, any award of compensation can be increased, although the total award cannot exceed the amount stipulated in section 124 ERA 1996 (£50,000 in 1999).

Finally, it should be noted that a trade union may be joined as a defendant in tribunal proceedings where an employer or agency maintains that it was induced to act in the manner complained of by union pressure.[32] If compensation is awarded, the union may be ordered to pay all or part of it.

Subject to detriment short of dismissal

Section 146 TULRCA 1992 gives employees the right not to be subjected to any detriment as an individual by any act, or any deliberate failure to act, by an employer if the act or failure takes place for the purpose of

(a) preventing or deterring them from being or seeking to become a member of an independent trade union or penalising them for doing so

(b) preventing or deterring them from taking part in the activities of an independent trade union at any appropriate time, or penalising them for doing so

(c) compelling them to become a member of any trade union or of a particular trade union or of one of a number of particular trade unions

(d) enforcing a requirement that in the event of their failure to become, or their ceasing to remain, a member of any trade union or a particular trade union or one of a number of particular trade unions, they must make one or more payments. For this purpose, any deduction from remuneration which is attributable to the employee's failure to become, or his or her ceasing to be, a trade union member will be treated as a detriment within the meaning of section 146 TULRCA 1992.

A deliberate failure to act by the employer can also be treated as a detriment if the purpose is one of the reasons above. As regards the requirement that the action must be taken against an employee as an individual, the Court of Appeal has offered the following guidance: 'If an employee is selected for discrimination because of some characteristic which he shares with others, such as membership of a particular trade union, then the action is ... taken against him as an individual.'[33] Thus de-recognition of an individual shop steward by an employer can be action taken against the shop steward as an individual, rather than action taken against the trade union.[34]

The words 'for the purpose of' connote an object that the employer seeks to achieve, and the purpose of an action must not be confused with its effect. Thus when a full-time union official was turned down for promotion, the Court of Appeal accepted that section 146 had not been infringed because the employer's purpose had been to ensure that only those with sufficient managerial experience were promoted.[35] It is clear that employees have the right to join any independent trade union of their choice.[36] Thus in *Carlson's* case[37] the EAT decided that the denial of a car-park permit to a member of a non-recognised independent trade union constituted a form of penalisation outlawed by the section. In this context 'penalising' was held to mean 'subjecting to a disadvantage'.

Because there is no statutory definition, tribunals have the task of determining what the 'activities of an independent trade union' are. The following have been accepted as such: attempting to recruit new members or form a workplace union branch, taking part in union meetings, and consulting a union official. Thus those claiming that they have suffered because of their activities do not have to show that they were authorised union representatives, although individual complaints or group meetings which have no union connection will not be protected. It is not conclusive that workers did not get together at a committee or formal branch meeting; it would appear sufficient that union members have discussed matters with which an independent trade union is concerned.[38] However, in *Therm-a-Stor v Atkins*[39] the Court of Appeal drew a distinction between the employer's reaction to a trade union's activities and reaction to an individual employee's activities in a trade union context. Where a union district secretary's letter asking for recognition led to dismissal it was therefore held that the reason for dismissal had nothing to do with anything which the employee concerned had personally done or proposed to do. As a result, the employment tribunal had no jurisdiction to hear Mr Atkins' complaint. The expression 'activities of an independent trade union' refers to the activities of a specific trade union rather than the activities of unions generally.

According to the EAT, an employment tribunal must establish:

(a) the belief held by the employer upon which the decision was taken

(b) that such a belief was genuinely held

(c) whether the facts upon which the belief was based, judged objectively, fell within the 'activities of an independent trade union'.[40]

Can industrial action be regarded as an activity? In *Rasool's* case[41] the EAT was prepared to accept that attendance at an unauthorised meeting for the purpose of considering the views of employees in relation to impending wage negotiations was such an activity. Nevertheless, such activity is not normally taken at an 'appropriate time' since this is defined as being outside working hours or within working hours in accordance with arrangements agreed with, or consent given by, the employer. Such consent may be express, for example in a collective agreement, or may be implied from the conduct of the parties. Unless there is an arrangement that covers the situation, however, it would seem that a shop steward who is unaccredited by management at the relevant time cannot be taken to have implied permission to call a meeting during working hours.[42] Activities carried out at an 'appropriate time' means activities occurring during the period of employment and excludes activities during a prior period. Nevertheless, the statute is infringed if the employee suffers detriment short of dismissal on the basis of previous trade union activities when the only rational basis for this is a subsequent employer's fear that those activities will be repeated in the present employment.[43] The phrase 'working hours' is defined as meaning any time when an employee is required to be at work, but in order to protect union activities carried out during paid tea breaks it has been construed as meaning the time when work is actually performed.[44]

A claim that there has been detriment short of dismissal must normally be presented within three months of the date on which the act complained of occurred, or if the act complained of is spread over a period, then the last day of that period.[45] A failure to act shall be treated as occurring on the date when it was decided upon. If there is an absence of evidence to the contrary, employers shall be deemed to have failed to act

(a) when they do something distinctly different from what they should have done (ie an act inconsistent with doing the failed act); or

(b) if there has been no inconsistent act, when the period expires within which the employer might have been expected to do the failed act.[46]

The burden is on the employers to show the purpose for which they acted or failed to act. In deciding on this purpose, the tribunal must not take into account any pressure exerted on the employer by the threat or organisation of industrial action.[47] Where an employment tribunal finds an employee's complaint to be well-founded, it must make a declaration to that effect and may make an award of compensation. The amount awarded must be such as the tribunal considers 'just and equitable in all the circumstances having regard to the infringement of the complainant's right' and 'to any loss sustained by the complainant which is attributable to that action'.[48] In this context 'loss' is taken to include any expenses reasonably incurred and any benefit which the applicant might have received but for the unlawful action. Compensation can be reduced if employees fail to mitigate their loss, or cause or contribute to the action taken against them. In *Brassington's* case[49] the EAT ruled that the statute did not impose a quasi-fine, so that compensation could be awarded only if the employee could show that an injury resulted. Yet this injury is not restricted to pecuniary loss. The stress engendered by the situation may have caused injury to the employee's health, or a sincere desire to join a union – with all the benefits of help and advice which that might entail – could have been frustrated. It might also include a sum for injury to feelings, as in *Cleveland Ambulance NHS Trust v Blane*[50] where a trade union activist was not short-listed for promotion because of trade union activities.

Dismissals relating to trade union membership

According to section 152(1) TULRCA 1992 a dismissal is unfair if the reason for it (or if more than one, the principal reason) was that the employee:

(a) was or proposed to become a member of an independent trade union; or

(b) had taken, or proposed to take, part in the activities of an independent trade union at any appropriate time; or

(c) was not a member of any trade union or of a particular trade union, or had refused or proposed to refuse to become or to remain a member.

Section 152(3) TULRCA 1992 states that dismissals are to be treated as falling within (c) above if one of the reasons for them was that employees:

(a) refused (or proposed to refuse) to comply with a requirement that in the event of their failure to become, or their ceasing to remain, a trade union member they must make some kind of payment; or

(b) objected, or proposed to object, to the operation of a provision under which their employer was entitled to deduct sums from their remuneration if they failed to become or remain a trade union member.

It would seem that if an employee is dismissed because of her or his proposal to leave an independent trade union, that will be unfair, even though the proposal is conditional on something occurring or not occurring.[51]

The usual qualifying period and upper age-limit for claiming unfair dismissal do not apply if the reason, or principal reason, for dismissal was one of those specified in section 152 TULRCA 1992.[52] This being so, the burden is on employees to prove that their dismissal related to trade union membership. However, where the question of jurisdiction does not arise, the only burden on the employee is to produce some evidence that casts doubt upon the employer's reason.[53]

Where employees allege that their dismissals were unfair by virtue of section 152 TULRCA 1992, they can seek 'interim relief'.[54] This is available where employees present their claims within seven days of the effective date of termination and, where sections 152(1)(a) or (b) TULRCA 1992 are relied on, they submit written certificates signed by an authorised union official which state that there appears to be reasonable grounds for supposing that the reason for dismissal was the one alleged in the complaints. The tribunal must hear such an application as soon as practicable,[55] and if it thinks it 'likely' (ie there is a pretty good chance) that the complainant will be found to have been unfairly dismissed by virtue of any of the above sections, it must ask whether the employer is willing to reinstate or (if not) to re-engage the employee pending the determination of the complaint. If the employer is willing to reinstate or the employee is willing to accept re-engagement, the tribunal shall make an order to that effect. Where the employer fails to attend the hearing or is unwilling to re-employ, the tribunal must make an order for the continuation of the employee's contract of employment. In essence, such an order amounts to suspension on full pay.[56]

Where there has been pressure to dismiss on the grounds of non-membership of a trade union, section 160 TULRCA 1992 enables the person who applied the pressure to be joined (by either the employer or the employee), ie be brought in as a party to the unfair dismissal proceedings. A request that a person be joined must be acceded to if it is made before the hearing but can be refused if it is made after that time. No such request can be entertained after a remedy has been awarded, and the tribunal is empowered to apportion compensation in a 'just and equitable' manner.

Refusal to opt out of a collective agreement
The ERel Act 1999 permits the Secretary of State to make regulations about cases where a worker is subject to detriment or dismissal on the grounds that the worker refuses to enter into a contract which includes terms which differ from an applicable collective agreement.[57] If an employer

wishes to persuade employees to agree to an individual contract of employment which excludes or changes the terms of a relevant collective agreement, the employer may try to do so as long as those that refuse to sign such contracts are not subjected to detriment or dismissal. Specifically excluded as a detriment, however, is the payment of higher wages or bonuses to those employees who sign, so long as they are not prevented, as a result, from being a member of any trade union.[58]

Compilation of lists of trade union members
Section 3 of the ERel Act 1999 allows the Secretary of State to make regulations prohibiting the compilation of lists which

(a) contain details of members of trade unions or persons that have taken part in the activities of trade unions, and

(b) are compiled with a view to being used by employers or employment agencies for the purposes of discrimination in relation to the recruitment or treatment of such workers.

This measure seeks to end the practice by some employers and employers' associations of maintaining lists of trade union members and activists who are seen as potential troublemakers and who are therefore turned down for any positions applied for with the employer or employers holding the list. It remains to be seen how effective such a measure can be against the informal exchange of information between employers, as against the keeping of formal lists.

AGE DISCRIMINATION IN EMPLOYMENT

In June 1999 the government introduced a Code of Practice on Age Diversity in Employment. The Code has no statutory basis and is entirely voluntary, but is intended to encourage employers to stop using age as a criterion in its human resource policies.

The purpose of the Code, according to its introduction, is to help employers 'to improve people management in their organisations and be better able' to

(a) recruit and retain staff

(b) eliminate unfair and short-sighted age discrimination

(c) introduce good practice

(d) understand how to make that good practice work within their organisation

(e) recognise the business benefits of an age-diverse workforce.

The government has identified six stages in the employment process in which good practice is required to create an age-diverse workforce and reduce discrimination. These are:

• recruitment

• selection

• promotion

• training and development

• redundancy

• retirement

Recruitment and selection
This is discussed in Chapter 4.

Promotion
This concerns the promotion of people based upon their ability or demonstrated potential. The principles put forward here are also those that apply to measures to stop all forms of discrimination. The same recommendations apply to those making decisions on promotion as those involved in selection, and there is the need to

(a) select on merit

(b) ensure that promotion opportunities are advertised through open competition and are available to all staff who have demonstrated the ability or the potential to do the job

(c) focus on the skills, abilities and potential of the candidates when sifting applications.

In the Code the government has highlighted the need for the senior management of any organisation to be committed to the policies put forward. This is perhaps especially important in the area of promotion. Promoting employees and possibly providing training and development for them is linked to any organisation's long-term objectives in respect of staff needed in the future. It is difficult to envisage a voluntary code that prevents a manager from promoting younger staff rather than older ones because of a perception that these younger staff will be around longer and provide much-needed skills in the future. This would be promotion based not upon the merits of the competing individuals but on the perceived long-term needs of the organisation.

Training and development

This category concerns the encouragement of all employees to take advantage of relevant and suitable training opportunities. Perhaps self-evidently, the Code states that the business with the most skilled, flexible and committed workforce has a more competitive edge. It then claims that skilled and motivated people are 'more productive, produce higher-quality work, reduce costs and wastage, and increase profitability'. The specific recommendations that follow are to

(a) ensure that the training and development needs of all staff are regularly reviewed and that age is not a barrier to training

(b) make sure that all staff are aware of the opportunities available and are encouraged to use them

(c) focus on the individual's and the organisation's needs when providing opportunities

(d) look at how training is delivered and to ensure that different learning styles and needs are addressed.

Redundancy

This looks at removing age as a criterion for making decisions on redundancy. The decisions are to be based on objective job-related criteria to ensure that skills needed to help the business are retained. There is also a recommendation that flexible options, such as part-time working, job-share, career breaks or short-term contracts, should be considered as an alternative to redundancy.

There is no mention of the more traditional approach to redundancy of 'last-in, first-out'. Such an approach may have favoured older workers with longer service.

Retirement

The Code states that retirement schemes should be fairly applied and business needs taken into account. Specific recommendations are to

(a) base retirement policy on business needs while also giving individuals as much choice as possible

(b) ensure that the loss to the company of skills and abilities is fully evaluated when operating early retirement schemes

(c) consider alternatives to early retirement

(d) perceive age as by no means the sole criterion in early retirement schemes

(e) use flexible retirement schemes wherever possible

(f) use phased retirement wherever possible

(g) make pre-retirement support available.

Section 156 of the Employment Rights Act 1996 deprives employees of any rights to redundancy payments if they continue working after normal retirement age. *Secretary of State v Levy*[59] concerned a female employee who had worked a few months past her retirement age. Despite the fact that she had 18 years' service with the employer, she was not paid any compensation for her dismissal through redundancy (her employer had become insolvent and she made a claim against the Redundancy Fund). The Employment Appeal Tribunal stated that

> The logic of choosing pensionable ages for the purpose of
> disentitlement ... must be that after retirement there can be no
> redundancy. The employee may cease to work, but the job may
> not cease to exist, and in any event there would be no dismissal
> caused by redundancy.

The implication of this is that every employee who reaches
normal or the state retirement age is deemed to have retired,
regardless of whether they continue to work. This means that
if the normal retirement age in an organisation is 55 years,
then after this age a worker will have lost all his or her rights
to redundancy payments and, indeed, rights to protection
against unfair dismissal, unless there is a contractual
obligation to the contrary. Such workers are likely to be
working entirely at their employer's discretion, who may
dispose of their services without any fear of costs arising out
of redundancy or unfair dismissal claims.

In *Secretary of State for Scotland v Taylor*[60] the Scottish
Prison Service was held to have 'embarked on a policy with
regard to retirement of older employees in order to achieve
a workforce generally of younger persons who could, as a
consequence, be paid less'. Mr Taylor argued that the
organisation's equal opportunities policy, which included
age discrimination, had become incorporated into the
contract of employment, and therefore the insistence on a
lower actual retirement age (of 55 years), and his own
consequent replacement by a younger person, was in breach
of that contractual term. He won his case at the employment
tribunal, but on appeal the Employment Appeal Tribunal
distinguished between the period before retirement and the
period following it. The EAT stated that

> In the final analysis, it is our decision that the protection in this
> case in respect of age discrimination subsisted in the contract to
> the benefit of the employee so long as he was working within
> the currency of the contract up to normal retirement age.
> Thereafter, the issue of age discrimination per se, whatever else
> may be the rights of an employee working after his retirement age
> at the discretion of the employer, simply disappears.

In other words, there was agreement that the equal

opportunities policy was incorporated into the contract of employment, but it could not be enforced when the employee reached retirement age. The age discrimination aspects of the equal opportunities policy applied only to those under retirement age (55 years) and ended when that age was reached. This decision was then upheld on appeal to the Court of Session.

In *Nash v Mash*[61] an applicant was dismissed from his post as a warehouse manager at the age of 69 years. He sought to claim unfair dismissal and a redundancy payment. His case was that sections 109 (which deprives people over normal retirement age of the right to claim unfair dismissal) and 156 of the Employment Rights Act 1996 are indirectly discriminatory against men, contrary to Article 119 EC (Article 141 in the Treaty of Amsterdam). Figures were produced which showed that in 1991 6.8 per cent of the male population aged 65 to 74 years were economically active, compared to 3.9 per cent of females. Figures from the Equal Opportunities Commission showed that 7.5 per cent of men over the age of 65 years were economically active whereas 3.1 per cent of women were also active. The employment tribunal concluded that the relevant sections of the Act were incompatible with Article 141 (previously Article 119 EC) of the EC Treaty. They were not willing to await the outcome of other judgments from the European Court of Justice because of the time they would take and with respect to the complainant's age.

The issue was further developed in a case at the Bedford employment tribunal.[62] This case concerned an 'over-age' employee who was attempting to claim a redundancy payment as in *Secretary of State v Levy*.[63] The tribunal in this instance decided to refer the case to the European Court of Justice for that court to decide on whether an upper age-limit is compatible with Article 141 EC. The decision in Levy's case was that the employee did not succeed in the claim because she had lost all her contractual rights when she reached retirement age: no new contractual rights existed that she might rely on, and all rights she might have had according to her previous contract no longer applied.

KEY POINTS 8
Disability, trade union membership and age discrimination

- It is unlawful for employers with 15 or more employees to discriminate against employees or applicants for reasons related to their disability.

- A disability, within the meaning of the Act, is a physical or mental impairment which has a substantial and long-term adverse effect on the ability to carry out normal day-to-day activities.

- A tribunal needs to approach the question of whether a person has a disability by reference to the impairment condition, the adverse effect condition, the substantial condition and the long-term condition.

- An employer has a duty to take steps and make adjustments in order not to place a disabled person at a substantial disadvantage.

- It is unlawful to refuse employment to a person because they are or are not members of a trade union.

- Employees have the right not to be subject to detriment short of dismissal for the purposes of preventing them from becoming a member or taking part in the activities of a trade union, or, conversely, for not wanting to be a member or to take part in union activities.

- A dismissal is unfair if the reason for it was that a person proposed to become a member of, or take part in the activities of, a trade union, or, conversely did not want to be a member or to take part in union activities.

- The Code of Practice on Age Diversity in Employment, which is voluntary, looks at all stages of the employment cycle and makes recommendations for good practice by employers.

NOTES

1 Reduced from twenty by the Disability Discrimination (Exemption for Small Employers) Order 1998 SI 1998/2618
2 See section 2 and Schedule 1 paragraph 2(2)
3 Section 64 DDA 1995
4 See the Disability Discrimination (Meaning of Disability) Regulations 1996 SI 1996/1455
5 See Schedule 1 paragraph 2 DDA 1995
6 Schedule 1 paragraphs 3 and 4 DDA 1995
7 Schedule 1 paragraph 6 DDA 1995
8 Schedule 1 paragraph 8 DDA 1995
9 (1999) IRLR 4
10 See the Disability Discrimination (Employment) Regulations 1996 (note 4)
11 *Clark v TGA Ltd t/a Novacold Ltd* (1999) IRLR 318
12 See note 11
13 See Code of Practice for the elimination of disability discrimination in employment 1996
14 See *Kenny v Hampshire Constabulary* (1999) IRLR 76
15 (1998) IRLR 628
16 See paragraphs 5.15 and 5.16
17 (1998) IRLR 233
18 The Code of Practice makes helpful suggestions about job specifications and interviews (note 14)
19 Section 4 DDA 1995. See *British Sugar v Kirker* (1998) IRLR 624
20 *Sheehan v Post Office Counters Ltd* (1999) ICR 734
21 See *Morse v Wiltshire County Council* (1998) IRLR 352
22 The Employment Tribunals (Constitution and Rules of Procedure) (Amendment) Regulations 1998 SI 1996/1757 oblige tribunals to give extended reasons for their decisions and enable them to make restricted reporting orders in DDA 1995 cases.
23 Section 8 and Schedule 3 DDA 1995
24 Section 11 DDA 1995
25 See *Clark v TGA Ltd t/a Novacold Ltd* (note 11). Section 6(7) DDA 1995 states that 'nothing in this part is to be taken to require an employer to treat a disabled person more favourably than he treats or would treat others'.
26 Section 58 DDA 1995
27 Disability Rights Commission Act 1999
28 See sections 53 and 60 DDA 1995
29 These provisions do not apply if the employee ordinarily works outside Great Britain
30 Defined by Section 143 TULRCA 1992
31 Section 140 TULRCA 1992
32 Section 142 TULRCA 1992
33 *Ridgway v NCB* (1987) IRLR 80
34 See *Farnsworth v McCoid* (1999) IRLR 626
35 *Gallagher v Department of Transport* (1994) IRLR 231
36 See *Ridgway v NCB* (note 33)
37 *Carlson v Post Office* (1981) IRLR 158
38 See *British Airways v Francis* (1981) IRLR 9

39 (1983) IRLR 78
40 See *Port of London Authority v Payne* (1992) IRLR 447
41 *Rasool v Hepworth Pipe Ltd* (No 2) (1980) IRLR 135
42 See *Marley Tile v Shaw* (1980) IRLR 25
43 See *Fitzpatrick v British Rail* (1991) IRLR 376
44 See *Zucker v Astrid Jewels* (1978) IRLR 385
45 Section 147(2) TULRCA 1992
46 Section 147(3) TULRCA 1992
47 Section 148(2) TULRCA 1992
48 Section 149 TULRCA 1992
49 See *Brassington v Cauldon Wholesale Ltd* (1977) IRLR 479
50 (1997) IRLR 332
51 See *Crossville Motor Ltd v Ashville* (1986) IRLR 475
52 Section 154(1) TULRCA 1992
53 See *Maund v Penwith District Council* (1984) IRLR 24
54 Section 161 TULRCA 1992
55 Section 162 TULRCA 1992
56 See section 164 TULRCA 1992
57 Section 17 ERel Act 1999
58 Section 17(4) ERel Act 1999
59 (1989) IRLR 469
60 (1999) IRLR 362
61 (1998) IRLR 168
62 *Simpson v British Timken Ltd* 29.5.98 case no. 1200143/98
63 See note 59

9 Parental rights

This chapter discusses the rights of parents in certain circumstances. The Employment Relations Act 1999 amended the rules on maternity leave and introduced rights to parental leave and time off for dependants. Firstly we deal with the issue of maternity leave. This is divided into the right to ordinary maternity leave, to compulsory maternity leave and to additional maternity leave. We then examine the right to return to work after maternity leave and the right to maternity pay, as well as the rights to parental leave contained in the Maternity and Parental Leave Regulations 1999 and time off for dependants contained in the Employment Relations Act 1999.

TIME OFF FOR ANTENATAL CARE

Irrespective of the length of service or the number of hours she works, a pregnant woman who, on the advice of a registered medical practitioner, midwife or health visitor, has made an appointment to receive antenatal care, has the right not to be unreasonably refused time off during working hours to enable her to keep the appointment. Apart from the first appointment, the woman may be required to produce a certificate and some documentary evidence of the appointment for the employer's inspection. A woman who is permitted such time off is entitled to be paid for her absence at the appropriate hourly rate.[1]

If time off is refused or the employer has failed to pay the whole or part of any amount to which she feels she is entitled, a woman can complain to an employment tribunal. Unless the 'time-limit escape clause' applies, her claim must be presented within three months of the date of the appointment concerned.[2] Where a tribunal finds that the complaint is well-founded, it must make a declaration to that effect, and if time off has been unreasonably refused, the employer will be ordered to pay a sum equal to that which she would have been entitled to had the time off not been refused. If the complaint is that the employer failed to pay the amount to which she was entitled, the employer must pay the amount that the tribunal finds due to her. Any contractual remuneration paid to a woman in respect of a period of time off under this section, however, goes towards discharging any statutory liability to pay that arises. Conversely, any payment made as a result of this section goes towards discharging any contractual liability to pay for the period of time off.[3]

MATERNITY LEAVE

Article 8 of the Pregnant Workers Directive[4] provides that pregnant workers, or those that have recently given birth, have a right to a period of maternity leave of at least 14 weeks, which must include a compulsory period of at least two weeks before and/or after confinement. Community law and the European Court of Justice have played an important part in developing rules that protect women during their pregnancy and maternity leave period. The ECJ has regarded discrimination against pregnant women as acts of sex discrimination which are in breach of Article 141 (previously Article 119), the Equal Treatment Directive[5] and the Equal Pay Directive.[6]

In *Pedersen*,[7] for example, the ECJ held that a policy which stated that workers who are unfit for work because of illness would receive full pay, but that pregnant women off sick from work for an illness related to the pregnancy would not, was in breach of Article 141 EC and the Equal Pay Directive. This developed further the view of the ECJ as expressed in *Brown v Rentokil*,[8] in which the Court of Justice held that the dismissal of a woman at any time during her pregnancy for absences caused by illness resulting from that pregnancy is direct discrimination on the grounds of sex contrary to the EC Equal Treatment Directive.[9] Part VIII of the ERA 1996, which was substantially amended by the Employment Relations Act 1999,[10] contains provisions for maternity rights and is more generous than the minimum requirements in the EU Directive.

The ordinary maternity leave period

Section 71 ERA 1996 provides a general right for all pregnant employees to be absent from work for a period of 18 weeks during an ordinary leave period. The Maternity and Parental Leave Regulations 1999 (the MPL Regulations 1999) state that an employee is entitled to ordinary maternity leave provided that[11] at least 21 days before the date on which she intends her ordinary maternity leave period to start, or as soon as is reasonably practicable, she notifies her employer, in writing if requested, of

(a)   her pregnancy

(b)   the expected week of childbirth[12]

(c)   the date on which she intends her ordinary maternity leave period to start. This date cannot be earlier than the beginning of the eleventh week before the expected week of childbirth.[13]

She must, if her employer so requests, produce a certificate for inspection from a registered doctor or midwife stating the expected week of childbirth.

Regulation 6 MPL Regulations 1999 provides that if the ordinary maternity leave has not commenced

(a)   by the first day after the beginning of the sixth week before the expected week of childbirth on which the employee is absent from work wholly or partly because of pregnancy, or

(b)   by the day on which childbirth occurs,

then the ordinary maternity leave will be deemed to have commenced on that day, provided that the employee notifies her employer, in writing if requested, as soon as reasonably practicable. Failure to provide this notification may result in the employee's losing her entitlement to ordinary maternity leave.[14]

Contractual rights during ordinary maternity leave

Section 71(4) ERA 1996 states that an employee on ordinary maternity leave is

(a) entitled to the benefit of the terms and conditions of employment which would have applied had she not been absent. This does not include terms and conditions relating to remuneration[15]

(b) bound by obligations arising under those terms and conditions

(c) entitled to return from leave to the job in which she was employed before her absence, with her seniority, pension and similar rights as if she had not been absent. She is also to return on terms and conditions not less favourable than those which would have applied if she had not been absent, unless there is a dismissal by reason of redundancy.[16]

The compulsory maternity leave period

An employer may not permit an employee to work during her compulsory maternity leave period. An employer who allows an employee to work during this period will be subject to a fine.[17] This compulsory period will not be less than two weeks in length, commencing with the day on which childbirth occurs, and it is included in the ordinary leave period (see above).[18]

The additional maternity leave period

An employee who is entitled to ordinary maternity leave and has, at the beginning of the eleventh week before the expected week of childbirth, been continuously employed for a period of not less than one year is also entitled to additional maternity leave.[19] This additional maternity leave period commences on the day after the last day of the ordinary maternity leave period and continues until the end of a period of 29 weeks beginning with the week in which childbirth occurred.[20]

The date of the return to work

Because the ordinary maternity leave period ends 18 weeks after the start date, both parties should know, at the time the employee notifies the start of her leave, precisely when she is due to return. There is no requirement for an employee returning to work after the ordinary leave period to give notice of her return to work. If the employee wishes to return early and not take her full entitlement of maternity leave, then she must give 21 days' notice, in writing, of her intended return date. If she does not give the required notice, the employer may delay her return for up to 21 days.[21]

Because the additional maternity leave period ends 29 weeks after childbirth, the date an employee is intending to return will not be known until the birth. There is therefore a requirement that the employee, if requested by her employer not earlier than 21 days before the end of her ordinary maternity leave period, notify the employer of the date on which childbirth occurred and of whether she wishes to return to work at the end of her additional maternity leave period. The employee then has 21 days, or as soon as reasonably practicable if that is not possible, in which to respond.[22] Failure to respond within the time period may result in the employee's losing the protection against detriment and unfair dismissal provided by the MPL Regulations (see below).

The employer's request for notification of the date of the birth and the expected date of return to work must be

(a) in writing, and

(b) accompanied by a written statement which, firstly, explains to the employee how, in accordance with the MPL Regulations, the date on which her additional maternity leave period may be determined to end, and which, secondly, contains a warning of the consequences of failing to respond within 21 days of receiving it.[23]

If an employee wishes to return to work early from her additional maternity leave, then the same rules apply as with returning early from ordinary maternity leave (see above). Apart from this ability to delay the return of an employee who wishes to return early without giving the proper notice, there are no provisions which enable an employer to postpone an employee's return after additional maternity leave. Nor are there provisions for an employee to postpone her return to work on the grounds of illness after the additional maternity leave. If she is ill, the normal sick leave procedures at her workplace will apply. This confirms the approach of the Court of Appeal in *Halfpenny v IGE Systems Ltd*,[24] which concerned the case of a woman who had given notice of an intention to return to work and then failed to do so because of illness. The employers treated her contract as coming to an end because of her failure to physically return. The Court of Appeal held that the right to return to work was complete once the notice had been given, and that she had been unfairly dismissed.

Where the employer has engaged a replacement for the absent woman, provided that person has been informed in writing that his or her employment will be terminated on the woman's return to work, the dismissal of the replacement will be regarded as having been for a substantial reason (see Chapter 14). This does not mean that such a dismissal will always be fair because a tribunal will have to be satisfied that it was reasonable to dismiss in the circumstances. For instance, it might be unfair to dismiss if the employer had a vacancy that the replacement could have filled.

If during ordinary or additional maternity leave it becomes clear that the employer cannot continue to employ the employee under her existing contract of employment by reason of redundancy, then the employee is entitled to be offered any other suitable employment which may be available. The work to be done needs to be both suitable and appropriate in the circumstances, and its provisions as to the capacity and place of work and other terms and conditions to be not substantially less favourable than if she had continued to be employed under the previous contract.[25]

PARENTAL LEAVE

An employee who has been continuously employed for a period of not less than one year and who has, or expects to have, responsibility for a child[26] is entitled to be absent from work on parental leave for the purposes of caring for that child.[27] This right applies only in respect of children who

(a) were born on or after 15 December 1999. The one exception to this is a child who is placed with the employee for adoption after this date and who may have been born before it.[28]

(b) have not passed their fifth birthday or the fifth anniversary of their placing for adoption with the employee. The exceptions to this are if the child is entitled to a disability living allowance or if the employee would have taken leave in time but for the employer's postponing it until after the birthday/anniversary had passed.[29]

The employee is entitled to 13 weeks' leave in respect of each child,[30] but this leave cannot be taken, under the default arrangements, in periods of less than one week,[31] or for more than four weeks in any one year.[32] A week's leave is defined as

(i) where an employee works for the same period each week, then that period, or

(ii) where an employee works variable hours under their contract of employment, or some weeks and not others, then a week's leave is calculated by adding the total hours required to be worked over one year and then dividing by 52.

Notice provisions

Before employees can exercise their rights to parental leave, they must, unless otherwise agreed by collective or workforce agreements (see Chapter 2),

(a) comply with a request from the employer to produce for inspection evidence of the employee's responsibility or expected responsibility for the child as well as evidence of the child's age

(b) give the employer notice of the period of leave that is proposed. This notice must specify the dates on which the leave is to begin and end and must be given at least 21 days before the date on which that period is to begin.[33]

If the employee is the father of the child, and the period of leave is to begin on the day on which the child is born, then the notice must specify the expected week of childbirth and the duration of the leave. It must also be given to the employer at least 21 days before the beginning of the expected week of childbirth.

If the child in respect of whom the leave is to be taken is one being placed with the employee for adoption, and the leave is to begin on the date of the placement, the notice must specify the expected week of placement and the duration of the period of leave. It must also be given at least 21 days before the beginning of that week, or, if that is not reasonably practicable, as soon as is reasonably practicable.[34]

(c)   ensure that the employer has not postponed the leave in accordance with the MPL Regulations (see below).

Postponing parental leave[35]

An employer may postpone a period of parental leave, subject to any collective or workforce agreements, where

(a)   the employee has applied and given the necessary notice; and

(b)   the employer considers that the operation of the business would be substantially prejudiced if the employee took leave during the period identified in the notice; and

(c)   the employer permits the employee to take a period of leave of the same length that had been requested within six months of the date on which it was due to begin. The actual dates to be determined by the employer in consultation with the employee, and

(d)   the employer gives notice in writing of the postponement stating the reasons for it and specifying the dates on which the employee may take parental leave. This notice must be given to the employee not more than seven days after the employer received the employee's notice.

An employee may complain to an employment tribunal if the employer has unreasonably postponed a period of parental leave or attempted to prevent the employee from taking it.[36] The tribunal may award such compensation that it considers 'just and equitable'.

Terms and conditions during periods of additional maternity leave and parental leave

Section 73(4) ERA 1996 declares that an employee who takes additional maternity leave is

(a) entitled to the benefit of the terms and conditions of employment which would have occurred had she not been absent. This does not include terms and conditions relating to remuneration[37]

(b) bound by obligations arising under those terms and conditions

(c) entitled to return to a job of a prescribed kind (see below).

Section 77(1) to (4) ERA 1996 makes the same provisions for those on parental leave. In addition, Regulation 17 MPL Regulations 1999 states that employees on additional maternity leave and parental leave are

(a) entitled to the benefit of the employer's implied obligation of trust and confidence (see Chapter 3) and any terms of employment relating to

   (i)   notice of the termination of the employment contract by the employer

   (ii) compensation in the event of redundancy

   (iii) disciplinary and grievance produres

(b) bound by an implied obligation of good faith to the employer and any terms and conditions of employment relating to

   (i)   notice of the termination of the employment contract by the employee

   (ii) the disclosure of confidential information

(iii) the acceptance of gifts or other benefits, or

(iv) the employee's participation in any other business.

The right to return to work after additional maternity leave or parental leave

Unless subject to dismissal through redundancy, an employee who takes additional maternity leave or parental leave is entitled to return from that leave to the job in which he or she was employed prior to the absence. If this is not reasonably practicable, the employer must permit the employee to return to another job which is both suitable and appropriate in the circumstances.[38] This right to return to work is a right to return

(a) on terms and conditions, relating to remuneration, not less favourable than those that would have applied had he or she not been absent from work since the beginning of ordinary maternity leave or the beginning of parental leave, as appropriate

(b) with seniority, pension and similar rights preserved as if there had been continuous employment

(c) on terms and conditions otherwise not less favourable than those that would have applied had there been no absence on additional maternity leave or parental leave.

TIME OFF FOR DEPENDANTS

Section 57A ERA 1996 states that an employee is entitled to take a reasonable amount of time off during the employee's working hours, in order to take action which is necessary

(a) to provide assistance on an occasion when a dependant falls ill, gives birth or is injured or assaulted

(b) to make arrangements for the provision of care for a dependant who is ill or injured

(c) in consequence of the death of a dependant

(d) because of the unexpected disruption or termination of arrangements for the care of a dependant, or

(e)   to deal with an incident which involves a child of the employee and which occurs unexpectedly in a period during which an educational establishment which the child attends is responsible for him or her.

There is an obligation for the employee to inform the employer of the reason for absence and of its duration as soon as reasonably practicable. The time off is limited to incidents involving a dependant, who is defined as[39]

(a)   a spouse

(b)   a child

(c)   a parent

(d)   a person who lives in the same household as the employee but who is not an employee, tenant, lodger or boarder

(e)   any person who reasonably relies on the employee for assistance if he or she is ill or assaulted[40]

(f)   any person who reasonably relies on the employee to make arrangements for the provision of care in the event of illness or injury.[41] The references to illness or injury include mental illness or injury.[42]

Section 57B ERA 1996 asserts that an employee may apply to an employment tribunal to complain about a failure to be allowed time off. A tribunal may make a declaration and award compensation which the tribunal 'considers just and equitable in the circumstances'.

PROTECTION FROM DETRIMENT[43]

An employee is entitled not to be subjected to any detriment by any act, or failure to act, on the part of the employer for one of the following reasons:

(a)   that she is pregnant or has given birth to a child

(b)   that the employee is subject to a relevant requirement or a relevant recommendation as defined by section 66(2) ERA 1996

(c) that she took ordinary maternity leave or availed herself of the benefits of her terms and conditions of employment during ordinary maternity leave

(d) that the employee took additional maternity leave, parental leave or time off under section 57A ERA 1996

(e) that the employee declined to sign a workforce agreement for the purposes of the MPL Regulations 1999

(f) that the employee was a representative of the workforce, a candidate for election as a representative or performed any activities or functions related to being a representative or a candidate.

UNFAIR DISMISSAL[44]

It is automatically unfair to dismiss an employee, irrespective of the length of service, if:

(a) the reason or principal reason for dismissal is that she is pregnant or is in any way connected with her pregnancy

(b) she is dismissed during her maternity leave period and the reason or principal reason for dismissal is that she has given birth or is connected with her having given birth[45]

(c) she is dismissed after the end of her maternity leave period and the reason or principal reason for dismissal is that she took, or availed herself of the benefits of, ordinary maternity leave

(d) the reason or principal reason for dismissal is a requirement or recommendation referred to in section 66 ERA 1996 (suspension on maternity grounds)

(e) she is dismissed during the MLP and the principal reason for dismissal is that she is redundant and the employer has not offered her any suitable alternative vacancy

(f) redundancy is the reason or principal reason for dismissal but the employee is selected for dismissal while other employees in similar positions are not, and the reason for selection is one of those set out in (a)–(e) above[46]

(g) the employee took time off for additional maternity leave, parental leave or time off for dependants in accordance with section 57A of the ERA 1996

(h) the employee refused to sign a workforce agreement for the purposes of the MPL Regulations 1999

(i) the reason is that, for the purposes of the MPL Regulations, the employee was a representative of the workforce, stood for election as a representative or performed any of the functions or activities of such a representative or a candidate for such representation.

Where an employee is dismissed while she is pregnant or during her ordinary maternity leave period, she is entitled to written reasons for her dismissal. This right does not depend on any qualifying period of service and the woman does not need formally to request the reasons.[47]

There are exceptions to the application of these automatically unfair dismissal rules. They do not apply if

(a) immediately before the end of the additional maternity leave period or dismissal, if earlier, the number of employees employed by the employer together with associated[48] employers does not exceed five; and if it is not reasonably practicable for the employer or associated employer(s) to offer her a suitable and appropriate job to return to

(b) it is not reasonably practicable for an employer to offer a suitable position, but an associated employer does offer her such a job and she accepts or unreasonably refuses that offer.

The onus for showing that these provisions are satisfied rests with the employer.

RISK ASSESSMENT

Where an employee is pregnant, has given birth within the past six months or is breast-feeding, the employer must assess the special risks which the woman faces in the workplace and take measures to avoid them.[49] If preventive action is impossible or would be inadequate to avoid the risk, the employee's working conditions or hours of work must be altered. If that would be unreasonable or would not avoid the risk, the employer must offer suitable alternative work, or where none is available, suspend her from work on full pay.[50] Alternative work will be suitable if it is both suitable in relation to the employee and appropriate for her to do in the circumstances. The terms and conditions applicable must not be substantially less favourable than those which apply to her normal work. An employment tribunal may award compensation to a woman if her employer fails to offer suitable alternative employment.[51]

A woman who is suspended on maternity grounds is entitled to be paid by her employer during the suspension. However, this right is lost if she unreasonably refuses an offer of suitable alternative work. The remuneration payable is a week's wage for each week of suspension and *pro rata* for any part of a week of entitlement. Any contractual remuneration paid goes towards discharging the employer's liability. Conversely, any suspension payment goes towards discharging any contractual obligation the employer may have. Where an employer fails to pay all or any of the amount due, an employment tribunal will order the employer to pay the remuneration owed.[52]

STATUTORY MATERNITY PAY

An employee who gives her employer the prescribed notice[53] that she is going to be absent from work wholly or partly because of pregnancy or confinement may be entitled to statutory maternity pay (SMP). This notice must be in writing if so requested. To qualify for SMP a woman must also:

(a) have at least 26 weeks' continuous employment with the same employer ending with 'the week immediately preceding the 14th week before the expected week of confinement'(EWC). Thus the 15th week before the EWC is known as the qualifying week for these purposes. A woman who has worked for less than 26 weeks for her employer may be able to claim state maternity allowance if she satisfies the contribution requirements

(b)   for the eight weeks immediately preceding the qualifying week have had normal (ie average gross) weekly earnings at or above the lower earnings limit for National Insurance contributions[54]

(c)   have reached the eleventh week before the EWC or have been confined.[55]

SMP is available for a maximum of eight weeks. It is not normally payable for a week in which the woman works, and the maternity pay period (MPP) is not extended to take account of such weeks.[56] Payment may begin 11 weeks before the EWC and is automatically triggered when a woman is absent from work wholly or partly because of pregnancy or confinement after the sixth week before the EWC. SMP is payable for complete weeks only. Women are entitled to receive nine tenths of their normal weekly earnings for the first six weeks,[57] but for the rest of the MPP they are eligible for the lower rate (£59.55 in 1999).[58] SMP should be paid on the normal pay day, and the 'set off' formula applies.[59] Employers will be reimbursed for the payments they make through deductions from their National Insurance remittances. The normal reimbursement rate is 92 per cent of the amount of SMP. However, small employers are entitled to be refunded the full amount plus 5 per cent to compensate for the additional National Insurance contributions.[60]

In respect of a period before the request is made, a woman can ask her employer for a written statement of one or more of the following:

(a)   the weeks in which the employer regards himself or herself as liable to pay SMP

(b)   the reasons she or he does not so regard other weeks in that period

(c)   the amount of weekly SMP to which the woman is entitled.

To the extent that this request is reasonable, an employer or former employer must comply with it in a reasonable time.[61] Where there is a dispute the matter can be referred to an officer of the Inland Revenue.[62] Ultimately, if an employer refuses to pay or is insolvent, the employee can recover what is due from the Secretary of State.[63]

KEY POINTS 9
Parental rights

- A pregnant woman is entitled to paid time off for antenatal care.

- The maternity leave period is divided into the ordinary, compulsory and additional leave periods.

- A woman has the right to return to her job under the original contract of employment and on terms and conditions not less favourable than those which would have applied had she not been absent.

- Where an employee is pregnant, has given birth within the last six months, or is breast-feeding, the employer must assess the special risks faced by the woman in the workplace and take measures to avoid those risks.

- It is automatically unfair, regardless of her length of service, to dismiss a woman for a reason connected with her pregnancy.

- A woman with at least 26 weeks' continuous service with the same employer is likely to have a right to statutory maternity pay.

- Parents with child responsibilities are entitled to time off for parental leave for a maximum of three months.

- Employees on parental leave are entitled to retain the benefit of their terms and conditions, apart from pay, as if they had not been absent.

- Employees are entitled to time off to provide assistance to dependants in certain circumstances.

NOTES

1 See section 56(1) ERA 1996
2 Section 57 ERA 1996
3 Section 56(6) ERA 1996
4 Directive 92/85/EEC of 19 October 1992
5 Directive 76/207/EEC
6 Directive 75/117/EEC
7 *Handelse-og-Kontorfunktionærernes Forbund i Danmark acting on behalf of Pedersen v Fællesføreningen før Danmarks Brugsføreninger acting on behalf of Kvicklyskive* (C-66/96) (1999) IRLR 55, ECJ
8 Case 394/96 (1998) IRLR 445
9 See also *Caledonia Bureau Investment & Property v Caffrey* (1998) IRLR 110
10 Schedule 4 Part 1 Employment Relations Act 1999
11 Regulation 3 MPL Regulations 1999
12 'Expected week of childbirth' means the week, beginning with midnight between Saturday and Sunday, in which it is expected that childbirth will occur – Regulation 2 MPL Regulations 1999
13 The provisions concerning maternity leave apply to employees whose expected week of childbirth begins on or after 30 April 2000; see Regulation 3(1) MPL Regulations 1999
14 Regulation 4(4)(b) MPL Regulations 1999
15 See Regulation 9 MPL Regulations 1999
16 Regulation 10 MPL Regulations 1999
17 Section 72(5) ERA 1996
18 Section 72(3) ERA 1996 and Regulation 7 MPL Regulations 1999
19 Regulation 5 MPL Regulations 1999
20 Regulation 7(4) MPL Regulations 1999
21 Regulation 11 MPL Regulations 1999
22 Regulation 12(1) MPL Regulations 1999
23 Regulation 12(2) MPL Regulations 1999
24 (1999) IRLR 177
25 Regulation 10 MPL Regulations 1999
26 Responsibility for a child means having or acquiring parental responsibility under the provisions of the Children Act 1989 or being registered as the child's father in accordance with the provisions of the Births and Deaths Registration Act 1953
27 Regulation 13(1) MPL 1999
28 Regulation 13(3) MPL Regulations 1999, although Regulation 2 puts a maximum age of under 18 years to the definition of a child
29 Regulation 15 MPL Regulations 1999
30 Regulation 14(1) MPL Regulations 1999
31 Schedule 2 section 7 MPL Regulations 1999
32 Schedule 2 sections 8 and 9 MPL Regulations 1999; a year is the anniversary of the date on which the employee first became entitled to parental leave or the date on which the employee most recently became entitled to such leave
33 Schedule 2 section 3 MPL Regulations 1999
34 Schedule 2 sections 4 and 5 MPL Regulations 1999
35 Schedule 2 section 6 MPL Regulations 1999
36 Section 80 ERA 1996

37 Section 73(5) ERA 1996
38 Regulation 18 MPL Regulations 1999
39 Section 57A(3) ERA 1996
40 Section 57A(4)(a) ERA 1996
41 Section 57A(4)(b) ERA 1996
42 Section 57B ERA 1996
43 Regulation 19 MPL Regulations 1999
44 See Regulation 20 MPL Regulations 1999
45 In *Rees v Apollo Watch Repairs* (1996) ICR 467 it was held that a woman was unfairly dismissed during her maternity leave after the employers hired a replacement whom they found to be more efficient
46 Sections 99 and 105(2) ERA 1996
47 Section 92(4) ERA 1996
48 'Associated employer' is defined by Regulation 2 MPL Regulations 1999
49 See the revised ACOP issued with the 1999 Health and Safety (Miscellaneous Modifications) Regulations; the revised ACOP refers employers to HSE guidance entitled *New and Expectant Mothers at Work: A guide for employers*
50 Regulation 13A of the Management of Health and Safety at Work Regulations 1992 SI 2051
51 Sections 66–7 ERA 1996
52 Sections 68–70 ERA 1996
53 Unless it is not reasonably practicable, in which case the notice must be given as soon as is reasonably practicable; section 164(4) SSCBA 1992
54 Section 164(2) SSCBA 1992
55 Regulation 3 of the SMP (General) Regulations 1986 SI No 1960 deals with dismissals 'solely or mainly for the purpose of avoiding liability for SMP'
56 Section 165 SSCBA 1992 and regulation 2 of the SMP (General) Regulations
57 According to *Gillespie v NHSSB* (1996) IRLR 214, a woman on maternity leave must receive any pay rise awarded before or during her leave if she is still employed. See the Statutory Maternity Pay (General) Amendment Regulations 1996 SI 1335
58 Section 10 the Social Security Benefits Up-Rating Order 1999 SI 264
59 See Schedule 13 SSCBA 1992
60 Section 167 SSCBA 1992 and SMP (Compensation of Employers) Amendment Regulations 1999 SI 363
61 Section 15(2) Social Security Administration Act 1992
62 See Social Security Contributions (Transfer of Functions) Act 1999, which transferred this responsibility from the DSS to the Inland Revenue
63 Regulation 7 SMP (General) Regulations (as amended)

10 Health and safety at work

In this chapter we examine some aspects of health and safety legislation. We look briefly at guidance, approved codes of practice and regulations issued by the Health and Safety Executive and the Health and Safety Commission. Consideration is then given to the Health and Safety at Work Act 1974 and the duties of employers to ensure the health, safety and welfare of their employees and others, and their duty to issue written statements. There is then an examination of the Management of Health and Safety at Work Regulations 1992 as amended, followed by the duty of employers to inform and consult safety representatives.

An important feature of the Health and Safety at Work Act 1974 (HASAWA 1974) and the Management of Health and Safety at Work Regulations 1992 (MHSW 1992)[1] is that they apply to people rather than premises and, with certain exceptions, all employed persons are covered. The Act sets out the general duties which employers have towards employees and members of the public, and which employees have towards themselves and each other.

The MHSW Regulations generally make more explicit what employers are required to do to manage health and safety under the Act. Like the HASAWA 1974 the MHSW Regulations apply to every work activity.[2] They also seek to protect persons other than those at work against risks to their health and safety arising out of, or in connection with, work activities. While a breach of HASAWA 1974 or regulations issued under it amounts to a criminal offence, civil liability arises only if there is a failure to comply with regulations.[3] Where the Health and Safety Commission (HSC) or Executive (HSE) consider action is necessary, they have three main options. They can issue:

(i) *guidance*, which has three purposes. It is intended firstly to help people understand the law by interpreting it; secondly, to help people comply with the law; and thirdly, to provide technical advice

(ii) *approved codes of practice* (ACOP), which offer practical examples of good practice. They also give practical advice on how to comply with the law. A failure to observe any provision of an approved code of practice does not of itself render a person liable to any civil or criminal proceedings. However, such a code is admissible in evidence, and proof of a failure to meet its requirements will be sufficient to establish a contravention of a statutory provision, unless a court is satisfied that the provision was complied with in some other way.[4] According to the HSC, a duty-holder who has complied with an ACOP will have done enough to satisfy the law on the specific issues addressed by the code.

(iii) *regulations*, which are made under the HASAWA 1974. Regulations identify specific risks and set out particular actions that need to be taken.[5]

HEALTH AND SAFETY AT WORK ACT 1974

According to section 2(1) HASAWA 1974, 'It shall be the duty of every employer to ensure, so far as is reasonably practicable, the health, safety and welfare at work of all his employees.' The matters to which this duty extends include:[6]

(a) the provision and maintenance of plant[7] and systems of work that are, so far as is reasonably practicable, safe and without risks to health

(b) arrangements for ensuring, so far as is reasonably practicable, safety and absence of risks to health in connection with the use, handling, storage and transport of articles and substances[8]

(c) the provision of such information, instructions, training and supervision as is necessary to ensure, so far as is reasonably practicable, the health and safety at work of employees

(d) so far as is reasonably practicable as regards any place of work under the employer's control, the maintenance of it in a condition which is safe and without risks to health and the provision and maintenance of means of access to and egress from it that are safe and without such risks

(e) the provision and maintenance of a working environment for his employees that is, so far as is reasonably practicable, safe, without risks to health, and adequate as regards facilities and arrangements for their welfare at work.[9] (On working time see Chapter 11.)

The responsibility under section 2(1) HASAWA 1974 is not confined to the employer centrally. In *R v Gateway Foodmarkets Ltd*[10] the employer, at head office level, had instituted procedures for the maintenance of lifts in its stores throughout the country, but failings at store management level led to the death of an employee. As a result the company was held to be in breach of its duties under section 2(1) HASAWA 1974.

It could be argued that these duties merely enact the employer's common law obligations. Although this is largely true, the extent to which detailed requirements are spelled out is of considerable consequence. The words 'reasonably practicable' do not mean that the employer must do everything that is physically possible to safeguard employees, only that the risks be weighed against the trouble and expense of eliminating or reducing them.[11] Employers are to be judged according to the knowledge they had or ought to have had at the time, and in any legal proceedings the accused has to prove that it was not reasonably practicable to do more than was in fact done.[12] The existence of a universal practice is evidence which goes to the question whether any other method was reasonably practicable but it does not necessarily discharge the onus on the employer.[13]

Written statements
Except where fewer than five employees are employed at any one time in an undertaking,[14] every employer must:

Prepare and, as often as may be appropriate, revise a written statement of his general policy with respect to the health and safety at work of his employees, and the organisation and arrangements for the time being in force for carrying out that policy, and bring the statement and any revision of it to the notice of all of his employees.[15]

The Act does not give any further indication of what the statement should contain, but advice and guidance notes, which are not legally enforceable, are available from the Health and Safety Executive. Clearly, it is intended that employers will seek solutions to their own particular safety problems and it will not be sufficient simply to adopt a model scheme drawn up by some other body. As an absolute minimum the safety policy should deal with the various responsibilities of all employees, from the board of directors down to the shop floor. Indeed, the statement may be used as evidence if a prosecution is launched under section 37 HASAWA 1974 (see below). It should also deal with general safety precautions, mechanisms for dealing with special hazards, routine inspections, emergency procedures, training and arrangements for consulting the workforce.

In industrial relations terms it is obviously desirable to reach agreement with employee representatives on the contents of the written statement, but this is not a legal requirement. No guidance is given as to how the statement should be brought to the notice of employees, although ideally a copy should be supplied to each person. Special precautions may have to be taken in relation to those who have language difficulties.

Persons other than employees
Section 3 HASAWA 1974 imposes a duty on employers and self-employed persons to conduct their undertakings in such a way as to ensure, so far as is reasonably practicable, that persons not in their employment who may be affected thereby are not exposed to risks to their health and safety. More specifically, Regulation 10 of the MHSW Regulations 1992 obliges employers and self-employed people to supply any person working in their undertaking who is not their employee with comprehensible information and instruction

on any risks which arise out of the conduct of the undertaking. It is clear that the word 'risk' should be given its ordinary meaning of denoting the possibility of danger rather than actual danger.[16] This may apply to subcontractors working on the employer's premises.

Employers cannot delegate their duty under Section 3 HASAWA 1974 and criminal liability is not limited to the acts of the 'directing mind' or senior management of a company.[17] In *R v Associated Octel*[18] the House of Lords held that the cleaning, repair and maintenance necessary for the carrying out of the employer's business is part of the conduct of the undertaking so as to impose a duty of care with regard to persons not in its employment, whether it is done by the employer's own employees or by independent contractors. It is unnecessary to show that the employer has some actual control over how the work is done. Nevertheless, as far as operations carried out by independent contractors are concerned, the question of control may be very relevant in that, in most cases, the employer has no control over how a competent contractor does the work and it may not be reasonably practicable to do other than rely on the contractor. Of course, there will be situations where it is reasonably practicable for the employer to give instructions.

The case of *R v Nelson Group Services (Maintenance) Ltd*[19] further considered the liability of employers for negligent work by employees. The company employed 800 fitters whose work was installing and maintaining gas installations. A small number of fitters had left appliances in an unsafe condition, thus exposing householders to risks to their health and safety. The question was to what extent the employer was responsible for this negligence. The obligation upon the employer, in section 3(1) HASAWA 1974, is to ensure that the business is conducted in such a way as not to expose persons not in its employment to such risks, as far as is reasonably practicable. The organisation had its own training centre and the Court of Appeal concluded that an employer could establish a defence against being held liable for its employees' carelessness if it had done everything that was reasonably practicable to discharge its duty under the

HASAWA 1974. The Court did not think it necessary, in order to safeguard the public, that an employer should always be held liable for a one-off piece of negligence by an employee. It was enough that the employer had shown that it had done everything that was reasonably practicable to ensure that the employee was trained, had a safe system of work, and was adequately supervised.

Safe premises
Section 4 HASAWA 1974 provides that a person who has control of non-domestic premises used as a place of work must take such measures as are reasonably practicable to ensure that the means of access and egress and any plant or substance in the premises is safe and without risks to health. According to the House of Lords, once it is proved that

(a) the premises made available for use by others are unsafe and constitute a risk to health

(b) the employer had a degree of control over those premises, and

(c) having regard to the employer's degree of control and knowledge of the likely use, it would have been reasonable to take measures to ensure that the premises were safe,

then the employer must demonstrate that, weighing the risk to health against the means (including cost) of eliminating it, it was not reasonably practicable to take those measures. However, if the premises are not a reasonably foreseeable cause of danger to people using them in circumstances that might reasonably be expected to occur, it is not reasonable to require further measures to be taken.[20]

Section 5 HASAWA 1974 obliges every person having control of prescribed premises to use the best practicable means for preventing the emission into the atmosphere of noxious or offensive substances and for rendering harmless and inoffensive such substances as may be emitted. It should be noted that the duty to use the best practicable means imposes a higher standard than in any of the preceding sections.

Employee duties

Section 7 of HASAWA 1974 imposes two general duties on employees while they are at work:[21]

(a) to take reasonable care of the health and safety of themselves and of others who may be affected by their acts or omissions

(b) as regards any duty imposed on employers or any other person by any of the relevant statutory provisions, to co-operate with them so far as is necessary to enable that duty to be performed.

THE MHSW REGULATIONS

The Management of Health and Safety Regulations 1992 were the principal method of enacting the EC Framework Directive on Health and Safety.[22] The Framework Directive places the primary responsibility for ensuring health and safety on employers. In carrying out their responsibilities employers must assess the risks at work and take measures to prevent or reduce them.[23] The Regulations were amended a number of times by

(a) the Management of Health and Safety at Work (Amendment) Regulations 1994 which implemented the health and safety provisions of the Pregnant Workers Directive[24] (see Chapter 9)

(b) the Health and Safety (Young Persons) Regulations 1997 which implemented the provisions of the Young Workers Directive[25] which allow for a specific risk assessment to be made for people under the age of 18 years

(c) the Fire Precautions (Workplace) Regulations 1997 which extended the requirement to undertake a risk assessment in respect of fire safety.

These amendments were incorporated into the proposals for the 1999 Health and Safety (Miscellaneous Modifications) Regulations together with a revised ACOP.[26]

Risk assessment

The MHSW Regulations impose a duty on all employers and the self-employed to conduct a risk assessment. This assessment must be both suitable and sufficient and must consider the risk to the health and safety of all employees and other persons arising from the conduct of the undertaking.[27] The purpose of the assessment is to identify the measures that need to be taken to ensure compliance with the relevant statutory provisions. These provisions are specified in the Approved Code of Practice and include the duties under HASAWA 1974 (see above). The risk assessment must be reviewed if there is reason to suspect that it is no longer valid or there has been a significant change in the matters to which it relates. Where the employer has five or more employees, the significant findings of the assessment must be recorded.[28]

Regulation 4 requires employers to give effect to appropriate arrangements for the effective planning, organisation, control, monitoring and review of the measures they need to take as a result of the risk assessment. Again, such arrangements must be recorded if the employer has five or more employees. Regulation 5 obliges employers to provide appropriate health surveillance for their employees.

Under Regulation 6 employers must appoint one or more 'competent persons' to assist them in implementing the measures they need to comply with the relevant statutory provisions. The number of people appointed, the time available for them to fulfil their functions and the means at their disposal must be adequate, having regard to the size of the undertaking and the risks to which employees are exposed. A 'competent person' is defined as someone who has sufficient training and experience or knowledge to enable him or her to assist properly in the undertaking.[29] In the amended Regulations, however, there is a requirement for the employer to give preference to the appointment of a 'competent person' in their employment over one from outside.[30]

Regulation 7 obliges an employer to establish appropriate

procedures to be followed in the event of 'serious and imminent danger to persons at work in his undertaking'. Employers must nominate a sufficient number of competent persons to implement these procedures and to be sure that employees are unable to enter dangerous areas without having received adequate health and safety instruction. It is made clear that this Regulation requires both the provision of information and procedures which enable employees to leave their work immediately in the event of 'serious and imminent danger'.[31]

PROVIDING INFORMATION

As regards the duty to provide information, the Health and Safety Information for Employees (Modifications and Repeals) Regulations[32] oblige employers to display a poster or distribute leaflets informing their employees in general terms about the requirements of health and safety law. This information must be kept up to date, and where a poster is displayed it must be in a reasonably accessible place and positioned so that it can be easily read. Regulation 8 of MHSW Regulations 1992 requires employers to provide employees with comprehensible and relevant information on the risks to which they are exposed and the measures that the employer has taken in accordance with the risk assessment that has been conducted. Information must also be given on the procedures to be taken in cases of serious and imminent danger. Regulation 7 of the Safety Representatives and Safety Committees Regulations 1977 (SRSC Regulations) obliges employers to make available to safety representatives information within their knowledge which is necessary to enable representatives to fulfil their functions.[33]

The Health and Safety (Consultation with Employees) Regulations 1996 (the HSCE Regulations 1996) were introduced to ensure that the information and consultation requirements of the SRSC Regulations were extended to those workplaces where there was no trade union recognised for collective bargaining purposes.

Regulation 5 requires employers to make available to those

employees or representatives such information as is necessary to enable them to participate fully and effectively in the consultation. Representatives of employee safety must also be given information to enable them to carry out their functions.[34] In addition, inspectors are obliged, in circumstances in which it is necessary to do so for the purpose of assisting in keeping employees adequately informed about health, safety and welfare matters, to give employees or their representatives factual information relating to an employer's premises, as well as information with respect to any action which they have taken or propose to take in connection with those premises. Such information must be conveyed to the employer, and inspectors can also give a written statement of their observations to anyone likely to be a party to any civil proceedings arising out of any accident, etc.[35]

The words 'instruction' and 'training' suggest that employees should be taught to understand the duties imposed by legislation. Indeed, Regulation 11 of the MHSW Regulations stipulates that in entrusting tasks to their employees, employers must take into account their capabilities in relation to health and safety. In particular, employers have a duty to ensure that their employees are provided with adequate health and safety training when recruited or if they are exposed to new or increased risks. As regards supervision, it would seem to follow that if the employer's efforts do not persuade an employee to adopt safe working practices, disciplinary or other action may have to be taken.

SAFETY REPRESENTATIVES

Section 2(4) HASAWA 1974 provides for the appointment by recognised trade unions of safety representatives from among the employees.[36] Where such representatives are appointed, employers have a duty to consult them with a view to the making and maintenance of arrangements which will enable the employer and employees to co-operate effectively in promoting and developing measures to ensure the health and safety at work of the employees, and in checking the effectiveness of such measures.[37] In particular, employers must consult union safety representatives in good time with regard to:

(a) the introduction of any measure which may substantially affect the health and safety of the employees represented

(b) the arrangements for appointing or nominating competent persons in accordance with Regulations 6(1) and 7(l)b of MHSW 1992

(c) any health and safety information that the employer must provide to the employees represented

(d) the planning and organisation of any health and safety training the employer is required to provide for the employees represented

(e) the health and safety consequences for the employees represented of the planning and introduction of new technologies.[38]

Union safety representatives may be elected or appointed. If there are employees who are not covered by union safety representatives under the SRSC Regulations, the employers must consult the employees directly or 'representatives of employee safety', who have been elected by employees, about the matters listed (a)–(e) above. In either case employers must make available such information within their knowledge as is necessary to enable full and effective participation in the consultation.[39] Where employers consult representatives of employee safety, they must inform the employees represented of the names of the representatives and the groups they represent.[40] Similarly, if employers discontinue consultation with a representative of employee safety, they must inform the employees in the group concerned of that fact.[41]

The SRSC Regulations stipulate that if an employer has received written notification from a recognised independent trade union of the names of the people appointed as union safety representatives, such persons have the functions set out in Regulation 4 of the SRSC Regulations (below). So far as is reasonably practicable, union safety representatives will either have been employed by their employer throughout the preceding two years or have had at least two years' experience in similar employment.[42] Employees cease to be union safety representatives for the purpose of these regulations when:

(a) the trade union which appointed them notifies the employer in writing that their appointment has been terminated

(b) they cease to be employed at the workplace[43]

(c) they resign.

Theoretically, there is no limit to the number of union safety representatives who can be appointed, but guidance notes published with the SRSC Regulations suggest appropriate criteria for assessment.[44] Similarly, employers must not consult a representative of employee safety if[45]

(a) that person has notified the employer that he or she does not intend to represent the group of employees for the purposes of such consultation

(b) that person has ceased to be employed in the group which he or she represents

(c) the period for which that person was elected has expired without that person's being re-elected, or

(d) that person has become incapacitated from carrying out his or her functions under the HSCE Regulations 1996.

Apart from representing all employees (not only trade union members) in consultation with the employer under section 2(6) HASAWA 1974, union safety representatives are given the following functions by Regulation 4(1) SRSC Regulations:

(a) to investigate potential hazards and dangerous occurrences at the workplace (whether or not they are drawn to their attention by the employees they represent) and to examine the causes of accidents at the workplace

(b) to investigate complaints by any employee they represent relating to that employee's health, safety or welfare at work

(c) to make representations to the employer on general matters affecting the health, safety or welfare at work of the employees at the workplace

(d) to carry out inspections in accordance with Regulation 5, 6 and 7 SRSC Regulations

(e) to represent the employees they are appointed to represent in consultation at the workplace with inspectors from the enforcing authorities

(f) to receive information from inspectors in accordance with section 28(8) of HASAWA 1974

(g) to attend meetings of safety committees where they attend in their capacity as safety representatives in connection with any of the above functions.

By way of contrast, representatives of employee safety have only the following functions:[46]

(a) to make representations to the employer on potential hazards and dangerous occurrences at the workplace which affect, or could affect, the group of employees represented;

(b) to make representations to the employer on general matters affecting the health and safety at work of the group represented and, in particular, on such matters as he or she is consulted about by the employer under Regulation 3 of the HSCE Regulations 1996; and

(c) to represent the group of employees in consultations at the workplace with inspectors appointed under section 19 HASAWA 1974.

Further points to note are:

(a) None of these functions imposes a duty on safety representatives, although they will be liable for the actions they take as ordinary employees.

(b) Employers who consult representatives of employee
safety have a duty to ensure that those representatives
are provided with such training in respect of their
functions as is reasonable in all the circumstances. The
employer must also meet any reasonable costs associated
with such training, including travel and subsistence
costs.[47]

Regulation 5 SRSC Regulations entitles safety representatives
to inspect the workplace at least every three months, but they
must give reasonable notice in writing of their intention to do
so. Of course, inspections may take place more frequently if
the employer agrees. Additional inspections may be made if
there has been a substantial change in the conditions of
work or new information has been published by the HSC or
HSE relevant to the hazards of the workplace. Inspections
may also be conducted where there has been a notifiable
accident or dangerous occurrence or a notifiable disease[48]
contracted, for the purpose of determining the cause. The
employer must provide reasonable facilities and assistance for
the purpose of carrying out an inspection, including facilities
for independent investigation by the union representatives
and private discussion with the employees. However, there
is nothing to prevent the employers or their representatives
from being present during an inspection.

Time off for safety representatives
According to regulation 4(2) of the Safety Representatives
and Safety Committee Regulations 1977[49] (SRSC
Regulations) and regulation 7(1)(b) of the Health and Safety
(Consultation with Employees) Regulations 1996 (HSCE
Regulations) a trade union safety representative or a
representative of employee safety[50] is entitled to time off,
with normal or average pay,[51] during working hours to
perform his or her functions and to undergo such training as
may be reasonable in the circumstances. In relation to trade
union safety representatives elected or appointed under the
SSRC Regulations, regard has to be had for the provisions
of an approved code of practice.[52] In *White v Pressed Steel
Fisher*[53] the EAT held that if employers provide an adequate

in-house course it is not necessarily reasonable for them to be required to grant paid time off for safety representatives to attend a union course. The Code recommends that as soon as possible after their appointment union safety representatives should be permitted time off with pay for basic training approved by the TUC or the independent union which appointed the representatives. Further training, similarly approved, should be undertaken where the safety representative has special responsibilities or where such training is necessary to meet changes in circumstances or relevant legislation. Aggrieved safety representatives or representatives of employee safety can complain to an employment tribunal that their employer has failed to permit them to take time off or that they have not been paid in accordance with the Regulations. If the complaint is well-founded, the tribunal must make a declaration and may make an award of compensation.[54]

Safety committees

Where at least two union safety representatives submit a written request, employers must establish a safety committee, but before doing so they must consult the union safety representatives who made the request and the representatives of recognised trade unions. Such a committee must be formed within three months of the request being made, and a notice must be posted stating the composition of the committee and the workplaces covered.[55] Under section 2(7) HASAWA 1974 the function of safety committees is to keep under review the measures taken to ensure the health and safety at work of employees.

It should be noted that the Code of Practice advises employers, recognised unions and union safety representatives to make full and proper use of existing industrial relations machinery to reach the degree of agreement necessary to achieve the purpose of the SRSC Regulations and to resolve any differences. However, where an employee suffers a detriment as a result of health and safety activities, a complaint may be brought under section 100 ERA 1996 (if the individual was dismissed) or section 44

ERA 1996. The remedies available for infringement of section 44 mirror those available from detriment on trade union grounds (see Chapter 20). In *Shillito v Van Leer*,[56] for example, an employee who was a safety representative for one production line became involved, in a belligerent way, in safety issues affecting another production line, for which the employee was not a representative. The employee was disciplined and given a formal warning. A complaint to the tribunal about suffering a detriment failed because the person involved was not a safety representative in the area concerned. In *Goodwin v Cabletel*[57] a construction manager had responsibility for health and safety matters on site, was unhappy with one subcontractor and took an aggressive approach. The manager's employer, however, wished to be more conciliatory. The construction manager was demoted and claimed constructive dismissal. The EAT subsequently confirmed that protection extended to the way duties were carried out.

REPORTING INJURIES

The Reporting of Injuries, Diseases and Dangerous Occurrences Regulations 1995[58] (RIDDOR 1995) apply to events which arise 'out of or in connection with work'[59] activities covered by HASAWA 1974. Whenever any of the following arises it must be reported to the enforcing authority in writing and a record kept.[60] If (a)–(d) happens, the enforcing authority must be notified by the quickest practicable means:

(a) the death of any person as a result of an accident, whether or not he or she is at work

(b) someone at work suffers a major injury as the result of an accident[61]

(c) someone who is not at work suffers an injury as the result of an accident and is taken to a hospital for treatment

(d) one of a list of specified dangerous occurrences takes place[62]

(e)   someone is unable to do his or her normal work for more than three days as the result of an injury caused by an accident at work

(f)   the death of an employee if this occurs after a reportable injury which led to the employee's death, but not more than one year afterwards

(g)   a person at work suffers a specified disease, provided that a doctor diagnoses the disease and the person's job involves a specified work activity.[63]

The duty to report the events listed above is imposed on the 'responsible person'.[64] Regulation 13 gives the HSE a limited power to grant exemptions from the requirements imposed by RIDDOR 1995.

OFFENCES

Apart from the Crown, any person or body corporate can be prosecuted for an offence under HASAWA 1974. However, if an offence is proved to have been committed with the consent or connivance of, or to have been attributable to neglect on the part of, any director, manager, secretary or other similar officer, then that person as well as the body corporate may be found guilty of an offence.[65] Thus in *Armour v Skeen*[66] a local authority Director of Roads was prosecuted for failing to prepare and carry out a sound safety policy. His neglect led to breaches of safety provisions that resulted in the death of a council employee.

Where the commission of an offence by any person is due to the act of default of some other person, that other person may be charged whether or not proceedings are taken against the first-mentioned person.[67] Crown servants may be prosecuted despite the immunity of the Crown itself. Proceedings under this Act can be brought only by an inspector or with the consent of the Director of Public Prosecutions.

The normal maximum penalty for a person found guilty of an offence on summary conviction (ie in a magistrate's court) is a fine not exceeding level 5 on the standard scale.

However, where there is a breach of sections 2–6 of HASAWA 1974, or of an improvement or prohibition notice, a fine of up to £20,000 can be imposed. If there is a breach of a notice or a court order under section 42 HASAWA 1974 (see below), an offender may receive a sentence of up to six months' imprisonment. When proceedings are brought on indictment (in a Crown court) there is the possibility of an unlimited fine and, in specified circumstances, up to two years' imprisonment.[68]

In deciding on the level of the fine to be imposed the court will take into account the ability of the company to pay. Generally, fines will not be so large as to endanger the earnings of employees or create a risk of bankruptcy, unless the offence is so serious that the firm should not be in business.[69] The questions to be asked, according to the Court of Appeal, which should guide courts in assessing fines were:

(a)   What financial penalty does the offence merit?

(b)   What financial penalty can a defendant reasonably be ordered to meet, and over what period? A longer period might be acceptable in the case of a company as opposed to an individual.[70]

In reaching a decision on the fine, the aggravating features to be taken into account will include:

(a)   whether the company has failed to heed warnings

(b)   whether the defendant deliberately profited financially from the failure to take the necessary health and safety measures.

Conversely, the features which might be taken in mitigation include:

(a)   prompt admission of responsibility and a timely plea of guilty

(b)   steps to remedy the deficiencies once they have been drawn to the defendant's attention

(c)   a good safety record.

Where people are convicted of offences in respect of any matters which appear to the court to be within their power to remedy, the court may, in addition to or instead of imposing any punishment, order them to take such steps as may be specified to remedy those matters.[71]

ENFORCING THE ACT

The HASAWA 1974 established two bodies, the HSC and the HSE. The HSC is appointed by the Secretary of State and consists of a chairperson together with three members appointed following consultations with employers' organisations, three members appointed after consultation with trade unions and three others appointed after local authorities and other appropriate organisations have been consulted. Apart from its general duty to 'do such things and make such arrangements as it considers appropriate', the HSC is required to:

(a) assist and encourage persons concerned with matters relevant to any of the general purposes of the Act to further those purposes

(b) make arrangements for carrying out research, provide information and training, and encourage others to perform these functions

(c) make arrangements for providing an information and advisory service

(d) submit proposed regulations.[72]

Except for the enforcement responsibilities of local authorities, HASAWA 1974 is enforced by the HSE, whose director is appointed by the HSC with the approval of the Secretary of State. Although the HSE is to give effect to any directions issued by the HSC, the former cannot be *directed* to enforce a statutory provision in a particular case.

The enforcing authorities appoint inspectors who may exercise the following powers:[73]

(a) at any reasonable time (or, if there is a dangerous situation, at any time) to enter premises

(b) to take with them a police officer, if they have reasonable cause to be apprehensive of any serious obstruction in the execution of their duty

(c) to take with them any other authorised person and any equipment or materials required

(d) to make such examination and investigation as may be necessary

(e) to direct that the premises be left undisturbed for so long as is reasonably necessary for the purpose of examination or investigation

(f) to take such measurements, photographs and readings as they consider necessary

(g) to take samples of any articles or substances found in any premises and of the atmosphere in, or in the vicinity of, any such premises[74]

(h) in the case of an article or substance which appears to have caused or to be likely to cause danger, to dismantle it or subject it to any process or test. The article or substance may be damaged or destroyed if it is thought necessary in the circumstances. However, if they are so requested by a person who is present and has responsibilities in relation to those premises, this power must be exercised in that person's presence unless the inspector considers that to do so would be prejudicial to the safety of the state

(i) in the case of an article or substance which appears to have caused or to be likely to cause danger, to take possession of it and detain it for so long as is necessary in order to examine it, to ensure that it is not tampered with before the examination is completed, and to ensure that it is available for use as evidence in any proceedings for an offence or any proceedings relating to a notice under section 21 or 22 HASAWA 1974 (see below). An inspector must leave a notice giving particulars of the article or substance stating that she or he has taken possession of it and, if it is practicable, she or he should give a sample of it to a responsible person at the premises.[75]

(j)   if carrying out examinations or investigations under (d), to require persons whom they have reasonable cause to believe to be able to give any information to answer such questions as the inspector thinks fit to ask and to sign a declaration of the truth of their answers

(k)   to require the production of, inspect and take copies of an entry in, any books or documents which are required to be kept and any other books or documents which it is necessary for them to see for the purpose of any examination or investigation under (d) above

(l)   to require any persons to afford them such facilities and assistance with respect to any matters within that person's control or responsibilities as are necessary for the inspectors to exercise their powers

(m) any other power which is necessary for the purpose of carrying into effect the statutory provisions.

Where an inspector is of the opinion that a person is contravening or has contravened a relevant statutory provision in circumstances that make it likely that the contravention will continue or be repeated, he or she may serve an 'improvement notice' stating that opinion. The notice must specify the provision, give particulars of the reasons why he or she is of that opinion and will require that person to remedy the contravention within such period as may be specified in the notice.[76] This period must not be less than the time allowed for appealing against the notice, ie 21 days.[77]

In respect of an activity covered by a relevant statutory provision, if any inspector believes that activities are being carried on or are about to be carried on which will involve a risk of serious personal injury, the inspector may serve a 'prohibition notice'. Such a notice will state the inspector's opinion, specify the matters which give rise to the risk, and direct that the activities to which the notice relates must not be carried on by or under the control of the person on whom the notice is served (unless the matters specified in the notice have been remedied). A prohibition notice will normally take effect immediately. Both types of notice may (but need not) include directions as to the measures to be taken to remedy the contravention or the matter to which the notice relates. Where a notice which is not to take immediate effect has been served, that notice may be withdrawn by the inspector within 21 days. Similarly, the period specified for rectification may be extended by an inspector at any time when an appeal against the notice is not pending.

A person on whom a notice is served may appeal to an employment tribunal, which has the power to cancel or affirm the notice or affirm it in a modified form.[78] For the purpose of hearing such appeals the tribunal may include specially appointed assessors. Bringing an appeal against an improvement notice has the effect of suspending the operation of that notice until the appeal is disposed of. Lodging an appeal against a prohibition notice suspends it only if the tribunal so directs and then only from the time when the direction is given.[79] Failure to comply with a notice is an offence.[80]

Because it is not possible to bring a prosecution against the Crown,[81] it is equally impossible to enforce improvement and prohibition notices against Crown bodies. However, the HSE has been prepared to issue 'Crown notices' where, in its opinion, an improvement or prohibition notice would have been appropriate. Such notices have no legal effect but may be of some value in so far as they put moral pressure on the employing body. Of course, trade union representatives who receive copies of these notices may be in a position to apply industrial pressure.

Finally, it is worth noting that the Environment and Safety Information Act 1988 requires enforcement authorities to keep public registers giving details of notices issued under HASAWA 1974 and other safety legislation. However, this statute does not apply to notices which 'impose requirements or prohibitions solely for the protection of persons at work'.[82]

KEY POINTS 10
Health and safety at work

- The HASAWA 1974 sets out the general duties which employers have towards employees and members of the public, and employees have towards themselves and each other.

- The HSC and HSE have the option to propose and issue guidance, ACOPs or regulations.

- Every employer with five employees or more must prepare and revise a written statement of their general policy on health and safety at work, and the organisation and arrangements for carrying out that policy.

- The HASAWA 1974 also places an obligation on employers to have regard for the health and safety of persons not in their employment.

- The MHSW Regulations 1992 have been amended by the Health and Safety (Miscellaneous Modifications) Regulations 1999, which cover pregnant women, young workers and fire precautions.

- All employers have an obligation to conduct a risk assessment. The purpose of this assessment is to identify the measures that need to be taken to ensure compliance with the provisions contained in the ACOP and the HASAWA 1974.

- There is a duty on employers to provide information and consult employees and their representatives who are either trade-union-appointed or directly elected.

- Employers must also distribute leaflets or display posters providing general information about the requirements of health and safety law.

- Certain injuries, incidents or accidents must be reported if they occur out of or in connection with work activities.

NOTES

1 SI 1992/2051; in 1999 these were amended by the Health and Safety (Miscellaneous Modifications) Regulations 1999
2 See *Health and Safety Regulations: A Short Guide*, HSE 1998
3 Except in so far as the regulations provide otherwise. See section 47(2) HASAWA 1974 and Regulation 15 MHSW Regulations 1992
4 Section 17 HASWA 1974
5 *Health and Safety Regulations: A Short Guide* (note 2)
6 Section 2(2) HASAWA 1974
7 Defined in section 53 HASAWA 1974 as including any machinery, equipment or appliance
8 Defined in section 54 HASAWA 1974 as 'any natural or artificial substance whether in solid or liquid form of a gas or vapour'
9 See *Pickford v ICI* (1998) IRLR 436 on the problems associated with caring for employees who carry out a large amount of typing
10 (1997) IRLR 189
11 See *West Bromwich Building Society v Townsend* (1983) IRLR 147
12 Section 40 HASAWA 1974
13 See *Martin v Boulton & Paul Ltd* (1982) ICR 366
14 An 'undertaking' is not statutorily defined for these purposes, but is likely to cover all enterprises or businesses
15 Section 2(3) HASAWA 1974
16 See *R v Trustees of the Science Museum* (1993) 3 All ER 853
17 See *R v British Steel* (1995) IRLR 310
18 (1997) IRLR 123
19 (1998) 4 All ER 331
20 See *Inspector of Factories v Austin Rover* (1989) IRLR 404
21 On the meaning of 'at work' see section 52(1) HASAWA 1974
22 Directive 89/391/EEC
23 See Consultative document on Proposals for the Health and Safety (Miscellaneous Modifications) Regulations 1999 HSE
24 Directive 92/85/EEC
25 Directive 94/33/EEC
26 The revised ACOP referred employers to two guides, in particular; these are *New and Expectant Mothers at Work* and *Young People at Work: A Guide for Employers*, HSE
27 See HSE Leaflet *Five Steps to Risk Assessment*
28 See Regulation 3
29 See Regulation 6(5)
30 Regulation 6(8) 1999 Regulations
31 See Regulation 7(2)
32 SI 1995/2923
33 For exceptions see Regulation 7(2) SRSC Regulations. See *A Guide to the Health and Safety (Consultation with Employees) Regulations* 1996. HSE 1996
34 For exceptions see Regulation 5(3) HSCE Regulations 1996
35 Section 28(8)(b) HASAWA 1974
36 In this context 'recognition' means recognition for the purposes of collective bargaining. See Regulation 2 SRSC Regulations and *Cleveland County Council v Springett* (1985) IRLR 131
37 Section 2(6) HASAWA 1974

38 Regulation 4A SRSC Regulations
39 Regulation 5(2) of HSCE 1996. 'Representatives of employee safety' are defined in Regulation 4(1)(b) HSCE Regulations 1996
40 Regulation 4(2) HSCE Regulations 1996
41 Regulation 4(3) HSCE Regulations 1996
42 Regulation 3(4) HSCE Regulations 1996
43 Defined by Regulation 2(1) SRSC Regulations
44 See Guidance notes 8 and 9
45 Regulation 4(3) HSCE Regulations 1996
46 Regulation 6 HSCE Regulations 1996
47 See Regulation 7(1)(a) HSCE Regulations 1996
48 For definitions see Regulations 6(3) SRSC Regulations
49 SI 1977/500
50 See Chapter 11
51 See the Schedule to the SRSC Regulations 1977 and the HSCE Regulations 1996
52 *Time Off for the Training of Safety Representatives*, HMSO 1978
53 (1980) IRLR 176
54 Regulation 11 SRSC Regulations and Schedule 2 HSCE Regulations 1996
55 Regulation 9 SRSC Regulations. See also the Guidance Notes on safety committees.
56 (1997) IRLR 495
57 (1997) IRLR 665
58 SI 1995/3163
59 Defined by Regulation 2(2)c RIDDOR 1995
60 Regulation 7 RIDDOR 1995
61 Major injuries are listed in Schedule 1 RIDDOR 1995
62 Dangerous occurrences are listed in Schedule 2 RIDDOR 1995
63 The specified diseases and corresponding work activities are listed in Schedule 3 RIDDOR 1995
64 Defined in Regulation 2
65 Section 37 HASAWA 1974. Directors who are convicted of an offence can be disqualified from office under the Directors Disqualification Act 1986
66 (1977) IRLR 310. See also *R v Boal* (1992) IRLR 420
67 Section 36 HASAWA 1974
68 Section 33(2)(5) HASAWA 1974
69 See *R v F Howe & Son* (1999) IRLR 434
70 See *R v Rollco Screw Co Ltd* (1999) IRLR 439
71 Section 42(1) HASAWA 1974
72 Section 11(1)(2) and section 50(3)
73 Section 20 HASAWA 1974
74 See *Laws v Keane* (1982) IRLR 500
75 See also section 25 HASAWA 1974 on the power to deal with an imminent cause of danger
76 See *West Bromwich Building Society v Townsend* (note 11)
77 Rule 2 Schedule 4 Employment Tribunal (Constitution and Rules of Procedure) Regulations 1993 SI 1993/2687
78 Section 24(2) HASAWA 1974. Section 82(1)(c) defines 'modifications' as including additions, omissions and amendments. See *British Airways v Henderson* (1979) ICR 77
79 Section 24(3) HASAWA 1974

80 See section 33(1)(g) HASAWA 1974 and *Deary v Mansion Hide Upholstery Ltd* (1983) IRLR 195
81 Section 48 HASAWA 1974
82 Section 2(3)

11 The regulation of working time

This chapter is concerned with the Working Time Regulations 1998 and those occasions when there is a statutory right to time off work. Issues relating to parental rights, including maternity leave, parental leave and time off for dependants, are dealt with in Chapter 9. There is an examination of the contents of the Regulations. This is followed by a consideration of the rights of trade unionists for time off to take part in trade union duties and activities. Finally we look at other rights to time off, including time off for safety representatives and for carrying out public duties.

THE WORKING TIME REGULATIONS 1998

The Working Time Regulations[1] (WT Regulations) came into force on October 1 1998. They implement the Working Time Directive[2] and provisions of the Young Workers Directive.[3] The preamble to the Working Time Directive states that 'in order to ensure the safety and health of Community workers, the latter must be granted minimum daily, weekly and annual periods of rest and adequate breaks' and that 'it is necessary in this context to place a maximum limit on working time'. Thus the legal basis for the Directive was Article 118a EC (now Article 138 EC) relating to health and safety. This was the subject of an unsuccessful challenge by the United Kingdom[4] who claimed that this was the wrong legal basis and that the regulation of working time was a matter for Member States and not a health and safety matter to be dealt with at Community level.

Certain activities are excluded from the scope of the WT Regulations. These are air, road, sea, inland waterway, and lake transport, sea fishing and other workers at sea.[5] Occupations that are excluded are doctors in training, the armed services and the police.[6] Special cases for exclusion are jobs in domestic service[7] and jobs involving unmeasured working time, which include managing executives, family workers and workers officiating at religious ceremonies in churches and religious communities.[8] There is the likelihood that some of these exemptions will be limited or removed. The European Commission has adopted proposals[9] to bring some 5 million excluded workers into the scope of the Directive. These include those working in transport in the air, rail, road, sea, inland waterways, in sea-fishing and those working at sea, as well as doctors in training.

Regulation 2 defines a 'worker' as an individual who has entered into, or works under, a contract of employment or 'any other contract, whether express or implied and (if it is express) whether oral or in writing, whereby the individual undertakes to do or perform personally any work or services for another party to the contract whose status is not by virtue of the contract that of a client or customer of any professional or business undertaking carried out by the individual'. Regulation 36 deals with agency workers, who are not otherwise workers, by deeming the agency or principal to be the employer depending upon who is responsible for paying the worker.

Working time, in relation to the worker, is defined[10] as:

(a) any period during which the worker is working, at the employer's disposal and carrying out the worker's activity or duties

(b) any period during which the worker is receiving relevant training

(c) any additional period which is to be treated as working time for the purpose of these Regulations under a relevant agreement (see below).

The maximum working week

Regulation 4 provides that a worker's working time, including overtime, must not exceed 48 hours per week (seven days) averaged over a reference period of 17 weeks. The employer is unable to insist that the employee works longer hours. In *Barber v RJB Mining (UK) Ltd*[11] the employees were granted a declaration by the High Court that having worked in excess of the permitted hours during the reference period, they need not work again until such time as their average working time fell within the limits specified in Regulation 4(1).

The Regulations supply a formula for calculating the average hours over the reference period.[12] The formula is

$$\frac{A + B}{C}$$

where A is the total number of hours comprised in the worker's working time during the reference period; B is the total number of hours comprised in the working time during the course of the period immediately after the end of the reference period and ending when the number of days in that subsequent period on which he or she has worked equals the number of excluded days during the reference period; and C is the number of weeks in the reference period. The excluded days in B are periods including annual leave, sick and maternity leave and periods in which an individual opting out agreement is in effect. For new employees the reference period is the number of weeks actually worked.

Regulation 5 allows a worker to opt out of the maximum working week provided that

(a) the agreement is in writing; and

(b) the agreement is terminable by the worker on seven days' notice, unless a different notice period is specified (subject to a maximum of three months); and

(c) the employer maintains up-to-date records which identify each of the workers concerned, set out the terms of the agreement, and specify the hours worked by the worker during each reference period since the agreement came into force (maximum two-year period), and makes those records, and any other information requested, available to an inspector from the Health and Safety Executive.

Night work

Regulation 2 defines 'night-time' as a period which is not less than 7 hours in length and includes the hours of 12 midnight to 5 am. A 'night-worker' is a worker who, as a normal course, works at least 3 hours of working time during 'night-time'[13] or is a worker who is likely, during 'night-time', to work a certain proportion of his or her annual working time as defined by a collective or workforce agreement (see below).

Regulation 6 states that a night-worker's normal hours of work must not exceed, in a reference period, an average of 8 in any 24-hour period. A night-worker's average normal hours of work for each 24 hours during a reference period are calculated by the formula:

$$\frac{A}{B-C}$$

A is the number of hours during the reference period which are the normal working hours for that worker; B is the number of days during the reference period; and C is the total number of hours during the reference period spent in rest periods (see below) divided by 24.

There is an obligation upon the employer to ensure that no night-worker whose work involves special hazards or heavy physical or mental strain works for more than 8 hours in any 24-hour period during which night work is performed.[14] Such hazards or strain can be identified in a collective or workforce agreement or as a result of a risk assessment carried out in accordance with Regulation 3 of the Management of Health and Safety at Work Regulations 1992 (see Chapter 10). Night-workers are also entitled to a free health assessment prior to taking up night work and at regular intervals thereafter.[15] Regulation 7(6) also stipulates that where a medical practitioner informs the employer that a worker is suffering from health problems connected with working night work, then, if it is possible, the employer should transfer the worker to more suitable work or work which is not night work. The employer also has an obligation to provide adequate rest breaks where the pattern of work is likely to cause health problems, such as where there is monotonous work or a predetermined work-rate.[16] Regulation 9 also ensures that employers keep adequate records for a period of at least two years.

Rest periods and rest breaks

According to Regulation 10, adult workers are entitled to a rest period of at least 11 consecutive hours in each 24-hour period. For young workers (ie those under the age of 18 years) this period constitutes at least 12 consecutive hours. The rest period can be interrupted in the case of activities which involve periods of work that are split up over the day or are of short duration. In addition,[17] adult workers are entitled to an uninterrupted weekly rest period of at least 24 hours in each seven-day period. The employer may change this to two uninterrupted rest periods of 24 hours in each 14 days or one uninterrupted rest period of 48 hours every 14 days. Young workers are entitled to an uninterrupted 48-hour rest period every seven days, although this may be interrupted in cases of activities which involve periods of work that are split up over the day or are of short duration, or where there are technical or organisational reasons for reducing it.[18]

Regulation 12 provides that where an adult worker's daily working time is more than six hours, the worker is entitled to a rest break. The details of this rest break can be in accordance with a workforce or collective agreement, provided that it is for at least 20 minutes and the worker is entitled to spend it away from the work station. Young workers are entitled to a break where their working time is more than four and a half hours. Their break is to be for at least 30 minutes and can be spent away from the work station. There is an additional complication for employers in Regulation 12(5), which states that where a young worker is employed by more than one employer, then the daily working time is the total number of hours that the young worker has worked.

Annual leave

In any leave year beginning after 23 November 1999 a

worker is entitled to four weeks' leave.[19] Unless there is a relevant agreement for another date, the worker's leave year begins on the date employment commenced and every anniversary thereafter. If the worker commences employment on a date that is different from the date agreed for the commencement of a leave year, he or she is entitled to a proportion for that first year. Workers are not entitled to this benefit until they have been continuously employed for at least 13 weeks. A worker is deemed to have been continuously employed if his or her relations with the employer have been governed by a contract during the whole or part of each of those weeks. The leave may only be taken in the leave year in respect of which it was due and cannot be replaced by a payment in lieu, unless the employment is terminated.[20]

A worker may give the employer notice of when he or she wishes to take the leave.[21] This notice must be given by a date which is equivalent to twice the amount of leave the worker is proposing to take. An employer can, however, stipulate when holidays can be taken by giving the worker concerned notice using the same formula. Regulation 16 provides that in respect of annual leave workers are entitled to be paid a sum equivalent to a week's pay for each week of leave.[22]

Records
There is an obligation, in Regulation 9, for employers to keep records in respect of the maximum weekly working time, night work and health assessment checks for night-workers. These records must be adequate to show that the relevant time-limits are being complied with in the case of each worker employed. These records must be retained for a period of two years.

The right not to suffer detriment
Sections 45A and 48(1ZA) were added to the ERA 1996 by the WT Regulations.[23] Workers have the right not to be subjected to any detriment by any act, or failure to act, on the part of the employer on the grounds that the worker

(a) refused, or proposed to refuse, to comply with any requirement in contravention of the WT Regulations

(b) refused, or proposed to refuse, to give up a right conferred by the WT Regulations

(c) failed to sign a workforce agreement (see below) or vary any other agreement with the employer which is provided for by the WT Regulations

(d) was a workforce representative or a candidate in an election for such representatives

(e) alleged that the employer had infringed the worker's rights under the WT Regulations

(f) was bringing proceedings to enforce rights under the WT Regulations.

The worker will be entitled to compensation, and if the detriment amounts to a dismissal for one of the above reasons, the worker may bring a complaint of unfair dismissal as in Part X ERA 1996.

Derogation by agreement

Apart from the individual's ability to opt out of the maximum working week (see above), the WT Regulations allow derogations, in some instances, by agreement between the employer and representatives of the employees. The types of agreement are

(i) *collective agreements*
which, according to Regulation 2, are collective agreements as defined in section 178 TULRCA. They are agreements between employers and independent trade unions recognised for collective bargaining purposes, which allow agreement to be reached on

(a) extension of the reference period for averaging the 48-hour week from 17 weeks up to a maximum of 52 weeks;[24]

(b) modifying or excluding the application of the

regulations concerning the length of night work, health assessments, daily and weekly rest periods and daily rest breaks;[25]

(ii) *workforce agreements*

according to schedule 1 to the Regulations, workforce agreements are valid if the following conditions are met:

(a) the agreement is in writing

(b) it has effect for a specified period not exceeding five years

(c) it applies to all the relevant members of the workforce or to a particular group within the relevant workforce

(d) the agreement is signed by representatives of the workforce or group

(e) before the agreement is signed, the employer provides a copy plus any necessary guidance to all the workers concerned.

If the employer has fewer than 20 workers, a workforce agreement can be reached either by representatives of that workforce or by obtaining the support of the majority of the workforce. Representatives of the workforce are the elected representatives of the workforce concerned. A workforce agreement will allow the same derogations as those for collective agreement.

Regulation 2 also contains a definition of a relevant agreement. It is an agreement which can be a provision of a collective agreement which forms part of a contract between the worker and the employer, or a workforce agreement, or any other agreement in writing that is legally enforceable as between employer and worker.

TIME OFF FOR TRADE UNION DUTIES AND ACTIVITIES

No minimum period of service is required before trade unionists can claim time off.

Trade union duties

According to section 168 TULRCA 1992, employers must permit employees who are officials of independent trade unions recognised by them to take reasonable time off with pay during working hours to enable them to:

(a) carry out their duties which are concerned with negotiations with the employer that are related to or connected with any of the matters specified in section 178(2) TULRCA and in relation to which the employer recognises the union,

(b) carry out any other duties which are concerned with the performance of any functions that are related to or connected with any matters listed in section 178(2) TULRCA 1992 and that the employer has agreed may be performed by the union

(c) receive information from the employer and be consulted under section 188 TULRCA 1992 or the Transfer Regulations 1981

(d) to undergo training in aspects of industrial relations which is both relevant to the carrying out of any of the duties mentioned in (a) and approved by their trade union or the TUC.

An official is defined as someone who is an officer of the union or branch of it, or someone who is elected or appointed in accordance with the rules to be a representative of its members or some of them.[26]

The amount of time off allowed, together with the purpose for which, the occasions on which, and any conditions subject to which, time off may be taken, depends on what is reasonable in all the circumstances having regard to any relevant provisions in the ACAS Code of Practice.[27] The Code does not lay down any fixed amount of time that employers should permit officials to take off. Employers and trade unions should reach agreements on arrangements for handling time off in ways appropriate to their situations.

Officials who are permitted time off should receive normal remuneration as if they had worked. Where the remuneration varies with the work done, average hourly earnings should be paid.[28] No claim can be made for overtime which would normally have been worked unless that overtime was contractually required, and there is no entitlement to be paid for time spent on trade union duties outside working hours.[29] It follows that an employee on the night shift who attends a works committee meeting during the day will not be entitled to a payment whereas a day shift worker would. Nevertheless, employees may reasonably require paid time off during working hours to enable them to undertake the relevant duties or training, for example to travel to or return from a training course.[30] Two further points should be noted. First, the 'set-off formula' applies here.[31] Second, employers who give their part-time employees paid time off only up to the limit of their normal working hours may be discriminating contrary to Article 141 EC (previously Article 119 EC).[32] The Code of Practice recommends that officials of recognised trade unions should be allowed reasonable time off for duties concerned with negotiations related to or connected with:[33]

(a) terms and conditions of employment, or the conditions in which employees are required to work, eg pay, hours of work, holiday pay and entitlement, sick pay arrangements, pensions, vocational training, equal opportunities, notice periods, the working environment and the utilisation of machinery and other equipment

(b) engagement or non-engagement, or termination or suspension of employment or the duties of employment, of one or more workers, eg recruitment and selection policies, human resource planning, redundancy and dismissal arrangements

(c) allocation of work, or the duties of employment as between workers or groups of workers, eg job grading, job evaluation, job descriptions and flexible working practices

(d) matters of discipline, eg disciplinary procedures, arrangements for representing trade union members at internal interviews, arrangements for appearing on behalf of trade union members, or as witnesses before agreed outside appeal bodies or employment tribunals

(e) trade union membership or non-membership, eg representational agreements, any union involvement in the induction of new workers

(f) facilities for officials of trade unions, eg accommodation, equipment, names of new workers to the union

(g) machinery for negotiation and consultation and other procedures, eg arrangements for collective bargaining, grievance procedures, joint consultation, communicating with members, communicating with other union officials also concerned with collective bargaining with the employer.

The Code states that where an official is not taking part in industrial action but represents members who are, normal arrangements for time off with pay should apply. Additionally, the code suggests that management should make available the facilities necessary for officials to perform their duties efficiently and to communicate effectively with members. The items mentioned are accommodation for meetings, access to a telephone, notice boards and the use of office facilities.[34]

Preparatory and explanatory work by officials may well be in fulfilment of duties concerned with any of the matters listed in section 178(2) TULRCA 1992.[35] What has to be demonstrated is that there is a sufficient nexus between the collective bargaining and the duty for which leave is sought.[36] Employment tribunals will have to decide whether the preparatory work is directly relevant to one of the matters specified in section 178(2), and if the employer does not negotiate on the issue, the employer's agreement to the performance of the duty will have to be demonstrated.[37] It also seems that the recognised union must, expressly or impliedly, require the performance of the duty, otherwise it would be impossible to hold that the individual was 'carrying out those duties ... as such an official'.[38] If no agreement on time off is reached in advance of a meeting, a sensible approach might be to determine claims for payment on the basis of what the minutes disclosed. Where only a proportion of the time was spent on section 168 TULRCA 1992 matters, a tribunal will probably find that only a proportion of the time should reasonably be paid for.

As regards industrial relations training, again no fixed amount of time is specified but the code recommends that officials should be permitted paid time off for initial basic training as soon as possible after their election or appointment. Time off should be allowed for further training where the official has special responsibilities or where it is necessary to meet changed industrial relations circumstances.[39] In determining whether a course meets the requirement of relevance to the specified duties, the description of people attending the course by those responsible for it will be pertinent.[40] Indeed, as a general principle it would seem wise for employers to insist on being shown a copy of course prospectuses.

Trade union activities

An employer must also permit a member of a recognised independent trade union to take reasonable time off during working hours for trade union activities and to represent the union. However, in the absence of any contractual term to the contrary, an employer does not have to pay for such time off. Trade union activities are not statutorily defined, although the code gives the following examples of the activities of a member:

(a) attending workplace meetings to discuss and vote on the outcome of negotiations with the employer

(b) meeting full-time officials to discuss issues relevant to the workplace

(c) voting in properly conducted ballots on industrial action

(d) voting in union elections.[41]

Paragraph 22 of the Code gives examples of activities where the member is acting as a representative of a union:

(a) branch, area or regional meetings of the union where the business of the union is under discussion

(b) meetings of official policy-making bodies such as the executive committee or annual conference

(c) meetings with full-time officials to discuss issues relevant to the workplace.

Section 170(2) TULRCA expressly excludes activities which consist of industrial action, although paragraph 39 of the code recommends that time off should be provided for the use of agreed procedures. Finally, in *Wignall v British Gas*[42] the EAT rejected the argument that the statute requires each proposed activity on the part of the employee in the service of his or her union to be weighed and tested on its own merits without regard to any other activities or duties on the union's behalf for which the employee might be taking time off. Thus every application for time off under section 170 should be looked at on its merits in the particular circumstances.

Employees wishing to complain of failure to permit time off or to pay the amount required by section 169 TULRCA 1992 must apply to an employment tribunal within three months of the date when the failure occurred.[43] According to the EAT, a complainant must establish on the balance of probabilities that a request for time off was made, that it came to the notice of the employer's appropriate representative, and that they refused it, ignored it or failed to respond to it.[44] If the tribunal finds that the claim is well-founded, it must make a declaration to that effect and may make an award of compensation of such amount as it considers 'just and equitable in all the circumstances having regard to the employer's default ... and to any loss sustained by the employee which is attributable to the matters complained of'.[45]

TIME OFF FOR PUBLIC DUTIES

Section 50 ERA 1996 permits employees who are:

(a) members of a local authority[46]

(b) members of any statutory tribunal

(c) members of a health authority, NHS trust or a Health Board

(d) members of a relevant education body[47]

(e) members of a police authority[48]

(f) the Service Authority of the National Crime Squad

(g) members of a board of prison visitors or a prison visiting committee[49]

(h) members of the Environment Agency or the Scottish Environment Protection Agency

to take time off during working hours for the purpose of performing any of the duties of their office or as members. Employees are eligible for time off irrespective of their length of service, but are not entitled to a payment from their employer by virtue of this section.

The duties referred to are attendance at meetings of the body (or its committees or sub-committees) and 'the doing of any other thing approved by the body' for the purpose of discharging its functions. The amount of time off which is to be allowed and the occasions on which and conditions subject to which it may be taken are those that are reasonable in the circumstances. No code of practice exists for these purposes but regard must be had to the following matters:[50]

(a) how much time off is required for the performance of the public duty as a whole and how much is required for the particular duty

(b) how much time off has already been permitted for trade union duties and activities (see above)

(c) the circumstances of the employer's business and the effect of the employee's absence on the running of it.

The EAT has commented that an employee who undertakes a variety of public and other duties may have some responsibility to plan the absences from work, and to scale down the level of commitment which such public duties involve, so as to produce a pattern which can be regarded as reasonable in the circumstances.[51] A complaint that an employer has failed to permit time off in accordance with the above provisions must be lodged in the same way as a claim that the employer has not complied with sections 168 or 170 TULRCA 1992, and the remedies available are identical. However, two observations may be helpful at this stage. First, rearranging employees' hours of work but requiring them to perform the same duties does not constitute giving time off. Second, it is not the function of employment tribunals to stipulate what amounts of, or conditions for, time off would be appropriate in the future.[52]

TIME OFF FOR EMPLOYEE REPRESENTATIVES[52a] AND EMPLOYEE TRUSTEES OF PENSION FUNDS

A person who is an employee representative for the purposes of consultation over redundancies or the transfer of undertakings (see Chapter 15), or a candidate in an election to be such a representative, is entitled to reasonable time off during working hours to perform the functions of such a representative candidate.[53] Employees who are permitted time off are entitled to be paid at the appropriate rate.[54] Those who feel that their rights have been infringed can use the enforcement mechanisms available in relation to time off for antenatal care.[55]

Section 58 (1) ERA 1996 allows employee trustees of a pension fund reasonable time off during working hours for the purpose of performing any of their duties as a trustee or undergoing training relevant to those duties. In ascertaining what is reasonable in all the circumstances regard must be had to:

(a) how much time off is required for the performance of the trustee's duties and undergoing relevant training, and how much time off is needed for undertaking the particular duty or training, and

(b) the circumstances of the employer's business and the effect of the employee's absence on the running of it.[56]

Employees who feel that this right has been infringed must normally complain to an employment tribunal within three months. The remedies available are identical to those that apply to time off for trade union duties (see above).[57]

It should also be noted that employee representatives (or candidates in an election) and trustees of pension funds have the right not to be subjected to any detriment on the ground that they performed (or proposed to perform) their functions or activities.[58] Claims must be lodged within three months of the act (or failure to act) complained of, and the remedies available are the same as for the right not to be subject to detriment on trade union grounds (see above).[59]

TIME OFF FOR STUDY OR TRAINING

Section 63A of the ERA 1996 permits certain young employees to have time off for study or training. The employees concerned are those who

(a)   are aged 16 or 17 years, and

(b)   are not receiving full-time or further education, and

(c)   have not attained such standard of achievement as is prescribed by regulations made by the Secretary of State.[60]

These standards of achievement are set out in the Right to Time Off for Study or Training Regulations 1999[61] (RTOST Regulations). Examples of the standards of achievement are: grades A–C in five subjects at GCSE or one intermediate level GNVQ or one GSVQ at level 2.[62]

In addition young employees who

(a)   are aged 18 years

(b)   are undertaking training or study leading to a relevant qualification

(c)   began that study before reaching the age of 18 years

are also entitled to time off during working hours.

The amount of time off permitted must be reasonable, taking

into account the requirements of the employee's study or training and the circumstances of the employer's business and the effect of the time taken off on that business.[63] An employee who has the right to take time off for study and training also has the right to be paid remuneration by the employer at the normal hourly rate.[64] If an employee has been unreasonably refused permission for time off or has not been paid correctly for that time off, he or she may make a complaint to an employment tribunal.[65] The complaint needs to be made within three months, unless not reasonably practicable, beginning with the day that the time off was taken or should have been taken. If the complaint is well-founded, the tribunal may make a declaration to that effect or order the employer to pay compensation equal to the amount of remuneration to which the employee would have been entitled.

TIME OFF TO LOOK FOR WORK

A person who has been continuously employed for two years or more and is under notice of dismissal by reason of redundancy is entitled to reasonable time off during working hours to look for new employment or make arrangements for training for future employment.[66] Such an employee should be paid at the appropriate hourly rate for the period of absence. This is one week's pay divided by the number of normal weekly hours, or, where the number of working hours varies, the average of such hours.[67]

A complaint that an employer has unreasonably refused time off or has failed to pay the whole or any part of any amount to which the employee is entitled must be presented to an employment tribunal, if reasonably practicable, within three months of the day in which it is alleged that the time off should have been allowed or paid for.[68] If the complaint is well-founded, the tribunal must make a declaration to that effect and order the employer to pay the amount which it finds due to the employee. Curiously, although the employee is entitled to be paid 'an amount equal to the remuneration to which he would have been entitled if he had been allowed the time off', the maximum that a tribunal can award is two-fifths of a week's pay. In *Dutton v Hawker Siddeley Aviation Ltd*[69] the EAT rejected the argument that employees had to give details of any appointments or interviews for which they wished to take time off.

KEY POINTS 11
The regulation of working time

- The WT Regulations implement the WT Directive and parts of the Young Workers Directive.

- The Regulations provide for a maximum 48-hour week during a 17-week reference period and provide rules on night work, rest periods and annual leave.

- The individual is able to agree to opt out of the 48-hour week and there are provisions for determining the rules by collective and workforce agreements.

- No minimum period of service is required before trade unionists can claim time off.

- Employers must permit employees who are officials of independent trade unions recognised by them to take reasonable time off with pay.

- Members of a recognised independent trade union are entitled to reasonable time off during working hours for trade union activities and to represent the union.

- Employees are to be permitted time off, without pay, for a variety of public duties such as being a member of a local authority or statutory authority.

- Young employees who are not receiving full-time education are entitled to time off to study and train for certain qualifications.

- A person who has been continuously employed for two years or more and is under notice of dismissal for redundancy is entitled to reasonable time off, during working hours, to look for new work.

NOTES

1   SI 1998/1833
2   Directive 93/104 concerning certain aspects of the organisation of working time
3   Directive 94/33 on the protection of young people at work
4   *UK v Council of the European Union* (1997) ICR 443
5   See Regulation 18(a) WT Regulations 1998
6   Regulations 18(b) and (c) WT Regulations 1998
7   Regulation 19 WT Regulations 1998
8   Regulation 20 WT Regulations 1998
9   18 November 1998
10 See Regulation 2 WT Regulations 1998
11 (1999) IRLR 308
12 Regulation 4(6) WT Regulations 1998
13 See *R v Attorney General for Northern Ireland* (1999) IRLR 315
14 Regulation 6(7) WT Regulations 1998
15 Regulation 7 WT Regulations 1998
16 Regulation 8 WT Regulations 1998
17 Regulation 11 WT Regulations 1998; regulation 11(7) states that the weekly rest period may not be in addition to the daily rest period 'where this is justified by objective or technical reasons or reasons concerning the organisation of work'
18 Regulation 11(8) WT Regulations 1998; the rest period may not be less than 36 consecutive hours
19 Regulation 13 WT Regulations 1998; see also *Gibson v East Riding of Yorkshire* (1999) IRLR 358 where a local authority employee relied upon the Working Time Directive being directly effective to claim four weeks' holiday
20 In which case the worker is entitled to a proportionate payment in lieu; see regulation 14
21 Regulation 15 WT Regulations 1998
22 A week's pay is as defined in sections 221–224 ERA 1996
23 Regulations 31 and 32 WT Regulations 1998
24 Regulation 23(b) WT Regulations 1998
25 Regulation 23(a) WT Regulations 1998, although regulation 24 allows for compensatory rest periods and rest breaks
26 Section 119 TULRCA 1992
27 *Time off for Trade Union Duties and Activities 1991*
28 Section 169(3) TULRCA 1992
29 Working hours are defined in the same way as section 146(2) TULRCA 1992
30 See *Hairsine v Hull City Council* (1992) IRLR 211
31 Section 169(4) TULRCA 1992
32 See *Davis v Neath Port Talbot Council* (1999) IRLR 769
33 Paragraph 12
34 Paragraph 28
35 See paragraph 13
36 See *London Ambulance Service v Charlton* (1992) IRLR 510
37 See *British Bakeries v Adlington* (1989) IRLR 218
38 See *Ashley v Ministry of Defence* (1984) IRLR 57
39 Paragraph 18

40 See *Ministry of Defence v Crook* (1982) IRLR 488
41 Paragraph 21
42 (1984) IRLR 493
43 Unless the 'time-lapse escape clause' applies; section 171 TULRCA 1992
44 *Ryford Ltd v Drinkwater* (1995) IRLR 16
45 Section 172 TULRCA 1992
46 Defined in section 50(5) ERA 1996
47 Defined in section 50(9) ERA 1996
48 Defined in section 50(6) ERA 1996
49 Defined in section 50(7) ERA 1996
50 Section 50(4) ERA 1996
51 *Borders Regional Council v Maule* (1993) IRLR 199
52 See *Corner v Buckinghamshire Council* (1978) IRLR 320
52a Workers must be permitted to take time off during working hours for the
    purpose of accompanying another worker at a disciplinary or grievance
    hearing: section 10 E Rel Act 1999
53 Section 68(1) TULRCA 1992 and section 61(1) ERA 1996
54 See section 62 ERA 1996
55 Section 63 ERA 1996
56 See section 58(2) ERA 1996
57 Section 60(3)(4) ERA 1996
58 See sections 47 and 46 ERA 1996 respectively. Dismissal on these grounds
    is unfair (see Chapter 14)
59 Sections 48–49 ERA 1996
60 Section 63A(1)(a)–(c) ERA 1996
61 SI 1999/986
62 Regulation 3 RTOST Regulations 1999; Regulation 4 lists the awarding
    bodies that are recognised for purposes of this section
63 Section 63A(5) ERA 1996
64 See section 63B(1) ERA 1996
65 Section 63C ERA 1996
66 Section 52 ERA 1996
67 Section 53 ERA 1996
68 Section 54 ERA 1996
69 (1978) IRLR 390

12 Variation, breach and termination of the contract of employment at common law

This chapter deals with various issues raised by the common law approach to the variation and ending of contracts of employment. To begin with we look at the consequences of unilateral variation of the contract by the employer. We then examine the options open when a breach of contract takes place by studying, firstly, the innocent party's choice whether or not to accept the breach, and secondly, the principal remedies for a breach. The issues concerned with the frustration of the contract and summary dismissal are considered. Finally we look at the consequences of termination without notice and the remedies for wrongful dismissal.

VARIATION

Theoretically, neither employer nor employee can unilaterally alter the terms and conditions of employment, for these can be varied only by mutual agreement. It follows that an employer cannot lawfully vary a contract simply by giving 'notice to vary'. Such a notice will have legal effect only if it terminates the existing contract and offers a new contract on revised terms.[1] Consent to change may be obtained through individual or collective negotiation or may be implied from the conduct of the parties. Thus if employees remain at work for a considerable period of time after revised terms have been imposed, they may be deemed to have accepted the changes.[2] Where the individual continues in employment but works 'under protest', it is a question of fact whether or not the variation has been accepted. In *WPM Retail v Lang*[3] it was held that the employer's obligation to pay a bonus in accordance with the terms when the employee was promoted remained in force until the employment was terminated three years later, notwithstanding that the bonus had been paid only in the first month after promotion and the employee had carried on working thereafter. As a general rule, courts and tribunals will be reluctant to find that there has been a consensual variation 'where the employee has been faced with the alternative of dismissal and where the variation has been adverse to his interest'.[4]

A unilateral variation which is not accepted will constitute a breach and could amount to a repudiation of the contract. However, there is no law that any breach which an employee is entitled to treat as repudiatory brings the contract to an end automatically.[5] Where there is repudiatory conduct by the employer, the employee has the choice of affirming the contract (by continuing in employment) or accepting the repudiation as bringing the contract to an end. If the latter option is exercised and the employee resigns within a short period, there will be a constructive dismissal for statutory purposes (see Chapter 13). In practice, developments in the law of unfair dismissal make it very difficult for an employee to resist a unilateral variation. Suffice it to say at this stage that employers can offer, as a fair reason for dismissal, the fact that there was a sound business reason for insisting on changes being put into effect. So long as a minimum amount of consultation has taken place, it is relatively easy to satisfy a tribunal, particularly where the majority of employees has been prepared to go along with the employer's proposals, that an employer has acted reasonably in treating a refusal to accept a variation as a sufficient reason for dismissing.[6]

BREACH OF CONTRACT

The options open to an innocent party will depend on whether the breach is of a minor or serious nature. An innocent party may choose to continue with the contract as if nothing had happened (ie waive the breach), may sue for damages, or, in the case of a serious or fundamental breach, may regard the contract as at an end (ie accept the other party's repudiation of it). Although the employer could sue or possibly dismiss for breach of contract, there are a number of reasons why disciplinary rather than legal action is preferred. First, the potential defendant may be unable to pay any damages awarded. Second, the amount likely to be obtained may not be worth the time and effort involved.

Third, taking legal rather than disciplinary action against individual employees is not conducive to harmonious industrial relations.

What options are open to employers when employees refuse to carry out all or part of their contractual obligations? Apart from the measures outlined in the previous paragraph, the employer may withhold pay on the grounds that employees who are not ready and willing to render the services required by their contracts are not entitled to be paid.[7] In *Wiluszynski v London Borough of Tower Hamlets*[8] the employee refused to perform the full range of his duties and had been told by the employer that until he did he would not be required for work, or be paid. Although he went to work and performed a substantial part of his duties, the Court of Appeal held that the local authority was entitled to withhold the whole of his remuneration. Clearly employees are not entitled to pick and choose what work they will do under their contracts, but if employers are prepared to accept part-performance they will be required to pay for such work as is agreed.

The principal remedies for breach of contract are an injunction (an order restraining a particular type of action), a declaration of the rights of the parties, and damages. Traditionally, great emphasis was placed on the personal nature of the contract of employment and courts were extremely reluctant to order a party to continue to perform the contract. However, in recent years the courts have been more willing to grant injunctions against employers who act in breach of contract. Nevertheless, they need to be satisfied not only that it would be just to make such an order but also that it would be workable.[9] The mere fact that the employer and employee are in dispute does not mean that mutual confidence has evaporated.[10] The position remains that an employee cannot be compelled to return to work,[11] although a tribunal has the power to order the re-employment of someone who has been unfairly dismissed and seeks this remedy (see Chapter 16). Those who seek damages can be compensated for the direct and likely consequences of the breach, although nothing can be recovered for the manner of the breach or for the mental stress, frustration or annoyance caused.[12] Compensation will not be recoverable for damage to an existing reputation unless pecuniary loss was sustained as a foreseeable consequence of the breach.[13]

Since July 1994 the jurisdiction of employment tribunals has been extended to breach of contract claims which have arisen or are outstanding at the end of employment. Under section 3(2) ETA 1996 the claim must be for:

(a) damages for breach of a contract of employment or any other contract connected with the employment.[14]

(b) a sum due under such a contract or the recovery of a sum in pursuance of any enactment relating to the terms or performance of such a contract.

The maximum that can be awarded in respect of claims relating to the same contract is £25,000.

Certain claims are excluded – for example personal injury, breach of confidence and restrictive covenant cases. Employers can bring proceedings (counterclaims) only if an employee has made a claim first, but the employer's claim can then continue even if the employee is unable to continue with the claim.[15]

An employee's claim must normally be brought within three months of the effective date of termination and an employer's counterclaim must be presented within six weeks of receiving a copy of the originating application. A case is heard by a chairperson sitting alone unless it is decided that a full tribunal should hear it. Although ACAS' services are available, the parties can reach their own agreement without any need for a conciliated settlement or compromise agreement.

AUTOMATIC TERMINATION: FRUSTRATION

A contract is said to have been frustrated where events make it physically impossible or unlawful for the contract to be performed, or where there has been a change such as to radically alter the purpose of the contract. Once a contract has come to an end by reason of frustration, it cannot be treated by the parties as still subsisting. If the parties come to an arrangement to continue the employment relationship, then this may constitute a new contract or some other arrangement. It will not be a continuation of the original contract which has been frustrated.[16] A contract which is still capable of being performed but becomes subject to an unforeseen risk is not frustrated.[17] As long as the frustrating event is not self-induced, there is an automatic termination of the contract, ie there is no dismissal.[18] This being so, it was not uncommon for an employer to resist a claim for unfair dismissal by alleging that the contract had been frustrated, eg on grounds of sickness. Although the EAT thought that the concept of frustration should normally only come into play where the contract is for a long term which cannot be determined by notice, the Court of Appeal has allowed this doctrine to be applied to contracts of employment which can be terminated by short periods of notice.[19]

The following principles are relevant to the application of the doctrine of frustration in the event of illness.[20] First, the courts must guard against too easy an application of the doctrine. Second, an attempt to decide the date that frustration occurred may help to decide whether it is a true frustration situation. Third, the factors below may help to decide the issue:

(a) length of previous employment

(b) how long the employment was expected to continue

(c) the nature of the job

(d) the nature, length and effect of the illness or disabling event[21]

(e) the employer's need for the work to be done and the need for a replacement employee

(f) whether wages have continued to be paid

(g) the acts and statements of the employer in relation to the employment. In *Hart v Marshall & Sons*[22] the EAT held that the employer's acceptance of sick notes did not prevent a tribunal from finding that the contract had been frustrated

(h) whether in all the circumstances a reasonable employer could have been expected to wait any longer

(i) the terms of the contract as to sick pay, if any

(j) a consideration of the prospects of recovery.

A prison sentence is a potentially frustrating event, but the circumstances of each case have to be examined to discover whether such a sentence has in fact operated to frustrate the contract or whether its termination was due to some other cause.[23]

TERMINATION WITHOUT NOTICE: SUMMARY DISMISSAL

A summary dismissal occurs where the employer terminates the contract of employment without notice. It must be distinguished from an instant dismissal, which has no legal meaning but normally refers to a dismissal without investigation or inquiry. Whereas an instant dismissal is likely to be procedurally defective in unfair dismissal terms (see Chapter 14), a summary dismissal may be lawful under both common law and statute.

In order to justify summary dismissal the employee must be in breach of an important express or implied term of the contract, ie be guilty of gross misconduct. Although certain terms are always regarded as important – for example the duty not to steal or damage the employer's property, the duty to obey lawful orders and not to engage in industrial action – the significance of other terms will depend on the nature of the employer's business and the employee's position in it. Thus smoking may not normally be viewed as an act of gross misconduct, but if it occurs at a gas-bottling plant it is likely to be so regarded! If an employer feels that a particular act or omission would warrant summary dismissal, this fact should be communicated clearly to all employees.[24]

One consequence of the contractual approach is that everything hinges upon the facts in the particular case and previous decisions usually have little bearing. Nevertheless, a number of general principles can be discerned:

(a) single acts of misconduct are less likely to give rise to a right of summary dismissal than a persistent pattern

(b) it is the nature of the act rather than its consequences which is relevant

(c) an employer is more likely to be entitled to dismiss summarily for misconduct within the workplace than outside it

(d) a refusal to obey instructions can still amount to repudiation even though the employee has mistakenly proceeded in the *bona fide* belief that the work which he or she had been instructed to do fell outside the scope of the contract.[25]

If employers do not invoke the right to end the contract within a reasonable period, they will be taken to have waived their rights and can only seek damages. What is a reasonable period will depend on the facts of the particular case. In *Allders International v Parkins*[26] it was held that nine days was too long a period to be allowed to pass in relation to an allegation of stealing before deciding what to do about the alleged repudiatory conduct. In *Gunton v London Borough of Richmond*[27] the Court of Appeal decided that the general doctrine that repudiation by one party does not terminate a contract applies to employment law. Thus an unlawful summary dismissal does not terminate a contract of employment until the employee has accepted the employer's repudiation and certain contractual rights and obligations will survive until that time, eg in relation to a disciplinary procedure (see Chapter 13 on the effective date of termination for statutory purposes). Nevertheless, in the absence of special circumstances a court will easily infer that the repudiation has been accepted.[28] Finally, at common law an employer is not required to supply a reason for dismissal, although this is now modified by statute[29] (see Chapter 14).

TERMINATION WITH NOTICE

Usually either party is entitled to terminate a contract of employment by giving notice[30] and once notice has been given it cannot be unilaterally withdrawn.[31] (Of course, an employer who makes a mistake could offer to re-employ.) The courts have consistently ruled that for notice to be effective it must be possible to ascertain the date of termination, and not infrequently employees have confused an advanced warning of closure with notice of dismissal.[32] The length of the notice will be determined by the express or implied terms of the contract and, if no term can be identified, both parties are required to give a reasonable period of notice. What is reasonable will depend on the circumstances of the relationship, eg the employee's position and length of service. Thus in *Hill v C. A. Parsons & Co. Ltd*[33] a 63-year-old engineer with 35 years' service was held to be entitled to at least six months' notice.

Apart from the situation where individuals are disentitled to notice by reason of their conduct,[34] section 86(1) ERA 1996 provides that certain minimum periods of notice must be given. After a month's service an employee is entitled to a week's notice and this applies until the employment has lasted for two years. At this point two weeks' notice is owed and from then on the employee must receive an extra week's notice for each year of service up to a maximum of 12 weeks. According to section 86(2) ERA 1996 an employee with a month's service or more need give only one week's notice to terminate, but there is nothing to prevent the parties from agreeing that both should receive more than the statutory minimum.

Although the statute does not prevent an employee from accepting a payment in lieu of notice, strictly speaking an employer must have contractual authority for insisting on such a payment. Without such authority a payment in lieu of notice will be construed as damages for the failure to provide proper notice. Thus a payment in lieu can properly terminate a contract of employment if the contract provides for such a payment or the parties agree that the employee will accept a payment in lieu, provided the payment relates to a period no shorter than that of the notice to which the employee would be entitled either under the contract of employment or section 86(1) ERA 1996.[35] The date of termination at common law is the day notice expires or the day wages in lieu are accepted. Except where the notice to be given by the employer is at least one week more than the statutory minimum, an employee is entitled to be paid during the period of notice even if:

(a)   no work is provided by the employer

(b)   the employee is incapable of work because of sickness or injury

(c)   the employee is absent from work wholly or partly because of pregnancy or childbirth

(d)   the employee is absent in accordance with the terms of his or her employment relating to holidays.[36]

Any payments by the employer by way of sick pay, maternity pay, holiday pay or otherwise go towards meeting this liability.[37] If employees take part in a strike after they have been given notice, payment is due for the period when they were not on strike. However, where employees give notice and then go on strike, they do not qualify for any payment under section 88 or 89 ERA 1996.[38]

REMEDIES FOR WRONGFUL DISMISSAL

Basically a wrongful dismissal is a dismissal without notice or with inadequate notice in circumstances where proper notice should have been given. The expression also covers dismissals which are in breach of agreed procedures. Thus where there is a contractual disciplinary procedure, an employee may be able to obtain an injunction or declaration from the courts so as to prevent a dismissal or declare a dismissal void if the procedure has not been followed.[39] However, an injunction will only be granted if the court is convinced that the employer's repudiation has not been accepted, that the employer has sufficient trust and confidence in the employee, and that damages would not be an adequate remedy.[40]

Judicial review is available where an issue of public law is involved, although employment by a public authority does not by itself inject any element of public law.[41] Indeed, where an alternative remedy is available, judicial review will only be exercised in exceptional circumstances. Factors to be taken into account in considering whether the circumstances are exceptional include the speed of the alternative procedure, whether it was as convenient, and whether the matter depended on some particular knowledge available to the appellate body.[42]

For the reason mentioned earlier the courts are reluctant to enforce a contract of employment, so in the vast majority of cases the employee's remedy will lie in damages for breach of contract. A person who suffers a wrongful dismissal is entitled to be compensated for such loss as arises naturally from the breach and for any loss which was reasonably foreseeable by the parties as being likely to arise from it. Hence an employee will normally recover only the amount of wages lost between the date of the wrongful dismissal and the date when the contract could lawfully have been terminated.[43] Examples of circumstances in which damages have been awarded include:

(a) an employee being allowed to keep share options, even though the terms of the share option scheme provided that the option to purchase lapsed on termination as a result of disciplinary action[44]

(b) a senior employee with a contract that allowed for a 10 per cent per annum salary increase and substantial annual bonuses during a three-year notice period was entitled to the benefit of those payments even though they were at the discretion of the board. For the board to exercise its discretion to reduce these payments to nil would have been capricious and a breach of contract[45]

(c) an employee wrongfully dismissed in breach of a contractual disciplinary procedure three weeks before the employee would have acquired enough service to claim unfair dismissal was entitled to compensation for the loss of the opportunity to make such a claim.[46]

Damages are not available for hurt feelings or the manner in which the dismissal took place, even though the manner might have made it more difficult to obtain other employment.

Except where employees have a contractual right to a payment in lieu of notice,[47] or are entitled to their full payments during a contractual notice period[48] they will have a duty to mitigate their loss, which means in effect that they are obliged to look for another job. Where there is a failure to mitigate, the court will deduct a sum which it feels the employee might reasonably have been expected to earn. As regards state benefits, it would appear that any benefit received by the dismissed employee should be deducted only where not to do so would result in a net gain to the employee.[49] Finally, the first £30,000 of damages is to be awarded net of tax, but any amount above this figure will be awarded gross since it is taxable in the hands of the recipient.

KEY POINTS 12
Common law approach to variation, breach and termination

- Theoretically, neither employer nor employee can unilaterally alter the terms and conditions of employment.

- A unilateral variation which is not accepted will constitute a breach and, if serious, could amount to a repudiation of the contract.

- An innocent party to a breach of contract may choose to waive the breach, sue for damages or, in serious cases, accept the repudiation and regard the contract as being at an end.

- Frustration of a contract occurs when it is physically impossible or unlawful for the contract to continue to be performed.

- In order to justify summary dismissal the employee

needs to be in breach of an important express or implied term of the contract.

- Once notice to terminate has been given it cannot unilaterally be withdrawn.

- For notice of termination to be effective, it must be possible to ascertain the date of termination.

- Wrongful dismissal is a dismissal without notice or with inadequate notice in circumstances where proper notice should have been given or where dismissals have been in breach of agreed procedures.

NOTES

1 *Alexander v STC Ltd* (1991) IRLR 286
2 *Aparau v Iceland Frozen Foods* (1996) IRLR 119
3 (1978) IRLR 343
4 See *Sheet Metal Components Ltd v Plumridge* (1979) IRLR 86
5 See *Boyo v Lambeth Borough Council* (1995) IRLR 50
6 See *Hollister v National Farmers Union* (1979) IRLR 238
7 See *Ticehurst v British Telecom* (1992) IRLR 219; section 14(5) ERA 1996 allows deductions to be made in respect of participation in industrial action
8 (1989) IRLR 279
9 See *Robb v London Borough of Hammersmith* (1991) IRLR 72
10 See *Hughes v London Borough of Southwark* (1988) IRLR 55
11 Section 236 TULRCA 1992
12 See *Bliss v South East Thames Regional Health Authority* (1988) IRLR 308
13 See *Malik v BCCI* (1997) IRLR 462
14 See *Raspin v United Newspapers* (1999) IRLR 9
15 See *Patel v RCMS Ltd* (1999) IRLR 161
16 See *GF Sharp & Co Ltd v McMillan* (1998) IRLR 632
17 See *Convefoam Ltd v Bell* (1981) IRLR 195
18 Where an employer dies or the business is destroyed a dismissal is deemed to occur for the purpose of safeguarding an employee's right to a redundancy payment; section 174 ERA 1996
19 See *Nottcutt v Universal Equipment Ltd* (1986) I WLR 641
20 See *Williams v Watsons Ltd* (1990) IRLR 164
21 Employers need to be aware of the possible implications of the DDA 1995; see Chapter 8 and *Goodwin v The Patent Office* (1999) IRLR 4 on when a person is considered to have a disability
22 (1977) IRLR 61
23 See *F Shepherd v Jerrom* (1986) IRLR 358
24 See ACAS Code of Practice on Disciplinary Practice and Procedures in Employment, paragraph 8

25 See *Blyth v Scottish Liberal Club* (1983) IRLR 245
26 (1981) IRLR 68
27 (1980) IRLR 321
28 See *Boyo v Lambeth Borough Council* (note 5)
29 Section 92 ERA 1996
30 A contract of apprenticeship is for a fixed term and the ordinary law relating to dismissal does not apply; see *Wallace v CA Roofing Ltd* (1996) IRLR 435
31 See *Harris & Russell Ltd v Slingsby* (1973) IRLR 221
32 See *ICL v Kennedy* (1981) IRLR 28
33 (1971) 3 WLR 995
34 See section 86(6) ERA 1996
35 See *Ginsberg Ltd v Parker* (1988) IRLR 483
36 Section 88(1) ERA 1996
37 Section 88(2) ERA 1996
38 Section 91(2) ERA 1996
39 See *Jones v Gwent County Council* (1992) IRLR 521
40 See *Dietman v London Borough of Brent* (1988) IRLR 299 and *Wall v STC* (1990) IRLR 55
41 See *R v East Berkshire Health Authority ex parte Walsh* (1984) IRLR 278 and *McLaren v Home Office* (1990) IRLR 338
42 See *R v Chief Constable of Merseyside Police ex parte Calveley* (1986) 2 WLR 144
43 See *Marsh v National Autistic Society* (1993) ICR 453
44 See *Lovett v Biotrace International Ltd* (1999) IRLR 375
45 *Clark v BET plc* (1997) IRLR 348
46 *Raspin v United News Shops Ltd* (see note 14)
47 See *Abrahams v Performing Rights Society* (1995) IRLR 486
48 See *Gregory v Wallace* (1998) IRLR 387
49 See *Westwood v Secretary of State* (1984) IRLR 209

13 Unfair dismissal (1)

Here we are concerned with the meaning of dismissal for statutory purposes and with the various qualifications that need to be achieved before an employee is entitled to protection against unfair dismissal. We start by looking at the hurdles to be overcome, such as the need to be below normal retirement age and have continuous service of one year for unfair dismissal protection. The ways in which a contract of employment can be ended are considered, such as termination with or without notice, by mutual agreement or by constructive dismissal. We then look at the importance of establishing the effective date of termination.

EXCLUSIONS AND QUALIFICATIONS

Every employee has the right not to be unfairly dismissed,[1] although there are a number of general exclusions and qualifications. Certain share fishers cannot lodge a complaint, but Crown employees are covered.[2]

Age-limits[3]

No claim can be made if on or before the effective date of termination (see below) the individual had attained the normal retiring age for an employee in his or her position or was 65 years old.[4] However, there is no age-limit if the reason or principal reason for dismissal is 'inadmissible' (see Chapter 14).[5] In *Secretary of State for Scotland v Taylor*[6] the Scottish Prison service was challenged after changing the retirement age of its employees to 55 years in order to save money, despite having an equal opportunities policy that excluded discrimination on the basis of age. The Court of Appeal accepted that this policy had become incorporated into the contract of employment, but that any retirement age was likely to discriminate on the grounds of age and that this could not fetter the employer's discretion. In

Nothman v London Borough of Barnet[7] the House of Lords ruled that there was one upper age-limit per person and that the 65 years restriction only applied when there is no normal retiring age fixed by the contract of employment. 'Normal retirement age' is the age at which employees in a group[8] can reasonably expect to be compelled to retire unless there is some special reason in a particular case for a different age to apply. In *Barclays Bank v O'Brien*[9] the Court of Appeal regarded a departure from the normal retirement age of 60 as being for a special reason. The exception was limited in time and was made for a relatively small category of employees in response to representations made on their behalf on the grounds of hardship.

The contractual retirement age does not conclusively fix the normal retirement age. Where there is a contractual retirement age there is a presumption that that age is the normal retirement age, but this presumption can be rebutted by evidence that there is in practice some higher age at which employees are regularly retired and which they have reasonably come to regard as their normal retirement age. According to the EAT, an employer cannot reduce the normal retirement age below the contractual age of retirement.[10] If the contractual retirement age is regularly departed from it is irrelevant that employment beyond that age was at management's discretion or that continued employment was subject to regular review.[11] Where there is evidence that employees retire at a variety of ages, there will be no normal retirement age and the statutory alternative applies. If there is no contractual retirement age, the correct approach is to consider whether there is evidence of a practice which establishes a normal retirement age.[12]

According to the Court of Appeal, in determining normal retirement age it is necessary to establish what, at the effective date of the termination of the employee's employment (see below), and on the basis of the facts then known, the age was at which employees of all ages in the employee's position could reasonably regard as the normal retirement age applicable to the group.[13] Thus the expectation is that of the group as a whole and need not be the universal expectation of each and every member of it.[14] Finally, it should be noted that the normal retirement age must be a definite age rather than an age-band.[15]

Continuous service

In order to complain of unfair dismissal one year's continuous service is required.[16] This qualification does not apply if the reason or principal reason for dismissal was 'inadmissible' (see Chapter 14). Continuity is to be calculated up to the effective date of termination in accordance with sections 210–219 ERA 1996. Employees who are wrongfully deprived of their statutory minimum entitlement to notice or receive a payment in lieu can add on that period of notice in ascertaining their length of service.[17] Longer contractual notice cannot be added, and it should be remembered that employees who are guilty of gross misconduct forfeit their entitlement to notice.[18] Two other exceptions should be noted. First, if an employee is dismissed rather than suspended on medical grounds, only one month's service is required.[19] Second, where sex or race discrimination is being alleged, no minimum period of service is needed because the case will be brought under the SDA 1975 or RRA 1976 rather than ERA 1996.

Contracting out

It is possible to contract out of the unfair dismissal and redundancy provisions in the following ways:

(a) An employee will be excluded if a dismissal procedures agreement has been designated by the Secretary of State as exempting those covered by it. An application must be made jointly by all the parties to the agreement and the Secretary of State must be satisfied about the matters listed in section 110(3) ERA 1996.

(b) An agreement to refrain from presenting a complaint will be binding if it has been reached after the involvement of a conciliation officer or satisfies the conditions regulating 'compromise agreements' (see Chapter 16).[20]

(c) An employee employed under a contract of employment for a fixed term of two years or more is not entitled to a redundancy payment if the dismissal consists only of the expiry of that term and, before the term expires, the employee has agreed in writing to exclude any right to a redundancy payment.[21]

THE MEANING OF DISMISSAL

Apart from the lay-off and short-time provisions, an employee is to be treated as dismissed for unfair dismissal and redundancy purposes if:[22]

(a) the contract under which he or she is employed is terminated by the employer with or without notice, or

(b) a fixed-term contract expires without being renewed under the same contract, or

(c) the employee terminates the contract with or without notice in circumstances such that he or she is entitled to terminate it without notice by reason of the employer's conduct.

For redundancy purposes section 174 ERA 1996 provides that a contract is terminated by the employer's death unless the business is carried on by the personal representatives of the deceased. Similarly, if the employee dies after being given notice of dismissal, she or he is to be treated as dismissed.[23] Finally, a court order for the compulsory winding up of a company, the appointment of a receiver by a court and a major split in a partnership can all constitute a termination by the employer.

Termination by the employer with or without notice

It is vitally important not to confuse a warning of impending dismissal – for example through the announcement of a plant closure – with an individual notice to terminate.[24] For the giving of notice to constitute a dismissal at law the actual date of termination must be ascertainable. Where an employer has given notice to terminate, an employee who gives counter-notice indicating that he or she wishes to leave before the employer's notice has expired is still to be regarded as dismissed.[25] However, in the case of redundancy this counter-notice must be given within the 'obligatory period' of the employer's notice. This 'obligatory period' is the minimum period which the employer is required to give by virtue of section 86(1) ERA 1996 (see Chapter 16) or the contract of employment.[26] Before the counter-notice is due to expire the employer can write to the employee and ask for it to be withdrawn, stating that unless this is done liability to make a redundancy payment will be contested.[27] If employees do not accede to such a request, a tribunal is empowered to determine whether they should receive the whole or part of the payment to which they would have been entitled. Tribunals decide what is just and equitable 'having regard to the reason for which the employee seeks to leave the employment and those for which the employer requires him to continue in it'.[28] Another possibility is that an employee leaves before the expiry of the employer's notice of termination for reasons of redundancy by mutual consent. This will not affect entitlement to a redundancy payment.[29]

Mutually agreed termination
A mutually agreed termination does not amount to a dismissal at law, although as a matter of policy tribunals will not find an agreement to terminate unless it is proved that the employee really did agree with full knowledge of the implications. Thus in *Hellyer Bros v Atkinson*[30] it was held that the employee was merely accepting the fact of his dismissal rather than agreeing to terminate his employment.

Whether a mutual agreement is void because of duress is a matter for the employment tribunal.[31] Moreover, where a provision for automatic termination is introduced by way of a variation to a subsisting contract, it may be declared void if its effect is to exclude or limit the operation of ERA 1996.[32] It is possible to have a mutual determination of a contract in a redundancy situation, and in *Birch and Humber v University of Liverpool*[33] the Court of Appeal held that there was no dismissal when the employer accepted the employees' applications for premature retirement. However, where an employer seeks volunteers for redundancy, those who are dismissed will be eligible for a payment despite their willingness to leave.[34]

Obviously, if people resign of their own volition there is no dismissal at law, yet if pressure has been applied, the situation will be different, eg where the employee is given the choice of resigning or being dismissed. However, an invitation to resign must not be too imprecise, and in *Haseltine Lake & Co. v Dowler*[35] it was held that there was no dismissal when the employee was told that if he did not find a job elsewhere his employment would eventually be terminated. It would also appear that there is no dismissal when an employee resigns on terms offered by an employer's disciplinary subcommittee. In *Staffordshire County Council v Donovan*[36] the EAT stated:

> It seems to us that it would be most unfortunate if, in a situation where the parties are seeking to negotiate in the course of disciplinary proceedings and an agreed form of resignation is worked out by the parties, one of the parties should be able to say subsequently that the fact that the agreement was reached in the course of disciplinary proceedings entitles the employee thereafter to say that there was a dismissal.

Problems can arise in determining whether the words used by an employee can properly be regarded as amounting to a resignation. Normally where the words are unequivocal and are understood by the employer as a resignation, it cannot be said that there was no resignation because a reasonable employer would not have so understood the words. However, exceptions will be made in the case of immature employees, decisions taken in the heat of the moment or under pressure exerted by an employer.[37] An objective test of whether the employee intended to resign applies only where the language used is ambiguous or where it is not plain how the employer understood the words. In *Southern v Franks Charlesly*[38] the Court of Appeal decided that the words 'I am resigning' were unambiguous and indicated a present intention of resigning. Equally, doubts can arise in relation to expressions used by an employer, and in *Tanner v Kean*[39] it was decided that the words 'You're finished with me' were merely spoken in annoyance and amounted to a reprimand rather than a dismissal. The EAT has advised tribunals that in deciding whether the employer's words constituted a dismissal in law they should consider all the circumstances of the case to determine whether the words were intended to bring the contract to an end.

Where a fixed-term contract expires

Here 'fixed-term' refers to a contract which has a defined beginning and a defined end. It is to be distinguished from a contract to complete a particular task which is discharged by performance when it is fulfilled,[40] or a contract which ends on the occurrence of a specified event.[41] Nevertheless, if the duration of the task can be established with reasonable precision, a court may hold that the contract was for a fixed term.[42] So long as it is for a specified period a fixed-term contract exists even though it is terminable by notice within that period.[43]

The Court of Appeal has concluded that a contract that has been extended for less than one year can amount to a fixed-term contract of one year or more. Where the period of a contract has been extended by a variation of that contract, the fixed term referred to in section 197(1) ERA 1996 is the whole period of the contract so varied. Thus in *BBC v Kelly-Phillips*,[44] where a temporary assistant's contract was renewed for a further three months, the Court of Appeal held that the employer was able to rely on the employee's agreement to waive the right to claim unfair dismissal.

In *Bhatt v Chelsea and Westminster Health Care Trust*[45] the EAT concluded that there are three possibilities when examining dismissal in the context of fixed-term contracts.[46] These were:

(a) the term expires without being renewed – dismissal

(b) the term expires and there is a renewal under a new contract – dismissal and re-engagement

(c) the term expires and there is a renewal or extension under the same contract – no dismissal.

The EAT held, therefore, that a number of extensions to a

research fellow's three-year contract over an eight-year period, including periods of less than one year, were extensions to the same contract, so that an employee's waiver of his or her rights to an unfair dismissal claim was still valid.

Constructive dismissal

The situation where the employee terminates the contract with or without notice in circumstances such that he or she is entitled to terminate it without notice by reason of the employer's conduct is commonly referred to as a 'constructive' dismissal. In these circumstances the employer's behaviour constitutes a repudiation of the contract and the employee accepts that repudiation by resigning.

Employees are entitled to treat themselves as constructively dismissed only if the employer is guilty of conduct which is a significant breach going to the root of the contract or which shows that the employer no longer intends to be bound by one or more of its essential terms.[47] Whether the repudiatory conduct of a supervisor binds the employer depends on whether the acts were done in the course of the supervisor's employment.[48]

If employees continue for any length of time without leaving, they will be regarded as having elected to affirm the contract and will lose the right to treat themselves as discharged.[49] However, provided that employees make clear their objection to what is being done they are not to be taken to have affirmed the contract by continuing to work and draw pay for a limited period of time.[50] Where the employer has allowed the employee time to make up his or her mind there is no need expressly to reserve the right to accept repudiation.[51] Even though a repudiatory breach of an express term has been waived it could still form part of a series of acts which cumulatively amounted to a breach of the employer's implied duty to show trust and confidence.[52] If there is merely a threat to repudiate, the employee is not to be treated as constructively dismissed unless there has been unequivocal acceptance of the repudiation before the threat is withdrawn.[53]

It is not necessary to show that the employer intended to repudiate the contract. The tribunal's function is to look at the employer's conduct as a whole and determine whether its cumulative effect judged reasonably and sensibly is such that the employee cannot reasonably be expected to tolerate it. The mere fact that a party to a contract takes a view of its construction which is ultimately shown to be wrong does not of itself constitute repudiatory conduct. It has to be shown that he or she did not intend to be bound by the contract as properly construed.[54] According to the Court of Appeal, whether or not there is a fundamental breach of contract is a question of fact, so the EAT cannot substitute its decision for that of an employment tribunal unless the latter misdirected itself in law or the decision was one which no reasonable tribunal could reach.[55]

A physical assault, demotion, or significant change in job duties or place of work[56] can amount to a constructive dismissal. In relation to the place of work, it is now established that even an express right to transfer may be subject to an implied right to reasonable notice, because employers must not exercise their discretion in such a way as to prevent employees from being able to carry out their part of the contract.[57] However, this does not mean that an employer repudiates a contract simply by introducing a general rule with which a particular employee is unable to comply – for example, a no-smoking policy.[58]

In *Millbrook Furnishing Ltd v McIntosh*[59] the EAT accepted that 'if an employer, under the stresses of the requirements of his business, directs an employee to transfer to other suitable work on a purely temporary basis and at no diminution in wages, that may, in the ordinary case, not constitute a breach of contract'. Nevertheless, the EAT has also held that for a breach to go to the root of the contract it need not involve a substantial alteration to terms and conditions on a permanent basis. A substantial alteration is sufficient by itself.[60] As regards demotion, even where this is provided for within a disciplinary procedure it may amount to repudiation if it can be said that the punishment was grossly out of proportion to the offence.[61]

It is clear that an employer is not entitled to alter the formula whereby wages are calculated, but whether a unilateral reduction in additional pay or fringe benefits is of sufficient materiality as to entitle the employee to resign is a matter of degree.[62] A failure to pay an employee's salary or wage is likely to constitute a fundamental breach if it is a deliberate act on the part of an employer rather than a mere breakdown in technology.[63] In *Gardner Ltd v Beresford*,[64] where the employee resigned because she had not received a pay increase for two years while others had, the EAT accepted that in most circumstances it would be reasonable to infer a term that the employer will not treat employees arbitrarily, capriciously or inequitably in the matter of remuneration. However, if a contract makes no reference at all to pay increases, it is impossible to say that there is an implied term that there will always be a pay rise.[65]

Many cases have been decided on the basis that the employer failed to display sufficient trust and confidence in the employee (see Chapter 3). Thus unjustified accusations of theft, foul language or a refusal to act reasonably in dealing with grievances, matters of safety or incidents of harassment could all give rise to a claim of constructive dismissal. According to the EAT, whatever the respective actions of employer and employee at the time of termination, the relevant question is: who really terminated the contract? So when an employer falsely inveigled an employee to resign and take another job with the express purpose of avoiding liability for redundancy it was held that there was a dismissal at law.[66] Similarly, where an employer unilaterally imposes radically different terms of employment, there will be a dismissal under section 95(l)(a) or section 136(1)(a) ERA 1996 if, on an objective construction of the employer's conduct, there is a removal or withdrawal of the old contract. This was held to be the case in *Alcan Extrusions v Yates*[67] where the employer imposed a continuous rolling shift system in place of the traditional shifts provided for in contracts of employment.

THE EFFECTIVE AND RELEVANT DATE OF TERMINATION

Whether a person is qualified to complain of unfair dismissal or has presented a claim within the prescribed time period (see Chapter 16) must be answered by reference to the effective date of termination. Similarly, entitlement to a redundancy payment and the computation of it, together with the time-limit for submitting a claim, all depend on ascertaining the 'relevant date' of dismissal. Thus, as a matter of policy, employers should ensure that there is no doubt as to what constitutes the effective or relevant date. Sections 97 and 145 ERA 1996 provide that:

(a) where the contract is terminated by notice, the effective or relevant date is the date on which the notice expires even though the employee does not work out that notice.[68] Where the employee gives counter-notice, the effective date is when the employee ceased working in accordance with that notice.[69] If the employee has given counter-notice in accordance with section 136(3) ERA 1996, the 'relevant date' is the date the counter-notice expires. However, once an employee has been given notice of redundancy to take effect on a specified date, there is nothing to prevent the employer and employee from altering that date by mutual agreement.[70] In *West v Kneels Ltd*[71] the EAT concluded that oral notice starts to run the day after it is given. Logically, the same should be true of notice in writing

(b) where the contract is determined without notice, the effective or relevant date is the date on which the termination takes effect,[72] although there is no reason why the date cannot be agreed between the parties, even if it is a date that is prior to the agreement itself.[73] The date of termination of people dismissed with payments in lieu of notice is the date on which they are told they are dismissed.[74] According to the Court of Appeal, where an employee is summarily dismissed during the course of a working day, and no question arises as to whether that dismissal constitutes a repudiation which the employee has not accepted, both the contract of employment and the status of employee cease at the moment when the dismissal is communicated to the employee.[75] Where employees are given notice of dismissal and told to work it, but the employer subsequently requires them to leave immediately, the effective or relevant date is the date when they stop working[76]

(c) where a fixed-term contract expires without being renewed under the same contract, the effective or relevant date is the date on which the term expires

(d) where under the redundancy provisions a statutory trial period has been served, for the purpose of submitting a claim in time the relevant date is the day that the new or renewed contract terminated. This is to be assessed in accordance with (a)–(c) above.

It is worth noting that the form P45 has nothing to do with the date on which employment terminates.[77]

Whether in a particular case the words of dismissal evince an intention to terminate the contract at once or an intention to terminate it only at a future date depends on the construction of those words. Such construction should not be technical but reflect what an ordinary reasonable employee would understand by the language used. Moreover, words should be construed in the light of the facts known to the employee at the time of notification.[78] If the language used is ambiguous, it is likely that tribunals will apply the principle that words should be interpreted most strongly against the person who uses them.[79] It should also be observed that where a dismissal has been communicated by letter, the contract of employment does not terminate until the employee has actually read the letter or had a reasonable opportunity of reading it.[80] What is the effective (or relevant) date where there is an appeal against dismissal? According to the House of Lords, unless there is a contractual provision to the contrary, the date of termination is to be ascertained in accordance with the above formula and is not the date on which the employee was informed that his or her appeal had failed.[81]

KEY POINTS 13
Unfair dismissal (1)

- Every employee has the right not to be unfairly dismissed, although there are a number of exclusions and qualifications, such as the need to be under normal retirement age and have one year's continuous service.

- An employee is to be treated as dismissed if his or her contract of employment is terminated by the employer with or without notice, a fixed-term contract expires without renewal or the employee terminates it as a result of the employer's conduct.

- Employees are entitled to treat themselves as constructively dismissed if the employer is guilty of conduct which is a significant breach going to the root of the contract of employment, or which shows that the employer no longer intends to be bound by one or more of its essential terms.

- In order to complain of unfair dismissal, one year's continuous service is required, unless the dismissal is for an inadmissible reason.

- Whether a person is qualified to complain of unfair dismissal or claim a redundancy payment must be answered by reference to the effective date of termination which in the case of termination by notice is the date on which notice expires, or otherwise the date on which termination takes effect.

NOTES

1 Section 94 ERA 1996
2 See sections 199(2) and 191 ERA 1996 respectively
3 See Chapter 8 for issues related to age discrimination in employment
4 Section 109(1) ERA 1996; 'Position' is defined in section 235(1) ERA 1996 as meaning the following matters taken as a whole: status, the nature of the work, and the terms and conditions of employment. See *Brookes v British Telecom* (1992) IRLR 67
5 See section 109(2) ERA 1996 and section 154 TULRCA 1992; for issues

about whether the upper age-limit is discriminatory against men, see Chapter 8

6 (1999) IRLR 362
7 (1979) IRLR 35
8 See *Barber v Thames TV* (1992) IRLR 410
9 (1994) IRLR 580
10 See *Bratko v Walmsley* (1995) IRLR 629
11 See *Whittle v MSC* (1987) IRLR 441
12 See *Waite v GCHQ* (1983) IRLR 341
13 See *Brookes v British Telecom* (note 4); on identifying the particular group see *Barber v Thames TV* (note 8)
14 See *Barclays Bank v O'Brien* (1994) IRLR 580
15 See *Swaine v HSE* (1986) IRLR 205
16 It should be noted that the qualification period was two years' continuous service until changed to one year by the Unfair Dismissal and Statement of Reasons For Dismissal (Variation of Qualifying Period) Regulations 1999 SI 1436; the compatibility of the two-year period with EU law was challenged at the ECJ in *R v Secretary of State for Employment ex parte Seymour-Smith and Perez* (1999) IRLR 253
17 Sections 97(2) and 213(1) ERA 1996; see *Staffordshire CC v Secretary of State* (1989) IRLR 117
18 See *Lanton Leisure v White* (1987) IRLR 119
19 Section 108(2) ERA 1996
20 Section 203(2)(e) and (f) ERA 1996
21 Section 197(3) ERA 1996
22 Sections 95 and 136 ERA 1996
23 See section 176 ERA 1996
24 See *Doble v Firestone Tyre* (1981) IRLR 300
25 Section 95(2) ERA 1996 and *Ready Case Ltd v Jackson* (1981) IRLR 312
26 Section 136(4) ERA 1996
27 Section 142(2) ERA 1996
28 Section 142(3) ERA 1996
29 See *CPS Recruitment Ltd v Bowen* (1982) IRLR 54
30 (1994) IRLR 88
31 See *Logan Salton v Durham CC* (1989) IRLR 99
32 See *Igbo v Johnson Matthey* (1986) IRLR 215 and ACAS Advisory Handbook *Discipline at Work*
33 (1985) IRLR 165; see also *Scott v Coalite* (1988) IRLR 131
34 *Burton v Peck* (1975) IRLR 87
35 (1981) IRLR 25
36 (1981) IRLR 108; see also *Logan Salton v Durham CC* (note 31)
37 See *Kwik Fit v Lineham* (1992) IRLR 156
38 (1981) IRLR 278
39 (1978) IRLR 110
40 See *Ironmonger v Movefield* (1988) IRLR 461
41 See *Brown v Knowsley BC* (1986) IRLR 461
42 See *Wiltshire County Council v NATFHE and Guy* (1980) IRLR 198
43 See *Dixon v BBC* (1979) IRLR 114
44 (1998) IRLR 295
45 (1997) IRLR 660
46 See section 95(1)(b) ERA 1996
47 See *Brown v Merchant Ferries Ltd* (1998) IRLR 682, where the employer's

conduct was not such that it could be interpreted as a constructive dismissal

48 See *Hilton Hotels v Protopapa* (1990) IRLR 316
49 See *Wilton v Cornwall Health Authority* (1993) IRLR 482
50 See *Rigby v Ferodo Ltd* (1987) IRLR 516
51 See *Bliss v South East Thames Regional Health Authority* (1985) IRLR 308
52 See *Lewis v Motorworld Garages* (1985) IRLR 465
53 See *Harrison v Norwest Holst* (1985) IRLR 240
54 See *Brown v JBD Engineering Ltd* (1993) IRLR 568
55 See *Martin v MBS Fastenings* (1983) IRLR 198
56 See *Aparau v Iceland Frozen Foods* (1996) IRLR 119
57 See *White v Reflecting Roadstuds* (1991) IRLR 332
58 See *Dryden v Greater Glasgow Health Board* (1992) IRLR 469
59 (1981) IRLR 309
60 See *McNeil v Crimin Ltd* (1984) IRLR 179
61 See *Cawley v South Wales Electricity Board* (1985) IRLR 89
62 See *Rigby v Ferodo Ltd* (note 50)
63 See *Cantor Fitzgerald International v Callaghan* (1999) IRLR 234
64 (1978) IRLR 63
65 See *Murco Petroleum v Forge* (1987) IRLR 50
66 See *Caledonian Mining Ltd v Bassett* (1987) IRLR 165
67 (1996) IRLR 327
68 See *TBA Industrial Products Ltd v Morland* (1982) IRLR 331
69 See *Thompson v GEC Avionics* (1991) IRLR 448
70 See *Mowlem Ltd v Watson* (1990) IRLR 500
71 (1986) IRLR 430
72 This principle was applied to a constructive dismissal in *BMK Ltd v Logue* (1993) ICR 601
73 See *Lambert v Croydon College* (1999) IRLR 346
74 See *R. Cort & Son Ltd v Charman* (1981) IRLR 437
75 See *Octavius Atkinson Ltd v Morris* (1989) IRLR 158
76 See *Stapp v Shaftesbury Society* (1982) IRLR 326
77 See *Leech v Preston BC* (1985) IRLR 337
78 See *London Borough of Newham v Ward* (1985) IRLR 509
79 See *Chapman v Letheby & Christopher Ltd* (1981) IRLR 440
80 See *McMaster v Manchester Airport plc* (1998) IRLR 112
81 See *West Midlands Co-op Ltd v Tipton* (1986) IRLR 112

14 Unfair dismissal (2)

We continue our examination of the rules concerning unfair dismissal by looking at the procedures to be followed after an employee has established that he or she qualifies to make a claim. We begin by looking at the burden on employers to show the reason for dismissal, and then consider those reasons that are automatically unfair. We study the potentially fair reasons of capability or qualifications, conduct, statutory ban and some other substantial reason. We consider the particular rules that apply to dismissals during industrial action and the amendments made by the Employment Relations Act 1999. Finally, we look at the ACAS Code of Practice on Disciplinary Practice and Procedures as well as the advisory handbook on *Discipline at Work*.

GIVING A REASON FOR DISMISSAL

Once employees have proved that they were dismissed, the burden shifts to the employer to show the reason, or, if there was more than one, the principal reason, for the dismissal and that it falls within one of the following categories.[1]

(a) It relates to the capacity or qualifications of the employee for performing work of the kind which he or she was employed to do.

(b) It relates to the conduct of the employee.

(c) The employee was redundant.

(d) The employee could not continue to work in the position held without contravention, either on the employee's part or that of the employer, of a duty or restriction imposed by or under a statute.

(e) There was some other substantial reason of such a kind as to justify the dismissal of an employee holding the position which the employee held.

Several points need to be made at this stage:

(a) Where no reason is given by the employer, a dismissal will be unfair simply because the statutory burden has not been discharged. Equally, if a reason is engineered in order to effect dismissal because the real reason would not be acceptable, the employer will fail because the underlying principal reason is not within section 98(1) or (2) ERA 1996.[2]

(b) The fact that an employer has inaccurately described the reason for dismissal is not necessarily fatal, for it is the tribunal's task to discover what reason actually motivated the employer at the time of dismissal. That the correct approach is the subjective one has been confirmed by the Court of Appeal: 'A reason for the dismissal of an employee is a set of facts known to the employer, or it may be of beliefs held by him which causes him to dismiss the employee.'[3] Subsequently the Court of Appeal has been prepared to attribute a reason for dismissal even where the employers had argued throughout the case that they had not dismissed but the employee had resigned.[4]

(c) The reason for dismissal must have existed and been known to the employer at the time of dismissal, which makes it impossible, for example, to rely on subsequently discovered misconduct.[5] The reason itself may be an anticipated event – eg if an employee is subject to a long period of notice, it is possible to give notice in anticipation of a decision and giving what the employer expects to happen as a reason for the dismissal.[6]

(d) Section 107 ERA 1996 provides that in determining the reason for dismissal, or whether it was sufficient to dismiss, a tribunal cannot take account of any pressure, in the form of industrial action or a threat of it, which was exercised on the employer to secure the employee's dismissal. It is not necessary that those exerting the pressure explicitly sought the dismissal of the employee: the test is whether it could be foreseen that the pressure would be likely to result in dismissal.[7]

According to section 92 ERA 1996, a person who has been continuously employed for one year[8] and has been dismissed or is under notice of dismissal has the right to be supplied with a written statement giving particulars of the reasons for dismissal. The employer must provide the statement within 14 days of a specific request being made. In *Gilham v Kent County Council*[9] the Court of Appeal held that the council had responded adequately by referring the employee's legal representative to two previous letters in which the reasons for dismissal were fully set out, enclosing copies of those letters and stating that their contents contained the reasons for dismissal. A claim may be presented to an employment tribunal on the ground that the employer unreasonably failed to provide such a statement or that the particulars given were inadequate or untrue. However, section 92 merely obliges employers to indicate truthfully the reasons they were relying on when they dismissed. Only if an unfair dismissal claim is brought will a tribunal have to examine whether the reasons given justify dismissal.[10] The same time-limit applies as for unfair dismissal claims (see Chapter 16).

The test for determining the reasonableness of an employer's failure is objective. Thus, where the employer maintains that there was no dismissal in law but the tribunal finds that there was, it must then decide whether there was an unreasonable failure to supply a statement.[11] If the complaint is well-founded, a tribunal may make a declaration as to what it finds the employer's reasons were for dismissing and must order that the employee receive two weeks' pay from the employer.[12] Perhaps the most important aspect of this section is that such a statement is admissible in evidence in any proceedings. This means that an employee who detects any inconsistency between the particulars given and the reasons offered as a defence to an unfair dismissal claim – eg on the employer's 'notice of appearance' – can exploit the situation to the full.

AUTOMATICALLY UNFAIR DISMISSAL

In certain circumstances a dismissal will be unfair because the reason for it was 'inadmissible'. Thus a dismissal will be automatically unfair if the reason for it related to any of the following:

(a) the assertion of a statutory right (see below)

(b) trade union membership or activities, or non-union membership (see Chapter 20)

(c) family reasons (see Chapter 9)

(d) certain health and safety grounds (see below)

(e) certain shop workers and betting workers who refuse to work on a Sunday[13]

(f) workers dismissed for refusing to comply with a requirement which is in contravention of the WT Regulations 1998 (see Chapter 11)[14]

(g) the reason, or the principal reason, for the dismissal is that the employee made a protected disclosure (see Chapter 3)[15]

(h) the employee is dismissed for trying to enforce the national minimum wage[16]

(i) the proposed or actual performance of any of the functions of an employee trustee of a pension scheme[17]

(j) the proposed or actual performance of any functions or activities as an employee representative or candidate[18]

(k) the dismissal of a worker for exercising rights in relation to the statutory recognition of a trade union (see Chapter 21)

(l) the dismissal of a worker within eight weeks of taking part in protected industrial action (see below)

(m) the application of the Tax Credit Act 1999[18a]

Additionally, if an 'inadmissible' reason was used to select a person for redundancy, then dismissal will also be unfair (see below). Other unfair reasons for dismissal are those connected to transfers of undertakings (see Chapter 15); to the SDA 1975 and the RRA 1976, which stipulate that it is unlawful to discriminate on the prohibited grounds by way of dismissal (see Chapter 7); to the Rehabilitation of Offenders Act 1974, which states that 'a conviction which has become spent . . . shall not be a proper ground for dismissing';[19] and finally to section 4(2) of the Disability Discrimination Act 1995, which states that it is unlawful to discriminate against disabled persons by dismissing them (see Chapter 8).

Asserting statutory rights

As regards the assertion of statutory rights, employees are protected if they have brought proceedings against the employer to enforce a 'relevant' statutory right or have alleged that the employer has infringed such a right. The 'relevant' statutory rights are:

(a) any right conferred by ERA 1996 which may be the subject of a complaint to an employment tribunal

(b) minimum notice rights under section 86 ERA 1996

(c) certain rights relating to the unlawful deduction of union contributions from pay, action short of dismissal on union membership grounds, and time off for union duties and activities

(d) rights afforded by the WT Regulations 1998

(e) rights afforded by the ERel Act 1999 in relation to statutory recognition of trade unions.

It should be noted that employees are protected irrespective of whether they qualify for the right that has been asserted or whether the right was actually infringed. All that has to be demonstrated is that the employee's claim was made in good faith.[20]

Health and safety

In relation to health and safety, section 100 ERA 1996 provides that a dismissal is unfair if the reason for it was that the employee:

(a) carried out, or proposed to carry out, activities designated by the employer in connection with preventing or reducing risks to the health and safety of employees

(b) performed, or proposed to perform, any of his or her functions as a safety representative or a member of a safety committee

(c) took part or proposed to take part in consultation with the employer pursuant to the HSCE Regulations 1996 (see Chapter 10) or in an election of representatives of employee safety within the meaning of those Regulations

(d) where there was no safety representative or committee or it was not reasonably practicable to raise the matter in that way, brought to the employer's attention, by reasonable means, circumstances connected with his or her work which he or she reasonably believed were harmful or potentially harmful to health and safety

(e) left or proposed to leave, or refused to return to (while the danger persisted), his or her place of work or any dangerous part of the workplace, in circumstances of danger which he or she reasonably believed to be serious and imminent and which he or she could not reasonably have been expected to avert

(f) took, or proposed to take, appropriate steps to protect himself or herself or other persons, in circumstances of danger which he or she reasonably believed to be serious and imminent. Whether those steps were 'appropriate' must be judged by reference to all the circumstances, including the employee's knowledge and the facilities and advice available at the time. A dismissal will not be regarded as unfair if the employer can show that it was, or would have been, so negligent for the employee to take the steps which he or she took, or proposed to take, that a reasonable employer might have dismissed on these grounds.

POTENTIALLY FAIR REASONS FOR DISMISSAL

Capability or qualifications

According to section 98(3) ERA 1996, 'capability' is to be assessed by reference to 'skill, aptitude, health or any other physical or mental quality', and it has been held that an employee's inflexibility or lack of adaptability came within his or her aptitude and mental qualities.[21] 'Qualifications' means 'any degree, diploma, or other academic, technical or professional qualification relevant to the position which the employee held'. In *Blue Star Ltd v Williams*[22] it was held that a mere licence, permit or authorisation is not such a qualification unless it is substantially concerned with the aptitude or ability of the person to do the job.

For our purposes it is convenient to consider capability in terms of competence and ill health. As regards competence, the ACAS advisory handbook *Discipline at Work* recommends that the following principles should be observed when employment commences:

(a) The standard of work required should be explained and employees left in no doubt about what is expected of them. Special attention should be paid to ensuring that standards are understood by employees whose English is limited and by young persons with little experience of working life.

(b) Where job descriptions are prepared, they should accurately convey the main purpose and scope of each job and the tasks involved.

(c) Employees should be made aware of the conditions which attach to any probation period.

(d) The consequences of any failure to meet the required standards should be explained.

(e) Where an employee is promoted, the consequences of failing to 'make the grade' in the new job should be explained.

It almost goes without saying that proper training and supervision are essential to the achievement of satisfactory performance and that performance should be discussed regularly with employees. Measures should be taken to ensure that inadequate performance is identified as soon as possible so that remedial action can be taken. In all cases, the cause of poor performance should be investigated, and the

ACAS advisory handbook *Discipline at Work* suggests the following guidelines to ensure that appropriate action is taken:

(a) the employee should be asked for an explanation and the explanation checked

(b) where the reason is a lack of the required skills, the employee should, wherever practicable, be assisted through training and given reasonable time to reach the required standard of performance

(c) where, despite encouragement and assistance, the employee is unable to reach the required standard of performance, consideration should be given to finding suitable alternative work

(d) where alternative work is not available, the position should be explained to the employee before dismissal action is taken

(e) an employee should not normally be dismissed because of poor performance unless warnings and a chance to improve have been given

(f) if the main cause of poor performance is the changing nature of the job, employers should consider whether the situation may properly be treated as a redundancy matter rather than a capability or conduct issue.

Finally, it is important to distinguish cases of sheer incapability owing to an inherent incapacity to function from those where there is a failure to exercise to the full such talent as is possessed. According to the EAT, cases where people have not come up to standard through their own carelessness, negligence or idleness are much more appropriately dealt with as cases of misconduct than of incapability.[23]

As regards ill health, it must be emphasised at the outset that the decision to dismiss is not a medical one but a matter to be determined by the employer in the light of the medical evidence available. The basic question is whether in all the circumstances the employer could have been expected to wait any longer for the employee to recover, and the factors taken into account in deciding whether a contract has been frustrated will be relevant here (see Chapter 12). Where an employee is absent owing to long-term illness the ACAS advisory handbook recommends that the following procedure be invoked:

(a) the employee should be contacted periodically and in turn should maintain regular contact with the employer[24]

(b) the employee should be kept fully informed if employment is at risk

(c) the employee's GP should be asked when a return to work is expected and what type of work the employee will be capable of

(d) on the basis of the GP's report the employer should consider whether alternative work is available

(e) the employer is not expected to create a special job for the employee concerned, nor to be a medical expert, but to take action on the basis of the medical evidence

(f) where there is reasonable doubt about the nature of the illness or injury, the employee should be asked if he or she would agree to be examined by a doctor to be appointed by the company

(g) where an employee refuses to co-operate in providing medical evidence or to undergo an independent medical examination, the employee should be told in writing that a decision will be taken on the basis of the information available and that it could result in dismissal

(h) where the employee is allergic to a product used in the workplace, the employer should consider remedial action or a transfer to alternative work

(i) where the employee's job can no longer be kept open and no suitable alternative work is available, the employee should be informed of the likelihood of dismissal

(j) where dismissal action is taken, the employee should be given the period of notice to which he or she is entitled and informed of any right of appeal.

In cases of intermittent absences owing to ill health, there is no obligation on an employer to call medical evidence. According to the EAT, an employer has to have regard to the whole history of employment and to take into account a range of factors including: the nature of the illness and the likelihood of its recurrence; the lengths of absences compared with the intervals of good health; the employer's need for that particular employee; the impact of the absences on the rest of the workforce; and the extent to which the employee was made aware of his or her position. There is no principle that the mere fact that the employee is fit at the time of dismissal makes that dismissal unfair.[25]

In deciding whether an employer acted fairly in dismissing, tribunals must determine as a matter of fact what consultation, if any, was necessary or desirable in the known circumstances; what consultation took place; and whether that consultation process was adequate in the circumstances.[26] Thus in *Eclipse Blinds v Wright*[27] the Court of Appeal ruled that it was not unfair to dismiss without consultation where the employer was genuinely concerned about giving the employee information about her health of which she seemed unaware.

Four further points need to be made:

(a) An employee's incapability need only 'relate to' the performance of contractual duties; there is no requirement to show that the performance of all those duties has been affected.[28]

(b) Although employees who are sick will hope to remain employed at least until their contractual sick pay entitlement (if any) is exhausted, this does not mean that a person cannot be dismissed before the period of sick pay has elapsed (see Chapter 6 on avoiding liability for SSP). Equally, it will be unfair to dismiss simply because the sick pay period has expired.

(c) The employer's duty to act fairly is unaffected by considerations as to who was responsible for the employee's unfitness to work.[29]

(d) An employee who has become incapable of work may have to be treated as a person with a disability within the meaning of section 1 of the Disability Discrimination Act 1995 (see Chapter 8).

Conduct

It is the function of tribunals to decide not whether misconduct is gross or criminal but whether the employer has, in the circumstances of the case, acted reasonably in dismissing. There is no necessary inference that because an employee is guilty of gross misconduct in relation to his or her particular job, he or she must necessarily be considered unsuitable for any employment whatsoever.[30] Clearly there will be cases where the misconduct is sufficiently serious that an employee can be dismissed without warning, and paragraph 8 of the ACAS *Code of Practice on Disciplinary Practice and Procedures in Employment* (1977) advocates that employees should be given 'a clear indication of the type of conduct which may warrant summary dismissal'.

According to the EAT, disciplinary rules which fail to follow the ACAS Code in specifying those offences that constitute gross misconduct and justify dismissal at the first breach will be defective. In *Lock v Cardiff Railway Company Ltd*[31] a train conductor was dismissed for gross misconduct when he asked a 16-year-old to leave the train because he did not have a valid ticket or sufficient money to pay the excess fare. The employer's disciplinary code did not specify which offences would be regarded as gross misconduct that would result in dismissal for the first offence. As a result the EAT held that no reasonable tribunal properly directing itself could have concluded that the dismissal was fair.

Fighting is an example of an area where it is not necessary to state that such behaviour will be regarded very gravely, since the courts have decided that whether or not to dismiss for this reason is essentially a matter for the employer. The test is what would be the reaction of a reasonable employer in the circumstances. Thus, if without proper inquiry an employer implements a policy of dismissing any employee who struck another, there could be a finding of unfairness.[32] Similarly, false clocking or claims in respect of hours done are serious offences which can justify dismissal without a warning if the employer has had due regard to all the circumstances.[33]

As a general rule, if an order is lawful, a refusal to obey it will be a breach of contract and amount to misconduct even though similar refusals have been condoned in the past. Nevertheless, in disobedience cases the primary factor to be considered is whether the employee is acting reasonably in refusing to carry out an instruction.[34] Acknowledging that employers are obliged to issue instructions in order to ensure compliance with health and safety legislation, tribunals have readily accepted that non-compliance with safety rules or procedures constitutes sufficient grounds for dismissal.

The intention to set up in competition with the employer is not in itself a breach of the implied duty of loyalty. Unless the employer has reasonable grounds for believing that the employee has done or is about to do some wrongful act, dismissal will not be justified.[35] Thus in *Marshall v Industrial Systems Ltd*[36] the EAT held that it was reasonable to dismiss a managing director after discovering that with another manager he was planning to set up in competition and take away the business of their best client, and that he tried to induce another key employee to join them in that venture.

Theft of an employer's property will amount to a fair reason for dismissal; far more difficult to handle are cases of *suspected* dishonesty. The Court of Appeal has approved of the approach taken to this delicate matter in *British Home Stores v Burchell*,[37] where it was stated that tribunals had to decide whether the employer entertained a reasonable suspicion amounting to a belief in the guilt of the employee at that time. There are three elements to this:

(a) the employer must establish the fact of that belief

(b) the employer must show that there were reasonable grounds upon which to sustain that belief

(c) at the stage at which the belief was formed the employer must have carried out as much investigation into the matter as was reasonable in the circumstances.

Thus the question to be determined is not whether, by an objective standard, the employer's belief that the employee was guilty of the misconduct was well-founded but whether the employer believed that the employee was guilty and was entitled so to believe having regard to the investigation conducted.[38] If these requirements are met, it is irrelevant that the employee is acquitted of criminal charges or that they are dropped. However, according to the EAT, *Burchell's* case[38a] should not be understood as saying that an employer who fails one or more of the three tests is, without more, guilty of unfair dismissal. There has been further consideration of this in *Haddon's* case (see below).[39]

Where there is a reasonable suspicion that one or more employees within a group have acted dishonestly, it is not necessary for the employer to identify which of them acted dishonestly.[40] Thus, provided certain conditions are satisfied, an employer who cannot identify which member of a group was responsible for an act can fairly dismiss the whole group, even where it is probable that not all were guilty of the act. These conditions are:

(a) the act must be such that if committed by an identified individual it would justify dismissal

(b) the employer had made a sufficiently thorough investigation with appropriate procedures

(c) as a result of that investigation the employer reasonably believed that more than one person could have committed the act

(d) the employer had acted reasonably in identifying the group of employees who could have committed the act and each member of the group was individually capable of doing so

(e)   between the members of the group the employer could not reasonably identify the individual perpetrator.

The fact that one or more of the group is not dismissed does not necessarily render the dismissal of the remainder unfair, provided the employer is able to show solid and sensible grounds for differentiating between members of the group.[41]

In certain cases it will be reasonable to rely on the results of extensive police investigation rather than carry out independent inquiries.[42] Similarly, where an employee admits dishonesty there is little scope for the kind of investigation referred to in *Burchell's* case. Where the probability of guilt is less apparent, the safer course may be to suspend until any criminal proceedings have been completed. Whether a conviction forms an adequate basis for dismissal will depend to some extent on the nature of the crime. Clearly there may be cases where the offence is trivial and dismissal would be unreasonable.[43]

The fact that employees have been charged with a criminal offence does not prevent the employer communicating with them or their representatives to discuss the matter. What needs to be discussed is not so much the alleged offence as the action which the employer is proposing to take. If the employee chooses not to give a statement to the employer, the latter is entitled to consider whether the evidence available is strong enough to justify dismissal.[44] However, it will not always be wrong to dismiss before a belief in guilt has been established, because involvement in an alleged criminal offence often involves a serious breach of duty or discipline. Even when charged by the police for a criminal offence, failure to give employees an opportunity to explain themselves may render the dismissal unfair.[45]

In the context of unfair dismissal, conduct may mean actions of such a nature, whether done in the course of employment or outside, that reflect in some way on the employer-employee relationship.[46] Thus it may cover the wilful concealment of convictions which are not 'spent', criminal offences outside employment, such as stealing or gross indecency, or even 'moonlighting'. Finally, in an appropriate case it may be unfair to dismiss without first considering whether the employee could be offered some other job.[47]

Statutory ban

Section 98(2)(d) ERA 1996 states that if it would be unlawful to continue to work in the position which the employee held, there is a valid reason for dismissing. In *Bouchaala v Trust House Forte*[48] the EAT held that the absence of the words 'related to' in this section were significant, and that a genuine but erroneous belief is insufficient for these purposes. Again, a tribunal must be satisfied that the requirements of section 98(4) ERA 1996 have been met. Thus the loss of a permit or licence may fall within section 98(2)(d) ERA 1996, but in deciding what is reasonable, attention will focus on whether the legal ban is permanent or temporary. If the former, an employer might be expected to consider the feasibility of redeployment, and if the latter, short-term alternative work might be offered. Whether such measures should be taken will depend on the type of business and the employee's work record. Of course, in some circumstances it may be possible for employees to continue in their normal job by making special arrangements – eg a sales representative who has been disqualified from driving may be prepared to hire a driver at his or her own expense in order to remain in employment.

Some other substantial reason

Section 98(1)(b) ERA 1996 was included in the legislative scheme so as to give tribunals the discretion to accept as a fair reason for dismissal something that would not conveniently fit into any of the other categories. It covers such diverse matters as dismissal for being sentenced to imprisonment,[49] being dismissed as manager of a public house because a partner had resigned from jointly holding the position,[50] refusing to sign an undertaking not to compete,[51] or because the employer's best customer was unwilling to accept the particular individual.[52] However, in *Wadley v Eager Electrical*[53] the EAT decided that an employee's dismissal on the grounds that there had been breaches of trust by his wife during her employment with the employer did not amount to a substantial reason.

Whether the non-renewal of a fixed-term contract amounts to some other substantial reason depends on whether the case is one where the employee has, to his or her own knowledge, been employed for a particular period or a particular job on a temporary basis. Tribunals have to draw a balance between the need to protect employers who have a genuine requirement for fixed-term employment which can be seen from the outset not to be ongoing and the need to protect employees.[54] When considering whether the ending of a fixed-term contract amounted to an unfair redundancy dismissal, the tribunal will take into account whether there has been unfair selection, a lack of consultation and a failure to seek alternative employment on the part of the employer – the latter two points being an indication of whether the employer had proceeded reasonably.[55]

According to the Court of Appeal, tribunals have to decide whether the reason established by the employer falls within the category of reasons which *could* justify the dismissal of an employee holding the position that the employee held.[56] Employers cannot claim that a reason for dismissal is substantial if it is whimsical or capricious. Nevertheless, if they can show that they genuinely believed a reason to be fair and that they had it in mind at the time of dismissal,[57] this would bring the case within section 98(1)(b) ERA 1996. It may be held that the reason was substantial even though more sophisticated opinion can be adduced to demonstrate that the belief had no scientific foundation.[58] The notion of genuine belief has also been invoked to assist employers who are unable to rely on any other reasons for dismissal owing to an error of fact. Thus this subsection could be relied on where an employee was dismissed as a result of the employer's mistaken belief that a work permit was needed.[59]

'Some other substantial reason' has frequently provided a convenient peg on which employees have been hung for dismissal as a result of a reorganisation of the business. The Court of Appeal has taken the view that it is not necessary for an employer to show that in the absence of a reorganisation there would be a total business disaster. It is sufficient if there is a sound business reason, which means only that there is a reason which management thinks on reasonable grounds is sound.[60] If the employer can satisfy a tribunal that a certain policy has evolved which was thought to have discernible advantages, then dismissal in accordance with that policy can be said to be for 'some other substantial reason'.

Where an employee refuses to agree changes consequent upon a reorganisation, the test to be applied by tribunals is not simply whether the terms offered were those which a reasonable employer could offer. Looking at the employer's offer alone would exclude from scrutiny everything that happened between the time the offer was made and the dismissal – eg a potentially significant factor is whether other employees accepted the offer.[61] Equally, there is no principle of law that if new contractual terms are much less favourable to an employee than the previous ones, dismissal for refusing to accept them will be unfair unless the business reasons are so pressing that it is vital for the survival of the business that the revised terms are accepted. In *Farrant v The Woodroffe School*[62] an employee was dismissed for refusing to accept organisational changes. The employer mistakenly believed that the employee was obliged to accept a new job description and that the dismissal was therefore lawful. The EAT held that dismissal for refusing to obey an unlawful order was not necessarily unfair. Of importance was not the lawfulness or otherwise of the employer's instructions but the overall question of reasonableness. In this case it was not unreasonable for them to act on professional advice, even if that advice was wrong. Tribunals will examine an employer's motive for introducing changes in order to ensure that they are not being imposed arbitrarily.[63] The reasonable employer will explore all the alternatives to dismissal but, like consultation with trade unions and the individual concerned, such a consideration is only one of the factors which must be taken into account under section 98(4) ERA 1996.

INDUSTRIAL ACTION AND LACK OF JURISDICTION

Protected industrial action

Prior to the ERel Act 1999, a tribunal was excluded from determining whether the dismissal of an employee during an 'official' strike was fair or unfair unless it could be shown that one or more 'relevant' employees of the same employer had not been dismissed, or that within three months of the complainant's dismissal any such employee had been offered re-engagement and the complainant had not.

This changed after the ERel Act 1999. The amended section 238A TULRCA is concerned with workers engaged in 'protected industrial action'.[64] This section states that a dismissal will be unfair if the reason is that the employee took part in protected industrial action and one of three situations applies:

(a) the dismissal takes place within a period of eight weeks from the day in which the employee first took part in the protected industrial action

(b) the dismissal takes place after that eight-week period and the employee had ceased to take part in protected industrial action before the end of that period

(c) the dismissal takes place after the end of the period and the employee has not ceased to take part in the protected industrial action before the end of that period and the employer has not taken such procedural steps as would have been reasonable for the purpose of resolving the dispute to which the action relates.

In deciding whether an employer has taken those steps mentioned in (c) above, tribunals will look at whether the employer or union[65]

(i) has followed procedures established by a collective agreement

(ii) had offered or agreed to start or resume negotiations after the start of the protected industrial action

(iii) unreasonably refused a request that conciliation services be used

(iv) unreasonably refused a request that mediation services be used.

The fact that employees are in breach of their duty to attend work is relevant to the question of whether they are taking part in a strike but it is not an essential ingredient. Thus employees who are off sick or on holiday could be held to be taking part in a strike if they associated themselves with it, for example by attending a picket line.[66] By way of contrast, if sick employees merely wish their colleagues well, this may be regarded as supportive but would not amount to taking part in industrial action.[67]

Although there is no statutory definition of a lock-out, dictionary definitions suggest that it means an employer's refusal to provide employees with work except on conditions which have to be accepted by the workforce collectively.[68] According to the EAT, if an employer does no more than insist that his employees should abide by their existing terms and conditions of employment if they are to return to work, that does not constitute a lock-out.[69]

An offer of re-engagement refers to an offer (made either by the employer, a successor or an associated employer) to re-engage either in the job which the employee held immediately before the date of dismissal, or in a different job which would be 'reasonably suitable in his case'.[70] In *Williams v National Theatre*[71] it was decided that treating employees who had been on strike as having received a second warning nevertheless constituted an offer to re-engage in the same job. However, a job may have conditions attached to it which are so disadvantageous compared to the position before the dismissal that it cannot realistically be suggested that the employee is being offered re-employment.

Unofficial action
The E Rel Act 1999 did not change the position with regard to those taking part in unofficial action. By virtue of section 237 TULRCA 1992 employees cannot complain of unfair

dismissal if at the time of dismissal they were taking part in an unofficial strike or other unofficial industrial action. For these purposes, a strike or other industrial action will be treated as unofficial unless the employee:

(a) is a union member and the action is authorised or endorsed by that union, or

(b) is not a union member but there are among those taking part in the industrial action members of a union by which the action has been authorised or endorsed within the meaning of section 20(2) TULRCA 1992 (see Chapter 21).

A strike or other industrial action will not be regarded as unofficial if none of those taking part in it is a union member. However, employees who were union members when they began to take industrial action will continue to be treated as such even if they have subsequently ceased to be union members.[72]

Section 237(4) TULRCA 1992 states that the issue of whether or not the action is unofficial is to be determined by reference to the facts at the time of the dismissal. Nevertheless, where the action is repudiated in accordance with section 21 TULRCA 1992 (see Chapter 21), the industrial action is not to be treated as unofficial before the end of the next working day after the repudiation has taken place. On the absence of statutory immunity for acts in support of those dismissed for taking unofficial action see Chapter 19.

REASONABLENESS IN THE CIRCUMSTANCES

Where the employer has given a valid reason for dismissal, the determination of the question whether the dismissal was fair or unfair

(a) depends on whether in the circumstances (including the size and administrative resources of the employer's undertaking) the employer acted reasonably or unreasonably in treating it as a sufficient reason for dismissing the employee, and

(b) shall be determined in accordance with equity and the substantial merits of the case.[73]

As a matter of law, a reason cannot be treated as a sufficient reason where it has not been established as true or that there were reasonable grounds on which the employer could have concluded that it was true.[74]

Under section 98(4) ERA 1996, tribunals must take account of the wider circumstances. In addition to the employer's business needs, attention must be paid to the personal attributes of the employee – for example, seniority and previous work record. Thus when all the relevant facts are considered, a dismissal may be deemed unfair notwithstanding the fact that the disciplinary rules specified that such behaviour would result in immediate dismissal.[75] Conversely, employers may act reasonably in dismissing even though they have breached an employee's contract.[76]

Employers will be expected to treat employees in similar circumstances in a similar way. The requirement that the employer must act consistently between all employees means that an employer should consider truly comparable cases which were known about or ought to have been known about. Nevertheless, the overriding principle seems to be that each case must be considered on its own facts and with the freedom to consider both aggravating factors and mitigating circumstances.[77] The words 'equity and the substantial merits' also allow tribunals to apply their knowledge of good industrial relations practice and to ensure that there has been procedural fairness (see below).[78]

Traditionally, employment tribunals were not encouraged to ask themselves whether they would have done what the employer did in the circumstances; their function was merely to assess the employer's decision to dismiss, to see whether it fell within a range of responses which a reasonable employer could have taken.[79] This view was challenged in *Haddon v Van Den Bergh*[80] when the EAT concluded that it was permissible for employment tribunals to form their own view, provided that they went on to consider the test of reasonableness. This requires the application of the ordinary meaning of the words contained in section 98(4)(a) and (b) ERA 1996.

THE CODE OF PRACTICE AND PROCEDURAL FAIRNESS

The ACAS *Code of Practice of Disciplinary Practice and Procedures in Employment* (revised 1997) does not have the force of law, so failure to comply with it does not make a dismissal automatically unfair. It will, however, weigh heavily against the employer if not followed.[81] Indeed, where there is a procedural defect the question to be answered is, did the employer's procedure constitute a fair process? A dismissal will be unfair either where there was a defect of such seriousness that the procedure itself was unfair or where the results of the defect taken overall were unfair. Thus in *Fuller v Lloyds Bank*[82] the failure to provide witness statements was a breach of company policy but the dismissal was fair because the employee knew exactly what was being alleged.

In certain circumstances there may be a good excuse for not following the Code – for example, if the inadequacy of the employee's performance is extreme or the actual or potential consequences of a mistake are grave, warnings may not be necessary.[83] Although it is management's responsibility to ensure that there are adequate disciplinary rules and procedures, the Code mentions the desirability of union involvement in agreeing procedural arrangements.[84] Naturally, tribunals tend to pay greater attention to agreed rather than unilaterally imposed procedures. The rules required will again depend on the nature of the employment but they should be reasonable in themselves, consistently enforced, and reviewed in the light of legal developments and organisational needs. Employees should know and understand the rules and be made aware of the likely consequences of breaking them.[85]

The essential features of a disciplinary procedure are outlined in paragraph 10 of the Code. They should:

(a) be in writing

(b) specify to whom they apply

(c) provide for matters to be dealt with quickly[86]

(d) indicate the disciplinary actions which may be taken

(e) specify the levels of management which have the authority to take the various forms of disciplinary action, ensuring that immediate superiors do not normally have the power to dismiss without reference to senior management

(f) provide for individuals to be informed of the complaints against them and to be given an opportunity to state their case before decisions are reached. (It is clear that allowing access to a grievance procedure does not constitute the giving of an opportunity to explain[87])

(g) give individuals the right to be accompanied by a trade union representative or by a fellow employee of their choice (see below)

(h) ensure that, except for gross misconduct, no employees are dismissed for a first breach of discipline

(i) ensure that disciplinary action is not taken until the case has been carefully investigated

(j) ensure that individuals are given an explanation for any penalty imposed

(k) provide a right of appeal and specify the procedure to be followed.[88]

It is clear from the above that natural justice is an important element in such procedures. Fairness requires that accused persons should know the case to be met; should hear or be told the important points of the evidence in support of that case; should have an opportunity to criticise or dispute that evidence and to adduce their own evidence and argue their case.[89] However, natural justice in this context does not include the automatic right to be present throughout a disciplinary hearing if the employee's interests are safeguarded by a representative. Similarly, employers are not required to conduct a quasi-judicial investigation, with cross-examination and confrontation of witnesses.[90]

According to the section 10 ERel Act 1999, workers will have the right to make a reasonable request to be accompanied during a disciplinary or grievance hearing. Where this happens, the worker may be accompanied by a single companion who

(a) is chosen by the worker

(b) is to be permitted to address the hearing

(c) is not to answer questions on behalf of the worker

(d) is to be allowed to confer with the worker during the hearing.

Such a person can be an official of a trade union or another of the employer's workers. A worker may propose an alternative time for the hearing if his or her chosen companion is unavailable at the time proposed by the employer. The employer must postpone the hearing to the time proposed by the worker, provided that the alternative time is reasonable and falls within a period of five working days beginning with the first working day after the day on which the worker was informed of the time by the employer. An employer must permit a worker to take time off during working hours in order to accompany another of the employer's workers.

If allegations are made by an informant, a careful balance must be maintained between the desirability of protecting informants who are genuinely in fear and providing a fair hearing of the issues for employees who are accused.[91] In *Rowe v Radio Rentals*[92] the EAT decided that the employer's appeal procedure did not conflict with the rules of natural justice because the person hearing the appeal had been informed of the decision to dismiss before it took place and the person who took that decision was also present throughout the appeal hearing. It was recognised as inevitable that those involved in the original decision to dismiss will be in daily contact with their supervisors who will be responsible for deciding the appeal. However, if it is not necessary for the same person to act as both witness and judge in the procedure leading to dismissal, there may be a finding of unfairness.[93]

Warnings are particularly appropriate in cases of misconduct but may also be useful in dealing with other types of case. Basically, there are two types of warnings which need to be distinguished: a 'rectifiable' warning means that the employee will be dismissed unless an existing situation is resolved, whereas a 'final' warning indicates that the employee will be dismissed if further unacceptable behaviour occurs. Final warnings are dealt with in paragraph 12 of the Code of Practice, where it is recommended that written warnings should set out the nature of the offence and the likely consequences of its being repeated. Because an ambiguous warning will be construed strictly against the employer who drafted it, the date and time on which a warning is to commence and expire should be specified clearly.[94]

According to the Court of Appeal, provided a formal disciplinary warning has been given on adequate evidence, and not for an oblique or improper motive, it is a relevant consideration to which an employment tribunal should have regard in deciding whether the dismissal was unfair, even where the warning was under appeal and the appeal had not been determined at the time of the dismissal.[95] It follows that systematic records will have to be kept by employers, although it is suggested in paragraph 19 of the Code of Practice that 'except in agreed special circumstances, breaches of disciplinary rules should be disregarded after a specified period of satisfactory conduct'. The ACAS advisory handbook indicates that warnings for minor offences may be valid for up to six months whereas final warnings may remain in force for a year or longer.

As regards appeal procedures, the House of Lords has confirmed that a dismissal is unfair if the employer unreasonably treats the reason for dismissal as a sufficient one, either when the original decision to dismiss is made or when that decision is maintained at the conclusion of an internal appeal.[96] Indeed, a dismissal may also be unfair if the employer refuses to entertain an appeal or to comply with the full requirements of the appeal procedure.[97] Where two employees are dismissed for the same incident, and one is successful on appeal and the other is not, in determining the fairness of the latter's dismissal the question is whether the appeal panel's decision was so irrational that no employer could reasonably have accepted it.[98] Whether procedural defects can be rectified on appeal will depend on the degree of unfairness at the original hearing. If there is to be a correction by the appeal, then that appeal must be of a comprehensive nature – in essence a rehearing and not merely a review.

Finally, paragraph 15 of the Code of Practice urges that special consideration be given to the way in which disciplinary procedures operate in exceptional cases. Three examples are given:

(a) employees to whom the full procedure is not immediately available, such as those who work on shifts or in isolated locations

(b) trade union officials: 'Although normal disciplinary standards should apply to their conduct as employees, no disciplinary action beyond an oral warning should be taken until the circumstances of the case have been discussed with a senior trade union representative or full-time official'

c) criminal offences outside employment should not be treated as automatic reasons for dismissal.

KEY POINTS 14
Unfair dismissal (2)

- Once employees have proved that they were dismissed, the burden shifts to the employer to show the reason for the dismissal.

- The employer must show that the reason for the dismissal relates to capability or qualifications, conduct, a statutory ban or some other substantial reason of a kind to justify the dismissal.

- There are certain reasons which are automatically unfair, such as those relating to trade union membership or activities or to pregnancy and maternity.

- Employees cannot claim unfair dismissal if they are dismissed while taking part in unofficial industrial action.

- Capability is assessed by reference to 'skill, aptitude, health or any other physical or mental ability'.

- Misconduct is a potentially fair reason for dismissal, but the employment tribunal will decide whether dismissal was a reasonable course of action taking into account all the circumstances.

- Some other substantial reason is a category which gives tribunals the discretion to accept as fair reasons which have not been defined by statute, such as reasons arising out of the reorganisation of a business.

- An employer must act reasonably in treating a reason as sufficient for dismissal and be guided by the ACAS Code of Practice and the ACAS advisory handbook *Discipline at Work*.

NOTES

1 Sections 98(1) and (2) ERA 1996
2 See *Maund v Penwith District Council* (1984) IRLR 24
3 See *Abernethy v Mott, Hay and Anderson* (1974) IRLR 213
4 See *Ely v YKK Ltd* (1993) IRLR 500
5 See *Devis & Sons Ltd v Atkins* (1977) IRLR 314
6 See *Parkinson v March Consulting* (1997) IRLR 308
7 See *Ford Motor Co. v Hudson* (1978) IRLR 66
8 No service qualification applies if a dismissal is on the grounds of pregnancy or maternity; see Chapter 9
9 (1985) IRLR 16
10 See *Harvard Securities v Younghusband* (1990) IRLR 17
11 See *Bromsgrove v Eagle Alexander* (1981) IRLR 127
12 Section 93(2) ERA 1996
13 Section 101 ERA 1996
14 Section 101A ERA 1996
15 Section 103A ERA 1996
16 Section 104A ERA 1996
17 Section 102 ERA 1996
18 Section 103 ERA 1996
18a Section 104B ERA 1996
19 Section 4(3)b Rehabilitation of Offenders Act 1974; see *Wood v Coverage Care* (1996) IRLR 264
20 Section 104 ERA 1996; see also *Mennell v Newell & Wright Ltd* (1997) IRLR 519
21 See *Abernethy v Mott, Hay and Anderson* (note 3)
22 (1979) IRLR 16
23 See *Sutton & Gates Ltd v Boxall* (1978) IRLR 486
24 See *Mitchell v Arkwood Plastics* (1993) ICR 471
25 See *Cereal Packaging Ltd v Lyncock* (1998) IRLR 510
26 See *Links v Rose* (1991) IRLR 353
27 (1992) IRLR 133
28 See *Shook v London Borough of Ealing* (1986) IRLR 46
29 See *London Fire Authority v Betty* (1994) IRLR 384
30 See *Hamilton v Argyll and Clyde Health Authority* (1993) IRLR 99
31 (1998) IRLR 358
32 See *Taylor v Parsons Peebles Ltd* (1981) IRLR 199
33 See *United Distillers v Conlin* (1992) IRLR 503
34 See *UCATT v Brain* (1981) IRLR 224
35 See *Laughton v Bapp Industrial Ltd* (1986) IRLR 245
36 (1992) IRLR 294; see also *Adamson v B&L Cleaning Ltd* (1995) IRLR 193
37 (1978) IRLR 379; see also *Scottish Daily Record v Laird* (1996) IRLR 665
38 *Scottish Midland Co-op v Cullion* (1991) IRLR 261
38a *British Home Stores v Burchell* (1978) IRLR 379
39 *Haddon v Van Den Bergh* (1999) IRLR 672
40 See *Parr v Whitbread plc* (1990) IRLR 39
41 *Frames Snooker v Boyce* (1992) IRLR 472
42 See *Parker v Dunn Ltd* (1979) IRLR 56
43 See *Secretary of State v Campbell* (1992) IRLR 263
44 See *Harris v Courage Ltd* (1982) IRLR 509
45 *Lovie Ltd v Anderson* (1999) IRLR 164

46 See *Thomson v Alloa Motor Co* (1983) IRLR 403
47 See *P v Nottingham County Council* (1992) IRLR 362
48 (1980) IRLR 382
49 See *Kingston v British Rail* (1984) IRLR 146
50 *Alboni v Ind Coope Retail Ltd* (1998) IRLR 131
51 See *RS Components Ltd v Irwin* (1973) IRLR 239
52 See *Scottpacking Ltd v Paterson* (1978) IRLR 166
53 (1986) IRLR 93
54 See *North Yorkshire County Council v Fay* (1985) IRLR 247
55 See *Langston v Cranfield University* (1998) IRLR 172
56 See *Dobie v Burns International* (1984) IRLR 329
57 See *Ely v YKK Ltd* (note 4)
58 See *Saunders v National Scottish Camps Association* (1981) IRLR 277
59 See *Bouchaala v Trust House Forte* (1980) IRLR 382
60 See *Hollister v National Farmers Union* (1979) IRLR 238
61 See *St John of God Ltd v Brooks* (1992) IRLR 546
62 (1998) IRLR 176
63 See *Catamaran Cruisers v Williams* (1994) IRLR 386
64 'Protected industrial action' consists of acts that are not actionable in tort; see section 219 TULRCA 1992
65 Section 238A(6) TULRCA 1992
66 See *Bolton Roadways Ltd v Edwards* (1987) IRLR 392
67 See *Rogers v Chloride Systems* (1992) ICR 198
68 See *Express & Star Ltd v Bunday* (1987) IRLR 422
69 See *Manifold Industries Ltd v Sims* (1991) IRLR 242 and (1993) EAT 223/91
70 Section 238(4) TULRCA 1992
71 (1982) IRLR 377
72 Section 237(6) TULRCA 1992
73 Section 98(4) ERA 1996
74 See *Smith v City of Glasgow DC* (1987) IRLR 326
75 See *Ladbroke Racing v Arnott* (1983) IRLR 154
76 See *Brandon v Murphy Bros* (1983) IRLR 54
77 See *London Borough of Harrow v Cunningham* (1996) IRLR 256
78 See *Williams v Compair Maxam Ltd* (1982) IRLR 83
79 See *British Leyland (UK) Ltd v Swift* (1981) IRLR 81
80 See note 39 above
81 See *Lock v Cardiff Railway Company* (1998) IRLR 358
82 (1991) IRLR 336
83 See *Alidair Ltd v Taylor* (1978) IRLR 82
84 See Code of Practice paragraph 5
85 See Code of Practice paragraphs 7 and 8
86 See *RSPCA v Cruden* (1986) IRLR 83
87 See *Clarke v Trimoco Ltd* (1993) IRLR 148
88 See *Vauxhall Motors Ltd v Ghafoor* (1993) ICR 376
89 See *Spink v Express Foods* (1990) IRLR 320
90 See *Ulsterbus Ltd v Henderson* (1989) IRLR 251
91 See *Linfood Cash and Carry v Thomson* (1989) IRLR 235
92 (1982) IRLR 177
93 See *Byrne v BOC Ltd* (1992) IRLR 505
94 See *Bevan Ashford v Malin* (1995) IRLR 360
95 See *Tower Hamlets Health Authority v Anthony* (1989) IRLR 394

96 See *West Midlands Co-op Ltd v Tipton* (1986) IRLR 112
97 See *Westminster City Council v Cabaj* (1996) IRLR 399
98 See *Securicor Ltd v Smith* (1989) IRLR 356

15 Redundancy and transfers of undertakings

In this chapter we consider dismissal as a result of redundancy. We begin by looking at the statutory definition and then consider the rules concerning offers of alternative employment and the opportunity for the employee to make a decision about them. There is then an examination of possible unfairness in the redundancy process. We look at the necessity for consultation with the employee and their representatives, while considering the particular rules concerning collective redundancies. Finally we examine the law relating to transfers of undertakings and the protection offered to employees in such situations.

THE DEFINITION OF REDUNDANCY

According to 139(1) ERA 1996, employees are to be regarded as being redundant if their dismissals[1] are attributable wholly or mainly to:

(a) the fact that the employer has ceased, or intends to cease, to carry on the business[2] for the purposes for which the employees were employed, or

(b) the fact that the employer has ceased, or intends to cease, to carry on that business in the place where the employees were so employed, or

(c) the fact that the requirement of that business for employees to carry out work of a particular kind, or for employees to carry out work of a particular kind in the place where they were so employed, has ceased or diminished or is expected to cease or diminish.

In this context 'cease' or 'diminish' mean either permanently or temporarily and from whatever cause.[3] The House of Lords has held[4] that the definition of redundancy requires two questions of fact to be answered. These are:

(a)   Had the requirements of the employer's business for employees to carry out work of a particular kind ceased or diminished, or were they expected to cease or diminish?

(b)   Was the dismissal of the employee attributable, wholly or mainly, to this state of affairs?

This means looking at the employer's overall requirements to decide whether there has been a diminution of need for employees, irrespective of the terms of the individual's contract or of the function that each performed. The House of Lords approved the approach of the EAT[5] in deciding that 'bumping' could give rise to a redundancy payment. 'Bumping' is where an individual's job may continue, but there is a reduction in requirement for the number of people to work in the business, and that individual is made redundant.

For these purposes, the place where an employee was employed does not extend to any place where he or she could contractually be required to work. The question of what is the place of employment concerns the extent or area of a single place, not the transfer from one place to another.[6] If there is no express term relating to mobility, a tribunal will have to examine all the evidence to see if a term should be inferred.[7] However, even though an employee may be contractually justified in declining to move, a request to do so may have to be considered as an offer of suitable alternative employment (see below).

One of the most onerous tasks of tribunals is to determine what constitutes 'work of a particular kind'. It is clear that a change in the time when the work is to be performed will not give rise to a redundancy payment,[8] nor will a reduction of overtime if the work to be done remains the same. Thus in *Lesney Products Ltd v Nolan*[9] the Court of Appeal held that the company's reorganisation, by which one long day shift plus overtime was changed into two day shifts, was done in the interests of efficiency and was not the result of any diminution in the employer's requirements for employees to carry out work of a particular kind. However, both the work that the employee actually carried out and the work that the employee was required to do by his or her contract will be considerations when an employment tribunal needs to decide on this issue.[10]

Three further points need to be made:

(a) Employees will be entitled to a payment notwithstanding that it could be seen from the commencement of the contract that they would be dismissed for redundancy. The fact that the contract was temporary and short term makes no difference in this respect.[11]

(b) The statutory definition of redundancy focuses on the employer's requirements rather than needs. Thus – even where there is still a need for the work to be done – if, owing to lack of funds, the requirement for the employee's service has ceased, the employee is redundant.[12]

(c) Section 163(2) ERA 1996 states that an employee who is dismissed is presumed to have been dismissed by reason of redundancy unless the contrary is proved.[13]

DISMISSAL FOR MISCONDUCT OR STRIKING DURING THE NOTICE PERIOD

If an employee who is working out notice of dismissal for redundancy commits an act of misconduct which justifies summary dismissal and is dismissed for that reason, a tribunal is empowered to determine whether it is just and equitable for him or her to receive the whole or part of the redundancy payment.[14] The burden is on the employer to show that the employee's conduct was such as to entitle the employer to terminate the contract without notice,[15] and the tribunal's discretion applies only if the misconduct occurred during the 'obligatory period' of the employer's notice or after the employee has given notice of an intention to claim a payment in respect of lay-off or short time. Where the misconduct takes place at any other time, the employee is not entitled to a payment.[16] Equally, section 140(2) ERA 1996 prevents employees who have been given notice of dismissal on the ground of redundancy from being denied a payment if they take part in a strike during the 'obligatory period'.[17] If the employee is sacked before redundancy notices have been issued, no payment is owed,[18] but the fact that redundancy is the result of industrial action will not bar an employee from obtaining a payment.

OFFERS OF ALTERNATIVE EMPLOYMENT

If, before the ending of a person's employment, the employer or an associated employer makes an offer, in writing or not, to renew the contract or to re-engage under a new contract which is to take effect either on the ending of the old one or within four weeks thereafter, then section 141 ERA 1996 has the following effect:

(a) if the provisions of the new or renewed contract as to the capacity and place in which the person would be employed, together with the other terms and conditions, would not differ from the corresponding terms of the previous contract, or

(b) the terms and conditions would differ, wholly or in part, but the offer constitutes an offer of suitable employment, and

(c) in either case the employee unreasonably refuses that offer, then he or she will not be entitled to a redundancy payment.

The burden is on an employer to prove both the suitability of the offer and the unreasonableness of the employee's refusal.[19] Offers do not have to be formal, nor do they have to contain all the conditions which are ultimately agreed.[20] However, supplying details of vacancies is not the same as an offer of employment.[21] Clearly, sufficient information must be provided to enable the employee to take a realistic decision.[22]

The suitability of the alternative work must be assessed objectively by comparing the terms on offer with those previously enjoyed. A convenient test has been whether the proposed employment will be 'substantially equivalent' to that which has ceased.[23] Merely offering the same salary will not be sufficient,[24] but short-term employment could be suitable if it is full-time.[25] The fact that the employment will be at a different location does not necessarily mean that it will be regarded as unsuitable.

By way of contrast, in adjudicating upon the reasonableness of an employee's refusal, subjective considerations can be taken into account, eg domestic responsibilities. In *Spencer v Gloucestershire County Council*[26] the employees had refused offers of suitable employment on the grounds that they would not be able to do their work to a satisfactory standard in the reduced hours and with reduced staffing levels. The Court of Appeal held that it was for employers to set the standard of work they wanted carried out but it was a different question whether it was reasonable for a particular employee, in all the circumstances, to refuse to work to the standard which the employer set. This is a question of fact for the tribunal. Similarly, it might be reasonable for an employee to refuse an offer of employment which, although suitable, involved loss of status.[27] Although in theory the questions of suitability and the reasonableness of refusal are distinct, they are often run together in practice.

To allow an employee to make a rational decision about any alternative employment offered, section 138(3) ERA 1996 states that if the terms and conditions differ, wholly or in part, from those of the previous contract, a trial period may be invoked. Such a period commences when the employee starts work under the new or renewed contract and ends four calendar weeks later[28] unless a longer period has been agreed for the purpose of retraining. Any such agreement must be made before the employee starts work under the new or renewed contract; it must be in writing, and specify the date the trial period ends, and the terms and conditions which will apply afterwards.[29] In order to have an agreement, an employee must do something to indicate acceptance. However, it is not necessary for the employer to provide all the information required by section 1 ERA 1996; the agreement need embody only important matters such as remuneration, status and job description.[30] If, during the trial period, the employee for any reason terminates or gives notice to terminate the contract, or the employer terminates or gives notice to terminate it for any reason connected with or arising out of the change, the employee shall be treated, for redundancy payment purposes, as having been dismissed on the date the previous contract ended. Of course, the employee's contract may be renewed again or he or she may be re-engaged under a new contract in circumstances which give rise to another trial period.[31] Indeed, the termination of a trial period could lead to a finding of unfair dismissal.[32]

The statutory trial period applies to those who have been dismissed by their employer and have unconditionally accepted a new or renewed contract. However, at common law if the employer is guilty of repudiating the contract, employees are allowed a reasonable period within which to decide whether or not to regard themselves as constructively dismissed (see above) or to carry on with the contract. In these circumstances the statutory trial period will not commence until after the expiry of the common-law period, so the employee gets the benefit of both.[33] Among the circumstances to be considered in determining the length of the common-law period are the steps taken by the employer to enquire what the employee is going to do. If the employer makes no such enquiries, the period continues until either the employee has announced a decision or a period expires which is long enough for it to be said that it would be unreasonable to consider the trial to be subsisting.[34]

UNFAIR REDUNDANCY

It is possible for a dismissed employee to claim both a redundancy payment and unfair dismissal, although double compensation cannot be obtained.[35] For unfair dismissal purposes the statutory presumption of redundancy does not apply, so it is up to the employer to establish this as the reason, or principal reason, for dismissal. However, tribunals will not investigate the background which led to the redundancy or require the employer to justify redundancies in economic terms. According to the EAT, employers do not have to show that their requirements for employees to carry out work of a particular kind have diminished in relation to *any* work that the employees could have been asked to do under their contracts. Thus where an employee is hired to perform a particular trade, it is that basic obligation which has to be looked at when deciding whether the employer's requirements have ceased or diminished, rather than any work that the employee could be required to carry out in accordance with a contractual flexibility clause.[36]

A dismissal on grounds of redundancy will be unfair if it is shown that 'the circumstances constituting the redundancy applied equally to one or more other employees in the same undertaking who held positions similar' and either the reason, or principal reason, for which the employee was selected was inadmissible (see Chapter 14).[37] A situation where a number of employees at a similar level are made to apply for a reduced number of jobs at that level may still result in a dismissal on the grounds of redundancy which is fair, even though the work of that particular employee still continues to be done.[38]

Because section 105 ERA 1996 is concerned purely with selection on grounds that are not permissible, a failure to comply with a procedural requirement to consult trade unions and to consider volunteers will not automatically be unfair.[39] Nevertheless section 98(4) ERA 1996 can still have a considerable impact on dismissals for redundancy, a point which has been emphasised by the decision in *Williams v Compair Maxam Ltd*.[40] In this case it was held that it is not enough to show that it was reasonable to dismiss *an* employee, a tribunal must be satisfied that the employer acted reasonably in treating redundancy as 'sufficient reason for dismissing *the* employee'. According to the EAT, where employees are represented by a recognised independent trade union reasonable employers will seek to act in accordance with the following principles:

(a) The employer will seek to give as much warning as possible of impending redundancies so as to enable the union and employees who may be affected to take early steps to inform themselves of the relevant facts, consider possible alternative solutions, and, if necessary, find alternative employment in the undertaking or elsewhere.

(b) The employer will consult the union as to the best means by which the desired management result can be achieved fairly and with as little hardship to the employees as possible.[41] In particular, the employer will seek to agree with the union the criteria to be applied in selecting the employees to be made redundant.[42] When a selection has been made, the employer will consider with the union whether the selection has been made in accordance with those criteria.[43]

(c) Whether or not an agreement as to the criteria to be adopted has been agreed with the union, the employer will seek to establish criteria for selection which so far as possible do not depend solely upon the opinion of the person making the selection but can be checked objectively against such things as attendance record, efficiency at the job or length of service.

(d) The employer will seek to ensure that the selection is made fairly in accordance with these criteria and will consider any representations the union may make as to such selection.

(e) The employer will seek to see whether instead of dismissing, an employee could be offered alternative employment.

In selecting employees for redundancy a senior manager is entitled to rely on the assessments of employees made by those who have direct knowledge of their work. Employers may need to show, however, that their method of selection was fair and applied reasonably. An absence of adequate consultation with the employees concerned or their representatives might affect their ability to do this[44] (consultation issues are considered below). It will not always be possible to call evidence subsequently to show that adequate consultation would not have made a difference to the decision on those selected for redundancy. If the flaws in the process had been procedural, it might be possible to reconstruct what might have happened if the correct procedures were followed. If, however, the tribunal decides that the flaws were more substantive, then this reconstruction may not be possible.[45] In practice many employers have established redundancy appeal procedures to deal with complaints that selection criteria have been unfairly applied.

It is now well established that employers have a duty to consider the alternatives to compulsory redundancy. Indeed, ACAS suggests the following methods of avoiding such redundancies:

(a) natural wastage

(b) restrictions on recruitment

(c) the retirement of employees who are beyond normal retiring age and the seeking of applicants for early retirement or voluntary redundancy

(d) reductions in overtime

(e) short-time working

(g) retraining and redeployment to other parts of the organisation

(h) termination of the employment of temporary or contract staff.[46]

As regards seniority, 'last-in, first-out' is frequently used as a criterion for selection and it is assumed to be based on periods of continuous rather than cumulative service.[47] Arguably, this form of selection indirectly discriminates against women and needs to be justified (see Chapter 7).[48]

As regards alternative employment, 'the size and administrative resources' of the employer will be a relevant consideration here. However, if a vacancy exists, an employer would be advised to offer it rather than speculate about the likelihood of the employee's accepting it. This is so even if the new job would entail demotion or other radical changes in the terms and conditions of employment. Nevertheless, only in very rare cases will a tribunal accept that a reasonable employer would have created a job by dismissing someone else. Finally, employers should consider establishing both redundancy counselling services, which would provide information on alternative employment, training, occupational and state benefits, and hardship committees, which would seek to alleviate 'undue hardship'.[49]

CONSULTATION

An important requirement in redundancy situations is the need for consultation (see below for specific requirements in relation to collective redundancies). Consultation may be directly with the employees concerned or with their representatives. In *Mugford v Midland Bank plc*[50] the EAT held that a dismissal on the grounds of redundancy was not unfair because no consultation had taken place with the employee individually, only with the recognised trade union. The EAT described the position with regard to consultation as follows:

(a) Where no consultation about redundancy has taken place with either the trade union or the employee, the dismissal will normally be unfair, unless the reasonable employer would have concluded that the consultation would be an utterly futile exercise.

(b) Consultation with the trade union over the selection criteria does not of itself release the employer from considering with the employee individually his being identified for redundancy.

(c) It will be a question of fact and degree for the tribunal to consider whether the consultation with the individual and/or the trade union was so inadequate as to render the dismissal unfair.

The overall picture must be viewed at the time of termination for the tribunal to decide whether the employer acted reasonably or not. The consultation must be fair and proper, which means that there must be:

(a) consultation when the proposals are still at a formative stage

(b) adequate information and adequate time to respond

(c) a conscientious consideration by the employer of the response to consultation.[51]

Although proper consultation may be regarded as a procedural matter, it might have a direct bearing on the substantive decision to select a particular employee, since a different employee might have been selected if, following proper consultation, different criteria had been adopted. It is not normally permissible for an employer to argue that a failure to consult or warn would have made no difference to the outcome in the particular case. It is what the employer did that is to be judged, not what might have been done. Nevertheless, if the employer could reasonably have concluded in the light of the circumstances known at the time of dismissal that consultation or warning would be 'utterly useless', he or she might well have acted reasonably.[52] While the size of an undertaking might affect the nature or formality of the consultation, it cannot excuse lack of any consultation at all.[53] It almost goes without saying that the obligation to consult is separate from the obligation to warn.[54]

COLLECTIVE REDUNDANCIES

Employers proposing to dismiss as redundant 20 or more employees at one establishment within a period of 90 days or less must consult appropriate representatives of employees affected by the proposed dismissals or who may be affected by measures taken in connection with those dismissals.[55] The consultation must begin 'in good time' and in any event

(a) where the employer is proposing to dismiss 100 or more employees, at least 90 days, and

(b) otherwise, at least 30 days before the first of the dismissals takes effect.[56]

Appropriate representatives are representatives of trade unions recognised for the purposes of collective bargaining. If there are no such representatives, then the employer may choose to consult either employee representatives who have been elected or appointed by the affected employees for the purpose of this consultation or existing employee representatives who may have been elected or appointed by the employees for another purpose.[57] Employers have a responsibility for ensuring that elections for employee representatives are fair and may determine the number of representatives to be elected.[58] If the affected employees fail to elect or appoint representatives, employers may fulfil their obligations by giving them the appropriate information.[59] Conversely, if there is a complaint that an employer has failed in its duty with regard to the election of employee representatives, then it is for that employer to show that it has satisfied the requirements in section 188 TULRCA 1992.[60] According to section 188(5A) TULRCA 1992, employers must allow appropriate representatives access to the employees whom it is proposed to dismiss and must provide the representatives with appropriate accommodation and facilities.[61]

In this context, redundancy is defined as 'dismissal for a reason not related to the individual concerned or for a number of reasons all of which are not so related'. This might include, for example, dismissals resulting from a refusal to accept a change in terms and conditions of employment. It will also be presumed that a dismissal is by reason of redundancy unless the contrary is proved.[62] It is important to note that the employees covered need not be employed for any minimum number of hours per week. However, those who work under a contract for a fixed term of three months or less will be excluded unless the employment lasted for more than three months.[63]

'Establishment' is not defined by the statute and the EAT has ruled that this is a question for the tribunal acting as an industrial jury using its common sense on the particular facts of the case. In *Bakers' Union v Clark's of Hove Ltd*[64] it was accepted that separate premises could be regarded as one establishment if there was common management and accounting. The ECJ has indicated that the word 'establishment' must be understood as designating the unit to which the workers made redundant are assigned to carry out their duties. It is not essential for that unit to be endowed with a management that can independently effect collective dismissals.[65]

The consultation required must include consultation about ways of:

(a)   avoiding the dismissals

(b)   reducing the numbers to be dismissed, and

(c)   mitigating the consequences of the dismissal,

and must be undertaken 'with a view to reaching agreement with the appropriate representatives'.

According to the EAT, employers are required to begin consultation before they give notice of dismissal,[66] but notices can be issued during the consultation period so long as the dismissals do not take effect until after the period has elapsed. Of course, if an employer gives notice of dismissal immediately after consultation has begun, it could be argued that no meaningful consultation took place.[67] A fundamental question in relation to these provisions is: how concrete does the intention to make employees redundant have to be before the duty applies? In *Hough v Leyland DAF*[68] the EAT suggested that the duty to consult arose when matters had reached a stage where a specific proposal had been formulated. This is a later stage than the diagnosis of a problem and the appreciation that one answer would be redundancies. Hence an employer must have formed some view as to how many employees are to be dismissed, when this is to take place and how it is to be arranged. It is important to note that Article 2 of the Collective Redundancies Directive[69] requires consultation where an employer is 'contemplating' collective redundancies.

The employer must disclose in writing the following matters at the beginning of the consultation period:[70]

(a)   the reason for the proposals

(b)   the number and description of employees whom it is proposed to dismiss

(c) the total number of employees of any such description employed by the employer at that establishment

(d) the proposed method of selecting the employees who may be dismissed

(e) the proposed method of carrying out the dismissals, with due regard to any agreed procedure, including the period over which the dismissals are to take effect

(f) the proposed method of calculating the redundancy payment if this differs from the statutory sum.

This information must be delivered to each of the appropriate representatives, or sent by post to an address notified by them or, in the case of union representatives, to the union head office. In *E. Green Ltd v ASTMS and AUEW*[71] it was held that items (d) and (e) had not been complied with when the method of selecting employees who might be dismissed was given as 'to be in consultation with union representatives'.

If there are 'special circumstances' which render it not reasonably practicable for the employer to comply with the above-mentioned provisions, an employer must take 'all such steps towards compliance' as are reasonably practicable in the circumstances. 'Special circumstances' mean circumstances which are uncommon or out of the ordinary, so insolvency by itself will not provide an excuse as it may well be foreseeable.[72] However, that the employer has continued trading in the face of adverse economic pointers in the genuine and reasonable expectation that redundancies would be avoided can justify non-compliance.[73] Additionally, a pending application for government financial aid, the withdrawal of a prospective purchaser from negotiations combined with a bank's immediate appointment of a receiver, and the need for confidentiality in negotiating a sale, have all constituted 'special circumstances'. By way of contrast, the following have not been accepted as being 'special':

(a) the alarm and chaos caused by the disclosure of information about the proposed redundancies

(b) a genuine belief that the union had not been recognised: in *Wilson & Bros v USDAW*[74] it was held that such a belief must be reasonable

(c) the fact that the employer had been informed by the relevant government department that there was no duty to consult in the particular case.[75]

Section 188(7) TULRCA 1992 also states that where the decision leading to the proposed dismissals is that of a person controlling the employer, a failure on the part of that person to provide information to the employer will not constitute 'special circumstances'. In addition, if the employer has invited any of the employees who may be dismissed to elect employee representatives and this invitation was issued long enough before the time when consultation must begin to allow them to elect representatives by that time, the employer is not in breach of the statute if he or she complies with the consultation requirements as soon as reasonably practicable after the election of the representatives.[76]

Where the employer has failed to comply with any of the requirements of section 188 TULRCA 1992, employee representatives can complain of any failure relating to them and the union can complain where there is a failure relating to its representatives. In any other case, employees who have been or may be dismissed as redundant can complain. Claims can be made to an employment tribunal before the proposed dismissal takes effect or within three months of its doing so unless the 'time-limit escape clause' applies (see Chapter 14).[77] Employers wishing to argue that there were 'special circumstances' justifying non-compliance must prove that these circumstances existed and that they took all such steps towards compliance as were reasonably practicable. If a complaint is well-founded, the tribunal must make a declaration to that effect and may also make a protective award. A protective award refers to the wages payable for a protected period to employees who have been dismissed or whom it is proposed to dismiss. The protected period begins with the date on which the first of the dismissals to which the complaint relates takes effect (ie the proposed date of dismissal)[78] or the date of the award (whichever is the earlier) and will be of such length as the tribunal determines 'to be just and equitable in all the circumstances having regard to the seriousness of the employer's default'. The protected period is a maximum of 90 days.[79]

The prevailing view appears to be that the object of an award is to compensate employees for their employer's failure to consult with the union even where compliance with the statute would have made no difference.[80] One consequence of focusing on the loss of days of consultation rather than the loss or potential loss of remuneration during the relevant period is that it becomes possible to make a protective award in favour of employees who have suffered no pecuniary damage – for example, where alternative employment was immediately secured.[81] The rate of remuneration payable under a protective award is a week's pay for each week of the protected period, with proportionate reductions being made in respect of periods less than a week.[82]

If during the protected period employees are fairly dismissed for a reason other than redundancy, or if they unreasonably resign, then their entitlement to remuneration under the protective award ceases on the day the contract is terminated. Similarly, employees who unreasonably refuse an offer of employment on the previous terms and conditions or an offer of suitable alternative employment will not be entitled to any remuneration under a protective award in respect of any period during which, but for that refusal, they would have been employed.[83] Employees who are of a description to which a protective award relates may complain to a tribunal, within three months unless the 'time-limit escape clause' applies, that their employer has failed, wholly or in part, to pay the remuneration under that award. If the complaint is well-founded, the employer will be ordered to pay the amount due to the complainant.[84]

Finally, it may be of interest to note that section 198 TULRCA 1992 enables the parties to a collective agreement to apply to the Secretary of State for an exemption order in respect of the consultation provisions.

Notification

An employer proposing to dismiss as redundant 100 or more employees at one establishment within a period of 90 days, or more than 20 employees within 30 days, must notify the Secretary of State in writing of the proposal within 90 or 30 days respectively.[85] Hence there is no obligation to notify if fewer than 20 employees are to be dismissed. In addition, the employer must give a copy of the notice to appropriate representatives. The written notice must be in such form and contain such particulars as the Secretary of State may direct, but it is expressly provided that where there are representatives to be consulted under section 188 TULRCA 1992 the employer must identify them and state when consultation began.[86] At any time after receiving a notice under this section the Secretary of State may require the employer to give further information.[87]

If there are special circumstances rendering it not reasonably practicable for an employer to comply with the requirements of section 193 TULRCA 1992, the employer must take all such steps as are reasonably practicable in the circumstances. Again, where the decision leading to the proposed dismissals is that of a person controlling the employer, a failure on the part of that person to provide information to the employer will not constitute 'special circumstances'.[88] Employers who fail to give notice in accordance with this section may be prosecuted and suffer a fine not exceeding level 5 on the standard scale.[89]

TRANSFERS OF UNDERTAKINGS

The Transfers of Undertakings (Protection of Employment) Regulations 1981[90] (the Transfer Regulations 1981) were introduced as a result of the Acquired Rights Directive.[91] The intention of the Directive and the Transfer Regulations 1981 was to protect the contract of employment and the employment relationship of employees who were transferred from one employer to another. When a transfer takes place, it is as if the employee's contract of employment was initially agreed with the transferee employer. All rights contained in the contract of employment, except pension benefits,[92] are transferred as are all outstanding claims and liabilities of the employer to the employees.[93] This may include non-contractual obligations such as in *DJM International Ltd v Nicholas*.[94] In this case the EAT held that liability for an alleged act of sex discrimination transferred from the transferor company to the transferee employer.

When does a relevant transfer of an undertaking take place?

There is no definition in the Directive or the Transfer Regulations of what a transfer actually consists of. The European Court of Justice supplied a definition in *Berg and Busschers v Besselsen*[95] in which it stated that a transfer happened as soon as a change occurs of the natural or legal person operating the undertaking and that a change of ownership is not needed. Thus a change in the natural or legal person running a business, or part of it, will constitute a transfer of an undertaking. Transfers have been held to take place in a wide variety of such situations as:

(a) the sale of an abattoir by an insolvent company to another, even though the abattoir was closed for a period during the sale[96]

(b) the outsourcing to a contractor of the internal catering operations of a company[97]

(c) the transfer of the work of caring for drug-dependent immigrants after the local authority switched its funding from one charity to another[98]

(d) the contracting out of a local authority refuse collection and street cleaning service.[99]

Because of the lack of a definition, the ECJ has developed the meaning of a transfer. In *Spijkers*[100] the ECJ stated that it was necessary to take all the factual circumstances of the transaction into account, including

(a) the type of undertaking or business in question

(b) the transfer or otherwise of tangible assets such as buildings or stocks

(c) the value of intangible assets at the date of transfer

(d) whether the majority of staff are taken over by the new employer

(e) the transfer or otherwise of customers

(f) the degree of similarity between activities before and after the transfer, and

(g) the duration of any interruption in those activities.

The Court of Justice held that one had to consider these factors and look at the entity before and after the transfer to see whether the operation continued. Since this case there have been a number of further cases at the ECJ which have developed this definition. In *Schmidt v Spar und Leihkasse*[101] this process led to the ECJ's concluding that the transfer of a contract using one part-time cleaner in a bank branch office constituted a transfer of an undertaking for the purposes of the Directive.

This has been qualified by the case of *Süzen*[102] which concerned the competitive tender for a school cleaning contract. The Court of Justice considered whether the taking over of a school cleaning contract could be a relevant transfer and concluded that one had to distinguish between the transfer of an entity (as in *Spijkers* above) and an activity only. If there is no transfer of tangible or intangible assets or the taking over by the new employer of a major part of the workforce, in terms of their numbers and skills, then there has not been a transfer of an entity, only the transfer of an activity (in this case the cleaning of a school). As a result of this judgment there was continuing uncertainty as to whether the Directive, and hence the Transfer Regulations, applied when one contractor took over a labour-intensive contract from another contractor. If there was no transfer of equipment or other assets and no transfer of the employees or their skills, then there appeared to be no protection offered to the affected employees.

This has led to apparently contradictory judgments in the English courts. In *Betts v Brintel Helicopters*[103] the question was whether the transfer of a helicopter contract ferrying supplies to North Sea oil rigs was a relevant transfer or not. The Court of Appeal decided that because no employees were transferred, nor any tangible assets, then according to the *Süzen* judgment there was no relevant transfer. Thus the employees working for the contractor who lost the contract received no protection from the Transfer Regulations. In *ECM Ltd v Cox*[104] there was a change of contractor running a car-delivery contract. Like *Betts* there was no transfer of employees or of tangible or intangible assets. In this case, however, the Court of Appeal concluded that there was a relevant transfer and concluded that employers could not escape the effects of the Transfer Regulations by failing to take on the previous contractor's employees. This latter view has had some support from the ECJ which looked at the transfer of a number of contracts which were labour only so that there could be no transfer of assets.[105] The ECJ concluded that there could be a transfer in circumstances where there were few assets to transfer, only employees who had been dedicated to a particular contract.

Who is protected by the Transfer Regulations?

Regulation 2 of the Transfer Regulations defines an employee as 'anyone who works for another person whether under a contract of service or otherwise, but [it] does not include anyone who provides services under a contract for services'. Thus the Regulations apply only to employees. Indeed, the ECJ has held that the Directive extends extra protection only to those who already receive protection under national law as employees.[106] There are a number of qualifications to be considered:

(a) Regulation 5(3) states that it is only employees who are employed immediately before the transfer who are protected. This has been interpreted broadly by the House of Lords. In *Litster v Forth Dry Dock Engineering*[107] an employer dismissed the workforce one hour before the transfer took place and claimed that there were no employees at the time of the transfer. The House of Lords took a purposive approach and held that being employed immediately before the transfer also included those who would have been so employed if they had not been unfairly dismissed before the transfer for a reason connected to the transfer.

(b) There is no obligation upon employees to transfer. Although employees employed immediately before the transfer are protected, those employees may choose not to move to the new employer.[108] Regulation 5(4B) of the Transfer Regulations states that 'Where an employee so objects, the transfer of the undertaking or part in which he is employed shall operate so as to terminate his contract of employment with the transferor but he shall not be treated, for any purpose, as having been dismissed by the transferor.'

The result is draconian, for the transferor no longer employs the worker concerned, who is now unemployed because his contract of employment has not transferred. There is no right of redress against the transferor because there has been no dismissal.[109]

(c) Regulation 8(1) of the Transfer Regulations states that if a person is dismissed for a reason connected to the transfer, he or she has a claim for unfair dismissal as in Part X of the ERA 1996. This only allows claims for employees with at least one year's continuous service.

(d) If a change to an employee's contract is for an economic, technical or organisational reason[110] (ETO reasons), then a change may be protected by the Transfer Regulations. In *Wilson v St Helens Borough Council*[111] a Community home was being transferred from one local authority to another. At the same time there was a reorganisation of staff and a number were made redundant while others suffered pay cuts. The claim that the employees were protected was not upheld by the House of Lords because the changes, which were aimed at making the homes economically viable, were held to be for economic, technical or organisational reasons even though they happened at the same time as the transfer. It is not always easy to distinguish between a change that results from the transfer and one that results from ETO reasons.

Information and consultation

Regulation 10 is concerned with the duty to inform and consult employee representatives and regulation 11 with the consequences of not doing so. The rules are that the appropriate representatives of the transferors' and the transferees' employees must be informed of

(a) the fact that a relevant transfer is to take place

(b) when that transfer is to take place

(c) the reasons for the transfer

(d) the legal, economic and social implications of the transfer for the affected employees

(e) the measures that the employer expects to take, in connection with the transfer, or in relation to the affected employees, or with the fact that there are no such measures envisaged.

This information will be given long enough before a relevant transfer in order for there to be opportunities for consultation. 'Long enough' before has been interpreted as meaning as soon as measures are envisaged and, if possible, long enough before the transfer.[112]

Appropriate representatives are representatives of a trade union recognised for collective bargaining purposes. If there are no such representatives, then they will either be representatives appointed or elected by the affected employees, or employee representatives elected or appointed for another purpose but who can also be consulted about transfers.[113] The onus is on the employer to make arrangements for elections of employee representatives, in the absence of a recognised trade union, and to decide on the number of representatives and to ensure that the election is fair.[114] If the employees fail to elect any representatives, the employer may just give the information required to each employee. If employers fail to consult, then, following a complaint to an employment tribunal, they may be required to pay compensation of up to 13 weeks' pay to each affected employee.[115]

KEY POINTS 15
Redundancy and transfers of undertakings

- Employees are to be regarded as redundant if the employer has ceased or intends to cease carrying on the business for the purposes for which the employees were employed, or in the place where they are employed there has been, or will be, a diminution in the requirement for work of a particular kind.

- If there is no express term relating to mobility in the contract of employment, the tribunal will have to examine the evidence to consider whether one should be inferred.

- The burden of proof is on the employer to show that any offer of alternative employment was suitable and that any refusal by the employee was unreasonable.

- A trial period may be invoked to consider offers of alternative employment if there is likely to be a difference in terms and conditions of employment.

- The employer should give as much warning as possible of impending redundancies to enable a union and the affected employees to take early steps to consider alternative solutions or possibly find alternative work in the undertaking or elsewhere.

- There are specific requirements for situations where an employer is proposing to dismiss as redundant 20 or more employees at one establishment within a period of 90 days or less.

- A transfer of an undertaking takes place as soon as there is a change in the natural or legal person operating the undertaking.

- Long enough before a relevant transfer the appropriate representatives of the employees must be informed of the fact that a transfer is to take place, when it is to take place, the reasons for it, the legal, social and economic implications, and the measures that the employer envisages taking in relation to the employees.

NOTES

1 On the meaning of dismissal for these purposes, see Chapter 14
2 'Business' is defined in section 235(1) ERA 1996
3 Section 139(6) ERA 1996
4 See *Murray v Foyle Meats Ltd* (1999) IRLR 562
5 *Safeway Stores v Burrell* (1997) IRLR 200
6 See *Bass Leisure v Thomas* (1994) IRLR 104; also *High Table Ltd v Horst* (1997) IRLR 514
7 See *Aparau v Iceland Frozen Foods* (1995) IRLR 119
8 See *Johnson v Nottingham Police Authority* (1974) ICR 170
9 (1977) IRLR 77
10 See *Shawkat v Nottingham City Hospital NHS Trust* (1999) IRLR 340
11 See *Pfaffinger v City of Liverpool College* (1996) IRLR 508
12 See *AUT v Newcastle University* (1987) ICR 317
13 See *Wilcox v Hastings* (1987) IRLR 299
14 Section 140(3) ERA 1996
15 See *Bonner v H. Gilbert Ltd* (1989) IRLR 475
16 Section 140(1) ERA 1996
17 On the possibility of extending the contract to make up for days lost, see section 143 ERA 1996
18 See *Simmons v Hoover Ltd* (1976) IRLR 266
19 See *Jones v Aston Cabinet Ltd* (1973) ICR 292
20 See *Singer Co. v Ferrier* (1980) IRLR 300
21 See *Curling v Securicor Ltd* (1992) IRLR 549
22 See *Modern Injection Mouldings Ltd v Price* (1976) IRLR 172
23 See *Hindes v Supersine Ltd* (1979) IRLR 343
24 See *Taylor v Kent County Council* (1969) 2 QB 560
25 See *Morganite Crucible v Street* (1972) ICR 110
26 (1985) IRLR 393
27 See *Cambridge and District Co-op v Ruse* (1993) IRLR 156
28 See *Benton v Sanderson Kayser* (1989) IRLR 299
29 Section 138(6) ERA 1996
30 See *McKindley v W. Hill Ltd* (1985) IRLR 492
31 Section 138(5) ERA 1996
32 See *Hempell v WH Smith & Sons Ltd* (1986) IRLR 95
33 See *Turvey v Cheyney Ltd* (1979) IRLR 105
34 See *Air Canada v Lee* (1978) IRLR 392
35 Section 122(4) ERA 1996
36 See *Johnson v Peabody Trust* (1996) IRLR 387
37 Section 105 ERA 1996; 'undertaking' is not defined in this context; 'position' is defined in note 7 Chapter 13; on 'positions similar' see *Powers and Villiers v A. Clarke & Co.* (1981) IRLR 483
38 See *Safeway Stores plc v Burrell* (1997) IRLR 200
39 See *McDowell v Eastern BRS Ltd* (1981) IRLR 482
40 (1982) IRLR 83; see also IPD Guide on Redundancy, London, IPD, 1996
41 See *Hough v Leyland DAF* (1991) IRLR 194
42 See *Rolls Royce Ltd v Price* (1993) IRLR 203
43 See *John Brown Engineering Ltd v Brown* (1997) IRLR 90
44 See *King v Eaton* (1996) IRLR 199
45 See *King v Eaton (No. 2)* (1998) IRLR 686

46 Advisory booklet no 12 page 7
47 See *International Paint Co v Cameron* (1979) IRLR 62
48 See *Brook v London Borough of Haringey* (1992) IRLR 478
49 See generally ACAS advisory booklet no 12 *Redundancy Handling*
50 (1997) IRLR 208
51 *King v Eaton Ltd* (1996) IRLR 199
52 See *Mugford v Midland Bank* (1997) IRLR 208
53 See *De Grasse v Stockwell Tools* (1992) IRLR 269
54 See *Rowell v Hubbard Group* (1995) IRLR 195
55 Section 188(1) TULRCA 1992 as amended by the Collective Redundancies and Transfers of Undertakings (Protection of Employment) (Amendment) Regulations 1999 SI 1999/1925
56 Section 188(1A) TULRCA 1992
57 Section 188(1B) TULRCA 1992
58 Section 188A TULRCA 1992
59 Section 188(7B) TULRCA 1992
60 Section 189(1B) TULRCA 1992
61 On time off for employee representatives, see Chapter 11
62 Section 195 TULRCA 1992
63 Section 282(1) TULRCA 1992
64 (1978) IRLR 366
65 *Rockfon* (1996) IRLR 168
66 See *NUT v Avon County Council* (1978) IRLR 55
67 See *TGWU v Ledbury Preserves* (1985) IRLR 412 and *Sovereign Distribution v TGWU* (1989) IRLR 334
68 (1991) IRLR 194
69 Directive 98/59
70 Section 188(4) TULRCA 1992
71 (1984) IRLR 135
72 See *GMB v Rankin* (1992) IRLR 514
73 See *APAC v Kirwin* (1978) IRLR 318
74 (1978) IRLR 20
75 See *UCATT v Rooke & Son Ltd* (1978) IRLR 204
76 Section 188(7A) TULRCA 1992
77 Section 189(1) and (5) TULRCA 1992
78 See *E. Green Ltd v ASTMS and AUEW* (1984) IRLR 435
79 Section 189(4) TULRCA 1992 as amended by the CRTUPEA Regulations 1999
80 See *Sovereign Distribution v TGWU* (1989) IRLR 334
81 See *Spillers-French Ltd v USDAW* (1979) IRLR 339
82 Section 190(2) TULRCA 1992
83 Section 191(1–3) TULRCA 1992
84 Section 192 TULRCA 1992
85 Section 193 TULRCA 1992
86 Section 193(4) and (6) TULRCA 1992
87 Section 193(5) TULRCA 1992
88 See section 193(7) TULRCA 1992
89 Section 194 TULRCA 1992
90 SI 1981/1794
91 Directive 77/187/EEC, now amended by Directive 98/50/EC
92 See *Adams v Lancashire County Council* (1996) IRLR 154
93 Regulation 5(1) Transfer Regulations 1981

94 (1996) IRLR 76
95 (1988) ECR 2559
96 *Spijkers v Gebroeders Benedik Abattoir* (1986) ECR 1119
97 *Rask v ISS Kantineservice* (1993) IRLR 133
98 *Sophie Redmond Stichting v Bartol* (1992) IRLR 366
99 *Wren v Eastbourne Borough Council* (1993) IRLR 425
100 See note 96
101 (1994) IRLR 302
102 *Süzen v Zehnacker Gebäudereinigung* (1997) IRLR 255
103 (1997) IRLR 361
104 (1999) IRLR 559
105 See *Francisco Hernandez Vidal v Gomez Perez* (1999) IRLR 132
106 See *Mikkelson* (1985) ECR 2639
107 (1989) IRLR 161
108 See *Katsikas v Konstantidis* (1992) ECR 6577
109 See *Hay v George Hanson Ltd* (1996) IRLR 427
110 Regulation 8(2) Transfer Regulations 1981
111 (1998) IRLR 706
112 See *Institution of Professional Civil Servants v Secretary of State* (1987) IRLR 373
113 See Regulation 11 Transfer Regulations 1981 (as amended)
114 10A Transfer Regulations 1981 (as amended)
115 Regulation 11(11) Transfer Regulations 1981 (as amended)

16 Unfair dismissal and redundancy claims

> This chapter looks at the rules for making a claim for unfair dismissal or a redundancy payment. We begin by discussing the time-limits for making a complaint to an employment tribunal and then look at the making of conciliation and compromise agreements or using arbitration procedures as an alternative to presenting the complaint to the tribunal. We go on to examine the remedies for unfair dismissal, which consist of reinstatement, re-engagement or compensation. There is then a consideration of how levels of compensation are arrived at and the method for calculating redundancy payments. The chapter concludes by outlining the rights of employees if the employer becomes insolvent.

MAKING A CLAIM

Unfair dismissal

Unless the 'time-limit escape clause' applies,[1] complaints of unfair dismissal must normally arrive at an employment tribunal within three months of the effective date of termination. However, where employees dismissed for taking part in industrial action allege that they should have been offered re-engagement, a complaint must be lodged within six months of the date of dismissal.[2] A time-limit expires at midnight on the last day of the stipulated period even when that is a non-working day.[3] A complaint can also be presented before the effective date of termination provided it is lodged after notice has been given. This includes notice given by an employee who is alleging constructive dismissal.[4] What is or is not reasonably practicable is a question of fact, and the onus is on the employee to prove that it was not reasonably practicable to claim in time. The meaning of 'reasonably practicable' lies somewhere between reasonable and reasonably capable of physically being done.[5] The tribunal will look at this issue of reasonableness in all the surrounding circumstances. Sickness may be taken into account, but will be more important if it falls within the critical latter part of the three-month period, rather than at the beginning.[6]

The courts have dealt with this jurisdictional point on several occasions and have taken the view that since the unfair dismissal provisions have been in force for over 20 years tribunals should be fairly strict in enforcing the time-limit. Nevertheless, the issue of reasonable practicability depends upon the awareness of specific grounds for complaint, not upon the right to complain at all. Thus there is nothing to prevent an employee who is precluded by lapse of time from claiming under one ground of complaint from proceeding with a second complaint under another ground raised within a reasonable period. According to the Court of Appeal, if employers want to protect themselves from late claims presented on the basis of newly discovered information they should ensure that the fullest information is made available to the employee at the time of dismissal.[7]

The fact that an internal appeal or criminal action is pending does not by itself provide a sufficient excuse for delaying an application.[8] The correct procedure is for employees to submit their applications, known as originating applications, and request that they be held in abeyance. It is a general principle of English law that ignorance does not afford an excuse. Nevertheless in *Wall's Meat Co. Ltd v Khan*[9] it was decided that ignorance or mistaken belief can be grounds for holding that it was not reasonably practicable if it could be shown that the ignorance or mistaken belief was itself reasonable. Thus in *Churchill v Yeates Ltd*[10] the EAT held that it was not reasonably practicable for an employee to bring a complaint until he or she had knowledge of a fundamental fact which rendered the dismissal unfair. In this case, after the three-month period had elapsed an employee who had been dismissed on the grounds of redundancy discovered that he had been replaced. Ignorance or mistaken belief will not be reasonable if it arises from the fault of complainants in not making such inquiries as they reasonably should have in the circumstances. However, the failure by an adviser – such as a trade union official, Citizen's Advice Bureau worker or solicitor – to give correct advice about a time-limit will not necessarily prevent an employee from arguing that it was not reasonably practicable to claim in time.[11]

The correct way to calculate the period of three months beginning with the effective date of termination is to take the day before the effective date and go forward three months. If there is no corresponding date (31st or 30th) in that month, the last day of the month is taken.[12] Where an application is posted within three months but arrives after the period has expired, the question to be determined is whether the claimant could reasonably have expected the application to be delivered in time in the ordinary course of the post.[13] The unexplained failure of an application to reach the tribunal is insufficient to satisfy the statutory test unless all reasonable steps were taken to confirm that the application was duly received.[14]

Redundancy

Employees who have not received a redundancy payment will normally be entitled to make a claim only if within six months of the relevant date they have:

(a) given written notice to the employer that they want a payment, or

(b) referred a question as to their right to a payment, or its amount, to a tribunal, or

(c) presented a complaint of unfair dismissal to a tribunal.[15]

The written notice to the employer does not have to be in a particular form. The test is whether it is of such a character that the recipient would reasonably understand in all the circumstances that it was the employee's intention to seek a payment.[16] In this context the words 'presented' and 'referred' seem to have the same meaning – ie an application must have been received by the employment tribunal within the six-month period.[17] Nevertheless, if any of the above steps are taken outside this period but within 12 months of the relevant date, a tribunal has the discretion to award a payment if it thinks that it would be just and equitable to do so. In such a case a tribunal must have regard to the employee's reasons for failing to take any of the steps within the normal time-limit.[18]

CONCILIATION AND COMPROMISE AGREEMENTS

Copies of unfair dismissal applications and redundancy claims and subsequent correspondence are sent to an ACAS conciliation officer who has the duty to promote a settlement of the complaint:

(a) if requested to do so by the complainant and the employer (known as the respondent), or

(b) if, in the absence of any such request, the conciliation officer considers that he or she could act with a reasonable prospect of success.

In *Moore v Duport Furniture*[19] the House of Lords decided that the expression 'promote a settlement' should be given a liberal construction capable of covering whatever action by way of such promotion is appropriate in the circumstances. Where the complainant had ceased to be employed, the conciliation officer must seek to promote that person's re-employment (ie reinstatement or re-engagement) on terms which appear to be equitable. If the complainant does not wish to be re-employed, or this is not practicable, the conciliation officer must seek to promote agreement on compensation.[20] In addition, section 18(3) ETA 1996 requires conciliation officers to make their services available before a complaint has been presented if requested to do so by either a potential applicant or respondent. However, conciliation officers have no statutory duty to explain to employees what their statutory rights are.[21]

Where appropriate, a conciliation officer is to 'have regard to the desirability of encouraging the use of other procedures available for the settlement of grievances', and anything communicated to a conciliation officer in connection with the performance of the above functions is not admissible in evidence in any proceedings before a tribunal except with the consent of the person who communicated it.[22] It should be noted that an agreement to refrain from lodging a tribunal complaint is subject to all the qualifications by which an agreement can be avoided at common law – for example on grounds of economic duress.[23] Where a representative holds himself or herself out as having authority to reach a settlement, in the absence of any notice to the contrary the other party is entitled to assume that the representative does in fact have such authority. In such circumstances the agreement is binding on the client whether or not the adviser had any authority to enter into it.[24] A conciliated settlement will be binding even though it is not in writing[25] and the employee will be prevented from bringing the case before a tribunal.[26]

Formerly, an agreement purporting to preclude a person from bringing an employment tribunal complaint was void unless action had been taken by a conciliation officer in accordance with the above provisions. However, an agreement to refrain from bringing certain tribunal proceedings will not be void if it satisfies the conditions governing 'compromise agreements'. These conditions are that:

(a)   the agreement must be in writing and must relate to the particular complaint

(b)   the employee must have received independent legal advice from a relevant independent adviser[27] as to the terms and effect of the proposed agreement and, in particular, its effect on the employee's ability to pursue his or her rights before a tribunal

(c)   at the time the adviser gives the advice there must be in force an insurance policy covering the risk of a claim by the employee in respect of loss arising in consequence of the advice

(d)   the agreement must identify the adviser and state that the conditions regulating compromise agreements under the relevant Act are satisfied.[28]

According to the EAT, an employment tribunal has

jurisdiction to enforce a compromise agreement relating to the terms on which employment is to terminate.[29]

ARBITRATION

The Employment Rights (Dispute Resolution) Act 1998 provided for ACAS to prepare an arbitration scheme which would be an alternative to an employment tribunal hearing for the resolution of unfair dismissal claims. The central feature of the scheme is that it is 'designed to be free of legalism'.[30] The arbitrator will decide on procedural and evidential matters and appeals will only be allowed on issues of alleged serious irregularity, rather than on points of law. The hearings are to be conducted in an inquisitorial manner, rather than an adversarial one, and the arbitrator is to have the same powers as an employment appeal chair in making witness orders or ordering the discovery/production of documents. Entry to the scheme is to be entirely voluntary, but the parties will opt for arbitration on the understanding that they will accept the arbitrator's decision as final. The arbitrator will decide whether the dismissal was fair or unfair, and in doing so will have regard to the ACAS Code of Practice on Disciplinary Practice and Procedures, and the ACAS handbook *Discipline at Work*. Where the dismissal is found to be unfair, the arbitrator may award reinstatement, re-engagement or compensation. Hearings will take place in a location convenient to all the parties, and the parties will be responsible for their own expenses.

THE REMEDIES FOR UNFAIR DISMISSAL

Re-employment

When applicants are found to have been unfairly dismissed, tribunals must explain their power to order reinstatement or re-engagement and ask employees if they wish such an order to be made.[31] Only if such a wish is expressed can an order be made, and if no order is made, the tribunal must turn to the question of compensation.[32] Where re-employment is sought, a tribunal must first consider whether reinstatement is appropriate, and in so doing must take into account the following matters:

(a) whether the complainant wishes to be reinstated

(b) whether it is practicable for the employer to comply with an order for reinstatement

(c) where the complainant caused or contributed to some extent to the dismissal, whether it would be just to order reinstatement.[33]

If reinstatement is not ordered, the tribunal must then decide whether to make an order for re-engagement, and if so, on what terms. At this stage the tribunal must take into account the following considerations:

(a) any wish expressed by the complainant as to the nature of the order to be made

(b) whether it is practicable for the employer or, as the case may be, a successor or associated employer to comply with an order for re-engagement

(c) where the complainant caused or contributed to some extent to the dismissal, whether it would be just to order re-engagement, and if so, on what terms.

Except in a case where the tribunal takes into account contributory fault under paragraph (c) it shall, if it orders re-engagement, do so in terms which are, so far as is reasonably practicable, as favourable as an order for reinstatement.[34] However, it would seem that tribunals cannot order that employees be re-engaged on significantly more favourable terms than they would have enjoyed had they been reinstated in their former jobs.[35] According to the Court of Appeal, a tribunal could approach the question of whether it would be practicable to order re-employment in two stages. The first stage would be before any order had been made, when a provisional decision could be taken. The second stage would arise if such an order was made but not complied with.[36]

If at least seven days before the hearing the employee has expressed a wish to be re-employed but it becomes necessary to postpone or adjourn the hearing because the employer does not, without special reason, adduce reasonable evidence about the availability of the job from which the employee was dismissed, the employer will be required to pay the costs of the adjournment or postponement.[37] In addition, section 116(5) ERA 1996 states that where an employer has taken on a permanent replacement, this shall not be taken into account unless the employer shows either:

(a) that it was not practicable to arrange for the dismissed employee's work to be done without engaging a permanent replacement, or

(b) that a replacement was engaged after the lapse of a reasonable period without having heard from the dismissed employee that he or she wished to be reinstated or re-engaged, and that when the employer engaged the replacement it was no longer reasonable to arrange for the dismissed employee's work to be done except by a permanent replacement.

Practicability is a question of fact for each tribunal. In *Boots plc v Lees*[38] the EAT agreed that it was practicable to reinstate notwithstanding that the employee's ultimate superior remained convinced that he was guilty of theft. In contrast, in *Wood Group Heavy Industrial Turbines Ltd v Crossan*,[39] the EAT held that an employer's genuine belief that an employee was dealing in drugs made re-engagement not a suitable option. In addition, the following arguments have been used to prevent an order being made: that the employee was unable to perform the work; that a redundancy situation arose subsequent to the dismissal; and that other employees were hostile to the complainant's return to work. It has also been suggested by the EAT that in a small concern where a close personal relationship exists reinstatement will be appropriate only in exceptional circumstances.[40]

For these purposes reinstatement is defined as treating the complainant 'in all respects as if he had not been dismissed', and on making an order the tribunal must specify:

(a) any amount payable by the employer in respect of any benefit which the complainant might reasonably be expected to have had but for the dismissal, including arrears of pay, for the period between the date of termination and the date of reinstatement

(b) any rights and privileges, including seniority and pension rights, which must be restored to the employee

(c) the date by which the order must be complied with.[41]

The complainant also benefits from any improvements that have been made to the terms and conditions of employment since dismissal.[42]

An order for re-engagement may be on such terms as the tribunal decides, and the complainant may be engaged by the employer, a successor or an associated employer in comparable or suitable employment. On making such an order the tribunal must set out the terms, including: the identity of the employer, the nature of the employment and the remuneration payable, together with the matters listed above in relation to reinstatement.[43]

Where a person is reinstated or re-engaged as the result of a tribunal order but the terms are not fully complied with,[44] a tribunal must make an additional award of compensation of such amount as it thinks fit, having regard to the loss sustained by the complainant in consequence of the failure to comply fully with the terms of the order.[45] It is a matter for speculation how long re-employment must last for it to be said that an order has been complied with. If a complainant is not re-employed in accordance with a tribunal order, he or she is entitled to enforce the monetary element in the employment tribunal.[46] Compensation will be awarded together with an additional award unless the employer satisfies the tribunal that it was not practicable to comply with the order.[47] According to the Court of Appeal, a re-engagement order does not place a duty on an employer to search for a job for the dismissed employee irrespective of the vacancies that arise.[48]

The additional award will be of between 26 and 52 weeks' pay.[49] The employment tribunal has discretion as to where, within this range, the additional compensation should fall, but it must be exercised on the basis of a proper assessment of the factors involved. One factor would ordinarily be the view taken of the employer's conduct in refusing to comply with the order.[50] Conversely, employees who unreasonably prevent an order being complied with will be regarded as having failed to mitigate their loss.

AWARDS OF COMPENSATION

Compensation for unfair dismissal will usually consist of a basic award and a compensatory award. It should be noted that if an award is not paid within 42 days of the tribunal's decision being recorded, it will attract interest.

Basic award

Normally this will be calculated in the same way as a redundancy payment and will be reduced by the amount of any redundancy payment received.[51] However, persons below the age of 20 are also entitled to a basic award, and the basic award is reduced for both men and women above the age of 64. Where the reason or principal reason for dismissal is related to union membership or the employee's health and safety responsibilities there is a minimum award of £2,900, subject to any deduction on the grounds stated below.[52] The basic award can be by such proportion as the tribunal considers just and equitable on two grounds:[53]

(a) the complainant unreasonably refused an offer of reinstatement. Such an offer could have been made before any finding of unfairness

(b) any conduct of the complainant before the dismissal, or before notice was given.[54] This does not apply where the reason for dismissal was redundancy unless the dismissal was regarded as unfair by virtue of section 100(1)(a) or (b), 101A(d), 102(1) or 103 ERA 1996. In that event the reduction will apply only to that part of the award which is payable because of section 120 ERA 1996. An award of two weeks' pay will be made to employees who were redundant but unable to obtain a redundancy payment in either of the following circumstances:

- they are not to be treated as dismissed by virtue of section 138 ERA 1996, which deals with the renewal of a contract or re-engagement under a new one, or

- they are not entitled to a payment because of the operation of section 141 ERA 1996, which is concerned with offers of alternative employment.[55]

Compensatory award

The amount of this award is that which a tribunal 'considers just and equitable in all the circumstances having regard to the loss sustained by the complainant in consequence of the dismissal insofar as that loss is attributable to action taken by the employer'.[56] This may include losses resulting from subsequent employment or unemployment if those losses can be attributed to the dismissal. In *Dench v Flynn & Partners*[57] an assistant solicitor was able to claim compensation for unemployment after a subsequent short-term job because it was attributable to the original dismissal. However, the mere fact that the employer could have dismissed fairly on another ground arising out of the same factual situation does not render it unjust or inequitable to award compensation.[58]

Section 123(3) ERA 1996 specifically mentions that an individual whose redundancy entitlement would have exceeded the basic award can be compensated for the difference, while a redundancy payment received in excess of the basic award payable goes to reduce the compensatory award. The compensatory award can be reduced in two other circumstances: where the employee's action caused or contributed to the dismissal, and where the employee failed to mitigate his or her loss. Before reducing an award on the ground that the complainant caused or contributed to the dismissal, a tribunal must be satisfied that the employee's conduct was culpable or blameworthy, ie foolish, perverse or unreasonable in the circumstances.[59] Thus there could be a finding of contributory fault in a case of constructive dismissal on the basis that there was a causal link between the employee's conduct and the employer's repudiatory breach of contract.[60] However, compensation in respect of discriminatory non-re-engagement following dismissal while taking part in industrial action will not normally be reduced on the grounds of contributory conduct.[61]

In determining whether to reduce compensation the tribunal must take into account the conduct of the complainant and not what happened to some other employee, for example one who was treated more leniently.[62] Not all unreasonable conduct will necessarily be culpable or blameworthy; it will depend on the degree of unreasonableness. Although ill-health cases will rarely give rise to a reduction in compensation on grounds of contributory fault, it is clear that an award may be reduced under the overriding 'just and equitable' provisions.[63] Having found that an employee was to blame, a tribunal must reduce the award to some extent, although the proportion of culpability is a matter for the tribunal.[64] According to the Court of Appeal, tribunals should first assess the amount which it is just and equitable to award because this may have a very significant bearing on what reduction to make for contributory conduct.[65] It should be noted that a payment made by an employer in lieu of notice must be deducted before applying a percentage reduction under Section 123(6) ERA 1996 to reflect the employee's contribution.[66]

Clearly, complainants are obliged to look for work, but there are stages that the tribunal must go through before it can decide what amount to deduct for an employee's failure to find work.[67] These are:

(a) to identify what steps should have been taken by the applicant to mitigate loss

(b) to find the date on which such steps would have produced an alternative income

(c) thereafter, to reduce the amount of compensation by the amount of income which would have been earned.

The onus is on the employer to prove that there was such a failure. While acknowledging that the employee has a duty to act reasonably, the EAT has concluded that this standard is not high in view of the fact that the employer is the wrongdoer.[68]

No account is to be taken of any pressure that was exercised on the employer to dismiss the employee,[69] and according to section 155 TULRCA 1992 compensation cannot be reduced on the grounds that the complainant:

(a) was in breach of or proposed to breach a requirement that he or she must be, or become, a member of a particular trade union or one of a number of trade unions; ceases to be, or refrains from becoming a member of any trade union or of a particular trade union or of one of a number of particular trade unions, or would not take part in the activities of any trade union, of a particular trade union or of one of a number of particular trade unions

(b) refused, or proposed to refuse, to comply with a requirement of a kind mentioned in section 152(3)(a) TULRCA 1992

(c) objected, or proposed to object, to the operation of a provision of a kind mentioned in section 152(3)(b).

Nevertheless, this section permits a distinction to be drawn between what was done by the complainant and the way in which it was done.[70]

The maximum compensatory award was raised by the Employment Relations Act 1999 to £50,000 and is linked to the retail price index. The limit applies only after credit has been given for any payments made by the employer and any reductions have been made,[71] but any 'excess' payments made by the employer over that which is required are deducted after the amount of the compensatory award has been fixed.[72] As regards deductions, normally an employer is to be given credit for all payments made to an employee in respect of claims for wages and other benefits. Thus payments in lieu of notice and *ex gratia* payments can be deducted.[73] Where an employee has suffered sex or race discrimination as well as unfair dismissal, section 126 ERA 1996 prevents double compensation for the same loss.

It is the duty of tribunals to inquire into the various grounds for damages, but it is the responsibility of the aggrieved person to prove the loss. The legislation aims to reimburse the employee rather than to punish the employer. Hence employees who appear to have lost nothing – eg where it can be said that, irrespective of the procedural unfairness which occurred, they would have been dismissed anyway – do not qualify for a compensatory award. However, if the employee puts forward an arguable case that dismissal was not inevitable, the evidential burden shifts to the employer to show that dismissal was likely to have occurred in any event.[74] Additionally, a nil or nominal award may be thought just and equitable in a case where misconduct was discovered subsequently to the dismissal.[75]

The possible grounds (heads) of loss have been divided into the following categories:

(i) *Loss incurred up to the date of the hearing*

Here attention focuses on the employee's actual loss of income, which makes it necessary to ascertain the employee's take-home pay. Thus tax and National Insurance contributions are to be deducted but overtime earnings and tips can be taken into account. Similarly, any sickness or invalidity benefits received may be taken into account.[76] It should also be noted that the loss sustained should be based on what the employee was entitled to, whether or not he or she was receiving it at the time of dismissal.[77] As well as lost wages, section 123(2) ERA 1996 enables an individual to claim compensation for the loss of other benefits, eg a company car or other perks. Similarly, 'expenses reasonably incurred' are mentioned in the statute – so, for example, employees will be able to recover the cost of looking for a new job or setting up their own business. However, complainants cannot be reimbursed for the cost of pursuing their unfair dismissal claims.

(ii) *Loss flowing from the manner of dismissal*

Compensation can be awarded only if the manner of dismissal has made the individual less acceptable to potential employers. There is nothing for hurt feelings.

(iii) *Loss of accrued rights*

This head of loss is intended to compensate the employee for the loss of rights dependent on period of continuous service, but because the basic award reflects lost redundancy entitlement, sums awarded on these grounds have tended to be nominal. Nevertheless, tribunals should include a sum to reflect the fact that dismissed employees lose the statutory minimum notice protection that they have built up.[78]

(iv) *Loss of pension rights*

Undoubtedly this presents the most complex problems of computation. Basically, there are two types of loss: the loss of the present pension position and the loss of the opportunity to improve one's pension position with the dismissing employer. When an employee is close to retirement, the cost of an annuity which will provide a sum equal to the likely pension can be calculated. In other cases the starting-point will be the contributions already paid into the scheme, and in addition to having their own contributions returned, employees can claim an interest in their employer's contributions, except in cases of transferred or deferred pensions. However, in assessing future loss the tribunal must take into account a number of possibilities – for example, future dismissal or resignation, early death, and the fact that a capital sum is being paid sooner than would have been expected. Although employment tribunals have been given actuarial guidelines on loss of pension rights, in each case the factors must be evaluated to see what adjustment should be made or whether the guidelines are safe to use at all.[79]

(v) *Future loss*

Where no further employment has been secured, tribunals will have to speculate how long the employee will remain unemployed. Here the tribunal must utilise its knowledge of local market conditions as well as considering personal circumstances. According to the EAT, employees who have become unfit for work wholly or partly as a result of unfair dismissal are entitled to compensation for loss of earnings, at least for a reasonable period following the dismissal, until they might reasonably have been expected to find other employment.[80] If another job has been obtained, tribunals must compare the employee's salary prospects for the future in each job and assess as best they can how long it will take the employee to reach in the new job the salary equivalent to that which would have been attained had he or she remained with the original employer.[81] Where the employee is earning a higher rate of pay at the time compensation is being assessed, the tribunal should decide whether the new employment is permanent, and if so, should calculate the loss as between the date of dismissal and the date the new job was secured.[82]

Finally, mention must be made of Employment Protection (Recoupment of Jobseeker's Allowance and Income Support) Regulations 1996,[83] which were designed to remove the state subsidy to employers who dismiss unfairly. Such benefits had the effect of reducing the losses suffered by dismissed persons. These regulations provide that a tribunal must not deduct from the compensation awarded any sum which represents jobseeker's allowance received, and the employer is instructed not to pay immediately the amount of compensation which represents loss of income up to the hearing (known as the 'prescribed element'). The National Insurance Fund can then serve the employer with a recoupment notice which will require him or her to pay the Fund from the prescribed element the amount which represents the jobseeker's allowance paid to the employee prior to the hearing.[84] When the amount has been refunded by the employer, the remainder of the prescribed element becomes the employee's property. It is important to note that private settlements do not fall within the scope of these Regulations.

CALCULATING A REDUNDANCY PAYMENT

The size of a redundancy payment depends on the employee's length of continuous service, his or her age and the amount of a week's pay. A week's pay is calculated in accordance with sections 220–9 ERA 1996 (see Chapter 17) and in this context means gross pay.[85] However, it does not take into account increased wage rates agreed subsequently to the employee's dismissal but backdated to a date prior to the dismissal.[86] Unless the contrary is shown, employment is presumed to have been continuous (see Chapter 17), but this only applies in relation to the dismissing employer (except when a business or undertaking has been transferred[87] or an employee has been taken into employment by an associated employer). If continuity is not preserved on a transfer, an assurance given by one employer that the obligations of another will be met will not confer jurisdiction on a tribunal to award a payment based on overall service. However, an employee may be able to show that there was a contract to the effect that he or she would retain the benefit of previous employment.[88]

Redundancy payments are calculated according to the following formula, with a maximum of 20 years' service being taken into account. Starting at the end of the employee's period of service and calculating backwards:

(a) one and a half weeks' pay is allowed for each year of employment in which the individual was between the ages of 41 and 64. Those who are aged 64 have their entitlement reduced by one-twelfth in respect of each month they remain in employment

(b) a week's pay for each year of employment in which the individual was between the ages of 22 and 40

(c) half a week's pay for each year of employment between the ages of 18 and 21.[89]

On making a redundancy payment the employer must give the employee a written statement indicating how the amount has been calculated. An employer who, without reasonable excuse, fails to do so can receive a fine not exceeding level 3 on the standard scale.[90]

EMPLOYEE RIGHTS ON INSOLVENCY

If an employer becomes insolvent or bankrupt, an employee's wages in respect of the four months beforehand, up to a maximum of £800, become a preferential debt.[91] In addition, Schedule 6 of the Insolvency Act 1986 provides that the following shall be treated as wages for these purposes: a guarantee payment; statutory sick pay; remuneration payable under suspension on medical grounds; remuneration payable during a protective award; and a payment for time off for union duties, antenatal care or to look for work or make arrangements for training in a redundancy situation.

The Insolvency Protection Directive[92] had as its purpose the 'protection of employees in the event of the insolvency of their employer, in particular in order to guarantee payments of their outstanding claims . . .'. Article 3 of the Directive requires Member States to set up guarantee institutions to enable outstanding claims to be paid in the event of an insolvent employer's being unable to do so. In the United Kingdom this guarantee institution is the DfEE.

Section 182 ERA 1996 gives employees the right to make a written request to the Secretary of State for a payment out of the National Insurance Fund to meet certain other debts which arise out of the employer's insolvency.[93] These debts are:

(a) arrears of pay up to a maximum of eight weeks. This includes any of the matters treated as wages for the purposes of the Insolvency Act 1986 (see above)

(b) wages payable during the statutory notice period. It should be noted that employees are still required to mitigate their loss

(c) holiday pay up to a maximum of six weeks, provided the entitlement accrued during the preceding 12 months

(d) a basic award of compensation for unfair dismissal

(e) any reasonable sum by way of reimbursement of the whole or part of any fee or premium paid by an apprentice or articled clerk.

A financial limit is imposed on the amount that can be recovered in respect of any one week[94] (£220.00 per week in October 1998).

Before reimbursing the employee the Secretary of State must be satisfied both that the employer has become insolvent and that the employee is entitled to be paid the whole or part of the debt claimed. The Secretary of State is liable only to the extent to which the employee is legally entitled to make a claim against the employer.[95] Also, a payment cannot be made unless a 'relevant officer' appointed in connection with the insolvency – eg a liquidator, receiver or trustee in bankruptcy – has supplied a statement of the amount owed to the employee. However, this requirement may be waived if the Secretary of State is satisfied that the statement is not necessary to determine the amount owing.[96] If the Secretary of State fails to make a payment or if it is less than the amount which the employee thinks should have been made,[97] a complaint may be presented to an employment tribunal within three months of the Secretary of State's decision being communicated.[98] Where a tribunal finds that a payment ought to have been made under section 182 ERA 1996, it must make a declaration to that effect and state the amount that ought to be paid. Finally, it should be noted that when the Secretary of State makes a payment to the employee, the rights and remedies of the latter in relation to the employer's insolvency are transferred to the Secretary of State.[99]

KEY POINTS 16
Making a claim

- Complaints of unfair dismissal must normally arrive at an employment tribunal within three months of the effective date of termination.

- Employees who have not received a redundancy payment will normally be entitled to make a claim within six months of the relevant date.

- ACAS will assist the employee and the employer by conciliating to try and reach an agreement to settle the complaint.

- Remedies for unfair dismissal include reinstatement, re-engagement and compensation.

- Compensation for unfair dismissal will consist of a basic award and a compensatory award.

- The maximum compensatory award was set at £50,000 in 1999 and is linked to the retail price index.

- The size of a redundancy payment depends upon the employee's age, length of service and the amount of a week's pay.

- If an employer becomes insolvent, some liabilities will pass to the Secretary of State for payment out of the National Insurance Fund.

NOTES

1 Section 111(2) ERA 1996
2 Section 239(2) TULRCA 1992
3 See *Swainston v Hetton Victory Club* (1983) IRLR 164
4 Section 111(4) ERA 1996; see *Patel v Nagesan* (1995) IRLR 370
5 See *Palmer v Southend BC* (1984) IRLR 119
6 See *Schultz v Esso Petroleum Co Ltd* (1999) IRLR 488
7 See *Marley Ltd v Anderson* (1996) IRLR 163
8 See *Palmer v Southend BC* (note 5)
9 (1978) IRLR 499
10 (1983) IRLR 187; see also *MTIRA v Simpson* (1988) IRLR 212
11 See *London International College v Sen* (1993) IRLR 333
12 See *Pruden v Cunard Ltd* (1993) IRLR 317
13 See *St Basil's Centre v McCrossan* (1991) IRLR 455
14 See *Camden & Islington NHS Trust v Kennedy* (1996) IRLR 381
15 Section 164(1) ERA 1996; see *Duffin v Secretary of State* (1983) ICR 766
16 See *Price v Smithfield Group Ltd* (1978) IRLR 80
17 See *Secretary of State v Banks* (1983) ICR 48 and *Swainston v Hetton Victory Club* (note 3)
18 Section 164(2) ERA 1996
19 (1982) IRLR 31
20 Section 18(4) ETA 1996
21 See *Slack v Greenham* (1983) IRLR 271
22 Section 18(6) and (7) ETA 1996
23 See *Hennessy v Craigmyle Ltd* (1985) IRLR 446
24 See *Freeman v Sovereign Chicken Ltd* (1991) IRLR 408
25 Se *Gilbert v Kembridge Fibres Ltd* (1984) IRLR 52

26 Section 203(2)(e) ERA 1996
27 Section 203(3A) ERA 1996 defines 'relevant independent adviser' as a qualified lawyer; an officer, official, member or employee of a trade union who has been certified to give advice by the union; an authorised advice centre worker; or others specified by the Secretary of State
28 See Sections 203(2)(f) and 203(3) ERA 1996
29 See *Rock-It Cargo Ltd v Green* (1997) IRLR 582
30 See ACAS Scheme for the resolution of unfair dismissal complaints, ACAS, July 1998
31 See *Cowley v Manson Timber* (1995) IRLR 153
32 Section 112 ERA 1996
33 Section 116(1) ERA 1996
34 Section 116(4) ERA 1996
35 See *Rank Xerox v Stryczek* (1995) IRLR 568
36 See *Port of London Authority v Payne* (1994) IRLR 9
37 Section 13(2) ETA 1996
38 (1986) IRLR 485
39 (1998) IRLR 680
40 See *Enessy Co v Minoprio* (1978) IRLR 489
41 Section 114(2) ERA 1996
42 Section 114(3) ERA 1996
43 Section 115(2) ERA 1996
44 See *Artisan Press v Strawley* (1986) IRLR 126 on the difference between not re-employing and not fully complying with an order
45 Section 117(2) ERA 1996
46 See section 124(4) ERA 1996
47 Section 117(3) and (4) ERA 1996
48 See *Port of London Authority v Payne* (note 36)
49 Section 117(3)(b) ERA 1996
50 See *Motherwell Railway Club v McQueen* (1989) ICR 419
51 Section 122(4) ERA 1996; see *Boorman v Allmakes Ltd* (1995) IRLR 553
52 Section 120 ERA 1996
53 Section 122(1) and (2) ERA 1996
54 See *RSPCA v Cruden* (1986) IRLR 83
55 Section 121 ERA 1996
56 Section 123 ERA 1996
57 (1998) IRLR 653
58 See *Devonshire v Trico-Folberth* (1989) IRLR 397
59 See *Nelson v BBC (No 2)* (1979) IRLR 304; *Morrison v ATGWU* (1989) IRLR 361
60 See *Polentarutti v Autokraft Ltd* (1991) IRLR 457
61 See *Crossville Wales Ltd v Tracey and Others (No 2)* (1997) IRLR 691
62 See *Parker Foundry Ltd v Slack* (1992) IRLR 11
63 See *Slaughter v Brewer Ltd* (1990) IRLR 426
64 See *Warrilow v Walker Ltd* (1984) IRLR 304
65 See *Rao v Civil Aviation Authority* (1994) IRLR 240
66 See *Heggie v Uniroyal Englebert Tyres Ltd* (1999) IRLR 802
67 See *Savage v Saxena* (1998) IRLR 182
68 See *Fyfe v Scientific Furnishings Ltd* (1989) IRLR 331
69 Section 123(5) ERA 1996
70 See *TGWU v Howard* (1992) IRLR 170
71 Section 124(5) ERA 1996; see *Braund Ltd v Murray* (1991) IRLR 100

72 See *Digital Equipment Co Ltd v Clements (No 2)* (1998) ICR 258
73 See *Cox v London Borough of Camden* (1996) IRLR 389
74 See *Britool Ltd v Roberts* (1993) IRLR 481
75 See *Tele-trading Ltd v Jenkins* (1990) IRLR 430
76 See *Puglia v James & Sons* (1996) IRLR 70 and *Rubenstein v McGloughlin* (1996) IRLR 557
77 See *Kinzley v Minories Finance Ltd* (1987) IRLR 490
78 See *Guinness Ltd v Green* (1989) IRLR 289 and *Puglia v James & Sons* (note 76)
79 See *Bingham v Hobourn Engineering Ltd* (1992) IRLR 298
80 See *Devine v Designer Flowers Ltd* (1993) IRLR 517
81 See *Tradewind Airways Ltd v Fletcher* (1981) IRLR 272
82 See *Fentiman v Fluid Engineering Ltd* (1991) IRLR 150
83 SI 1996/2439; see also sections 16 and 17 ETA 1996
84 See *Homan v A1 Bacon Ltd* (1996) ICR 846
85 See *Secretary of State v Woodrow* (1983) IRLR 11
86 See *Leyland Vehicles Ltd v Reston* (1981) IRLR 19
87 See *Lassman v Secretary of State* (1999) ICR 416 where continuity was preserved by the Transfer Regulations 1981, even though, at the time of the transfer, the employees received statutory redundancy payments
88 See *Secretary of State v Globe Elastic Ltd* (1979) IRLR 327
89 Section 162(1) and (2) ERA 1996
90 Section 165 ERA 1996; see *Barnsley MBC v Prest* (1996) ICR 85
91 Section 386 Insolvency Act 1986
92 Directive 80/987
93 Insolvency is defined in section 183 ERA 1996; see *Secretary of State v Stone* (1994) ICR 761
94 See *Morris v Secretary of State* (1985) IRLR 297
95 See *Mann v Secretary of State* (1999) IRLR 566
96 Section 187(2) ERA 1996
97 See *Potter v Secretary of State for Employment* (1997) IRLR 21 on the ability of the Secretary of State to set off protective awards against the claims of the employees
98 Section 188(2) ERA 1996; the 'time-limit escape clause' applies here
99 Section 189 ERA 1996

17 Calculating continuous service, normal working hours and a week's pay

In this chapter we are concerned with the important concepts of continuity of service, normal working hours and a week's pay. They are important because many statutory rights are dependent upon minimum length of service, and payments are related to statutory concepts of normal working hours and a week's pay. We begin by looking at continuity of employment and what impact different types of gaps in continuity have on these statutory rights. We then look briefly at normal working hours. (Aspects of the regulation of working time are dealt with in Chapter 11.) Lastly we examine the concept of a week's pay which is used for computing many payments under ERA 1996, such as redundancy payments and compensation for unfair dismissal.

CONTINUITY OF EMPLOYMENT

Continuous employment is an important concept because many statutory rights are dependent on a minimum service qualification, and certain benefits – for example redundancy payments and basic awards – are calculated by reference to length of service. For the purposes of ERA 1996 an individual's period of employment is to be computed in accordance with sections 210–219. Continuity of employment is a statutory concept[1] and the courts will look to see whether there has been a break in service. In *Morris v Walsh Western UK Ltd*[2] the employer agreed to ignore a month's break in employment and treat the employee as having been continuously employed. Despite this, the EAT held that the month's gap had constituted a break in service.

Section 210(5) ERA 1996 states that employment is presumed to have been continuous unless the contrary is shown, although this is not so where there is a succession of employers.[3] Apart from redundancy payment purposes, these provisions also apply to periods of employment wholly or mainly outside Great Britain.[4] Continuity is normally assessed in relation to the particular contract on which a claim is based. However, it may be possible for an employer to deliberately subject employees to a combination of separate contracts which amount to a series of fixed-term contracts with a break in between.[5] The EAT concluded that any anomalies or avoidance of the legislation is a matter for Parliament rather than the Courts.

A period of continuous employment, which begins with the day on which the employee 'starts work',[6] is to be computed in months, and except in so far as is otherwise provided, a week which does not count breaks the period of continuous employment.[7] A person accrues a period of continuous service only if he or she is employed under a legal contract of employment. Thus, if for a period of time the contract is illegal, then for that period the contract cannot be relied on.[8] Where there is a dispute over continuity, employees have to establish that there was a week which counted, but in respect of subsequent weeks they can rely on the presumption contained in section 210(5) ERA 1996 that employment is continuous (unless there is evidence to the contrary).[9]

Weeks that count

According to section 212(1) ERA 1996, any week[10] during the whole or part of which a person has a contract of employment will count. In *Sweeney v J & S Henderson Ltd*[11] an employee resigned on a Saturday and was re-engaged on the following Friday. Despite the fact that the employee had left voluntarily, continuity was preserved for the purposes of a subsequent unfair dismissal claim. A week counts if one of the following applies for the whole or part of that week:

(a) The employee is incapable of work as a consequence of sickness or injury.[12] Not more than 26 consecutive weeks can be counted under this head.[13] In this context the expression 'incapable of work' does not mean incapable of work generally, nor does it refer to the particular work provided for in the contract which has ended. According to the Court of Appeal, where the work on offer by the employer differs from that for which the employee was previously employed, the tribunal must consider whether the work offered was of a kind which the employee was willing to accept or, even if the employee was unwilling, was suited to his or her particular circumstances.[14]

(b) The employee is absent from work on account of a temporary cessation of work.[15] In this context the phrase 'absent from work' does not necessarily mean physical absence but means not performing in substance the contract that previously existed between the parties.[16] The words 'on account of' refer to the reason when the employer dismissed, and the fact that the unavailability of work was foreseen and the employee took another job will not prevent a tribunal's holding that this provision applies. 'Cessation of work' denotes that a quantity of work has for the time being ceased to exist and was therefore no longer available to be given to the employee. Thus, when a member of a pool of casual cleaners was not allocated work under a pool arrangement, that absence was not on account of a temporary cessation of work.[17]

According to the House of Lords, 'temporary' means lasting a relatively short time and whether an interval can be so characterised is a question of fact for the employment tribunal. Where there is a succession of fixed-term contracts with intervals between them, continuity is not broken unless 'looking backwards from the date of expiry of the fixed-term contract on which the claim is based, there is to be found between one fixed-term contract and its immediate predecessor an interval that cannot be characterised as short relative to the combined duration of the two fixed-term contracts'.[18] In *Flack v Kodak Ltd*[19] the EAT held that where an employee has worked intermittently over a period of years in an irregular pattern, tribunals ought to have regard to all the circumstances and should not confine themselves to the mathematical approach of looking at each gap and immediately adjoining periods of employment. The fact that cessation is not permanent does not mean that it must be temporary for these purposes.[20]

(c) The employee is absent from work in circumstances such that by arrangement or custom he or she is regarded as continuing in the employment of the employer for all or any purposes.[21] Although an arrangement must normally exist at the time the absence began, the EAT has held that the period between dismissal and voluntary reinstatement may be covered by this provision.[22] It should be noted that unfair dismissal complainants who are re-employed following a tribunal or arbitrator's decision, a compromise agreement (see Chapter 16), or action taken by a conciliation officer have their continuity preserved by special regulations.[23]

It would appear that the cause of the absence is immaterial. Thus employees who have been loaned to a third party may be protected as well as those given leave of absence for personal reasons. In *Colley v Corkindale*[24] the EAT held that employees who worked alternate weeks were to be regarded as being absent by arrangement on their weeks off.

Finally, note should be taken of the fact that continuity of employment where employees are absent from work for family reasons is now dealt with under the Maternity and Parental Leave Regulations 1999. Readers wishing to know more about these Regulations should turn to Chapter 9 (Parental Rights), pages 158–175, where the relevant issues are discussed in some detail.

Strikes and lock-outs

Days on which an employee is on strike neither count nor break the employee's period of continuous service.[25] By virtue of section 235(5) ERA 1996 for this purpose 'strike' means

(a) 'the cessation of work by a body of persons employed acting in combination, or

(b)   a concerted refusal or a refusal under a common understanding of any number of persons employed to continue to work for an employer in consequence of a dispute

(c)   done as a means of compelling their employer or any person or body of persons employed, or to aid other employees in compelling their employer or any person or body of persons employed, to accept or not to accept terms and conditions of or affecting employment'.

Where an employee is absent from work because of a lock-out, again continuity is not broken and if the contract of employment subsists, the period of absence could be counted under section 212(1) ERA 1996.[26] 'Lock-out' means

(a)   'the closing of a place of employment,

(b)   the suspension of work,

(c)   the refusal by an employer to continue to employ any number of persons employed by him in consequence of a dispute, or

(d)   done with a view to compelling those persons, or to aid another employer in compelling persons employed by him, to accept terms or conditions of or affecting employment'.[27]

It makes no difference that employees were dismissed during a strike or lock-out; as long as they were subsequently re-engaged, their period of continuous employment will be preserved. Any attempt to provide otherwise – for example, by introducing a specific term relating to previous employment – will be construed as an attempt to exclude or limit the operation of this paragraph and will be ineffective as a result of section 203 ERA 1996.[28]

Change of employer

Usually when an employee leaves one employer and starts working for another, his or her period of continuous service will be broken. However, in certain circumstances a person will be regarded as having been employed by the new employer as from the date his or her previous employment commenced. Apart from the situation where an employer voluntarily agrees to give credit for service with a previous employer (which does not bind the Secretary of State),[29] there are six main types of case in which employment is deemed to be continuous despite a change of employer:

(a) if there is a transfer of a trade, undertaking, business or part of a business.[30] The words 'trade' and 'undertaking' are not defined in ERA 1996, but 'business' includes a trade or profession and any activity carried on by a body of persons, whether corporate or unincorporated.[31] In relation to business transfers the critical question is whether there has been the transfer of a 'going concern' which could be carried on without interruption or merely the disposal of assets. If the latter, continuity of employment is not maintained. A transfer is not an event that necessarily happens all at once. A trade or business has different elements such as goodwill, property and stock in trade, as well as the employees. The transfer, for continuity purposes, does not therefore take place at a precise moment in time.[32]

If the transfer is a relevant transfer for the purposes of the Transfer Regulations 1981 (see Chapter 15), the fact that the employees were dismissed and given redundancy payments at the time of the transfer will not necessarily affect continuity of employment.[33]

(b) if an Act of Parliament results in one corporate body replacing another as employer[34]

(c) if the employer dies and the employee is then re-employed by the personal representatives or trustees of the deceased[35]

(d) if there is a change in the partners, personal representatives or trustees who employ the individual[36]

(e) if the individual is taken into the employment of an associated employer.[37] 'Associated employer' is defined in section 231 ERA 1996 as follows: 'Any two employers are to be treated as associated if (a) one is a company of which the other (directly or indirectly) has control; or (b) both are companies of which a third person (directly or indirectly) has control.' The expression 'has control' is used in the company law sense of controlling 51 per cent or more of the shares. However, the register of shares does not conclusively establish the identity of the possessor of control because the person registered as owner might be a nominee.[38] While there must not be a gap between the employments (unless it is covered by the statute), it is not necessary that the move to an associated employer be made with the acquiescence of either employer.

(f) if the employee is employed by the governors of a school maintained by a local education authority or by the authority itself and he or she is transferred to another school or local education authority.[39]

NORMAL WORKING HOURS[40]

For all statutory purposes normal working hours and a week's pay are to be ascertained by reference to section 234 and sections 220–229 ERA 1996. Normal working hours are the number of hours employees are required to work by their contracts, and where they are expressly stated, this will usually be conclusive even if longer hours are actually worked.[41] Where the contractual terms have not been expressed by the parties, to determine the number of hours the contract normally involves it is necessary to look at the way the parties have acted. If it was a term that employees should work the hours they were asked to, then one looks at the hours actually worked.[42] Normal working hours will not include overtime unless that overtime is included in the minimum number of hours of employment.[43]

A WEEK'S PAY

This concept is used for computing many payments under ERA 1996 – for example, redundancy payments and the basic award of compensation for unfair dismissal. Where there are normal working hours,

(a) if remuneration does not vary with the amount of work done, a week's pay is the gross amount payable for a week's work under the contract of employment in force on the calculation date.[44] Calculation dates are laid down in section 225 ERA 1996 and vary according to the particular statutory rights being enforced.

(b) if the remuneration varies with the amount of work done, a week's pay is the remuneration for the number of normal working hours payable at the average hourly rate.[45] The average hourly rate is ascertained by calculating the total number of hours actually worked in the 12 calendar weeks preceding the calculation date, the total amount of remuneration paid for these hours, and then deducing the average hourly payment. The 12 calendar weeks preceding the calculation date consist of weeks during which the employee actually worked even though for some of this time he or she might have earned less than usual. However, a week in which no remuneration was required to be paid must be disregarded.[46] In *British Coal v Cheesebrough*[47] the average hourly rate was calculated by taking into account all remuneration paid in respect of all hours worked, including overtime, except that the premium element in respect of overtime was disregarded.

(c) and the normal working hours are worked at varying times and in varying amounts in different weeks – for example, in the case of shift-workers – both the average rate of remuneration and the number of hours worked in a week will have to be computed, again in the 12 calendar weeks preceding the calculation date. In these circumstances, a week's pay is the average weekly number of normal working hours payable at the average hourly rate of remuneration.[48]

Where there are no normal working hours, a week's pay is the average weekly remuneration received over the period of 12 calendar weeks preceding the calculation date.[49]

If an employee has not been employed for a sufficient period to enable a calculation to be made under any of the above provisions, a tribunal must decide what amount 'fairly represents a week's pay'. Section 228(2)–(3) ERA 1996 sets out some matters for consideration in this respect.

Annualised hours contracts can present a problem here. In *Ali v Christian Salvesen Food Services Ltd*[50] the employees agreed a total number of hours per annum as part of a collective agreement. The arrangement, however, did not deal with the situation where employees left during the year, after they had worked in excess of the notional weekly hours on which their standard rate of pay was based. The Court of Appeal refused to fill the gap in the agreement so that the employees could claim for the hours actually worked.

Finally, the word 'remuneration' has not been statutorily defined for these purposes but it has been held to include any payments made on a regular basis, eg commission, bonuses and attendance allowances. Payments in kind are excluded – eg free accommodation – as are payments received from a third party, such as tips. However, gratuities added to cheques and credit card vouchers are paid to the employer and may be treated as remuneration for these purposes.[51]

KEY POINTS 17
Continuity, normal working hours and a week's pay

- Continuity of employment is a statutory concept and the courts look to see whether there has been a break in service.

- A person accrues a period of continuous service only if he or she is employed under a legal contract of employment.

- Any week during the whole or part of which a person has a contract of employment will count. One day's employment in a week is sufficient to preserve continuity.

- Days on which an employee is on strike neither count nor break the employee's period of continuous service.

- There are circumstances in which an employee leaves one employer and starts working for another and continuity is preserved, for example in the Transfer Regulations 1981.

- Normal working hours are the number of hours employees are required to work by their contracts of employment and exclude non-contractual overtime.

- A week's pay is normally the gross amount payable for a week's work under the contract of employment. Where there is a variation in the amount paid for work, the average hourly rate will apply.

NOTES

1 See *Collison v BBC* (1998) IRLR 239
2 (1997) IRLR 562
3 See *Secretary of State v Cohen* (1987) IRLR 169
4 See section 215 ERA 1996 and *Weston v Vega Space Ltd* (1989) IRLR 509
5 See *Booth v United States of America* (1999) IRLR 16 and note Directive on Fixed-term Work COM (1999) 203
6 See *General of the Salvation Army v Dewsbury* (1984) IRLR 222
7 Section 210(4) ERA 1996
8 See *Hyland v J. Barker Ltd* (1985) IRLR 403
9 See *Nicoll v Nocorrode Ltd* (1981) IRLR 163
10 'week' means a week ending with Saturday; see section 235(1) ERA 1996
11 (1999) IRLR 306
12 Section 212(3)(a) ERA 1996
13 Section 212(4) ERA 1996
14 See *Pearson v Kent County Council* (1993) IRLR 165
15 Section 212(3)(b) ERA 1996
16 See *Stephens & Son v Fish* (1989) ICR 324
17 *Byrne v City of Birmingham DC* (1987) IRLR 191
18 *Ford v Warwickshire County Council* (1983) IRLR 126
19 (1986) IRLR 255
20 See *Sillars v Charrington Ltd* (1989) IRLR 152 on seasonal work
21 Section 212(3)(c) ERA 1996
22 *Ingram v Foxon* (1985) IRLR 5
23 See Employment Protection (Continuity of Employment) Regulations 1993 SI 1993/2165
24 (1995) ICR 965
25 Section 216(1) and (2) ERA 1996
26 Section 216(3) ERA 1996
27 Section 235(4) ERA 1996

28 See *Hanson v Fashion Industries* (1980) IRLR 393

39 See *Secretary of State v Globe Elastic Thread Co. Ltd* (1979) IRLR 327

30 Section 218(2) ERA 1996; for a generous interpretation of this provision see *Tuck Ltd v Bartlett* (1994) IRLR 162 and *Justfern Ltd v D'Ingerthorpe* (1994) IRLR 164

31 Section 235(1) ERA 1996

32 See *Clark & Tokeley Ltd v Oakes* (1998) IRLR 577

33 See *Lassman v Secretary of State* (1999) ICR 416

34 Section 218(3) ERA 1996

35 Section 218(4) ERA 1996

36 Section 218(5) ERA 1996; see *Jeetle v Elster* (1985) IRLR 227

37 Section 218(6) ERA 1996

38 See *Payne v Secretary of State* (1989) IRLR 352 and *Strudwick v JBL* (1988) IRLR 457

39 Section 218(7) ERA 1996; see also section 218(8)–(10) on certain types of employment in the health service

40 See also Chapter 11 on the regulation of working time

41 See *Gascol Conversions v Mercer* (1974) IRLR 155

42 See *Dean v Eastbourne Fishermen's Club Ltd* (1977) IRLR 143

43 Section 234(3) ERA 1996; see *Lotus Cars Ltd v Sutcliffe and Stratton* (1982) IRLR 381

44 Section 221(2) ERA 1996; see *Keywest Club v Choudhury* (1988) IRLR 51

45 Section 221(3) ERA 1996

46 Section 225 ERA 1996; see *Secretary of State v Crane* (1988) IRLR 238

47 (1990) IRLR 148

48 Section 221 ERA 1996

49 Section 224 ERA 1996

50 (1997) IRLR 17

51 See *Nerva v RL&G Ltd* (1996) IRLR 461

18 Human rights and data protection

Article 8(1) of the European Convention on Human Rights, now incorporated into UK law by the Human Rights Act 1998 (see below), states that 'Everyone has the right to respect for his private and family life, his home and his correspondence.' We examine here the provisions of the Human Rights Act 1998, the Data Protection Act 1998 and the Access to Medical Records Act 1988, and consider their effect upon employment law and practice.

THE HUMAN RIGHTS ACT 1998

The Human Rights Act 1998 (HRA 1998) incorporates a substantial part of the European Convention for the Protection of Human Rights and Fundamental Freedoms, which was originally agreed in Rome in 1950. It is unlawful for public authorities, which include courts and tribunals, to act in a way that is incompatible with a Convention right.[1] From October 2000 courts and tribunals in the United Kingdom must take into account any 'judgment, decision, declaration or advisory opinion' of the European Court of Human Rights[2] (ECHR) or the European Commission of Human Rights. In addition, all primary and subordinate legislation must be read and interpreted in a way that is compatible with Convention rights.[3] If a court is satisfied that a piece of legislation is incompatible with a Convention right, it may make a declaration of incompatibility,[4] after which the government may amend the legislation concerned to bring it into line.[5]

The Articles of the Convention that might have an effect on employment law in the United Kingdom are listed below, with some illustrations of how they may, or may not, impact:

Article 8: The right to respect for private and family life

This Article has two parts. The first, quoted in the introductory paragraph to this chapter, states the right to privacy (see also the Data Protection Act 1998 below). Article 8(2) forbids the interference by any public authority in the exercise of this right, except for

(a) the interests of national security

(b) public safety or the economic well-being of the country

(c) the prevention of disorder or crime

(d) the protection of health and morals

(e) the protection of the rights and freedoms of others.

These are important exceptions. In *Halford v United Kingdom*[6] the Assistant Chief Constable of Merseyside Police brought a claim that she had been discriminated against on the grounds of her sex when, on a number of occasions, she unsuccessfully applied for promotion. During the proceedings, Ms Halford complained to the ECHR that the interception of telephone calls from her office and home breached her rights to privacy and freedom of expression.[7] The UK Government argued that interception of office telephone calls fell outside the protection of Article 8 because there could not be a reasonable expectation of privacy in relation to them. They argued that in principle employers should be able to monitor phone calls without the employees' knowledge on equipment provided by them. The Court refused to accept this argument and awarded her compensation. Because she had received no warning, Article 8 applied to protect her privacy. Thus the entitlement to privacy extends to calls made from the office as well as home, unless there has been prior warning that such calls are liable to be monitored.

Article 9: Freedom of thought, conscience and religion

Article 9(1) establishes the right of a person to 'freedom to change his religion or belief, and freedom, either alone or in community with others and in public or private, to manifest his religion or belief, in worship, teaching, practice and observance'. The limitations to this right are those:

(a) in the interests of public safety

(b) for the protection of public order, health or morals

(c) for the protection of the rights and freedoms of others.

One issue is when the practice of religion or religious beliefs clashes with the requirements of a contract of employment. It is not clear whether Article 9 will be helpful in this respect.

In *Ahmad v Inner London Education Authority*[8] a school teacher who was a devout Muslim worked under a contract of employment which required his full-time service. The contract incorporated a staff code which allowed for time off with pay on special days in which a religion held that no work should be done. The employers would not allow him a 45-minute period of absence each Friday for him to be able to attend at a mosque. The claim for unfair dismissal was lost in the Court of Appeal, which held that the dismissal was fair because the employee absented himself during working hours, and was not for reasons of religious belief. Lord Denning considered the issue with regard to Article 9 and concluded that 'It is drawn in such vague terms that it can be used for all sorts of unreasonable claims and provoke all sorts of litigation.' He then stated that he could see nothing in the Convention that would give an employee the right to participate in religious activity on Friday afternoons in derogation of a contract of employment. Lord Scarman dissented from the majority view and decided that the Convention required a broad view to be taken, and that Article 9 would help people exercise their religious beliefs during working hours without losing pay.

In *Stedman v United Kingdom*[9] an employee lost a claim for breach of Article 9 as a result of her dismissal for refusing to work on a Sunday, which was against her religious beliefs. A similar case was cited of an employee of Finnish State Railways who had lost a job because a requirement to work after sunset on a Friday clashed with the employee's beliefs as a member of the Seventh Day Adventist Church. The Court had held that this was for economic reasons and had nothing to do with the person's religious beliefs. Ms Stedman lost for similar reasons.[10]

Article 10: Freedom of expression

According to Article 10(1), the right to freedom of expression shall include the right to hold opinions and receive and impart information and ideas without interference from public authorities and regardless of frontiers. Again there is an important list of limitations to this right. They are restrictions in the interests of:

(a) national security

(b) territorial integrity or public safety

(c) the prevention of disorder or crime

(d) the protection of health or morals

(e) the protection of the reputation or the rights of others

(f) the prevention of disclosure of information received in confidence

(g) maintaining the authority and impartiality of the judiciary.

Camelot v Centaur Communications[11] concerned a leak of information about Camelot, who ran the national lottery, to the press. The information was a draft set of accounts which contained potentially embarrassing information. Amongst other matters, Camelot sought the return of the documents partly to help them identify the source of the leak, which they believed to be an employee. The Court of Appeal stated that weight had to be given to the Convention and decisions of the ECHR. The Contempt of Court Act of 1981 restricted the Court's right to compel disclosure unless it was in the interests of, amongst other factors, justice or national security.[12] The Court decided that the public interest in enabling the employer to discover the identity of the person who had made the leak outweighed the public interest in 'enabling the person to escape detection'. A slightly broader approach was evident in a case which concerned employees distributing leaflets outside a supermarket to urge the public not to buy their employer's goods.[13] Lord Justice Neill stated that the Court should bear in mind the Convention whenever it is asked to exercise its discretion in a way which restricts freedom of expression.

In *Ahmed v United Kingdom*[14] there was a challenge by local government officers against regulations which restricted the right of senior local government employees to participate in political activities. They claimed that the regulations were in breach of Article 10 of the Convention. The ECHR held that such restrictions were not in breach because they were prescribed by law for a legitimate aim, namely to protect the rights of others, such as local councillors and the electorate, to effective political democracy at the local level. The ECHR accepted that for a restriction of Article 10 there had to be a pressing need and that States had a certain 'margin of appreciation'. This restriction was a valid response to a social need within the UK's margin of appreciation.

Article 11: Freedom of assembly and association

Article 11(1) states that everyone has the 'right to freedom of peaceful assembly and to freedom of association with others, including the right to form and to join trade unions for the protection of his interests'. There is an exception allowed for the armed forces, the police and 'the administration of the state'.[15] Other restrictions are:

(a)   for the interests of national security or public safety

(b)   for the prevention of disorder or crime

(c)   for the protection of health or morals

(d)   for the protection of the rights and freedom of others.

The attitude of the United Kingdom towards this Article was tested in the decision, in 1984, to forbid employees at the Government Communications Headquarters to be members of a trade union. The UK government argued that there was a national security justification for this action.[16] The matter was subsequently considered by the European

Commission of Human Rights.[17] The trade unions argued that the exceptions should be strictly interpreted and that assertions of national security did not create a 'blanket exception to the Convention guarantees'. The Commission accepted that the staff serving at GCHQ could be considered members of the administration of the state and that 'they were concerned with vital functions of national security'. As a result the measures were held to come within the exceptions in Article 11(2).

Nor does this Article, according to the House of Lords, give a trade union a right to recognition, even where it can show that it has members employed in the place of work concerned. In a case where in the interests of good industrial relations ACAS refused to recommend recognition even though the trade union had majority support, the trade union was unable to rely on the Convention to claim a right to recognition.[18]

DATA PROTECTION

The collection and holding of information on workers is an important role of management. The potential for misuse of this information is evident. Employers will hold much personal and other information which, if used for the wrong purposes, may have a detrimental effect upon employees' working and personal lives. In the United Kingdom the Data Protection Act 1984 provided some protection by giving rights to individuals about whom information is recorded on computers. The Directive on the Protection of Personal Data[19] 1995 (PPD Directive) led to the passing of the Data Protection Act 1998, which replaced the 1984 Act.

The Directive on personal data protection
The PPD Directive is aimed at seeking a high level of protection in the European Community and is partly justified by Article 8 of the European Convention on Human Rights, which is concerned with the right to privacy.[20] Article 1(1) of the Directive states that

Member States shall protect the fundamental rights and

freedoms of natural persons, and in particular their right to privacy with respect to the processing of personal data.

It applies not only to the processing of personal data wholly or partly by automatic means, but also to data that is part of a non-automated filing system.[21] Obligations are imposed upon the data controller, ie the natural or legal person or body 'which determines the purposes and the means of the processing'.[22] Data controllers are required to observe a number of principles. These are that data should be processed fairly and lawfully; it should be collected for specified purposes and used accordingly; it should be adequate, relevant and not excessive for the purpose proposed; it should be accurate and up to date; and individuals should not be identifiable from the data longer than is necessary.[23]

The Directive also sets out the criteria which makes the processing of data legitimate.[24] These are that:

(a) the data subject has unambiguously given his or her consent

(b) data processing is necessary for the performance of a contract or in order to enter into a contract requested by the data subject

(c) processing is required by law

(d) processing is necessary to protect a vital interest of the data subject

(e) processing is necessary in the performance of tasks carried out in the public interest or by official authorities where necessary

(f) data can be processed where the data controller has a legitimate interest to do so and this interest is not overridden by the interest of protecting the fundamental rights, including that of privacy, of data subjects.

More stringent rules apply to the processing of sensitive data relating to racial or ethnic origin, political opinions, religious or philosophical beliefs, and trade union membership, and the processing of data concerning personal health or sex life.[25]

The Data Protection Act 1998

The use, or misuse, to which information held by employers can be put was illustrated by *Dalgleish v Lothian and Borders Police Board*.[26] In this case an employer was asked by the local authority to provide details of employee names and addresses in order to help the local authority in identifying those who were in arrears with their community charge.[27] The employees succeeded in obtaining an interim interdict (injunction) stopping the employer revealing this information. The Court of Session held that the names and addresses of employees were confidential and therefore protected against disclosure. The information was held by the employer for the purpose of the employment relationship. That an individual residing at a particular address was an employee of the employer was information that was generally not available to the public.

'Data' in the Data Protection Act 1998 (DPA 1998) means information which

(a) is processed by equipment operating automatically in response to instructions given for that purpose

(b) is recorded with the intention that it should be processed by means of such equipment

(c) is recorded as part of a relevant filing system or with the intention that it should be part of that system[28]

(d) is not one of the above, but is an accessible record such as a health, educational or other accessible public record.[29]

It is important to note that the Act applies to data that is kept in a manual filing system which is structured 'either by reference to individuals or by reference to criteria relating to individuals, in such a way that specific information relating to a particular individual is readily accessible'.[30]

The Data Protection Commissioner has the power to conduct assessments on behalf of individuals who believe themselves to be directly affected by the processing of personal data[31] or to help individuals in bringing proceedings.[32]

Exceptions to the rights of data subjects to access information include personal data consisting of references for education, training or employment purposes[33] and personal data which consists of records in relation to any negotiations between the data controller and the data subject to the extent that the information is likely to prejudice those negotiations.[34]

The Act has a number of transitional measures, which means that its full effect will not be felt for some years after its introduction – eg some manual data is exempt until October 2001, and manual data held before 24 October 1998 is exempted until October 2007.

THE ACCESS TO MEDICAL REPORTS ACT 1988

This Act provides a right of access to any medical report relating to an individual which is to be, or has been, supplied by a medical practitioner for employment or insurance purposes. The AMRA 1988 applies to 'medical reports' which are commissioned both before employment commences and during employment from 'a medical practitioner who is or has been responsible for the clinical care of the individual'.[35]

An employer who wishes to apply for a medical report covered by this legislation is required to notify the individual that he or she proposes to make an application, and must obtain that person's consent.[36] In addition, the employer must inform the individual in writing of the following rights created by the Act:

(a) the right to withhold consent to such an application[37]

(b) if the individual does consent, the right to state that he or she wants access to the report. Where the individual so states, the employer must notify the medical practitioner of this fact at the time the report is sought[38]

(c)   the right of access is to the report before it is supplied to the employer[39] and to any medical report relating to him or her that the practitioner has supplied during the previous six months.[40] A person who wants access to the report before it is supplied to the employer has 21 days to contact the medical practitioner about arrangements for access. For these purposes, giving access to a report means supplying the individual with a copy of it or making the report (or a copy) available for inspection. A reasonable fee may be charged for the cost of supplying a report

(d)   the right to request the amendment of, or record a difference of opinion over, any details contained in the report which the individual regards as misleading or incorrect. If the individual requests in writing that the medical practitioner should attach to the report a statement of that individual's views about any part of the report which the doctor refuses to amend, the doctor is obliged to do so[41]

(e)   the right to refuse consent to the disclosure of the report to the employer.[42]

An employer who applies for a medical report from a doctor must also inform that doctor of certain matters.[43] However, there is nothing to prevent employers from using standard forms for notifying either employees or doctors. The Court of Appeal has held that medical practitioners who carry out pre-employment medical assessments and examinations do not owe a duty of care to the potential employee. The duty of care is owed to the person for whom the report is made and who is relying on it. Thus in *Kapfunde v Abbey National plc*[44] a potential employee who was assessed by a medical practitioner as not being suitable for permanent employment failed in an attempt to bring negligence proceedings against the doctor. The doctor owed a duty of care to the employer, not to the employee.

Individuals can be denied access to the whole or part of a report if the medical practitioner thinks that its disclosure would be likely:

(a) to cause serious physical or mental harm to the individual involved, or

(b) to reveal information about another individual, or

(c) to reveal the intentions of the practitioner in relation to the individual, or

(d) to reveal the identity of another non-medical person who has supplied information to the medical practitioner.[45]

Where the medical practitioner decides that access to the report should be withheld (wholly or in part) because of one or more of the statutory exemptions, he or she must notify the individual of that fact. If a person is unhappy about the disclosure of information in these circumstances, he or she may choose to refuse consent to the report's being supplied to the employer. Obviously, both jobseekers and job-holders will think hard about the conclusions that employers might draw from the withholding of consent to a medical report.

People who feel that their rights under this Act have been infringed can complain to the County Court.[46] If the court is satisfied that a person has failed (or is likely to fail) to comply with a requirement relating to the complainant, it may order compliance. Thus if a medical report has already been supplied without the individual's consent or access to it has been denied, all that can be enforced is the right of access to the report and to have a statement of views attached to it.

KEY POINTS 18
Human rights and data protection

- The Human Rights Act 1998 incorporates a substantial part of the European Convention for the Protection of Human Rights and Fundamental Freedoms into UK law.

- The Articles that may have particular effect upon employment law are Article 8 on respect for private and family life, Article 9 on freedom of thought, conscience and religion, Article 10 on freedom of expression, and Article 11 on freedom of assembly and association.

- Employment tribunals and courts must interpret legislation in a way that is compatible with Convention rights.

- The Directive on the Protection of Personal Data 1995 aims to achieve a high level of protection of the 'fundamental rights and freedoms of natural persons, and in particular their right to privacy with respect to the processing of personal data'.

- The Data Protection Act 1998 regulates the processing of data whether done automatically or through a manual filing system.

- The Access to Medical Records Act 1988 provides some rules for employers and medical practitioners seeking a pre-employment medical assessment or examination.

- Medical practitioners who carry out such assessments owe a duty of care not to the employee but to the employer who is relying on the report.

NOTES

1 Section 6 HRA 1998
2 Section 2(1)(a) HRA 1998
3 Section 3(1) HRA 1998
4 Section 4 HRA 1998; the courts referred to include the House of Lords, the Court of Appeal, the High Court and the Court of Sessions
5 Section 10 HRA 1998
6 (1997) IRLR 471
7 Articles 8 and 10 of the Convention, respectively
8 (1977) ICR 490
9 (1997) 23 EHRR CD 168
10 Sections 45 and 101 ERA 1996 protect shop workers and betting workers who refuse to work on a Sunday from suffering detriment or dismissal because of this refusal
11 (1998) IRLR 81
12 Section 10 Contempt of Court Act 1981
13 *Middlebrook Mushrooms Ltd v TGWU* (1993) IRLR 232
14 (1999) IRLR 188
15 Article 11(2) HRA 1996
16 See *CCSU v Minister for the Civil Service* (1985) ICR 374
17 See *CCSU v United Kingdom* (1987) EHRR 269
18 See *ACAS v UKAPE* (1980) IRLR 124
19 Directive 95/46/EC
20 Preamble, paragraph (10) DPP Directive 1995
21 Article 3 DPP Directive 1995
22 See Article 2(d) DPP Directive 1995
23 Article 4 DPP Directive 1995
24 See Article 7 DPP Directive 1995
25 Article 8 DPP Directive 1995
26 (1991) IRLR 422
27 Community charge was the method of collecting local taxes at the time. It was levied on the individual, rather than the household
28 Section 1(1) DPA 1998
29 See section 68 DPA 1995
30 Section 1(1) DPA 1998
31 Section 42 DPA 1998
32 Section 53 DPA 1998
33 See schedule 7 section 1
34 See schedule 7 section 7
35 Section 2(1) AMRA 1988
36 Section 3(1) AMRA 1988
37 Section 3(2) AMRA 1988
38 Section 4(1) AMRA 1988
39 Section 4(2) AMRA 1988
40 Section 6(2) AMRA 1988
41 Section 5(2) AMRA 1988
42 Section 5(1) AMRA 1988
43 Section 4(1) and (2) AMRA 1988
44 (1998) IRLR 583
45 Section 7 AMRA 1988
46 Section 8 AMRA 1988

19 The legal framework of collective bargaining

The general and specific duties of ACAS, the functions of the Central Arbitration Committee (CAC) and the role of the Certification Officer were all outlined in Chapter 1. In this chapter we examine the legal definition of an employers' association and a trade union, and describe the mechanism by which a union can obtain a certificate of independence. We also consider the question of recognition, including the statutory right to recognition of trade unions, and the duty placed upon employers to disclose information for the purpose of collective bargaining. Finally, the legal enforceability of collective agreements is discussed.

EMPLOYERS' ASSOCIATIONS

According to section 122 TULRCA 1992 an employers' association means an organisation which consists either:

(a) wholly or mainly of employers or individual proprietors whose principal purposes include the regulation of relations between employers and workers (or trade unions), or

(b) wholly or mainly of constituent or affiliated organisations with these purposes or representatives of such organisations,

and in either case is an organisation whose principal purposes include the regulation of relations between employers and workers (or trade unions) or between constituent and affiliated organisations.[1]

Thus whether a trade association is or is not to be legally regarded as an employers' association will depend on its particular objectives. The Certification Officer is responsible for maintaining a list of employers' associations containing the names of those organisations which are entitled to have their names entered on it.[2] Whether listed or not, employers' associations are granted immunity in respect of the doctrine of restraint of trade, although the immunity of incorporated associations is only in connection with the regulation of relations between employers (or employers' associations) and workers (or trade unions).[3] Like trade unions, employers' associations are required to keep accounting records, to make annual returns and to have their accounts audited.[4] Part 1 Chapter 3 of TULRCA 1992 deals with the administrative provisions relating to employers' associations and trade unions.

TRADE UNIONS AND CERTIFICATES OF INDEPENDENCE

A trade union is an organisation, whether permanent or temporary, which consists either:

(a) wholly or mainly of workers whose principal purposes include the regulation of relations between workers and employers (or employers' associations), or

b) wholly or mainly of constituent or affiliated organisations with those purposes, or representatives of such organisations,

and in either case is an organisation whose principal purposes include the regulation of relations between workers and employers (or employers' associations) or include the regulation of relations between its constituent or affiliated organisations.[5]

This definition covers not only individual and confederated unions and the TUC, but also the union side of a joint negotiating committee. Section 10 TULRCA 1992 states that a trade union 'shall not be, or be treated as if it were, a body corporate', yet it is capable of making contracts, suing and being sued in its own name, and being prosecuted. However in *EETPU v Times Newspapers*[6] it was held that the union could not sue for libel because it did not have the necessary legal personality to be protected by an action for defamation. All property belonging to a trade union must be vested in trustees, and any judgment, order or award is enforceable against the property held in trust.[7] Trade unions are protected against the doctrine of restraint of trade, in respect of both their purposes and their rules[8] (on immunity from certain actions in tort, see Chapter 21).

The Certification Officer maintains a list of trade unions, and a trade union which submits the appropriate fee, a copy of its rules, a list of officers, the address of its head office and the name under which it is known may apply for inclusion on this list.[9] A listed union is entitled to a certificate stating that its name is included on the list and such listing is a prerequisite for obtaining a certificate of independence. The Certification Officer makes copies of the lists of trade unions and employers' associations available for public inspection and must remove the name of an organisation if requested to do so by that organisation or if he or she is satisfied that the organisation has ceased to exist.[10] Any organisation which is aggrieved by the refusal of the Certification Officer to enter its name on the relevant list, or by a decision to remove its name, may appeal to the EAT on a question of fact or law.[11]

A trade union whose name is on the relevant list can apply to the Certification Officer for a certificate that it is independent. The Certification Officer is responsible for keeping a record of all applications and must decide whether the applicant union is independent or not.[12] Section 5 TULRCA 1992 deems a trade union to be independent if:

(a) it is not under the domination or control of an employer or a group of employers or of one or more employers' associations, and

(b) it is not liable to interference by an employer or any such group or association, arising out of the provision of financial or material support or by any other means whatsoever, tending towards such control.

A certificate constitutes conclusive evidence for all purposes that the union is independent. If a question arises in any proceedings as to whether a trade union is independent and there is no certificate in force and no refusal, withdrawal or cancellation of a certificate recorded, the body before whom the issue arose cannot decide the matter but may refer it to the Certification Officer.[13]

Over the years, certain criteria have evolved for assessing whether a union is under the domination or control of an employer. In *A. Monk Staff Association v Certification Officer and ASTMS*[14] the EAT confirmed that the following matters should be considered:

(a) the union's history (was it originally the employer's creation?)

(b) its organisation and structure (is it likely to be controlled by senior members of management?)

(c) its finances (to what extent is it subsidised by the employer?)

(d) the extent of employer-provided facilities (are there free premises, etc?)

(e) its collective bargaining record.

Here there had been significant changes since the Certification Officer investigated the matter, including the appointment of an independent consultant/negotiator. In this case it was also held, on appeal against the Certification Officer's decision, that the question of independence should be decided on all the evidence available and not confined to the material that was before the Certification Officer.

As regards 'liable to interference', the Court of Appeal has ruled that the Certification Officer is not required to assess the likelihood of interference by the employer. The Certification Officer's interpretation of the words as meaning 'vulnerable to interference' was the correct one – ie the degree of risk is irrelevant so long as it is recognisable and not insignificant. Thus in *GCSF v Certification Officer*[15] the staff federation was denied a certificate because its continued existence depended on the approval of the GCHQ director.

Finally, it is worth documenting the major advantages that accrue to independent trade unions:

(a) If recognised, they have the right to appoint safety representatives (see Chapter 10).

(b) If recognised, their representatives are entitled to receive information for collective bargaining purposes (see below).

(c) If recognised, their representatives may be consulted in respect of redundancies and transfers of undertakings (see Chapters 13 and 15).

(d) If recognised, their officials can take time off for union activities (see Chapter 11).

(e) They can make and apply for exemption for a 'dismissal procedures agreement' (see Chapter 14).

(f) Employees cannot have action taken against them because they seek to join, have joined, or have taken part in the activities of such a union. Interim relief is available to members who have been dismissed.

RECOGNITION

An independent trade union must be recognised by the employer in order to enjoy a number of statutory rights. The same definition applies in respect of each of these rights, namely, 'Recognition in relation to a trade union means the recognition of the union by an employer, or two or more associated employers, to any extent for the purpose of collective bargaining.'[16]

Collective bargaining means negotiations relating to or connected with one or more of the matters specified in section 178(2) TULRCA 1992.[17] Although the question of recognition is one of fact for a court or employment tribunal to decide, it would appear that there must be an express or implied agreement between the union and the employer (but see statutory rights to recognition below) to negotiate on one or more of the matters listed in section 178(2) TULRCA 1992. For agreement to be implied there must be clear and unequivocal conduct over a period of time.[18] Thus although recognition has been inferred from consultations on discipline and facilities for union representatives despite the absence of formal agreement,[19] a discussion on wages which took place on a particular occasion was held to be insufficient to establish recognition, particularly when the employer's attitude was one of refusing to bargain.[20] Neither the fact that the union has a right of representation on a national body responsible for negotiating pay[21] nor the fact that the employers' association to which the employer belongs recognises the union will, by itself, constitute recognition by the employer.[22]

According to Regulation 9 of the Transfer Regulations 1981, where the transferred undertaking retains a distinct identity, any trade union recognised by the transferor must be recognised by the transferee to the same extent.[23] There is no guidance as to what constitutes 'an identity distinct from the remainder of the transferee's undertaking', but it is clear that once a transfer has occurred the transferee can open negotiations about whether recognition should be continued. Similarly, Regulation 6 provides that collective agreements which exist at the time of transfer continue in force after the transfer in relation to the employees transferred as if the agreements had been made with the new employer. This means that any provisions of a collective agreement which apply to individual employees will continue to operate and could include non-contractual disciplinary or grievance procedures.

STATUTORY RECOGNITION PROCEDURES

The rules regarding the statutory right of trade unions[24] to recognition for collective bargaining purposes were introduced by the ERel Act 1999 and are now contained in Schedule A1 of TULRCA 1992. In this the meaning given to collective bargaining by section 178(1) TULRCA 1992 (see above) does not apply. Unless otherwise agreed by the parties, collective bargaining that is the result of the statutory recognition procedure relates to negotiations on pay, hours and holidays only.[25]

Request for recognition

A union seeking recognition must make a request for recognition to the employer. The request must be in writing, identify the union and the bargaining unit and state that it is made under this Schedule.[26] The basic rules concerning the parties are:

(a) The union must have a certificate of independence (see section 6 TULRCA 1992).[27]

(b) The employer, including associated employers, must employ at least 21 workers on the day of the request, or have employed an average of 21 workers in the 13 weeks ending on the day of the request.[28]

The parties agree[29]

If, before the end of a 10-day period, starting on the day the employer received the request, the parties agree on a bargaining unit and that the union is to be recognised for collective bargaining purposes on behalf of that unit, then the matter is complete.

If, before the end of the first period of 10 working days the employers inform the union that they do not accept the request but are willing to negotiate, then negotiations may continue into a second period. This second period lasts for 20 working days, starting on the day after the first period ends, or longer if both parties agree.

Negotiations fail[30]

If, before the end of the first period of 10 days the employers fail to respond or inform the union that they do not accept the request (and show no willingness to negotiate), then the union may apply to the Central Arbitration Committee (CAC) to decide two important issues. These are:

(a) whether the proposed bargaining unit is appropriate or some other bargaining unit is appropriate

(b) whether the union has the support of a majority of the workers constituting the bargaining unit.

If the employers refuse the request for recognition or no

agreement is reached by the end of the second period of 20 working days, then the union may apply to the CAC to decide the two issues described above.

If the employers inform the union that they intend to request ACAS to assist in the negotiations and this proposal is rejected by the union or the union fails to respond, the application to the CAC must be delayed.

Appropriate bargaining unit[31]

If the CAC accepts an application from a trade union (see above), it is obliged to help the parties reach an agreement, within the appropriate period, on what the appropriate bargaining unit is.

The appropriate period is 20 working days, beginning with the day after that on which the CAC accepts the application, or a longer period, if the CAC specifies, with reasons. If there is no agreement within the appropriate period, then the CAC has 10 working days, or a longer period, if the CAC specifies, beginning with the day after the end of the appropriate period, to make a decision.

In making the decision the CAC must take into consideration the need for the bargaining unit to be compatible with effective management and, provided they do not conflict with this consideration, with

(a) the views of the employer and the union

(b) existing national and local bargaining units

(c) the desirability of avoiding small fragmented bargaining units within an undertaking

(d) the characteristics of workers falling within the proposed bargaining unit and of any other employees the CAC considers relevant

(e) the location of the workers.

Ballots for union recognition[32]

Once the appropriate bargaining unit has been decided upon by agreement between the parties or by CAC decision, the CAC must decide whether the union is likely to have the support of a majority of the workers in the unit. The CAC can only proceed if it is satisfied that the union is likely to have support.

If the union shows that a majority of the workers in the unit are members of the union, then the CAC must issue a declaration that the union is recognised for collective bargaining purposes.

If one of three qualifying conditions is fulfilled, the CAC will hold a ballot rather than make a declaration. The three qualifying conditions are:

(a)   the CAC is satisfied that a ballot is in the interests of good industrial relations

(b)   a significant number of union members within the bargaining unit inform the CAC that they do not want the union to conduct collective bargaining on their behalf

(c)   membership evidence is produced which leads the CAC to doubt whether a significant number of union members want the union to represent them. This evidence is about the circumstances in which employees became members and evidence about the length of time for which union members have belonged.

The CAC will appoint a qualified independent person to conduct the ballot within a period of 20 working days, starting the day after the appointment. If it gives reasons, the CAC may specify a longer period. The ballot can be conducted at a workplace, or workplaces, or by post. In deciding which method to select, the CAC must take into account:

(a)   the likelihood of unfairness or malpractice if the ballot is conducted at a workplace

(b)   costs and practicality

(c)   any other matters it thinks appropriate.

As soon as practicable the CAC must inform the parties of its decisions. Once the employers are informed, they must comply with three duties:

(a) to co-operate with the union and the independent person in connection with the ballot

(b) to give the union access to the workers so that they can inform them of the ballot and seek support

(c) to provide the CAC, within 10 working days, with the names and home addresses of the workers concerned, together with the names and addresses of any workers who join or leave after this.

The CAC will pass this information to the independent person who is conducting the ballot. This person will send out material provided by the union to the workers concerned, at the union's expense. If the CAC is satisfied that the employer has failed to comply with any of the three duties it may order the employer to take steps to do so, or it may declare that the union is recognised for collective bargaining purposes. The costs incurred in the ballot will be shared equally between the employer and the union.

As soon as practicable the CAC will inform the parties of the result of the ballot. It will issue a declaration that the union is recognised if:

(a) a majority of those voting support recognition, and

(b) at least 40 per cent of the workers constituting the bargaining unit supported recognition.

The consequences of recognition[33]

Following the declaration from the CAC the parties may negotiate, within a certain period, about the way in which they will conduct collective bargaining. The negotiating period is 30 working days from when the parties were notified of the declaration. The parties may agree to a longer period.

If no agreement is reached, the employer or the union may ask the CAC for assistance. There is then an agreement period of 20 working days, or longer if the CAC decides (with the agreement of the parties), in which the CAC will try to help the parties reach an agreement. If no agreement is reached, the CAC may specify the method by which they are to conduct collective bargaining.

This agreement will be a legally enforceable contract between the parties. It may be varied by the parties agreeing, but it will remain a legally enforceable agreement. The only remedy available for breach of this agreement will be that of specific performance, by which the court will order an employer to carry out the terms of the agreement. The CAC may stop the whole process prior to issuing its ruling at the joint request of the parties.

General provisions
The CAC will not accept an application

(a)   if it is satisfied that there is already a union recognised on behalf of any of the workers in the bargaining unit

(b)   if it decides that members of the union constitute at least 10 per cent of the workers and there is prima facie evidence that a majority of the workers are likely to favour recognition. The CAC will decide whether this is so within 10 working days of receiving the application

(c)   if the employer alleges that they are below the 21-employee threshold (see above). In this case they may have up to 10 working days in which to produce the evidence. The CAC will consider the views of the union before making a decision

(d)   where there is more than one union involved, if the CAC is not yet satisfied that the unions 'will co-operate with each other in a manner likely to secure stable and effective bargaining' or will make if the employer so wishes, joint negotiating arrangements

(e)   where there is another application within a period of three years for substantially the same bargaining unit by the same union.

VOLUNTARY RECOGNITION

If the parties reach a voluntary agreement on recognition, they may still apply to the CAC to specify the method by which collective bargaining is to be carried out.[34] The CAC will accept the application, provided the employee threshold has been met (see above) and it is clear that the parties have either not agreed a method or have failed to implement a method to which they have agreed. There is an agreement period of 20 working days, or longer if both the parties agree, in which the CAC will help them to reach an agreement. If no agreement is reached, the CAC may specify the method to be used. The same rules about legally enforceable contracts and the remedy of specific performance apply (see above).

CHANGES AFFECTING THE BARGAINING UNIT[35]

There will be situations where the original bargaining unit becomes inappropriate. If either the employer or the trade union believe that this has happened, they may apply to the CAC to make a decision as to what the appropriate bargaining unit should be. For such an application to be admissible, the reason must be that there has been:

(a) a change in the organisation or structure of the business carried on by the employer

(b) a change in the activities pursued by the employer in the course of the employer's business

(c) a substantial change in the number of workers employed in the original unit.

If the parties cannot agree on new arrangements, then the CAC is empowered to issue a declaration on the changes to be made.

Employers may also give notice to the union, with a copy to the CAC, that they believe that the original bargaining unit has ceased to exist. If the CAC accepts this, it may make a declaration ending the bargaining arrangements or may make a decision on a more appropriate bargaining unit.

DE-RECOGNITION[36]

This applies where the CAC has issued declarations on

recognition and/or the method to be used for collective bargaining purposes. The process is the reversal of that for recognition, albeit with different initiators and a different question in the application to the CAC. The relevant date is the expiry of a three-year period after the date of the CAC's declaration or the parties' agreement.

PROTECTION AGAINST DETRIMENT AND DISMISSAL[37]

Detriment

A worker has the right not to be subject to any detriment by any act, or any deliberate failure to act, by the employer if the act or failure takes place on any of the following grounds:

(a) the worker acted with a view to obtaining or preventing recognition of a union

(b) the worker indicated that he or she supported or did not support recognition of a union

(c) the worker acted with a view to securing or preventing the ending of bargaining arrangements

(d) the worker indicated that he or she supported or did not support the ending of bargaining arrangements

(e) the worker influenced or sought to influence the way in which votes were to be cast by other workers in a ballot

(f) the worker influenced or sought to influence other workers to vote or abstain in the ballot

(g) the worker voted in such a ballot

(h) the worker proposed to do, failed to do, or proposed to decline to do, any of the above.

The worker is not protected, however, if the ground is an unreasonable act or omission by the worker.

The only remedy available to a worker is complaint to an employment tribunal, normally within three months of the act, or failure to act, which constitutes the detriment. The tribunal may issue a declaration and award compensation 'such as the tribunal considers just and equitable in all the circumstances having regard to the infringement complained of and to any loss sustained by the complainant which is attributable to the act or failure'.

Workers have a duty to mitigate their loss, and there will be a reduction in compensation if the worker contributed to the act or failure. Compensation for ending a contract is subject to the limits on compensation for unfair dismissal specified in the ERA 1996.

Dismissal

For the purposes of Part X of the ERA 1996, which is concerned with the right not to be unfairly dismissed (see Chapter 13), the dismissal of an employee shall be regarded as unfair if it takes place for any of the reasons listed above (under Detriment). This applies only to employees rather than those covered by the wider definition of worker, as in Section 296(1) TULRCA 1992, but includes those on fixed-term contracts.

The dismissal of an employee for redundancy shall also be unfair if it is shown to be for one of the reasons listed above or if it is shown that there are others in a similar position and the same circumstances who were not dismissed for reasons of redundancy.

DISCLOSURE OF INFORMATION FOR COLLECTIVE BARGAINING

For the purposes of all the stages of collective bargaining between employers and representatives of recognised independent trade unions, employers have a duty to disclose to those representatives, on request, all such information relating to their undertakings as is in their possession or that of any associated employer which is both:[38]

(a) information without which the union representatives would be to a material extent impeded in carrying on with such collective bargaining, and

(b) information which it would be in accordance with good industrial relations practice that they should disclose.

An employer can insist that a request for information must be made in writing, and likewise the information itself must be in written form if that is the wish of the union representatives.[39] According to section 181(1) TULRCA 1992, a 'representative' is an 'official or other person authorised by the trade union to carry on such collective bargaining'. However, an 'undertaking' is not defined for these purposes.

The phrase 'of all the stages' means that information can be sought in order to prepare a claim, although it must relate to matters in respect of which the union is recognised. In *R v CAC ex parte BTP Tioxide*[40] the High Court held that the CAC had misdirected itself in concluding that the union was entitled to information relating to a job evaluation scheme in respect of which it had no bargaining rights but only the right to represent its members in re-evaluation appeals:

> There is no obstacle under the Act to an agreement which recognises the union's right to collective bargaining, that is negotiating, in respect of one aspect of terms and conditions of employment and also recognises a right to some form of dealings with employers which does not answer to the description of collective bargaining, about another aspect.

In essence, for information to be disclosed under these provisions it must be both relevant and important. Although each case must be judged on its merits, unions may be entitled to information about groups not covered for collective bargaining purposes. Thus in Award 80/40 the CAC held that information about a productivity scheme for management not covered by the union, was relevant and important to negotiations over a scheme for technical staff because of the similarity of the work of some employees within both groups.

In determining what constitutes 'good industrial relations practice' attention must be paid to the ACAS Code of Practice,[41] although other evidence is not to be excluded.[42] Thus unions may seek to demonstrate good practice by referring to the approaches taken by comparable employers. To decide what information will be relevant, negotiators are advised to take account of the subject matter of the negotiations and the issues raised during them, the level at which negotiations take place, the size of the company, and its type of business.[43] There is no list of items which should be disclosed in all circumstances but the following examples of information which could be relevant in certain situations are given as a guide:[44]

(a) pay and benefits

(b) conditions of service

(c) manpower

(d) performance

(e) finance.

This is not an exhaustive list and other items may be relevant in particular negotiations. The underlying philosophy of the code is that employers and unions should endeavour to reach a joint understanding on how the disclosure provisions can be implemented most effectively: 'In particular, the parties should endeavour to reach an understanding on what information could most appropriately be provided on a regular basis.'[45]

The duty to disclose is subject to the exceptions detailed in section 182 TULRCA 1992. Employers are not required to disclose:

(a) any information the disclosure of which would be against the interests of national security

(b) any information which could not be disclosed without contravening other legislation

(c) any information which has been communicated to the employer in confidence

(d) any information relating specifically to an individual unless he or she has consented to its disclosure

(e) any information the disclosure of which would cause substantial injury to the employer's undertaking for reasons other than its effect on collective bargaining

(f) information obtained by the employer for the purpose of bringing or defending any legal proceedings.

Although (c) applies to standard form tenders headed 'In confidence',[46] it should be noted that it does not protect an employer who discloses information in confidence to lay union representatives and restricts them from communicating it to union members and full-time officials. Where a union seeks disclosure about individual salaries without the consent of the individuals concerned, in order to avoid the impact of (d) it must be clear that the information relates to the posts involved and not to the individuals who fill them. As regards (e), paragraph 14 of the Code offers some examples of information which, if disclosed in particular circumstances, might cause substantial injury. This would cover such matters as cost information on individual products, detailed analysis of proposed investment, marketing or pricing policies, price quotas, and the make-up of tender prices. Further guidance is offered in paragraph 15:

> ... substantial injury may occur if, for example, certain customers would be lost to competitors, or suppliers would refuse to supply necessary materials, or the ability to raise funds to finance the company would be seriously impaired as a result of disclosing certain information. The burden of establishing a claim that disclosure of certain information would cause substantial injury lies with the employer.

By virtue of section 182(2) TULRCA employers are not obliged to produce, allow inspection of, or copy, any document other than a document conveying or confirming the information disclosed, and are not required to compile any information where to do so would involve an amount of work or expenditure out of reasonable proportion to the value of the information in the conduct of collective bargaining.

A union which feels that its representatives have not received the information to which they are entitled can complain in writing to the CAC, and if the CAC is of the opinion that the complaint is 'reasonably likely to be settled by conciliation' it must refer it to ACAS. Where no reference to ACAS is made or no settlement or withdrawal is achieved, the CAC must hear the complaint, make a declaration stating whether it is well-founded, wholly or in part, and give reasons for its finding. If the complaint is upheld, the declaration will specify the information in respect of which the CAC believed the complaint to be well-founded, the date on which the employer refused or failed to disclose information, and the period within which the employer ought to disclose the information specified.[47]

At any time after the expiry of this period the union may present a 'further complaint' that the employer has failed to disclose the required information. Again, the CAC must hear and determine the complaint and declare whether it holds it to be well-founded.[48] On or after presenting the further complaint the union may submit a claim that the employees' contracts should be amended to include the terms and conditions detailed in the claim, eg for more pay. However, no such claim can be lodged, or if presented it will be treated as withdrawn, if the relevant information is disclosed at any time before the CAC has adjudicated on the further complaint. If the further complaint is well-founded, the CAC may, after hearing the parties, award the terms and conditions detailed in the claim or others which it considers appropriate. Such an award will relate only to matters in respect of which the trade union is recognised. The terms and conditions awarded take effect as part of the contracts of employment of the employees covered, except in so far as they are superseded or varied by:

(a) a subsequent award under these provisions

(b) a collective agreement between the employer and the union

(c) an individual agreement, express or implied, effecting an improvement in the terms and conditions laid down in the award.[49]

It should be observed that these statutory provisions do not enable a union to force the disclosure of information.

THE LEGAL ENFORCEABILITY OF COLLECTIVE AGREEMENTS

In this section we are concerned with the legal enforceability of collective agreements between employers and trade unions and not the effect of such agreements on individual contracts of employment. It is important to remember that the legal status of the arrangements made between the employer and the union has no bearing on the relationship between the employer and his or her workers. The mechanisms by which the terms of a collective agreement may be enforced between the parties to a contract of employment have been described in Chapter 2.

A collective agreement is statutorily defined as any agreement or arrangement made by or on behalf of one or more trade unions[50] and one or more employers, or employers' associations, which relates to one or more of the matters mentioned in section 178(2) TULRCA 1992.[51] A collective agreement is conclusively presumed not to have been intended by the parties to be a legally enforceable contract unless the agreement is in writing and contains a provision which states that the parties intend the agreement to be a legally enforceable contract.[52] Equally, the parties may declare that one or more parts only of an agreement are intended to be legally enforceable.[53] Nevertheless, it should not be assumed that a collective agreement which declares the parties' intention to create legal relations is necessarily legally binding, because agreements exist which are too vague or uncertain to be enforced as contracts.

THE DIRECTORS' REPORT ON EMPLOYEE INVOLVEMENT

Schedule 7 paragraph 11 of the Companies Act 1985 requires companies with more than 250 employees working in the UK to include in their directors' report a statement describing the action that has been taken during the financial year to introduce, maintain or develop arrangements aimed at:

(a) providing employees systematically with information on matters of concern to them

(b) consulting employees or their representatives regularly so that employees' views can be taken into account in making decisions which are likely to affect their interests

(c) encouraging employee involvement in the company's performance through an employees' share scheme or by some other means

(d) achieving a common awareness on the part of all employees of the financial and economic factors affecting the company's performance.

It is worth noting that the Act does not actually oblige companies to take any measures to bring about involvement.

KEY POINTS 19
The legal framework of collective bargaining

- The Certification Officer maintains a list of employers' associations and of trade unions and makes them available for public inspection.

- The Certification Officer decides if a trade union is entitled to a certificate of independence.

- An independent trade union must be recognised by an employer in order to enjoy a number of statutory rights, such as the right to the disclosure of information for collective bargaining purposes.

- The statutory recognition procedures apply to firms with 21 or more employees on the day an independent trade union requests recognition.

- Establishing the bargaining unit is a necessary prerequisite for the recognition procedure. The CAC will assist and take into account, amongst other factors, the need for bargaining units to be compatible with effective management and the desirability of avoiding small fragmented units within an undertaking.

- Employers have a duty to disclose to trade unions recognised for collective bargaining purposes such information without which the union representatives would be to a material extent impeded in carrying on collective bargaining with them.

- A collective agreement is conclusively presumed not to be a legally enforceable contract unless it is in writing and contains a provision that the parties intend it to be a legally enforceable contract.

NOTES

1 The words 'employee', 'employer' and 'worker' are defined in sections 295–6 TULRCA 1992; the expression 'associated employer' is defined in section 297 TULRCA 1992
2 Section 123 TULRCA 1992
3 Section 128 TULRCA 1992
4 Section 131 TULRCA 1992
5 Section 1 TULRCA 1992
6 (1980) 1 All ER 1097
7 Sections 12 and 13 TULRCA 1992
8 Section 11 TULRCA 1992
9 Section 3 TULRCA 1992
10 Section 4 TULRCA 1992
11 Section 9(1) TULRCA 1992
12 Section 6(2) and (5) TULRCA 1992
13 Section 8 TULRCA 1992
14 (1980) IRLR 431
15 (1993) IRLR 260
16 Section 178(3) TULRCA 1992
17 Section 178(1) TULRCA 1992
18 See *NUGSAT v Albury Bros* (1978) IRLR 504
19 See *J. Wilson & Albury Bros v USDAW* (1978) IRLR 20
20 See *NUGSAT v Albury Bros* (note 18)
21 See *Cleveland County Council v Springett* (1985) IRLR 131
22 See *NUGSAT v Albury Bros* (note 18)
23 On the meaning of a relevant transfer see Chapter 15
24 All references in this section to a trade union should also be taken as references to more than one union if there is more than one union involved in the application for recognition
25 Schedule A1 para 3(3) TULRCA 1992
26 Schedule A1 para 8 TULRCA 1992
27 Schedule A1 para 6 TULRCA 1992
28 Schedule A1 para 7 TULRCA 1992
29 Schedule A1 para 10 TULRCA 1992
30 Schedule A1 para 12 TULRCA 1992

31 Schedule A1 para 18 TULRCA 1992
32 Schedule A1 paras 20–29 TULRCA 1992
33 Schedule A1 paras 30–31 TULRCA 1992
34 Schedule A1 paras 58–63 TULRCA 1992
35 Schedule A1 Part III TULRCA 1992
36 Schedule A1 Part IV TULRCA 1992
37 Schedule A1 Part VIII TULRCA 1992
38 Section 181(1) and (2) TULRCA 1992
39 Section 181(3) and (5) TULRCA 1992
40 (1982) IRLR 61
41 *Disclosure of Information to Trade Unions for Collective Bargaining Purposes*, HMSO, 1977
42 Section 181(4) TULRCA 1992
43 Paragraph 10 Code of Practice
44 Paragraph 11 Code of Practice
45 Paragraph 22 Code of Practice
46 See *CSU v CAC* (1980) IRLR 274
47 Section 183 TULRCA 1992
48 Section 184 TULRCA 1992
49 Section 185(5) TULRCA 1992
50 See *Edinburgh Council v Brown* (1999) IRLR 208, where an agreement between the employer and the joint consultative committee constituted a collective agreement
51 Section 178(1) TULRCA 1992
52 Section 179(1) TULRCA 1992
53 Section 179(3) TULRCA 199

20 Trade unions and their members

In this chapter we look at the way in which the relationship between trade unions and their members is regulated. This includes controls over what discretion trade unions have to admit, discipline and expel members. We also look at the detailed statutory rules that exist to regulate union elections. We then look at the important role played by the Certification Officer in settling disputes. Finally we consider union political funds and the settlement of inter-union disputes.

ADMISSION

A union is entitled to stipulate the descriptions of persons who are eligible for membership, but provided it observes its own rules no union can be ordered by a court to admit a particular applicant. However, the Sex Discrimination Act 1975 and the Race Relations Act 1976 make it unlawful for an organisation of workers to discriminate in the terms on which it is prepared to admit into membership, or on which it refuses or deliberately omits to accept an application for membership. Equally, it is unlawful for an organisation of workers to discriminate on the prohibited grounds against a member in the way it affords access to any benefits, facilities or services, or subjects him or her to any detriment including deprivation of membership.[1]

Section 174 TULRCA 1992 gives employees the right to join the union of their choice. It states that an individual may not be excluded from a union unless the reason is one of the following:

(a) The individual fails to satisfy an enforceable membership requirement in the union's rules. A requirement is 'enforceable' if it restricts membership solely by reference to one or more of the following criteria:

- employment in a specified trade, industry or profession

- occupational description (including grade, level or category)

- possession of specified qualifications or work experience.[2]

(b) The individual does not qualify for membership by reason of the union's operating only in particular parts of Great Britain.

(c) The union operates only in relation to one employer or a number of associated employers, and the individual is not employed by that employer or one of those employers.

(d) The exclusion is entirely attributable to the individual's conduct. For these purposes conduct does not include being or ceasing to be:

- a member of another trade union

- employed by a particular employer or at a particular place

- a member of a political party.

Nor does it include any conduct for which an individual may not be disciplined by a trade union (see below).[3]

In this context 'exclusion' refers to a refusal to admit into membership, not to suspension of the privileges of membership.[4]

A person excluded in contravention of these provisions can complain to an employment tribunal. This must normally be done within six months of the date of exclusion. However, where a tribunal finds that it was not reasonably practicable to comply with this time-limit, the period may be extended by such amount as is considered reasonable.[5] If the claim is upheld, the tribunal will make a declaration to that effect. Complainants who are admitted or re-admitted to the union can apply to the tribunal for compensation after a four-week period and must do so before six months have elapsed from the date of the declaration. If there is no admission or re-admission, applications for compensation must be made to the EAT. The employment tribunal and EAT will award such compensation as is considered 'just and equitable in all the circumstances' subject to a maximum as set out in section 176(6) TULRCA 1992. However, compensation fixed by the EAT must be at least £5,000.[6]

DISCIPLINE, EXPULSION AND RESIGNATION

The rules of a trade union constitute a contract between the union and its members and must be strictly adhered to. A trade union wishing to take disciplinary action must therefore ensure that its rule-book contains the necessary powers.[7] Although a court can infer a power to discipline a member, it will do so only where there are compelling circumstances to justify it.[8]

Section 64 TULRCA 1992 gives members the right not to be unjustifiably disciplined by the union, and section 65 deems disciplinary action by a union to be unjustifiable for the following types of conduct:

(a) failing to participate in industrial action or criticising such action. What 'industrial action' is for these purposes is a mixed question of fact and law. It is necessary to look at all the circumstances, including the contracts of the employees concerned and whether any breaches of the terms are involved, the effect on the employer of what is done or omitted, and the object that the union or employees seek to achieve[9]

(b) alleging that the union or an official is acting unlawfully. This protects members who bring legal proceedings against the union

(c) encouraging or assisting others to perform their contracts of employment (for example, during industrial action) or encouraging others to make an allegation of the type mentioned in (b)

(d) asking the Certification Officer for advice or assistance on any matter, or consulting another person about an allegation against the union or its officers

(e) refusing to comply with a requirement imposed by a union (for example, during disciplinary proceedings) which amounts to an infringement of the above rights

(f) proposing or preparing to engage in any conduct mentioned above

(g) resigning or proposing to resign from the union or another union, joining or proposing to join another union, refusing to join another union, or being a member of another union

(h) working with, or proposing to work with, individuals who are not members of the union or who are not members of another union

(i) working for, or proposing to work for, an employer who employs or has employed individuals who are not members of the union, or who are not members of another union

(j) requiring the union to do an act which it is required to do under TULRCA 1992 when requested to do so by a member.

In this context disciplinary action covers virtually all forms of detrimental treatment.[10] Thus in *NALGO v Killorn*[11] a member was subjected to a detriment when suspension deprived her of the benefits of membership and she was named as a strike-breaker in a branch circular with the intention of causing her embarrassment.

Those wishing to complain about unjustifiable discipline may choose between making a complaint to an employment tribunal or the Certification Officer (see below). The complainant must normally apply to an employment tribunal within three months of the relevant union decision.[12] Not surprisingly, individuals cannot be prevented from complaining by their union rule-book and any settlement will be binding only if ACAS has been involved or the conditions regulating compromise agreements are satisfied.[13] If a tribunal upholds a complaint, it will make a declaration to that effect. Compensation is available if a separate application is lodged not earlier than four weeks and not later than six months from the date of the tribunal's declaration.[14] If the union has revoked its disciplinary action, compensation will be assessed by an employment tribunal; otherwise, applications must go to the EAT.[15] Both tribunals are empowered to award such compensation as is just and equitable in the circumstances. As with unfair dismissal, compensation can be reduced on the grounds of contributory fault or a failure to mitigate loss.[16] The remedies for unjustifiable discipline are not available where the complainant could bring an action under section 174 TULRCA 1992 (see below). However, if the exclusion or expulsion is for any of the reasons listed under (a)–(j) (see above), it is not to be attributed to the conduct of the individual.[17]

If the rules specify the grounds on which disciplinary action may be taken, it will be unlawful for the union to rely on any other grounds, and where the rules provide for a procedure to be adopted, that procedure must be rigidly followed. Ultimately, a court's interpretation of the rules will take precedence over that of the union, although occasionally the judges have acknowledged that union rules should not be construed literally but should be given a reasonable interpretation which accords with their intended meaning.[18]

The court's jurisdiction as final arbiters on questions of law cannot be ousted. Thus a rule which purports to make a decision of a union appeal body 'final and binding' will be of no effect if challenged.[19] Even where there is an express provision that internal remedies must be exhausted before a member goes to law, a court will not be bound by such a requirement. Indeed, section 63 TULRCA 1992 gives union members a right to start legal proceedings in connection with any matter which can be dealt with under the rule-book so long as a valid application to resolve the matter within the union's rules has previously been made. However, the court proceedings cannot be commenced within six months of the date of the application to the union, and this period can be extended if a court is satisfied that any delay in operating the internal procedure resulted from the applicant's unreasonable conduct. If these conditions are met, the court is bound to deal with the matter, but if they are not, the burden will be on complainants to show why they should not first exhaust the internal procedures.[20]

At one time, judges were of the opinion that the essential fairness or otherwise of union rules was not for them to decide, although a different view is that if such rules are contrary to natural justice they should be declared invalid. In this context natural justice requires that a member should be given notice of the charge and a reasonable opportunity of meeting it. However, there is no legal obligation on a union to give notice of a decision to terminate membership or to grant an opportunity of being heard if there is nothing the member could say which would affect the outcome.[21] Where hearings are granted they must be fairly conducted and bona fide decisions reached on their merits – in other words, without even the appearance of bias.[22] However, unless contained in the rule-book, there would appear to be no right to legal representation. As regards appeals, the courts have decided that since they do not constitute a rehearing, appeals cannot correct defects at the initial hearing.

Under common law a person who is wrongfully expelled may seek a declaration that he or she is still a union member, an injunction to prevent the expulsion's being put into effect, and damages for breach of contract. In addition, section 174 TULRCA 1992 establishes a right not to be expelled from a trade union unless there is a statutory permitted reason for expulsion.[23] This precisely parallels the right not to be excluded, and the method of enforcement is as described in relation to a refusal to admit (see above). It should be noted that although the employment tribunal procedure will be cheaper, the common law remedies may prove more attractive. There are three main reasons for this: first, an injunction may be obtained to compel the union to treat the plaintiff as still being a member; second, damages cannot be reduced on the grounds of contributory fault; third, a court is unlikely to condone breaches of the union's rules and procedures.

As regards resignation, section 69 TULRCA 1992 implies into every contract of membership of a trade union a term conferring a right on the member, on giving reasonable notice and complying with reasonable conditions, to terminate his or her membership of the union.

ELECTIONS

Section 46 TULRCA 1992 stipulates that irrespective of its rule-book, every trade union must elect its president, general secretary and members of its executive by ballot at least once every five years.[24] The election results must be given effect within a reasonable period (not exceeding six months), although the actions of the principal executive committee remain valid even if that body is not elected in accordance with the statute.[25] In conducting such elections unions must satisfy the following conditions:

(a) members must be given equal entitlement to vote unless they belong to a specified class which is excluded by the union rules from voting

(b) members who are entitled to vote must be allowed to do so in secret by marking a voting paper without interference from the union (or any of its members, officials or employees), and so far as is reasonably practicable they should do so without incurring any direct cost to themselves[26]

(c) ballot papers and a list of candidates must be sent by post to a member's address and each member must be given an opportunity to vote by post

(d) votes must be fairly and accurately counted, although any inaccuracy can be disregarded if it is 'accidental and on a scale which could not affect the result of the election', and the result of the election must be determined solely by counting the number of votes cast directly for each candidate[27]

(e) no member must be unreasonably excluded from standing as a candidate, unless she or he belongs to a class which has been excluded by the union rules, and no candidate can be required to be a member of a political party.[28] In *Ecclestone v National Union of Journalists*[29] the claimant was held to have been unreasonably excluded from a short-list for election to the post of deputy general secretary. The national executive committee of the union had imposed a qualification which amounted to having the confidence of that committee. The High Court held that this created a class of excluded persons which was created purely by reference to whom the executive committee decided to exclude. This was deemed to be arbitrary and not in accordance with good employment practice.

Section 48 TULRCA 1992 gives candidates in union elections the right to prepare an election address and to have it distributed with the ballot papers. Unions cannot impose a word-limit of fewer than 100 words, and the address can be edited only with the permission of the candidate. There is also a duty to ensure, so far as is practicable, that the same facilities apply equally to all candidates. Section 24 TULRCA obliges trade unions to compile and maintain a register of the names and addresses of their members and to secure, so far as is reasonably practicable, that entries in the register are accurate and kept up to date.

Prior to an election being held, a trade union must appoint a qualified independent person (a 'scrutineer').[30] Before the scrutineer begins performing his or her functions, a trade union must either personally inform all its members, so far as is reasonably practicable, of the scrutineer's name or notify the members of the name in such other way as is in keeping with the union's practice. A trade union must supply the scrutineer with a copy of the register of members' names and addresses as it applies to the particular election. The scrutineer must inspect the register (see above) whenever it appears appropriate to do so and, in particular, if requested to do so by a member who suspects that the register is not accurate or up to date. The latter requirement does not apply where the scrutineer considers that the suspicion is ill-founded.[31]

The scrutineer must supervise the production and distribution of voting papers; make a detailed report on the conduct of an election, indicating any matters about which he or she is dissatisfied; and retain custody of the returned voting papers for at least a year after the ballot result has been announced. Once the candidate with the largest number of votes has been declared elected, following a favourable report by the scrutineer, a trade union cannot cancel the election unless there is express power under the union rules to do so or it can be shown that the whole election process was a nullity.[32]

The storage and distribution of the voting papers and the counting of votes must be undertaken by 'independent persons' appointed by the union. Such a person may be the scrutineer or a person whom the union believes will carry out his or her functions competently, and whose independence cannot reasonably be called into question.[33] Finally, in addition to the detailed statutory provisions, the Secretary of State is empowered to issue codes of practice on union elections.[34]

If a trade union fails to comply with any of the above provisions, within a year from the date the election result was announced a member may apply to the Certification Officer or the High Court for a declaration. The High Court can also make an enforcement order requiring the union to take remedial action. The period for ensuring compliance with an enforcement order will be specified by the court, and any person who was a member when the order was made is entitled to enforce obedience to it.[35]

THE ROLE OF THE CERTIFICATION OFFICER

The ERel Act 1999 added a new Chapter VIIA to Part I TULRCA 1992. The effect was to establish an alternative to the courts for trade union members to seek remedies in relation to certain alleged breaches of union rules. Chapter VIIA consists of three sections: 108A, 108B and 108C.

Section 108A specifies the circumstances under which a complaint can be made to the CO and gives the CO the authority to make declarations dealing with the complaint. The alleged breach or intended breach of union rules must relate to:

(a) the appointment or election of a person to any office in the union

(b) the removal of a person from an office of the union

(c) disciplinary proceedings by the union against a member of the union (including expulsion)

(d) the balloting of union members other than in respect of industrial action

(e) the constitution or proceedings of union executive committees and other decision-making meetings

(f) any other matter which the Secretary of State may specify from time to time.

Complaints to the CO on these matters can be made only by members of the union or individuals who were members of the union at the time of the alleged or threatened breach.[36] Complaints about a breach of the rules concerning dismissal or disciplining employees of the union, however, are excluded from the CO's jurisdiction.[37] Sections 108A(6) and (7) TULRCA 1992 set out the timetable for complaints to the CO. In cases where the internal disputes procedure of the union was not used, complaints must be made within six months of the alleged breach or intended breach. Where the internal complaints procedure of the union was used within six months of the alleged or intended breach, the complaint to the CO must be made within six months of the ending of that internal procedure, or 12 months after the procedure was commenced, whichever is the sooner. It is not possible to complain to the court and the CO. A complainant will need to choose, and having made that choice will not be able to take parallel action with either the court or the CO.

According to section 108B the CO may refuse to accept applications unless the applicant satisfies the CO that all reasonable steps have been taken to use the union's internal complaints procedure.[38] The CO also has the power to make declarations.[39] Sections 108B(3) and (4) give the CO the power to make enforcement orders imposing requirements on the union to remedy the breach or withdraw the threat of a breach within a specified time period. Any declarations of the CO are to be relied upon as if they were a declaration of the court and can be enforced as if they were court orders.[40]

Section 108C allows for appeals against the CO's decisions to be made to the EAT. These appeals can be made only on questions of law.

POLITICAL FUNDS

Contribution to a union's political fund cannot be made a condition of admission to a union, and members who wish to contract out of a political levy must be free to do so. Similarly, the contracted-out members cannot be excluded from any benefit or disqualified from holding any office, except for a position connected with the management of a political fund.[41] According to sections 73–8 TULRCA 1992, unions wishing to maintain political funds must ballot their members at least once every 10 years and observe the same conditions as apply to elections (see above). Where a political fund resolution has ceased to have effect, members who were exempt from the obligation to contribute must not be excluded from any benefits or placed in any respect, either directly or indirectly, under any disadvantage compared with other union members by reason of being so exempt.[42] Similarly, where a resolution has lapsed but the union has continued to collect contributions, it must pay a refund of any contribution made after the date of cessation to any member who applies for one.[43]

Unions must first seek the approval of the CO for the rules under which they propose to conduct the ballot. The CO will give an opportunity for both the complainant and the union to be heard and take into account decisions on similar issues that have previously been made by the courts. The CO has the power to make an enforcement order on the union to remedy a failure to comply with the law on political fund ballots and/or to abstain from repeating the failure in the future. The CO's order can be enforced in the same way as an order from the court.

Section 86 TULRCA 1992 imposes a duty on employers not to deduct contributions to a political fund from the emoluments payable to a member who has either informed the employer in writing that he or she is exempt from paying the political levy or has given written notification to the union of his or her objection to paying it. Employers must comply as soon as is reasonably practicable and will be in breach of the Act if they simply deduct any union dues from the pay of the person who submitted a certificate under this section. Aggrieved employees may apply to the county court for a declaration that the employer has failed to comply and the court can make an order requiring the employer to take remedial action within a specified period.[44]

INTER-UNION DISPUTES

There is no legal machinery for handling inter-union disputes, and relations between TUC-affiliated unions are regulated by the Bridlington Principles.[45] According to Principle 2, TUC affiliates 'accept as a binding commitment ... that they will not knowingly and actively seek to take into membership the present or 'recent' members of another union by making recruitment approaches, either directly or indirectly, without the agreement of that organisation'. Where there is dispute over recruitment, 'The effort at resolution will include a moral obligation on the part of the respondent union to offer compensation to the complainant union for any loss of income that it has suffered as a consequence of any knowingly and active recruitment of its members.' Principle 3 provides that 'No union shall commence organising activities at any establishment or undertaking in respect of any grade or grades of workers in which another union has the majority of workers employed and negotiates terms and conditions, unless by arrangement with that union.'[46] Principle 4 obliges unions to involve the TUC before industrial action occurs over an inter-union dispute and, where necessary, to take steps to secure a return to normal working. Where unions are unable to resolve a dispute and it is referred to the TUC, the General Secretary may refer it to a Disputes Committee which is empowered to make an award. Finally, it should be noted that an employer who is affected by an inter-union problem may seek assistance from ACAS.

UNION AMALGAMATIONS

The CO is able to hear complaints from trade union members that their union is in breach of statute or rules in connection with gaining members' approval for union amalgamations. The CO is able to make declarations and orders concerning this subject matter.[47] The CO may make such enquiries as are seen to be necessary and can ask the interested parties to supply information by specified dates. The CO is able to make declarations which can be enforced in the same way as court orders, thus enabling union members to apply to the court to force the union to comply.

KEY POINTS 20
Trade unions and their members

- Employees have the right to join the union of their choice and cannot be excluded unless they fail to meet an enforceable membership requirement, unless the union only operates in another part of Great Britain, unless the union only deals with one employer, or unless the exclusion is attributable to the individual's conduct.

- The rules of a trade union constitute a contract between the union and its members and must be strictly adhered to, so a trade union wishing to discipline a member must have the power to do so in its rule-book.

- If the union rules specify the grounds on which

disciplinary action may be taken, and the procedures to be taken, it will be unlawful for the union to rely on other grounds, or not rigidly follow its own procedures.

- Irrespective of its rule-book, every trade union must elect its president, general secretary and members of its executive by ballot at least once every five years.

- There are detailed rules governing union elections, including candidates having the right to prepare election addresses and have them distributed with the ballot papers, plus the need to appoint independent persons to distribute and store ballot papers, and the need for an independent scrutineer.

- The Certification Officer can be used as an alternative to the courts for union members who wish to make complaints about disciplinary actions by their union. The Certification Officer has the power to make enquiries, hear the parties and issue declarations which can be enforced in the same way as court orders.

- Contributions to a union's political fund cannot be made a condition of admission, and members who wish to contract out of a political levy must be free to do so.

NOTES

1 Section 12 SDA 1975, section 11 RRA 1976; see also EOC Code of Practice, paragraph 6–8, and CRE Code of Practice, part 3
2 Section 174(3) TULRCA 1992
3 Section 174(4) TULRCA 1992
4 See *NACODS v Gluchowski* (1996) IRLR 252
5 Section 175 TULRCA 1992
6 Section 176 TULRCA 1992
7 See *Clarke v Chadburn* (1984) IRLR 350
8 *McVitae v Unison* (1996) IRLR 33
9 See *Knowles v Fire Brigades Union* (1996) IRLR 617
10 Section 64(2) TULRCA 1992
11 (1990) IRLR 464

12 Section 66(2) TULRCA 1992
13 Section 288 TULRCA 1992
14 Section 67(3) TULRCA 1992
15 On the requirement to take all necessary steps to secure the reversal of an expulsion, see *NALGO v Courtney* (1992) IRLR 114
16 Section 67(6) and (7) TULRCA 1992
17 Section 174(4) TULRCA 1992
18 See *Jacques v AUEW* (1986) ICR 683
19 See *Leigh v NUR* (1970) IRLR 60
20 See *Longley v NUJ* (1987) IRLR 109
21 *Cheall v APEX* (1983) IRKLR 215
22 See *Roebuck v NUM* (1976) ICR 573 and *Hamlet v GMBATU* (1986) IRLR 293
23 See *McGhee v TGWU* (1985) IRLR 199 on the meaning of expulsion
24 Section 46(3) TULRCA 1992 defines a 'member of the executive'. On exemptions for certain presidents and general secretaries, see section 46(4) TULRCA 1992
25 Sections 59 and 60 TULRCA 1992
26 See *Paul v NALGO* (1987) IRLR 43
27 See *R v Certification Officer ex parte EPEA* (1990) IRLR 98
28 Section 47 TULRCA 1992
29 (1999) IRLR 166
30 Defined by section 49(2) TULRCA 1992
31 See sections 49 and 52 TULRCA 1992. On the confidentiality of the register, see section 24A TULRCA 1992
32 See *Douglas v GPMU* (1995) IRLR 426
33 Section 51A TULCRA 1992
34 Section 203 TULRCA 1992
35 Section 54 TULRCA 1992; on a contractual right of a member to complain of a breach of the rules, see *Wise v USDAW* (1996) IRLR 609
36 Section 108A(3) TULRCA 1992
37 Section 108A(5) TULRCA 1992
38 Section 108B(1) TULRCA 1992
39 Section 108B(2) TULRCA 1992
40 Sections 108B(6) and (8) TULRCA 1992
41 Section 82 TULRCA 1992
42 Section 91(4) TULRCA 1992
43 Section 90 TULRCA 1992
44 Section 87 TULRCA 1992
45 See TUC booklet *TUC Disputes, Principles and Procedures, 1993*
46 The process of statutory recognition of trade unions is stopped if there is an unsettled dispute between unions about representation (see Chapter 19)
47 Section 103 TULRCA 199

21 Liability for industrial action

It has already been explained that all forms of industrial action are likely to constitute a breach of an individual's contract of employment. In this chapter we shall be concentrating more on the liability of those who organise industrial action than those who participate in it. In this respect we shall be examining the nature of the common-law liabilities and the extent to which statutory provisions can be used to negate their effect. We begin with an examination of the economic torts and then consider the protection offered by statute for action that takes place in contemplation or furtherance of a trade dispute. This is followed by a consideration of the statutory hurdles that have to be overcome before official action can take place. We shall be focusing mainly on the civil law, but it will also be necessary to deal with the possibility of criminal prosecutions.

THE 'ECONOMIC' TORTS

Inducing a breach of contract

There are two forms of inducement: direct and indirect.

Direct inducement may occur when a union official puts direct pressure on an employer to breach a commercial contract. Thus if A induces B to break the contract of supply with C and C suffers loss as a result, C could sue B for breaking the contract (but is unlikely to in the circumstances), or could sue A if the following matters are shown:

(a) that A knew of the contract which would be broken or was 'recklessly indifferent' as to its existence

(b) that A's conduct was intentional. Here, once sufficient knowledge has been established, the intention to produce a breach will be presumed

(c) that there was clear evidence of inducement. In this

Figure 21.1

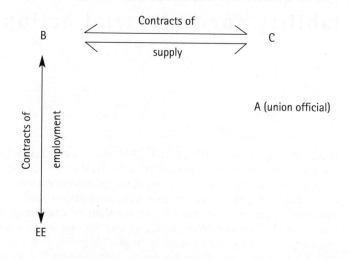

context inducement means pressure, persuasion or procuration and must be distinguished from the giving of advice, information or a warning.[1]

Indirect inducement is when A induces union members to break their contracts of employment so that B is forced to break the contract with C. C can sue A if the requirements of knowledge, intention and inducement are met and the use of unlawful means is proved. It makes no difference that A believed that the functions performed by the members were voluntary rather than contractual.[2] For the purposes of all the economic torts, unlawful means may be either tortious, eg breaking a contract or inducing a breach of statutory duty, or criminal acts, eg the use of violence.

Thus the essential difference between direct and indirect inducement is one of causation. Where the person immediately responsible for bringing the pressure to bear was the defendant or someone for whose acts he or she was legally responsible, the inducement is direct. If it was a third party responding to the defendant's inducement or persuasion but exercising his or her choice (and not being a person for whom the defendant was legally responsible), the inducement is indirect.[3]

Section 219(1)(a) TULRCA 1992 provides that an act done in contemplation or furtherance of a trade dispute – the so-called 'golden formula' (see below) – will not be actionable in tort on the ground only that it induces another to break a contract. In *Norbrook Ltd v King*[4] it was pointed out that the effect of the phrase 'on the ground only' is that the use of unlawful means to induce a breach of contract deprives the user of statutory protection. However, it is clear that section 219 does not provide immunity against prosecution in respect of acts which are in themselves criminal.[5]

Intimidation

This tort is committed where C suffers as a result of action taken by B in response to an unlawful threat made to B by A. In this situation C or B can sue A at common law, whether the threat is of tortious or criminal conduct.[6] However, section 219(1)(b) TULRCA 1992 states that an act done in contemplation or furtherance of a trade dispute shall not be actionable in tort on the ground only that it consists of a person 'threatening that a contract (whether one to which he is a party or not) will be broken or its performance interfered with, or that he will induce another person to break a contract or interfere with its performance'.

Conspiracy

Again, this tort could take one of two forms:

(a) A combination to injure with illegitimate objectives. This is where two or more persons combine in order to harm the plaintiff by use of means which are lawful in themselves but with a predominant purpose other than that of advancing their own legitimate interests. Thus if those combining can show a genuine trade union reason behind their action (for example, protecting jobs), the conspiracy will not be actionable despite any loss caused to an employer.[7]

(b) A situation in which people combine in order to harm the plaintiff by using unlawful means: in this way a tort is committed irrespective of the purpose of the combination. The use of unlawful means eliminates the justification of self-interest.

Because almost all strikes involve combinations of workers inflicting loss on employers, section 219(2) TULRCA 1992 provides that a combination to do any act in contemplation or furtherance of a trade dispute is not actionable in tort if the act is one which, if done by one person alone, would not be actionable.

Interference with business by unlawful means

This tort was developed to take account of the practice of inserting *force majeure* clauses into commercial contracts. The effect of such a clause is to exempt a party from liability where a breach of contract would otherwise have arisen as a result of industrial action. The Court of Appeal has stated that to succeed in establishing the tort of wrongful interference with contractual rights, five conditions must be fulfilled. These are:

(a) It must be shown that the defendant persuaded or procured or induced a third party to break its contract with the plaintiff.

(b) It must be shown that the defendant when so acting had knowledge of that contract.

(c) The defendant must be shown to have had the intent to persuade or induce a breach of that contract.

(d) The plaintiff must show that it suffered more than nominal damage.

(e) If justification is put forward as a defence, the plaintiff must be able to rebut this.[8]

Statutory immunity is provided by section 219(1)(a) TULRCA 1992, which states that so long as the 'golden formula' applies, an act is not to be actionable in tort on the ground only that it 'interferes or induces any other person to interfere' with the performance of a contract. In *Hadmor Productions v Hamilton*[9] the House of Lords held that inducing, or threatening to induce, a breach of contract could not be regarded as unlawful means for the purpose of establishing liability for interference with the business of a third person.

Inducing a breach of statutory duty

In *Meade v Haringey LBC*[10] two Court of Appeal judges expressed the opinion that persons inducing a public body to act in breach of its statutory duty would be committing a tort for which there would be no statutory immunity. If this view were adopted, it would be relatively easy to restrain action taken by workers in the public sector.

ECONOMIC DURESS

If the financial consequences to an employer of not acceding to the request of a trade union or another person are catastrophic, it could be argued that there was such coercion of the employer's will as to vitiate consent to any agreements made with, or payments made to, the union (or person) applying the pressure. Contracts made in these circumstances will be voidable and it will be possible to claim restitution of money paid under them. The rationale is that the employer's apparent consent was induced by pressure exercised by that other party which the law does not regard as legitimate. In *Universe Tankships Inc of Monrovia v ITWF*[11] the House of Lords accepted that sections 219 and 244 TULRCA 1992 afforded an indication of where public policy requires the line to be drawn between the kind of commercial pressure by a trade union which ought to be treated as legitimised and the kind that amounts to economic duress. The events which gave rise to this case occurred in 1978 and it is safe to say that subsequent legislation will have encouraged the judiciary to take a narrower view of what is regarded as legitimate pressure.

THE 'GOLDEN FORMULA'

We have observed that statutory immunity in tort for various types of industrial action depends on that action's taking place *in contemplation or furtherance of a trade dispute*. Although we shall be outlining later the requirement to conduct a ballot before industrial action (see below), it should be noted that so long as the action taken is in contemplation or furtherance of a trade dispute the TULRCA 1992 immunities apply irrespective of whether or not the action is in breach of a disputes procedure. However, if the 'golden formula' does not apply, it will be relatively easy for an employer to show that one of the economic torts is being committed, and to obtain an interlocutory injunction on that basis.

The meaning of 'trade dispute'

Section 244 TULRCA 1992 defines a trade dispute as a dispute between workers and their employer which relates wholly or mainly to one or more of the following:

(a)   terms and conditions of employment, or the physical conditions in which any workers are required to work. These are not confined to contractual terms and conditions[12]

(b)   engagement or non-engagement, or termination or suspension of employment, or the duties of employment of one or more workers. However, if the reason or more of the reasons for calling industrial action is 'the fact or belief that the employer has dismissed one or more employees in circumstances such that by virtue of section 237 TULRCA 1992 (dismissal in connection with unofficial industrial action) they have no right to complain of unfair dismissal', the immunity provided by section 219 TULRCA 1992 is lost[13]

(c)   allocation of work or the duties of employment as between workers or groups of workers

(d)   matters of discipline

(e)   the membership or non-membership of a trade union on the part of a worker. Nevertheless, there will be no immunity from liability in tort where the purpose of the industrial action is to enforce union membership or persuade employers to insert recognition or consultation requirements in contracts for the supply of goods or services[14]

(f)   facilities for officials of trade unions

(g)   the machinery for negotiation or consultation and other procedures relating to any of the foregoing matters, including the recognition by employers or employers' associations of the right of a trade union to represent workers in any such negotiation, or consultation, or in the carrying out of such procedures.

In *University College London Hospital NHS Trust v Unison*[15] the union gained an overwhelming majority in favour of strike action in support of a demand for employment guarantees associated with the building of a new hospital under the Private Finance Initiative. This would involve the transfer of some workers to a new employer. The Court of Appeal held that the dispute was about terms and conditions which would apply to workers not currently employed by the NHS Trust and that such a dispute about future employment with a new employer was outside the provisions of section 244.

Clearly, where there is a dispute between a union and an employer there is a dispute between those workers on whose behalf the union was acting and that employer.[16] In addition, section 244(2) TULRCA 1992 provides that in certain circumstances a dispute between a Minister of the Crown and any workers is to be treated as a dispute between those workers and their employers.[17]

A 'worker' is defined to cover only those employed by the employer in dispute.[18] However, the 'golden formula' will not apply if the dispute concerns a former employee unless either the employment was terminated in connection with the dispute or the termination was one of the circumstances giving rise to the dispute. A realistic view of who is an employer was taken in *Examite Ltd v Whittaker*[19] where it was stated that 'the Act applies to employers whatever particular hat these particular employers may wear from time to time.'

A trade dispute can exist even though it relates to matters occurring outside the UK:

> so long as the person or persons whose actions in the UK are said to be in contemplation or furtherance of a trade dispute relating to matters occurring outside the UK are likely to be affected in respect of one or more of the matters specified in section 244(1) TULRCA by the outcome of that dispute.[20]

It is also stated that an act, threat or demand done or made by a person or organisation against another which, if resisted, would have led to a trade dispute with that other, shall, notwithstanding that because that other submits to the act or threat or accedes to the demand no dispute arises, be treated as being done or made in contemplation or furtherance of a trade dispute.[21]

Contemplation or furtherance

The word 'contemplation' refers to something imminent or likely to occur, so the 'golden formula' cannot be invoked if the action was taken too far in advance of any dispute. 'Furtherance' assumes the existence of a dispute and an act will not be protected if it is not for the purpose of promoting the interests of a party to the dispute (for example, if it is in pursuit of a personal vendetta) or occurs after its conclusion.[22] In *MacShane and Ashton v Express Newspapers*[23] the House of Lords held that while the existence of a trade dispute had to be determined objectively, the test for deciding whether an act is in furtherance of such a dispute is a subjective one: 'If the person doing the act honestly thinks at the time he does it that it may help one of the parties to the dispute to achieve their objective and does it for that reason, he is protected.' Apparently there is no requirement that a union should act exclusively in furtherance of a trade dispute; it is sufficient if the furtherance of a trade dispute is one of its purposes. Indeed, the presence of an improper motive is relevant only where it is so overriding that it negates any genuine intention to advance the trade dispute.[24]

SECONDARY ACTION

In this book 'primary action' refers to action taken directly against the employer in dispute and 'secondary action' is that taken against the employer's suppliers and customers. Section 244 defines secondary action as being an inducement to break or interfere with a contract of employment or a contract for personal services, or a threat to do so, where the employer under that contract is not party to the dispute.

For these purposes an employer is not to be regarded as a party to a dispute between another employer and its workers. Similarly, where more than one employer is in dispute, the dispute between each employer and its workers is to be treated as a separate dispute.[25]

The protection afforded against certain tort liabilities by section 219 TULRCA 1992 will not be available unless the secondary action satisfies the requirements of section 224. These can be met only if the secondary action is taken in the course of such attendance as is declared lawful by section 220 TULRCA 1992

(a) by a worker employed (or last employed) by the employer who is party to the dispute, or

(b) by a union official whose attendance is lawful by virtue of section 220(1)(6) TULRCA 1992 (on peaceful picketing and section 220 TULRCA 1992, see below).

UNION RESPONSIBILITY FOR THE ACTS OF THEIR MEMBERS AND OFFICIALS

Trade unions are to be treated in law as ordinary persons. This means that they get the benefit of the immunities conferred by section 219 TULRCA 1992 but can be sued if they are responsible for unlawful industrial action. However, a union will be held liable for the torts mentioned in section 20(1) TULRCA 1992 only if the acts in question were authorised or endorsed by the union. Where other torts are committed, the ordinary principles or vicarious liability apply.[26] Irrespective of union rules, acts are to be regarded as authorised or endorsed if there was authorisation or endorsement by:[27]

(a) any person empowered by the rules to do, authorise or endorse acts of the kind in question

(b) the principal executive committee or the president or general secretary, or

(c) any other committee of the union or any other official of the union (whether employed by it or not).

In this context 'rules' means the 'written rules of the union and any other written provisions forming part of the contract between a member and other members'. 'President' and 'general secretary' are defined to include, where there is no such office in the union, the person who holds the 'nearest equivalent' office.[28] For these purposes any group of persons constituted in accordance with the rules of the union is a committee of the union and 'an act shall be taken to have been done, authorised or endorsed by an official if it was done, etc' by any member of a group whose purposes include organising or co-ordinating industrial action.[29] These provisions apply irrespective of anything in the union rules which prevents particular officials or committees calling industrial action.

A union can avoid liability for the actions of union committees and officials if those actions are repudiated by the principal executive committee or the president or general secretary 'as soon as reasonably practicable after coming to the knowledge of any of them'. However, a repudiation will be effective only if:

(a) written notice of the repudiation is given to the official or committee in question without delay, and

(b) the union has done its best to give individual written notice of the fact and date of repudiation without delay to every member whom the union has reason to believe is taking part, or might otherwise take part, in the industrial action. The notice to members must contain the following statement: 'Your union has repudiated any call for industrial action to which this notice relates and will give no support to such action. If you are dismissed while taking unofficial industrial action, you will have no right to complain of unfair dismissal.' This notice must also be given to the employer of every such member.[30]

An act shall not be treated as repudiated if the union's principal executive committee, president or general secretary subsequently behaves in a manner inconsistent with that repudiation. Additionally, if a request is made to any of these bodies within three months by a person who is party to a commercial contract that has been, or may be, interfered with and who has not been given notice of the repudiation, that body must immediately confirm the repudiation in writing.[31] Finally, in any injunction proceedings arising out of this section, the courts are empowered to require unions to take such steps as are considered appropriate for ensuring that:

(a) there is no inducement of persons to take part in industrial action, and

(b) no person engages in any conduct after the grant of the injunction by virtue of having been induced before it was granted to take part in industrial action.[32]

BALLOTS AND NOTICE OF INDUSTRIAL ACTION

Trade unions and their officials can benefit from immunity provided by section 219 TULRCA 1992 only if the union has authorised or endorsed the industrial action, having gained majority support in a ballot of the members concerned not more than four weeks before the start of the action.[33] It is the Court of Appeal's view that once industrial action has begun it should continue 'without substantial interruption' if reliance is to be placed on the result of the original ballot. Whether the original action has come to an end is a matter of fact and degree.[34]

For section 219 TULRCA 1992 immunity to be available, the following requirements must be met:

(a) Trade unions must take such steps as are reasonably necessary to ensure that at least seven days before the start of the ballot a written notice is received by 'every person who it is reasonable for the union to believe ... will be the employer of persons who will be entitled to vote in the ballot'. This notice must

• state that the union intends to hold a ballot

• specify the date which the union reasonably believes will be the opening day of the ballot

- provide the employer with such information in the union's possession which 'would help the employer to make plans and bring information to the attention of those of his employees whom the union intends to induce or has induced to take part, or to continue to take part, in the industrial action'.[35] If the union possesses information as to the number, category or workplace of the employees concerned, then this information should be included in the notice.[36] Additionally, at least three days before the opening of the ballot, the union must take such steps as are reasonably necessary to ensure that the same employer receives a sample voting paper.[37]

(b) Conditions (b) and (d) on union elections must be satisfied (see Chapter 20).

(c) Entitlement to vote must be given equally to those, and only those, whom the union reasonably believes will be called upon to take strike or other industrial action.[38] In *London Underground v RMT*[39] the Court of Appeal accepted that a union could call for newly recruited members to take part in industrial action even though they had not been balloted.

(d) There must be a separate ballot at each workplace unless the ballot is limited to all the members of a union who

- according to the union's reasonable belief have an occupation of a particular kind or have any of a number of particular kinds of occupation, and

- are employed by a particular employer, or by any number of particular employers, with whom the union is in dispute.[40]

(e) So far as is reasonably practicable, all members entitled to vote must be sent a voting paper at his or her registered address, and be given a convenient opportunity to vote by post.[41]

(f) The voting paper must:

- state the name of the independent scrutineer appointed to carry out the functions described above[42]

- specify the address to which, and the date by which, it is to be returned

- be marked with a number which is one of a series of consecutive whole numbers

- contain the following statement:

> If you take part in a strike or other industrial action you may be in breach of your contract of employment. However, if you are dismissed for taking part in a strike or other industrial action which is called officially and is otherwise lawful, the dismissal will be unfair if it takes place fewer than eight weeks after you started taking part in the action, and depending on the circumstances may be unfair if it takes place later.

- invite a 'yes' or 'no' answer to the question whether members are prepared to participate in a strike or other industrial action. According to the Court of Appeal, the questions on the ballot paper must be framed so that members can draw a distinction between their willingness to take strike action and their willingness to take action short of a strike.[43] In *Connex South Eastern Ltd v NURMTW*[44] employees voted for strike action and the employer was notified by the union that they proposed to start a ban on overtime and rest day working. The employer claimed that this discontinuous action was not strike action and was therefore unlawful. The Court of Appeal held that the action was lawful because strike action was not restricted to stoppages of all work, but could include stoppages on particular days and at particular hours. The position has been modified by the ERel Act 1999 which states that overtime bans and call-out bans are forms of industrial action short of a strike.[45] Each question has to be voted on individually and the majority in respect of each question considered separately[46]

- identify the person(s) authorised to call industrial action and that person must be one of those specified in section 20(2) TULRCA (see above)

Industrial action will not be regarded as having the support of a ballot if a member, who was likely to be induced into taking part in the action, was not accorded the right to vote.[47]

(g) As soon as is reasonably practicable after the ballot, the union must take such steps as are reasonably necessary to ensure that all those entitled to vote and every relevant employer are informed of the number of votes cast, the numbers voting 'yes' and those voting 'no', and the number of spoiled ballot papers.[48] If there is a failure to inform one or more relevant employers, the ballot and subsequent action will still be valid in relation to the other employers who were informed correctly.[49]

(h) Trade unions must take all reasonably necessary steps to ensure that the employer of those to be called upon to take industrial action receives written notice of the action. This notice must be received after the employer has been informed of the ballot result and at least seven days prior to the date on which the action is to commence. The notice must contain:

- such information 'as would help the employer to make plans and bring information to the attention of those of his employees it is reasonable for the union to believe...will be entitled to vote in the ballot'[50]

- a statement of whether the industrial action is intended to be continuous or discontinuous[51]

- where there is continuous action, the date on which it is intended to start; where the action is discontinuous, the dates on which it is intended to take place. The ballot will cease to be effective after a period of four weeks, or up to eight weeks if the union and the employer agree[52]

- a statement that the notice is given for the purposes of section 234A TULRCA 1992.

If there are accidental and minor failures to comply with all the balloting requirements, these may be ignored as long as they are unlikely to affect the ballot outcome.[53]

Where industrial action ceases to be authorised or endorsed (other than in compliance with a court order or undertaking), and is subsequently re-authorised or re-endorsed, the union must give another notice to the employer before the industrial action is resumed.

Finally, where a member has been (or is likely to be) induced by the union to take part in any industrial action which does not satisfy the ballot requirements of Part V TULRCA 1992, he or she can apply to the High Court for an order requiring the union to stop authorising or endorsing the industrial action without the support of a valid ballot.[54] It should be noted that although a court can order the union to ensure that there is no further inducement, it has no power to compel the union to conduct a valid ballot.

REMEDIES

Damages
Section 22(2) TULRCA 1992 limits the amount of damages that can be awarded 'in any proceedings in tort' against a trade union which is deemed liable for industrial action.[55] The words 'in any proceedings' are crucial, since separate proceedings may be brought by all those who have suffered from the industrial action. The limits set are:

(a) £10,000, if the union has fewer than 5,000 members

(b) £50,000, if the union has 5,000 or more members but fewer than 25,000

(c) £125,000 if the union has 25,000 or more members but fewer than 100,000

(d) £250,000 if the union has 100,000 or more members.

It should be noted that interest on such damages may be available.[56] Finally, it should be noted that damages, costs or expenses cannot be recovered from certain 'protected property'. This includes union provident funds and political funds, which cannot be used for financing industrial action.[57]

Injunctions

If an employer is suffering economic harm as a result of unlawful industrial action, the logical remedy is to seek an injunction so as to prevent further loss being incurred. An injunction may be sought against a trade union or some other person, although section 236 TULRCA 1992 prevents a court from compelling an employee to do any work. The general principle that if damages would provide an adequate remedy an injunction must be refused will not apply in this context: 'Where it is clear that the defendants were acting unlawfully, it would require wholly exceptional circumstances to be a proper exercise of discretion to allow such conduct to continue.'[58]

There are three basic types of injunction that should be mentioned:

(a) In situations of extreme urgency an *interim* injunction can be sought. This is a temporary measure which endures until a named day and can be obtained on the basis of sworn statements submitted by the applicant alone. If the respondent is absent, this is known as an *ex parte* (one-sided) injunction.

   According to section 221 TULRCA 1992, a court shall not grant an application if the party against whom the injunction is sought claims (or in the court's opinion might claim) that the act was done in contemplation or furtherance of a trade dispute unless all reasonable steps have been taken to give that party notice of the application and an opportunity of being heard.

(b) An *interlocutory* injunction (see below) restrains the commission of an act until the issue comes to trial. Again, no witnesses will be called but there will be legal argument and sworn statements from both sides.

(c) A *permanent* injunction is one which is granted at the end of the trial.

Before granting an interlocutory injunction, a judge will have to consider the following questions:

(a) Is there a serious question to be tried?

(b) Does the balance of convenience lie with the plaintiff? In *NWL v Nelson*[59] Lord Diplock argued that judges should not blind themselves to the practical realities by pretending that an injunction merely preserves the *status quo* until the trial is heard: 'It is the nature of industrial action that it can be promoted effectively only so long as it is possible to strike while the iron is hot; once postponed, it is unlikely that it can be revived ... The grant or refusal of an interlocutory injunction generally disposes finally of the action.' In such a case the court has to balance the risk of doing an injustice to either party and evaluate the public interest.[60]

(c) Where the party against whom the injunction is sought claims that the action was in contemplation of furtherance of a trade dispute, is there a likelihood of the defendant's establishing a defence to the action under section 219 or 220 TULRCA 1992?[61] It has been held by the House of Lords that the effect of section 221(2) TULRCA 1992 is that in exercising its discretion a court should put into the balance of convenience the degree of likelihood of the defendant's succeeding in establishing a trade dispute defence.[62] Thus in *Health Computing v Meek*[63] no injunction was granted because there was a 'substantial probability' that the defendants would establish that they were acting in contemplation or furtherance of a trade dispute. By way of contrast, in *RJB Mining v NUM*[64] an interlocutory injunction was granted because it was at least arguable that the union was in breach of section 227 TULRCA 1992 by omitting to ballot all of its members who might be involved in the industrial action. However, that it is likely that a trade dispute defence would be established should not be regarded as an overriding or paramount factor precluding the granting of an injunction. There may be cases where the consequences to the plaintiff or to others may be so serious that the court feels it necessary to grant this form of remedy. In the *Duport Steels* case[65] the Law Lords confirmed that there is a residual discretion to grant an injunction notwithstanding the likelihood of a trade dispute defence succeeding at trial. Nevertheless, the opinion was expressed that it required an exceptional case in which the consequences of the threatened act might be disastrous.

(d) What good will be done to the plaintiff by the grant of the injunction sought? In *Hadmor Productions v Hamilton*[66] the House of Lords held that the High Court judge had been entitled to attach great weight to the view that an injunction would not have been of practical use to the plaintiff. It is not sufficient ground for granting an injunction to argue that if the defendants had no intention of engaging in unlawful conduct the injunction would do them no harm![67]

Failure by union officials to comply with an injunction may amount to contempt of court, for which the union is vicariously liable. Indeed, it would appear that a delay in complying with a court order cannot be justified by reference to the union's internal constitution.[68] Where there is deliberate defiance of a court order, a substantial fine may be imposed.[69] In this context it should be observed that section 15 TULRCA 1992 makes it unlawful for a union to use its property to indemnify an individual on whom a penalty has been imposed for contempt or a criminal offence. Additionally, where it is alleged that a union's trustees have unlawfully applied union property or complied with an unlawful direction given under the union rules, a member can seek a High Court order to remove the trustees, recover the property or appoint a receiver.[70]

INDUSTRIAL ACTION THAT AFFECTS THE SUPPLY OF GOODS OR SERVICES TO AN INDIVIDUAL

Section 235A TULRCA 1992 gives an individual the right to apply to the High Court for an order if:

(a) a trade union or other person has done, or is likely to do, an unlawful act to induce a person to take part in or continue with industrial action, and

(b) an effect, or likely effect, of the industrial action is, or will be, to prevent or delay the supply of goods or services, or to reduce the quality of goods or services supplied to the claimant.

For these purposes an act is unlawful if it is actionable in tort by anyone, or if it could form the basis of an application by a union member under section 62 TULRCA 1992 (see above). It is immaterial whether or not the individual concerned is entitled to be supplied with the goods or services in question.

PICKETING

Civil law aspects

According to section 220 TULRCA 1992, it shall be lawful for a person in contemplation or furtherance of a trade dispute to attend:

(a) at or near their own place of work, or

(b) if they are an official of a trade union, at or near the place of work of a member of that union whom they are accompanying and whom they represent

for the purpose only of peacefully obtaining or communicating information, or peacefully persuading any person to work or abstain from working.

'Place of work' is not statutorily defined but it would seem to refer to a person's principal place of work or base.[71] As regards the words 'at or near', the Court of Appeal has confirmed that a geographical approach should be taken and that the matter will be one of fact and degree in each case.[72] If people normally work at more than one place or at a place where it is impracticable to picket, their place of work shall be any of their employer's premises from which they work or from which their work is administered.[73] Unemployed workers whose last employment was terminated in connection with a trade dispute, or whose dismissal was one of the circumstances giving rise to a trade dispute, are entitled to picket at their former place of work. It should be observed that section 220 TULRCA 1992 does not necessarily provide employees with a place that they can effectively picket – for example, if their place of work is closed down. A trade union official who has been elected or appointed to represent some of the members is to be regarded for the purposes of picketing as representing only those members; otherwise, a union official is regarded as representing all the union's members.[74]

Section 220 TULRCA 1992 protects mere attendance only for one of the designated purposes. If an act is done in the course of picketing which is not lawful by virtue of section 220, then section 219 TULRCA 1992 will not prevent an action in tort from being brought. Thus pickets acting within the scope of section 220 TULRCA 1992 may be liable for conspiracy to use unlawful means if they are accompanied by pickets who are not so acting. Equally, a person who is not picketing at a permitted place may be sued for trespass to the highway as well as all the economic torts. This is so even if the employer at the premises picketed has accepted the work of the primary employer in dispute. Peaceful picketing at one's own place of work may also result in civil liability – for example, if it is in support of workers in dispute with another employer.

In *Thomas v NUM (South Wales)*[75] Mr Justice Scott refused to distinguish between 'so-called pickets who are stationed close to the gates of the colliery and the rest, so-called demonstrators, who stand near by'. The judge held that whether the presence or conduct of pickets represents a tortious interference with the right of those who wish to go to work depends on the particular circumstances of the case. In his view, where feelings run high substantial numbers of pickets are almost bound to have an intimidatory effect on those going to work. Thus while picketing *per se* is not a common-law nuisance, mass picketing is – ie picketing so as by sheer weight of numbers to block the entrance to premises or prevent the entry of vehicles or people.[76]

An employer whose contracts are interfered with by picketing which falls outside section 220 TULRCA 1992 may bring an action for damages against those responsible and ask a court to make an order stopping the unlawful picketing. An injunction will normally be sought against the person or union on whose instructions or advice the picketing is taking place, but it will also restrict the activities of any others who act on behalf of that person or union (see above on a union's responsibility for the acts of its officials). While the police are not obliged to help an employer identify pickets, a court can ask the police to assist its officers in enforcing injunctions.

The impact of the criminal law

The immunity provided by the civil law cannot protect a picket who commits a criminal offence, and even peaceful picketing can lead to criminal proceedings if it is not lawful by virtue of section 220 TULRCA 1992:

> The criminal law protects the right of every person to go about his lawful daily business free from interference by others. No one is under any obligation to stop when a picket asks him to do so, or if he does stop, to comply with the picket's request, for example, not to go into work. Everyone has the right, if he wants to do so, to cross a picket line to go into his place of work or to deliver or collect goods. A picket may exercise peaceful persuasion, but if he goes beyond that and tries by means other than peaceful persuasion to deter another person from exercising those rights, he may commit a criminal offence.[77]

Paragraph 43 of the Department of Employment *Code of Practice on Picketing* lists a range of criminal offences that may be committed by pickets:

(a) using threatening, abusive or insulting words or behaviour, or disorderly behaviour within the sight or hearing of any person . . . likely to be caused harassment, alarm or distress by such conduct

(b) using threatening, abusive or insulting words or behaviour towards any person with intent to cause fear of violence or to provoke violence

(c) using or threatening unlawful violence

(d)   obstructing the highway or the entrance to premises or to seek physically to bar the passage of vehicles or persons etc

(e)   being in possession of an offensive weapon

(f)   intentionally or recklessly damaging property

(g)   engaging in violent, disorderly or unruly behaviour or taking any action which is likely to lead to a breach of the peace

(h)   obstructing a police officer in the execution of his duty.[78]

Although it is not the function of the police to take a view of the merits of a particular trade dispute, the law gives them the discretion to take whatever measures may reasonably be considered necessary to ensure that picketing remains peaceful and orderly. Hence the police are entitled to limit the number of pickets at any one place where they have reasonable cause to fear disorder.[79] Having identified the main causes of violence and disorder on the picket line as excessive numbers, the Code of Practice exhorts pickets and their organisers to ensure that 'in general the number of pickets does not exceed six at any entrance to, or exit from a workplace; frequently a smaller number will be appropriate'.[80] The code also has paragraphs dealing with the functions of a picket organiser and the safeguarding of essential supplies and services.[81]

Apart from the law relating to picketing, the criminal law does not generally play an important role in regulating industrial conflict. However, if employees occupy their employer's premises they become trespassers under the civil law and the employer may invoke a specified procedure to regain possession. In addition, persons occupying a workplace may be charged under the Criminal Law Act 1977 with using violence to secure entry and trespassing with a weapon of offence, eg ordinary working tools if they are intended to be used offensively.[82] Of the remaining statutory provisions which could give rise to criminal liability, the most important today are probably sections 240–1 TULRCA 1992. According to section 240:

A person commits an offence who wilfully and maliciously breaks a contract of service or hiring, knowing or having reasonable cause to believe that the probable consequence of his so doing, either alone or in combination with others, will be (a) to endanger human life, or cause serious bodily injury, or (b) to expose valuable property whether real or personal to destruction or serious injury.

Anyone found guilty of such an offence is liable to pay a fine not exceeding level 2 on the standard scale or to be imprisoned for up to three months, or both. This provision is less likely to form the basis of a prosecution than an action for an injunction to prevent a breach of it by someone who expects that serious injury will result from industrial action.

Section 241 TULRCA 1992 states that:

A person commits an offence who, with a view to compelling another person to abstain from doing or to do any act which that person has a legal right to do or abstain from doing, wrongfully and without legal authority:

(a) uses violence to or intimidates such other person or his wife or children, or injures his property, or

(b) persistently follows such other person about from place to place, or

(c) hides any tools, clothes or property owned or used by such other person, or deprives him of or hinders him in the use thereof, or

(d) watches or besets the house or other place where such other person resides, or works, or carries on business, or happens to be, or the approach to such house or place, or

(e) follows such other person with two or more other persons in a disorderly manner in or through any street or road.

A person found guilty of this offence is liable to imprisonment for a term not exceeding six months or a fine not exceeding level 5 on the standard scale, or both.

To establish guilt under this section it must be proved that the conduct relied on was wrongful and that the intention with which it was done was, at least in part, to compel others from doing specified acts which they had a legal right to do.[83] In *Galt v Philp*[84] it was held that employees who locked and barricaded the entrance to the premises where they were employed so as to prevent others from working were guilty of 'besetting' within (d) above.

KEY POINTS 21
Liability for industrial action

- The economic torts considered here are inducing a breach of contract, intimidation, conspiracy, interference with business by unlawful means and inducing a breach of statutory duty.

- Statutory immunity from these torts depends on the action's taking place in contemplation or furtherance of a trade dispute. This is known as the 'golden formula'.

- A union will be held liable for the actions of its committees and officials unless those actions are repudiated by the principal executive committee, the president or the general secretary and the union has done its best to inform the officials, and those taking part in the industrial action, of its repudiation.

- Trade unions and officials can only claim immunity if the union has authorised and endorsed the industrial action after a ballot of members has shown a majority in support of that action.

- Trade unions must take all reasonably necessary steps to ensure that the employer of those to be called upon to take part in industrial action receives written notice of the action. The union must also provide information which would help the employer to make plans and bring information to the attention of those employees that the union believes will be entitled to vote in the ballot.

• Remedies available for unlawful action are damages, and interim, interlocutory and permanent injunctions.

• Picketing is lawful in contemplation or furtherance of a trade dispute if it takes place near the employee's own place of work, or if the picket is an official of the union accompanying a member, with the intention of peacefully persuading someone to work or abstain from working.

NOTES

1 See *Camellia Tanker Ltd v ITWF* (1976) IRLR 183
2 See *Metropolitan Borough of Solihull v NUT* (1985) IRLR 211
3 See *Middlebrook Mushrooms v TGWU* (1993) IRLR 232
4 (1984) IRLR 200
5 See *Galt v Philp* (1984) IRLR 156
6 See *Messenger News Group v NGA* (1984) IRLR 397
7 See *Crofter Harris Tweed Co v Veitch* (1942) AC 435
8 See *Timeplan Education Group Ltd v NUT* (1997) IRLR 457
9 (1982) IRLR 103
10 (1979) ICR 494; see also *Barrets & Baird Ltd v IPCS* (1987) IRLR 3
11 (1982) IRLR 200; see also *Dimskal Shipping v ITWF* (1992) IRLR 78
12 See *Hadmor Productions v Hamilton* (1982) IRLR 103 (note 9)
13 Section 223 TULRCA 1992; see Chapter 14 on dismissal during industrial action
14 Sections 222 and 225 respectively TULRCA 1992
15 (1999) IRLR 31
16 ABP v TGWU (1989) IRLR 291
17 See *London Borough of Wandsworth v NAS-UWT* (1993) IRLR 344
18 Section 244(5) TULRCA 1992
19 (1977) IRLR 312; compare *Dimbleby & Sons v NUJ* (1984) IRLR 161
20 Section 244(3) TULRCA 1992
21 Section 244(4) TULRCA 1992
22 See *Huntley v Thornton* (1957) 1 WLR 321; also *Stratford v Lindley* (1965) AC 307
23 (1980) IRLR 35
24 See *ABP v TGWU* (1989) IRLR 305
25 Section 224(4) TULRCA 1992
26 See *News Group v SOGAT* (1986) IRLR 227
27 Section 20(2) TULRCA 1992
28 Section 119 TULRCA 1992
29 Section 20(3)(b) TULRCA 1992
30 Sections 21(1)–(3) TULRCA 1992

31 Section 21(5) and (6) TULRCA 1992
32 Section 20(6) TULRCA 1992
33 This can be extended to eight weeks with agreement by the employer; section 234 TULRCA 1992; see also *RJB Mining v NUM* (1997) IRLR 621
34 *Post Office v UCW* (1990) IRLR 143
35 See section 234(3)(a) TULRCA 1992
36 Section 226A(3A) TULRCA 1992
37 Section 226A TULRCA 1992
38 Section 227 TULRCA 1992
39 (1995) IRLR 636
40 Section 228A TULRCA 1992
41 Section 230(2) TULRCA 1992
42 See sections 226B and 131B TULRCA 1992
43 *Post Office v UCW* (note 34)
44 (1999) IRLR 249
45 See section 229(2A) TULRCA 1992
46 See *West Midlands Travel v TGWU* (1994) IRLR 578
47 Section 232A TULRCA 1992
48 See sections 231 and 231A TULRCA 1992
49 Section 226(3A)
50 Section 226A(2)(c) TULRCA 1992; this means that there is no requirement for the trade union to actually reveal the names of its members to the employer in these circumstances
51 See *Connex South Eastern Ltd v NURMTW* (1999) IRLR 249 (note 44)
52 See section 234(1) TULRCA 1992
53 Section 232B TULRCA 1992
54 Section 62 TULRCA 1992
55 For exceptions see section 22(1) TULRCA 1992
56 See *Boxfoldia Ltd v NGA* (1988) IRLR 383; on aggravated and exemplary damages, see *Messenger News Group v NGA* (note 6)
57 Section 23 TULRCA 1992
58 *Express Newspapers v Keys* (1980) IRLR 247 per Griffiths J
59 (1979) IRLR 478
60 ABP v TGWU (note 24)
61 See section 221(2) TULRCA 1992
62 See *NWL v Nelson* (1979) IRLR 478
63 (1980) IRLR 437
64 See note 33
65 *Duport Steels v Sirs* (1980) IRLR 112
66 See note 12
67 See *Shipping Company Uniform Inc v ITWF* (1985) IRLR 71
68 See *Kent Free Press v NGA* (1987) IRLR 267
69 See *Read Transport v NUM* (South Wales) (1985) IRLR 67
70 Section 16 TULRCA 1992
71 See *Union Traffic v TGWU* (1989) IRLR 127
72 See *Rayware Ltd v TGWU* (1989) IRLR 134
73 See section 220(2) TULRCA 1992
74 See section 220(4) TULRCA 1992
75 (1985) IRLR 136
76 See also *News Group v SOGAT* (note 26) where the torts of nuisance and intimidation were committed

77 Paragraph 42 Department of Employment *Code of Practice on Picketing*
78 See also the Public Order Act 1986 for the offences of disorderly conduct, riot, violent disorder, affray and threatening behaviour
79 See *Moss v McLaughlan* (1985) IRLR 76
80 Paragraph 51 Department of Employment Code; see *Thomas v NUM (South Wales)* (1985) IRLR 136
81 Paragraphs 54–7 and 62–4 Department of Employment Code
82 See sections 6 and 8 Criminal Law Act 1977
83 See *Elsey v Smith* (1983) IRLR 293
84 See note 5

Further resources

BOOKS

Butterworth's Employment Law Handbook. London, Butterworth's, 1999.

FOSTER N. *EC Legislation.* London, Blackstone Press, 1999.

KIDNER R. *Statutes on Employment Law.* London, Blackstone Press, 1999.

USEFUL WEBSITES

Acts of Parliament	www.hmso.gov.uk/acts.htm
Commission for Racial Equality	www.cre.gov.uk
DTI Internet Service	www.dti.gov.uk
Equal Opportunity Commission	www.eoc.org.uk
European Court of Justice	www.europa.eu.int/cj/en/
European Trade Union Confederation	www.etuc.org
European Union	www.europa.eu.int
Health and Safety Executive	www.open.gov.uk/hse/hsehome.htm
Statutory instruments	www.hmso.gov.uk/stat.htm
Trades Union Congress	www.tuc.org.uk

CIPD PUBLICATIONS

All the titles listed below are available from Plymbridge Distributors (01752–202 301).

The *Legal Essentials* series by Hammond Suddards Solicitors:

> *Contracts of Employment*
> *Data Protection*
> *Disability Discrimination*
> *Dismissal*
> *Employment Relations Act*
> *Maternity Rights*
> *Redundancy*
> *Sex and Race Discrimination*

Transfer of Undertakings
Working Time Regulations

Other titles

FOWLER A. *Managing Redundancy*. 1999.
GENNARD J. *and* JUDGE G. *Employee Relations*. 2nd edn. 1999.

THE CIPD EMPLOYMENT LEGAL ADVISORY SERVICE

This service, which is provided free of charge to CIPD members only, is available five days a week from Hammond Suddards Solicitors (tel. 0990 561 251). For more information, see the CIPD's website: www.cipd.co.uk

Index